SWAHILI MUSLIM PUBLICS AND POSTCOLONIAL EXPERIENCE

SWAHILI MUSLIM PUBLICS AND POSTCOLONIAL EXPERIENCE

Kai Kresse

Indiana University Press

This book is a publication of

Indiana University Press
Office of Scholarly Publishing
Herman B Wells Library 350
1320 East 10th Street
Bloomington, Indiana 47405 USA

iupress.indiana.edu

Manufactured in the United States of America

Cataloging information is available from the Library of Congress.
ISBN 978-0-253-03753-4 (hardback)
ISBN 978-0-253-03754-1 (paperback)
ISBN 978-0-253-03755-8 (ebook)

1 2 3 4 5   23 22 21 20 19 18

Contents

Preface   *vii*

Acknowledgments   *xiii*

Part I: Conceptualizations

1 Introduction: Past Present Continuous: Postcolonial Experience,
   Intellectual Practice, and the Struggle for Meaning   *3*

2 Muslim Publics, Postcolonial Imaginations, and the Dynamics of
   Self-Positioning   *34*

Part II: Readings

3 Colonial Experience and Future Anticipations: Sheikh Al-Amin
   Mazrui and Swahili Islamic Pamphlets, 1930–32   *61*

4 *The Voice of Justice*: An Islamic Newspaper in Postcolonial
   Kenya, 1972–82   *105*

5 "Get Educated with Stambuli!": An Open Discussion Platform
   on Local Islamic Radio, 2005–07   *147*

6 Conclusion: Toward the Understanding of Understanding:
   Elements of a Swahili Intellectual Tradition   *190*

References   *213*

Index   *233*

Preface

The *time of existence and experience*, the *time of entanglement* . . . this time of
African existence is neither a linear time nor a simple sequence in which each
moment effaces, annuls, and replaces those that preceded it, to the point where
a single age exists within society. This time is not a series but an *interlocking* of
presents, pasts, and futures that retain their depths of other presents, pasts and
futures, each age bearing, altering, and maintaining the previous ones.

   . . . It may be supposed that the present *as experience of a time* is precisely
that moment when different forms of absence become mixed together: absence
of those presences that are no longer so and that one remembers (the past), and
absence of those others that are yet to come and are anticipated (the future).

   A. Mbembe, *On the Postcolony* (2001, p. 16)

The thoughts of a people distant in time or space cannot be at all deeply shared
without our becoming acquainted with things and ideas important to them but
of which we have no exact equivalent. As far as possible, one wants to read the
works themselves in which the thoughts have been expressed; in these, even
in translation, the special concepts and categories of the writers, as well as the
personalities and places referred to, must be reproduced (if the translation is
serious) in forms alien to the usual flow of English, no matter how much the
resources of English may have been adapted or even twisted to do duty for what
remain alien conceptions.

   The same is, in some degree, true of any work treating of the alien
civilization. The serious reader must be prepared to think in novel ways. To
this end, he must be prepared to absorb as readily as possible a whole range of
new concepts and terms. Otherwise he cannot expect to profit seriously by a
study of the culture; at most he will receive an impression of exotic quaintness,
romance, or incongruity which does no justice to the human reality.

   "On Making Sense of Islamicate Words, Names and Dates,"
   M. Hodgson, *The Venture of Islam: Conscience and History in a World
Civilization*, vol. I (1977 [orig. 1958], p. 3)

Two Entry Points

At the turn of this century, the Cameroonian philosopher and anthropologist
Achille Mbembe (1992; 2001) presented us with critical inventories and stimulating conceptualizations of postcolonial experience in Africa. He combined a
critique of autocratic rule, narrated as a description of its common patterns (and
those of popular resistance in response), with a critique of a history of Eurocentric

scholarship that continued dismissing and obscuring Africa's lived subjectivities and actual realities. Mbembe's vivid accounts are full of perceptive observations on political dynamics and everyday life that feed into a critique that is frank, piercing, and stimulating, often picking up on the real-life satires that the postcolony creates and ordinary people have to endure. On the research front, he criticized an increasing lack of fieldwork, a lack of knowledge of local languages, and a low sense of (and sensitivity for) human and intellectual agency in Africa (2001, 7). My study here speaks to these points (which have also been flagged by other critical Africanist researchers), as I provide ethnographically contextualized readings and discussions of postcolonial experience and intellectual practice on the Kenyan Swahili coast.[1]

In the second epigraph, from almost half a century earlier, Marshal Hodgson called upon researchers to acquire familiarity with and convey a deep understanding of Muslim societies and life-worlds,[2] in their own terms and through the words used by social actors (and thus sensitive to language in a way that is no longer self-understood). Reminding ourselves of Hodgson's commitment is not a bad entry point for a study such as this one. This book explores how coastal Muslims in postcolonial Kenya address and negotiate the conceptual and political challenges they confront in their everyday lives, by drawing from the rich resource of genres and discursive strategies that Swahili language and culture provide. Such creative conceptual (and largely discursive) activity occurs in response to practical demands, is framed in political or religious terms, and is embedded in historical continuities of language use, forms of interaction, and mutual normative expectations among community members. In short, it happens in a social field of intellectual practice.

Around the time of Hodgson's writing, Seyid Qutb was one of the most critical and most influential modern Islamic thinkers, an author whom some of my Swahili interlocutors pointed to as inspirational. Qutb lamented that colonized Muslims around the world had neglected their own forms and histories of intellectual practice, which they could have used to reassert themselves and to counter the pressing global political imbalance. Instead, he wrote, they were simply copying the principles and practices pursued by the representatives of the European empires: "Here in Egypt and in the Muslim world as a whole, we pay little heed to our native spiritual resources and our own intellectual heritage; instead, we think first of importing foreign principles and methods, or borrowing customs and laws from across the deserts and from beyond the seas" (Qutb 2000 [orig. 1953], 19). Qutb's regret about such neglect of one's own intellectual heritage that should have been brought to bear in struggles against external domination and for the building of future political visions for one's society was shared, among others, by East African Muslims. In the early 1930s, already Sheikh Al-Amin Mazrui's pamphlets voice similar sentiments. This book discusses the discursive activity of individual figures advocating religiously guided forms of social reform on the Swahili coast at different points in time both before and after Qutb made this statement. Overall, this book works through the dynamics of continuity and change within the wider field of intellectual practice on the Swahili coast, in terms of language use and the verbal arts, as well as the ongoing social significance of poetic genres, but also in terms of its use for religious and/or political expression, discussion, and contestation.

In the opening chapter, I develop and introduce my take on intellectual practice as an ethnographic and conceptual entry point to the study of society that also lends itself to understanding the facets of postcolonial experience of coastal Muslims in Kenya, and the ways they struggle to find their place in the world, in dynamic processes of self-positioning. When seeking to understand (and convey to others) the back-and-forth of arguments going on among social actors, we need to acquire a good sense of both the key concepts and the ways of speaking and arguing that people employ in specific situations, in similar (and yet individually significantly different) ways. This is what this book works through, and what it works toward, looking at three differently situated case studies of Swahili Muslim publics.

Sources and the Research Process

A useful and important tradition in anthropological research is to account for one's research process, the collection of materials, and one's relations (interactions and dependencies) with one's interlocutors and advisers. In this case, the main materials on which the following chapters are based have been collected over a period of over ten years, in collaboration with friends, interlocutors, and colleagues in Mombasa, Kenya, Europe, the United States, and Canada. Further primary sources are worked into the chapters that follow. Here I account for the main materials used in each of the three main ethnographic chapters.

Chapter 3—Uwongozi/*Guidance*

I received a copy of Sheikh Al-Amin Mazrui's *Uwongozi* collection from Abdilatif Abdalla, with whom I have been in close touch over the last years. This collection of his *Sahifa* essays from 1930–32 was a local reprint from 1955 that was originally published in 1944. Abdalla connected me to Muhammad bin Yusuf, a grandson of Sheikh Al-Amin and the author of the first English translations of the *Uwongozi* essays. They had been published between March and June 2009 in the *Friday Bulletin*, Kenya's most important weekly news bulletin for Muslims, distributed countrywide from Nairobi's central Jamia Mosque. Bwana Muhammad kindly sent me a complete set of his translations. Therein, he used a popular voice targeting a contemporary youthful audience, thus illustrating some of the currency of Sheikh Al-Amin's writings. Together, with my Kenyan colleague Hassan Mwakimako (Associate Professor at Pwani University, Kilifi), I began to work on a more academic translation that would render the text more closely and make Sheikh Al-Amin's thinking accessible to a wider Anglophone audience worldwide. This translation was completed with linguistic help and guidance from Abdilatif Abdalla and Alamin Mazrui, and it was approved by the Mazrui family. It is now published (Mazrui 2017) as a bilingual Swahili-English edition with Brill's series African Sources for African History, and it will be reprinted in due course as an East African edition by Mkuki na Nyota in Dar es Salaam.

During my visits in Mombasa over the years, I always went to see the local historian and former teacher *marehemu* Sayyid Abdulrahman Saggaf Alawy (commonly called Mwalimu Saggaf), who passed away in spring 2018. Mwalimu Saggaf had been a student of Sheikh Al-Amin, and he had grown up and lived in his house for some years. During our meetings, I tried to zoom in on particular texts and thematic aspects of the essay collection, but due to his old age and frail health, it was rare to have extensive focused conversations. While I collected a valuable cluster of comments and impressions, I did not succeed in pursuing regular sessions with systematic joint readings and close discussions of selected texts and topics with him, as would have been desirable (see Eickelman 1985; Messick 1993). Nevertheless, I am very grateful to have had the privilege of many conversations with Mwalimu Saggaf, who rarely turned down a request. Acquiring some firsthand information on the texts and the author from these sessions (some of them jointly with Sheikh Abdilahi Nassir), I caught some important glimpses of a fuller picture of Sheikh Al-Amin, as writer, scholar, and human being, impressions that were complemented also by Ghalib Tamim's biographical book (Tamim 2006)—a picture that I tried to put together in my chapter narrative below.

Chapter 4—Sauti ya Haki

As for the *Sauti ya Haki* materials, my collection grew gradually over the years. I had come across several issues in SOAS Library during my early postdoctoral research phase, and I found the newspaper particularly intriguing. Reading it for me enlivened a research perspective I had already started to build, on Sheikh Muhammad Kasim Mazrui and his booklets of collected pamphlets, called *Hukumu za Sharia* (Mazrui 1970; 1971; see Kresse 2003). I saw that *Sauti ya Haki* was a direct (and more stable) continuation of these—and that it also obviously developed the project of public education (for social and religious reform) that his teacher and mentor Sheikh Al-Amin had engaged in. Interesting to note is that Sheikh Muhammad was one of the editors of Sheikh Al-Amin's *Uwongozi* volume. At a conference in 2007 where I presented a talk on Sheikh Muhammad Kasim, Gerard van de Bruinhorst generously offered access to his sizable collection of the newspaper in Leiden. In the same year, I was kindly sent another set of collected *Sauti ya Haki* newspapers, by Prof. Alamin Mazrui, Sheikh Muhammad Kasim's son (now at Rutgers University). I had first met him in 2001 when I gave my first conference talk on his father's pamphlets, and he had heard that I was continuing to work on his father's oeuvre. Some years later, Abdilatif Abdalla gave me access to his collection of the newspapers, so that overall, my overview was almost complete. I feel fortunate to have received such kind attention to my research interests, with these provisions of materials and the recognition of my efforts as worthy of support. This became a binding obligation for me in turn, to complete an in-depth account and a serious study on them. During a visit to Mombasa, in 2010, I interviewed Munir Mazrui about *Sauti ya Haki* (he had also been involved in editorial assistance and other tasks for it), and he kindly supplied me with a photocopy of the maiden issue, which I had not seen until then. Again, like with *Uwongozi*, it was not possible for me to pursue intensive and systematic research on the ethnography of reading with former readers or producers of the newspaper, although I did speak to some of them. But I did benefit a lot from direct conversations with people who were involved with the paper or close to it, including Sheikh Muhammad's sons, Sheikh Hamad Muhammad Kasim and Alamin Mazrui. I have tried to make good use of the information and comments received and, guided by them, to convey a vivid reconstruction of the public debates and their dynamics that resonates well enough with people's memories—while I have, of course, built my own interpretation of the texts and the matters discussed, the respective editor at work, and the relevant contexts.

Chapter 5—Radio Rahma and Elimika na Stambuli!

Finally, my work on *Radio Rahma* was to continue another related strand of previous research. I focus here on the broadcast *Elimika na Stambuli!*, "Get Educated with Stambuli!" (early on, it was also called *Jielimishe na Stambuli*," or "Educate Yourself with Stambuli"). In my first book (Kresse 2007, chapter 7), I had discussed Stambuli as one of three representative figures of the younger generation (there anonymized as "Saidi"), in contrast and comparison to the older Swahili scholars whom I had examined in depth in chapter-length discussions. Since my earlier fieldwork and my annual visits from 2004 to 2007, he had developed his political activities further, voicing critique of coastal Muslim elites and political representatives (whom he regarded as having let their community down). He continued, through public talks and discussions, to stimulate people's thinking and provoke reactions, working toward the building of a coastal historical consciousness and the cultivation of a general political sensitivity among coastal Muslims. He addressed practical matters in everyday life that needed attention (by the authorities or the citizens, whether garbage disposal and ecological conscience or water supply and the care of existent hydrants). His project had turned from a kind of local lecturing tour on these matters (as it had been in the late 1990s) to a carefully conceptualized radio show, for which open access and participation of people through live phone-in discussions was a major feature. This became *Elimika na Stambuli!* The show was generally well received, and Stambuli became a household name in Mombasa.

For my research, in addition to hours spent listening to Radio Rahma and this particular program (both alone and with friends), Stambuli gave me a selection of recordings, and I conducted a number of conversations and interviews with him and the professional moderator of his show, Abubakar Amin.[3] During my visits to Mombasa, I also stimulated some conversations and informal discussions of the radio show with my friends, acquaintances, and regular interlocutors. Stambuli and Abubakar read and approved of a draft of the chapter and, upon my query, both independently decided they wanted to be mentioned and described by their full and proper names here, Stambuli Abdilahi Nassir and Abubakar Amin Baalawy, fully recognizable and not anonymized (as is common convention).

What I wish to convey here, in conclusion, is a sense of my long-term commitment to the issues explored in this project, and the long and progressive character of the research process involved. From its early conception and at almost every stage of its pursuit, this was often stimulated, influenced, or guided by communications and interactions with Swahili (and other Kenyan, and international) interlocutors, advisers, and friends.

Acknowledgments

Fieldwork, interviews, and conversations in Mombasa were carried out in short-term visits, lasting between two and five weeks, annually between 2004 and 2007, and again in 2010, 2011, 2012, and 2014. Over the years, many people have helped me in my research, both in Kenya and in my places of residence, in St Andrews (Scotland), Berlin (Germany), and more recently New York (USA). First, I would like to express my gratitude to all my East African friends and interlocutors, in Mombasa, Lamu, and elsewhere. The oldest among them, *marehemu* Sayyid Abdulrahman Saggaf Alwy (Mwalimu Saggaf), passed away in May 2018. He made himself readily available during each of my Mombasa visits since my doctoral fieldwork and was generous with his knowledge. It was always good to converse and consult with my two *wazee* in Mombasa, Sheikh Abdilahi Nassir and Ustadh Ahmad Nassir, and it was such a pleasure to have been able to invite them to Berlin in summer 2008 for two weeks for conversations, a *baraza*, and a truly unforgettable public lecture and reading event at the ZMO, with funding by ZMO and the University of St Andrews. I am also grateful for all the personal interactions I have had with two other mentors, *marehemu* Profesa Ahmed Sheikh Nabhany (sadly missed), and Ustadh Mahmoud Abdoulkader (known as "Mau"), both *washairi*, in Mombasa and Lamu, whenever there was a chance to meet up. And I appreciate the opportunity for conversations, in East Africa, with Stambuli A. Nassir, Abubakar Amin, Zahir Bhalloo, Saad Yahya, Farouk Topan, Mohamed Bakari, Adulqadir A. Nassir, and, long ago, with *marehemu* Sharif Khitamy.

Marehemu Mzee Bashir Chandoo is sorely missed too; he was gracious in passing on knowledge and always eager to learn more and discuss. I thank him and his family for their hospitality and kindness, and Shoeb for staying in touch. Sorely missed is also my former neighbor *marehemu* Mzee Abdulkarim, and I thank his son Akasha and family for continuing to interact in his spirit. Fuad and Nuru and family have been wonderful friends and hosts, and it was a joy to have been able to see their family, and Abbas's and Abdalla's, grow and develop over the years; here, Farouk is sorely missed. Between Kenya and Berlin, Hassan Mwakimako became colleague, friend, and collaborator on projects, and I thank him for many exchanges and discussions, and his family for delicious food and good company. More good company was readily given by Kadara Swaleh, in conversations and discussions, with and without *wazee*. I am grateful for conversations with Ustadh Harith, Sheikh Ahmed Msallam, Sheikh Hammad M. K.

Mazrui, Munir Mazrui, and Ghalib Tamim. Over time, Abdilatif Abdalla has been a great help, as well as friend and mentor, and I cannot thank him enough. I thank Mohamed Lali for conversations and generous hospitality in Lamu.

In Berlin, at ZMO, I was happy to pursue research in the company of Katrin Bromber, Roman Loimeier, Ulrike Freitag, Heike Liebau, Katharina Lange, Samuli Schielke, Knut Graw, Bettina Graef, Saadi Nikro, Birgit Krawietz, Niels Riecken, Marloes Janson, Abdoulaye Sounaye and Birgit Meyer, among others, in good spirits and with mutual encouragement. Working with Lutz Diegner also on the Berlin Swahili Baraza we established was always a pleasure. And being able to interact in Berlin with like-minded researchers from various disciplines, including Franziska Duebgen, Stefan Skupien, Hanna Nieber, Roman Seidel, and Schirin Amir-Moazami, has been a great experience.

Related presentations on aspects of the book project in its early stages were given in lectures in Oxford and Cape Town. Individual presentations were given, among other places, in New York, Stanford, Michigan, Vancouver, Toronto, Gainesville, Lamu, Bayreuth, Bergen, Muenster, Leiden, Napoli, and Berlin. For related invitations and fruitful discussions over the years, I also thank Clarissa Vierke, Markus Verne, Julia Verne, Helene Basu, Abdulkader Tayob, Shamil Jeppie, Zulfikar Hirji, Sean Henretta, Terje Ostebo, Rose Marie Beck, Alena Rettová, Benedetta Lanfranchi, and Benedikt Pontzen.

Funding for the different stages of fieldwork and write-up during a sabbatical was provided by DAAD, BMBF, DFG, University of St Andrews, ZMO, the Berlin Graduate School for the Study of Muslim Cultures and Societies (BGSMCS) at the Freie Universität Berlin, and Columbia University. I am immensely grateful for the sabbatical year 2015–16 that made a proper writing process possible, for the Visiting Fellowship at the BGSMCS at Freie Universität Berlin, and extra writing time at ZMO.

Friendship, feedback, and food for thought, at different stages of this project, were also given by Scott Reese, Mark Harris, Trevor Marchand, Edward Simpson, John D. Y. Peel (who is sadly missed), Ruediger Seesemann, Kelly Askew, Atreyee Sen, Anne Bang, Ridder Samsom, Sauda Barwani, Andrew Eisenberg, Katharina Zoeller, Liese Hoffmann, and Jasmin Mahazi. At Columbia, they were given by Mahmood Mamdani, Brinkley Messick, and Timothy Mitchell, who also commented on chapters, as did Birgit Meyer, Roman Loimeier, Katrin Bromber, Sadi Nikro, Abdoulaye Sounaye, Stambuli A. Nassir, and Hassan Mwakimako. I am grateful for their valuable time and attention. Two anonymous reviewers also provided immensely helpful feedback for revisions. At Indiana University Press, I am most grateful to Dee Mortensen for early and continued interest in the book, and good sense in the process. I also thank Paige Rasmussen for her help.

The good fortune of continued (often occasional) conversations and discussions on African philosophy and intellectual culture over the years, with

Bruce Janz, Gail Presbey, Anke Graness, D. A. Masolo, Oriare Nyarwath, Paulin Hountondji, Barry Hallen, Kwasi Wiredu, and S. Bachir Diagne, as well as Bertold Bernreuter, Franz Wimmer, Elmar Holenstein, and, earlier on, Jens Heise, was enriching and has fed into this book too. I also thank my teachers from long ago, Johannes Ratzek and Gottfried Lorenz, for instilling desire and dedication to study. And I am grateful to Louis Brenner and Sean O'Fahey for guidance and support, early on. Gerard van der Bruinhorst deserves gratitude for his selfless help with his collected Swahili materials, especially the *Sauti ya Haki* volumes. Such copies I also received from Alamin Mazrui, whom I also thank for encouragement, and advice on the *Uwongozi* translations and the permission to translate and work with them.

In New York, I thank Annmarie Drury, Mandana Limbert, and Meena Alexander for new exchanges. At Columbia particularly, I thank Mahmood Mamdani, Abdul Nanji, Brink Messick, Tim Mitchell, Gregory Mann, Rhiannon Stephens, Brian Larkin, Mamadou Diouf, Sheldon Pollock, Allison Busch, Manan Ahmed, and Sara Weschler for their supportive interactions and related intellectual exchanges. For clerical support, I thank Irys Shenker, Charles Jester, Michael Fishman, and Jessica Rechtschaffer in the MESAAS office, and for work toward the manuscript preparation at different stages, I thank Brianna Alston, Teresa Schloegl, Constanze Fertig, Lillian Ren-Tsevo, and Hannah Schoening.

Finally, I thank my parents Christian Kresse and Toni Kresse for their encouragement and support from early days onward, for cultivating curiosity and travel, and my siblings Uta and Klaas for being there whenever needed.

Last but not least, I would never have been able to complete this project without the help of my wife, Joy Adapon. I cannot thank her enough for her critical comments, stimulating questions, encouragement, and editorial help on the one hand, and a lot of patience and companionship over the years on the other. For their vivid presence and supportive distractions, and their overall confidence in me, I thank Saskia, Oscar, Otto, and Pascal. I am looking forward to spending more time with you all.

A Note on Swahili Language Terms

There are a number of Swahili terms, often referring to Muslim practices or to positions or social roles in local Muslim society, that I include in the text and for which I use a common form of spelling as used by local authors. These spellings differ from the standard transcription of Arabic Islamic terms, but they are preferable to me as they represent the local, established communication and understanding more adequately. (The same applies to Muslim names and their spellings.) Terms of this kind include: *baraza*; *bidaa*; *dhikri*; *elimu*; *kadhi*; *maulidi*; *sharifu* (pl., *masharifu*); *sheikh* (pl., *masheikh*); *ustadh*; *wabara*; *wapwani*; *waungwana*; *ziyara*.

Notes

1. Among these are Karin Barber, Johannes Fabian, and Richard Werbner, as shall be seen in the following chapters.

2. Here, "Islamicate" was the term Hodgson coined to characterize languages, cultural practices, or social contexts that were marked and influenced by Islam while not strictly speaking "Islamic" (1977, 56–60).

3. Abubakar Amin has moved to Tanga in Tanzania in the meantime, where he has been a show host and general manager for the newly established Islamic radio station Radio Maarifa for some years now. Stambuli has remained in Mombasa, and is currently operational manager of the new radio station Pwani FM.

PART I
CONCEPTUALIZATIONS

1 Introduction

Past Present Continuous: Postcolonial Experience, Intellectual Practice, and the Struggle for Meaning

THIS BOOK EXPLORES particular case studies of selected Swahili Muslim publics and the texts and discourses shaping them. "Past present continuous" refers to actions and experiences that have started in the past and are ongoing in the present (and possibly beyond). Here, this expression encapsulates the postcolonial experience of coastal Muslims in Kenya (i.e., Muslims who identify as belonging to the Swahili coast)[1] making persistent, recurrent references to the colonial past in everyday life. Picking up on such references witnessed during my fieldwork, I use the expression as a leitmotif with which to think through postcoloniality from the perspective of coastal Muslims. They generally feel marginalized by the ongoing external "Christian upcountry" rule of their home region, and I have often come across expressions of what seems like nostalgic longing for an imaginary colonial past, a period that is depicted in stark contrast to the frustrating postcolonial present.[2] "Past present continuous" here also refers to people being enveloped in loops of experience, feeling stuck, as things are not changing despite an acute sense of the time that is passing.

The chapters of this book focus on local Islamic media initiatives pushed by engaged individuals, and their attempts to provide guidance for personal and communal self-positioning at different points in time in Kenyan postcolonial (and colonial) history. Here, close readings are combined with ethnographic contextualization of pamphlets and newspapers, as well as lectures, speeches, and radio discussions. The struggles of self-positioning are explored from the perspective of coastal Muslims vis-à-vis each other and in relation to the state. As we shall see, the effects of the latter have largely been experienced as "external rule," imposed on coastals (*wapwani*) by upcountry people (*wabara*) who are predominantly Christian; this experience can be seen in continuation of previous phases of external dominance.

Before the current postcolonial (i.e., post-Independence) upcountry rule that began in 1963, from the late nineteenth century, the Kenyan coast was ruled and/or administered by Christian British colonials, and before that, from the end of

the seventeenth century, by Ibadi Muslim Omani Arabs and governors (the Mazrui, for Mombasa); and before that, from the early sixteenth century, by Christian
Portuguese invaders.[3] These constellations illustrate the long-term external political domination that also characterized Swahili society from early on as a kind
of "middlemen society" (Middleton 1992). Rarely completely in charge of its own
region politically, the "Swahili corridor" (Horton 1987) long fulfilled a crucial
two-way mediating role (in terms of trade, religion, knowledge, etc.) between
faraway places across the Indian Ocean and a variety of peoples of East Africa,
already pointed to by the visiting Ibn Battuta in the fourteenth century (Ham-
doun and King 1994). We may speak of a sequence of multiple colonial (and qua-
sicolonial) as well as consecutive postcolonial experiences here over the course
of five centuries. Along these lines, politically, the sphere of the coastal towns
can be seen as an enduring and historically layered "serial post-colony," illustrating various dimensions of its regionally specific "post-post-postcolonial experience" of sorts, shaped by the effects of Portuguese, Omani, British, and Kenyan
rule. Sensitive to the effects of such long-term external domination in relation to
the sense of self of coastal Muslims as expressed in public discourse, this book
also works on the rhetorical and argumentative patterns in such processes of
self-positioning, which are made within a wider field of "intellectual practice" in
social interaction.

In this way, the book critically maps out the ways in which topics representative of postcolonial experience are tackled and negotiated at specific points
in time. Ordinary Muslims as well as scholars evoke imaginary memories of
coastal society under colonial rule (and sometimes, prophetic futures of postcolonial rule), in the face of what is seen as coastal Muslims' decline and desperation. The phrase "past present continuous," therefore, effectively captures
the flow of experience of local actors, as they themselves describe it as oriented
toward a significant (meaningful) past. The book proceeds by continuing to pay
attention to the particular kind of "double periphery" in which many coastal
Muslims in postcolonial Kenya see themselves placed (Kresse 2009).[4] On the
one hand, they face neglect by their own government, whichhas continuously
excluded them from certain rights and benefits as citizens. On the other, they
feel regarded as somewhat lesser members of the *umma* (the worldwide community of Muslim believers), which seems dominated by a Middle Eastern
Arabocentric perspective. As the Mombasa-based scholar Sheikh Abdilahi Nassir once put it, when discussing the relationship between Muslims and the state
in Kenya, "Kenya is a secular state—but it is Christian."[5] This kind of upcountry rule has also been described, by local human rights activists, as "Christocentric politics" pursuing "(internal) colonial ends" (KHRC 1997, 11, 17). On the
coast, this trope is often invoked in public when airing grievances.[6] In this book
I explore the way in which coastal Swahili Muslims verbalize and intellectualize

their conceptions of the past in the present and how they envisage possibilities for the future.

To this end, I examine textual case studies of selected Swahili Muslim publics to analyze the social and discursive dynamics shaping them. Working closely with local texts—in different genres, by diverse speakers, using various perspectives—opens up windows of social experience as entry points and foci for analysis. Combining ethnography and textual study has much to contribute to the study of postcolonial contexts, for in order to make well-founded comments on the postcolonial condition more generally, one needs to work through the scope of available sources in regional languages. There is no substitute for this, despite tendencies in postcolonial studies to be confined to Europhone sources, which may be lacking or misleading, as they often represent exceptions or minority positions within African (or other) societies (Barber 2007, 223–225). A researcher with substantial fieldwork experience who listens closely to what is said in those texts, can engage in strategies of understanding and contextualization, participating (in a mediatory, interpretive capacity) in the social life he or she observes. The researcher can thus tune in and follow public debates in an informed manner, when "texts' meanings are held to be publicly available, accessible (in principle) to anyone in command of the relevant language and conventions" (Barber 2007, 203). Gaining insight into the specific dynamics of communication mediated by specific kinds of texts between social actors leads to "forms of social knowledge, and clues to how society is locally conceptualized and constituted" (Barber 2007, 202). Increasing such an understanding of coastal Kenyan society (linked to the longer history of Swahili society) is a goal of my study here. As I work through particular themes, modes, and patterns of internal debate and discussion, I seek to convey a sense of how society is thought and negotiated.

Three Quotations: Voicing Discontent, Verbalizing Postcolonial Experience

The three quotations discussed in this section are drawn from a religious sermon, an educational poem, and a political manifesto, respectively. All from the recent past, they convey a sense of the mutual tensions between coastal Muslims and the state, and they serve as entry points to the scope of discussion in this book.

I: A Maulidi Sermon in Lamu, 2006

"Until today there continue to be doubts about our Kenyan-ness," a leading local Islamic scholar said in the conclusion of his sermon on the night of the main festivities of *maulidi* in Lamu, after the communal recitations of the *maulidi al-Habshi* had been performed together by thousands of participants, male and female (who attended in divided sections), inside and outside one of the main mosques of Lamu Town.[7] This speaker had been elaborating his concerns in the following terms, and encouraged his audience to be critical of the government:

> The time has come for us coastals in general to think about a solution—this solution should not be on the level of councils, nor on the level of parliaments, nor on the level of being given ministries in the government. All these approaches have been shown to be useless. . . . We need to plan a new "strategy" [English in the original]. *We should recognize ourselves as coastals;* and that we have these cards that we can use. . . . Coastals, we have to think hard. We have to place ourselves anew in politics. And we should make it clear to those others that *we are we* (*sisi ni sisi*), we are who we are. We must not wait for them to tell us. We should recognize ourselves and declare ourselves, and not wait to be recognized. . . . *Until today there continue to be doubts about our "Kenyan-ness."*

He continued by pointing, with much frustration, to the ongoing problems of practical neglect by the state that the people of Lamu had been enduring over the years: "Look at the problems with light and electricity, year-in, year-out. It's such kinds of problems and struggles we are in. Water is a problem; streets are a problem, all kinds of things come together. Until when will we continue to sing the same song? And each of the politicians knows how to use us because of this song" [emphasis added].[8]

Clearly, he indicated that the time was ripe for change, as the coastal people's endurance had not helped them one bit. I had attended the festivities and this particular sermon in person, and I bought the cassette recording of the sermon the next day, at one of the little stalls known to be a distributing platform. The sermon had struck a fine balance between the expected dedicated call to follow and praise Prophet Muhammad (whose qualities were being remembered and celebrated through the joint recitation of religious praise poetry) and a critical response to political developments in Lamu after recent oil findings off the coast, when the national government had sent assistant ministers to inform local representatives about prospective procedures (and notably, not to consult with them). In clear language, the speaker here expressed coastal people's common discontent about the lack of basic provisions (water, transport, etc.) and the lack of recognition by the government. He implored his audience, a sizable mix of Lamu residents and other coastal Kenyans and Muslims from the wider region visiting for the occasion, that the time had come for coastal Muslims to change their attitude. They needed to reflect upon who they were and who they wanted to be, as coastals vis-à-vis the state, and to take initiative to find and formulate their own position. No longer should they accept being told what to do.

A little earlier, in the same sermon, the speaker had already formulated a clear sense of coastal people's mistrust of successive postcolonial Kenyan governments that had consistently taken away income earned in the region. The point was about trust, and he stated repeatedly, "We have no trust in the government" (*hatuna amani na serikali*). In the light of these experiences, he said, coastals were no longer interested in being taken advantage of:

> We don't trust you [the government]. *Don't waste your time: we don't trust you.* What did we get, my friends, from these governments that have changed, we as coastal people, or as Muslims? [pause] My friends, the oil that could be drawn from here, will it turn out like all that money earned from Kilindini Harbour in Mombasa? . . . Let's try to follow something we should know, namely how much money is earned there in one day, each day? Where is Kilindini? In Mombasa? What did the people of Mombasa, or of the coast, get from there that they could use for themselves? . . . The big offices for Kilindini Harbour are in Nairobi.[9]

He went on to describe the severe ecological dangers and risks of pumping oil in this area, commenting on the likelihood that all profits would go outside, to others, and all the risks and effects and potential environmental catastrophes would affect the Lamu area and have to be shouldered by its people. Then he reported what else he told those assistant ministers who came to Lamu to speak with local representatives (including himself) about the recent oil findings and the government's plans to let a Japanese company survey the area to exploit the resources: "Tell the minister that we are praying to God to give us a special prayer (*dua*) with which we ask that the oil will all dry up the moment you leave Lamu [later today]."[10]

II: A Poem in Lamu, 2010/11

The second sample text is a pamphlet in poetic form, published a few years later in Lamu. It was written and self-published by a town elder and former education officer who called this *utendi* "Regionalism: True Freedom to Save the Coastal People" (*Majimbo: uhuru kamili kuwaokoa wapwani*). An *utendi* (also called *utenzi*) is a long poem written in the classical *tendi* (or *tenzi*, the plural form) genre that follows clear rules of rhyme and meter, and is commonly used for extensive didactic messages in Swahili, and disseminated in both oral and written form.[11] This composition of 137 stanzas circulated in Lamu in the form of a small photocopied and stapled booklet in 2011. It called upon coastal people to stand up and support a change to regionalism as a system of government, and to strive for coastal independence from Kenya. The composition was introduced thus, loaded with references to the special character and nature of coastal people and their region:

> "Majimbo" (Regionalism) is a little booklet of guidance about the determination to wake up the coastal people to show them that there has now been enough of pain, warnings, poverty and oppression that they have suffered for the goals of making the coastals stand up for the coast [lit., "in a coastal manner"] in order for their region, the coast, to achieve true freedom of the coastal strip (*mwambao*), our region belonging to the coastal people. Thank you. The author.[12]

This *utendi* makes reference to numerous examples of the suffering of the coastal people (not only Muslims per se) under upcountry governments throughout the postindependence period. Here, the Kenyan government is repeatedly addressed as "the colonizers" (*wakoloni*) who took over the country after the previous colonizers (the British) left in 1963. Along the lines of broader demands at the time, the poem calls for the coastal people to be granted political self-determination; that is, self-rule within a framework of so-called *majimbo* politics of decentralized regional administration. The effect would be a kind of "independence" of the coast.

III: *The Mombasa Republican Council (MRC) Manifesto, 2010*

Around the same time, the "Manifesto of MRC" was published by the Mombasa Republican Council, a movement striving for coastal independence. In 2010, this manifesto formalized the MRC principles in writing, in both an English and a Swahili version (which differ in their wording), making the following opening statement:

> *We, the coast people are not concerned with the Kenya constitution* [sic]; the Coast Region (Mombasa) has a separate legal status as a protectorate.
>
> The country Mombasa which extends right from the Indian Ocean to Sultan Hamud, from Lungalunga to Kismayu and owned by natives [sic], namely: the Mijikendas, Taitas, Pokomos, Bajunis, Arabs, Hindus and other Coastal tribes, has suffered a lot since 1963. . . . This country (Mombasa) has become a field of *Kenyans looting our wealth*.
>
> DEMAND—The original communities as named above are now demanding *their colonial masters, Kenyans*:
>
> 1. To repeal the 8/10/1963 Agreement
> 2. Remove their administration
> 3. To grant our independence[13] (p.2; my emphasis)

The final paragraph ends with the following appeal, after a long sequence of 67 points of demands: "Let us join hands and change the said Agreement. Hello coastals, *wake up* and get all that we have mentioned in this manifesto, and many other good things which the coastals cannot do under the leadership of the present ruling of *the selfish masters* (the government of Kenya) and in the 8/10/1963 Agreement which stated that the government of Kenya entered into certain undertakings concerning their protection after Kenya had attained Independence"[14] (p.12, my emphasis).

A clear rhetorical difference is marked between coastals and their "others"— above all the Kenyan government and its upcountry peoples, who are literally cast as alien foreigners who exploit coastal lands and resources as if they are "colonialists." In fact, the Swahili version of the document explicitly criticizes "the bad colonial leadership from Kenya" (*uongozi mbaya wa kikoloni kutoka Kenya*). A direct and confrontational tone is used, explicitly demanding independence within the boundaries of the colonial protectorate of the Kenyan coastal strip (*mwambao*), which the British had administered for the sultan of Zanzibar (and not ruled directly, like the "Kenyan Colony" proper), until the formal agreement about Kenya's independence was reached. The political slogan coined by the MRC, "*Pwani si Kenya!*" (The coast is not Kenya!), was popular on the coast, often heard and seen as graffiti in the streets, between 2010 and 2013. In the buildup to the general elections in September 2013, however, when it was the MRC's declared goal to boycott the elections on the coast, there was no sizable support for this among the population.[15] Nevertheless, the movement had left a clear mark expressing coastal sentiments of discontent and frustration with upcountry governments.

The three examples above, in three different genres, vividly illustrate the marked tensions in political discourse, between coastal people (*watu wa pwani*, or in short, *wapwani*) and upcountry people (*watu wa bara*, in short, *wabara*). They depict a postcolonial history of marginalization and rejection, of exclusion and discrimination, and they mark instances of a fundamental turning point in their consciousness and behavior. The simple message is that there have been too many years of meek compliance, submission, and "singing along" with the government.[16] It is now time to redefine their relationship, separate from each other, with coastals as self-conscious, confident, independent political actors, unlike in the past.

Or just like in the past—for in the early 1960s, there was a previous coastal independence movement, called Mwambao (Coastal Strip). Then, as part of Kenya's preindependence negotiations with Great Britain and the Sultanate of Zanzibar, coastal representatives anticipated political marginalization by the future KANU–Kenyatta government,[17] and thus campaigned for a separate coastal polity. This had some enthusiastic support for a while but was ultimately doomed to failure, as the parameters for a postcolonial future had been set between the colonial government and KANU. All that the two coastal delegates could do during the final deliberations at the Lancaster House Conference in London was refuse to sign the agreement that the coast was to be taken over and ruled by an upcountry Kenyan government—a process that, as they saw it, actually perpetuated the terms of the previous colonial administration.[18]

Thus, within coastal experience between colonial preindependence and the late postcolonial period, we can observe what look like recurring loops of thematic reference points. Yet to be sure, coastal Kenyans were not alone in their discontentment with their government, nor were they intrinsically more marginalized than all other Kenyans—this may well apply to the Kenyan Somali community, whose members faced tough restrictions and military measures by the state from independence until the present.[19] Yet even those who identified strongly as Kenyan nationalists in the early postcolonial era, and who were engaged in democratic politics and the idea of shaping their young nation, would soon sober up when the autocratic features of the KANU–Kenyatta government that would not tolerate any oppositional parties or individuals became more and more visible.[20]

Notably, in December 1968, the young oppositional KPU (Kenya People's Union) activist Abdilatif Abdalla from Mombasa was jailed for writing and distributing a pamphlet with the heading, "Kenya: Where Are We Going?" (*Kenya: Twendapi?*). There he emphatically criticized the "dictatorial" (*kidikteta*) features of the government's behavior. He called those in power "black Boers" who had, by obstructing democratic election processes, become even worse than the British colonials. This term was borrowed from racist apartheid South Africa, and it underlined his utter disgust with the government. Expressing immense frustration on behalf of ordinary Kenyans, the pamphlet even said that "the times of the colonial ruler were better (*ni afadhali wakati wa Mkoloni*)" (Abdalla 2016, 31). Abdalla had signed off the anonymous KPU pamphlets with the generic name "The Discontented" (*Wasiotosheka*). He had to spend three years in solitary confinement in Kenya's high-security prison as punishment for speaking out. So, as we can see, discontentment with and disapproval of the national government was present in both the early and late phases of Kenya's postcolonial history.[21]

Intellectual Traditions, Intellectual Practice, and the Critique of Eurocentrism

Groups of human beings in cultures and societies anywhere in the world are qualified as "communities" through the discursive traditions in which they partake (like Islam), and which in turn shape them, in a historical continuum of shared social experience. It is also helpful to understand these (more pointedly) as intellectual traditions with not only their own norms but also, correlatively, their specific conceptual frameworks (and key terms) that illuminate and underpin social norms while also providing a flexible grid of orientation for social actors (as Talal Asad has shown for Islam). We can then better perceive the creative potential of thinking and being-in-the-world from an internal point of view in each case (including our own society). The conceptual grid people use for their normative orientation is grounded in historical social experience, and linked to established patterns of language use. Yet it is still open to constant negotiation within society, in response to internal or external challenges and disputes.

Thus, part of my bigger point here is that if we are able to identify and understand specific aspects and performances of intellectual practice in a particular society, in relation to its intellectual traditions and social norms, we can understand and appreciate this society better (even if it is not our own) as the kind of valuable, precarious, and potentially rewarding project that internal actors regard it as. We can also identify with internal agents who need to continue to be critical and wary, because what their society will become depends on their mindful activities in shaping it, in social interaction. This applies to communities around the world, and to the respective responsibilities of their members to organize and shape them into the envisaged sociopolitical spaces they want them to be, seeking to keep them in balance while keeping them open for the potential participatory efforts of others. Boosting awareness about these dynamics more generally, and providing illustrative discussions about the East African (Kenyan) coastal Muslim community as a case in point, this book seeks to contribute to the project of overcoming Eurocentric frameworks of analysis and moving toward Chakrabarty's idea of "provincializing Europe," taking Europe as only one particular regional strand of human experience among others in history—albeit one that comes with a particular history of power—and a correlative set of analytic ways of understanding the world, and society.

From this perspective, European thought had made itself indispensable for understanding society and human experience across the world, since as a colonial power it had fundamentally contributed to the conditions of the experience that was to be analyzed. At the same time, it was inherently inadequate for such analysis because its lens, its perspective on social life elsewhere, was from the outset incapable of understanding and representing it in appropriate terms. What is needed, then, is a thorough understanding of intellectual traditions from elsewhere and their visions of "society" and "the human," to provide alternative (and more adequate) regional models to think with, thus making sure that "the European intellectual tradition" is no longer the only paradigmatic one for understanding human social life (Chakrabarty 2007, 4–5). Therefore, in order to convey a rich and appropriate understanding of intellectual traditions elsewhere, the kinds of intellectual practice underpinning them need to be studied: the specific internal dynamics of how knowledge is mediated—how people argue, reason with, and contest each other in a social context—need to be explored; familiarity with key terms, incidents, texts (and their authors), and their respective meanings in social practice needs to be acquired.

Knowledge and Intellectual Practice

With a view to the ethnographic task of making understandable what is seen and represented as "knowledge" in the social contexts that we study, the term "intellectual practice" is useful to think with, as the status of what counts as knowledge (and what kind of knowledge) is precisely what is contested across social and cultural boundaries—and often within them. Thus it can be crucial to us as researchers to be able to investigate a surrounding, wider field of social processes and (inter-)actions that are motivated by knowledge, or its critique, and therefore affirm or question what is presented by some social actors as knowledge to others. "Intellectual practice" denotes this wider field, which conceptually links up the specific fields of ethnographic and conceptual investigation with intellectual history and the study of religion.[22]

My ethnographic interest in the wider social field of knowledge-seeking or -mediating and otherwise knowledge-related practices in the Swahili context pushed me to work more and more on understanding a wider range of specific and partly overlapping practices or fields of inquiry that also underpin this study. These are local interpretations of Islam (in relation to practical concerns); the transmission of such interpretations, through particular Swahili genres of educational discourse (in speeches, poems, sermons, or pamphlets); and the specific kinds of narratives and ways of saying things that go along with them. The latter are an intricate part of what I have been coming to terms with in order to get a fuller sense of what I was seeking to study in the first place—a local but also transregionally shaped universe of intellectual practice, as part of a wider regional intellectual culture.

In order to convey a sense of this universe, I briefly discuss social and linguistic interrelations that concern social obligations and their negotiations in the Swahili context. In the concluding chapter, I return to reflections on this specific universe and its intellectual culture. My analysis is situated between philosophy, intellectual history, postcolonial critique, and ethnographically grounded social theory. Building on such discussions of the three illustrative case studies in the main chapters, I address a related and bigger question. This concerns the ongoing task in the humanities and social sciences of overcoming a Eurocentric bias. By rethinking the ways in which we are thinking society, we thus rethink the world, by means of alternative conceptual paradigms from elsewhere. Indeed, a challenge that we may face productively is to work out (in this case) a "Swahili model" for rethinking society more generally—as the basis for an alternative, coherent social theory that uses a Swahili conceptual framework and its key terms. Here, it is intriguing to consider the idea of "recalibrating" our thinking (readjusting social theory), in terms of how we best pursue "thinking society" from here, from a geographical and conceptual elsewhere to Eurocentric paradigms.[23] To this bigger project, my approach to the anthropological study of intellectual practice as a pathway into studying society has something to contribute.

There are some illuminating Africanist conceptual frameworks to think with, such as Wyatt MacGaffey's work on Bakongo society, which recounts fundamental cosmological, religious, and political perspectives through regional key terms and discusses their significance in relation to social experience. His studies show that regional political culture needs to be understood historically, and with a view to the conceptual dynamics of society—or, in other words, with a view to intellectual culture more widely.[24] At this point, it is useful to turn to general reflections on knowledge and intellectual practice before laying out the specifics of the Swahili case.

An Anthropological Approach to Swahili Intellectual Practice

In his comprehensive and globally oriented "sociology of philosophies," Randall Collins (1998) indicates how important the social dimensions are for an adequate understanding of philosophy as an academic discipline and long-standing systematic intellectual endeavor. He goes beyond a narrow focus on philosophy in order to show how it is socially embedded. He points at the roles that social contexts and networks (of peers, rivals, followers, supporters, and audiences) play, to show the ways that ideas of particular individual thinkers at specific points in time can lead, and somewhat reshape, the intellectual community. Most importantly for our interests here, Collins illustrates how much the social dimensions of direct face-to-face interactions matter, in the specific "intellectual rituals" (Collins 1998, 28) that academics perform (e.g., seminars, talks, and lectures).[25] Their performances shape the respective communities of intellectuals, and produce the needed critical dynamics for the development and reshaping of academic groups and debates. Group members gather around leading figures who, delivering a sustained discourse, may negate or affirm (and thus degrade or recharge) the current "sacred objects" of the intellectual community—the respective "scientific truths" or insights that (for a while, respectively) appear as guiding lights and center-points of such communities.[26]

Collins shows us how there are specific, ritualized rules of engagement for intellectual exchange and success, and for the behavior and communication (and potential exclusion) among the "initiated" of an intellectual community. Specific patterns of systematization and sustained references to earlier (related mindful) historical discourse brought about and shaped, for instance, philosophy as an established academic field.[27] Similarly, different foci and systematizations of intellectual practice, anywhere in the world, will also build, shape, and sustain other relevant traditions of knowledge and socially recognized schools of knowledge, with their own particular communities of initiates, practitioners, leading figures, and followers, who believe in, create, and further the "truth" or efficacy of their approach to knowledge in practice.

This description is similarly applicable to other knowledge systems, groups of specialists, and related practices elsewhere, such as described, for instance, in research on healing practices in Africa. Collins's approach resonates with and could be applied, for instance, to the ways in which John Janzen (1992) has analyzed the widespread *ngoma* healing ritual, concurrently as a network of initiates and practitioners with internal hierarchies; as a school of thought, even as a kind of "discipline"; and as a ritual process, involving participation in required forms and prescribed ways.[28] Collins's framework of the sociology of knowledge can also be related to Michael Lambek's hermeneutical approach to the constitution and cultivation of knowledge as a "social fact" in Mayotte. There, schools of knowledge relate to specific theories and practices of healing and harming, and to experts and qualified practitioners employing their knowledge to cure the afflicted. Again, we can say that a systematized body of knowledge-oriented practices has been cultivated, to shape and govern, for instance, the *ilim ny lulu* knowledge complex that Lambek studied as "spirit possession" (Lambek 1993, part III).

These examples show how, analytically, an approach that focuses on intellectual practice is useful to think with because it operates on a relatively underdetermined descriptive level that provides us with the opportunity to employ the same kind of basic analytical vocabulary for different kinds of intellectual traditions and knowledge-oriented practices—thus avoiding double standards and other kinds of established conceptual prejudice that still plague studies of other cultures in the humanities and social sciences, and that have also burdened research on African philosophical traditions for a long time. This could be seen pointedly in the heated ideological debate about "ethno-philosophy." Hountondji (1996) rejected this term as a simplified notion of philosophy for Africa, one that was derived at through collectivizing descriptions of African peoples as supposedly intellectually homogenous and static social entities. This misconception, to follow Hountondji (1983), was also related to a mistaken understanding of "tradition" as fixed, prescribed, and somewhat frozen in time, and of supposedly "traditional" societies as closed, static, and irrational.[29] This issue also pertains to the study of the Muslim world, as we have already covered above.

Swahili Sociality: Intertwining the Discursive, the Social, and the Religious

We can conceive of intellectual practice as the way in which social actors move conceptually through socially mediated (largely discursive) space, concerned about their practical orientation. This discursive space, as much as it is accessible (*offen zugaenglich—oeffentlich*), constitutes a kind of "public" within which people interact, through mediated discourses of their own making and shaping. In the main ethnographic chapters below, I examine the examples of a pamphlet, a newspaper, and a radio broadcast as case studies. Their internal debates and the performances of self-positioning by members of the coastal Muslim community proceed differently within local Islamic media at specific points in the colonial and postcolonial era. But before engaging with case studies, I need to lay out the basic settings and the kind of sociality we are dealing with here. In the historically Muslim urban contexts on the Swahili coast, the social, the discursive, and the religious are mutually interlinked in everyday communication.

When describing social relationships within the Swahili-speaking Muslim community—as they are or as they should be—people employ idioms of speech that express mutual concern for each other. This is done by adding the "reciprocal" linguistic marker for mutuality, the suffix *-an*, at the end of the stem of a Swahili verb, and thus qualifying it as "doing something with each other." The following key terms can be taken as common illustrative examples:

-ju-an-a[30]	*to know each other*
-wasili-an-a	*to communicate (with each other)*
-faham-i-ana (also: -elew-an-a)	*to understand each other*
-kumbush-an-a	*to remind each other*
-elimish-an-a	*to educate each other*
-heshim-i-an-a	*to respect each other*

In this straightforward linguistic way, we may say, the fundamental in-between of the social is expressed, mediating between people and marking what is, after all, social "inter-action." These words, as constructions that point to basic aspects of mutual relatedness in social interaction, also indicate implications of specific fundamental obligations that members of the community have for each other, and these pertain to mutual recognition as moral human beings who should be known, interacted with, respected, and taken care of. In other words, the mutual cultivation of social relationships is expected. In particular, knowledge (informational, educational, and moral) is to be shared. The obligations to remind and to educate each other (*-kumbushana; elimishana*) are the most morally loaded and are often invoked with specific actions in mind (what someone should be reminded of, or taught, in order to avoid outright conflict), while mutual respect marks a general rule of proper behavior. The other expressions underline the value of basic social interaction among members of the community, in being in communication (or "in touch") with each other (*-wasiliana*), knowing each other (*-juana*) and thus being able to understand each other (*-fahamiana*). Thus in everyday life, sociality and language use are fundamentally intertwined, through mutual reference to, and knowledge of, each other.

Of course, this group of words is only indicative on one level (the verbal) of the specific kind of mutually oriented sociality that it expresses, and in which it is embedded. These verbal expressions are complemented by nonverbal ones, such as bodily movements, gestures, and spatial arrangements and positioning. As forms or conventions of self-presentation, ways of walking or standing (or even sitting), as well as ways of speaking (of address, of toning one's voice), in relation to age, gender, descent, and educational background, represent the significant habitus of people within the community interacting with each other. In combination, they indicate and constitute a dynamic whole.[31] In any case, the words above are often invoked and appealed to in everyday social interaction.

They are part of a distinct recognizable vocabulary of, and for, Swahili sociality, as it is commonly conceived. While some express and underline Islamic features, like the obligatory acts of greeting each other and praying together, other quotidian expressions like the common word for good-bye, *tutaonana* (lit., "we will see each other"), and the mutual appeal to stay in communicative touch (lit., "let us communicate"), *tuwasiliane*, also attest to an established emphasis on reciprocity and mutual inclusion.[32]

Thus, when social processes of mutual familiarity, recognition, care, and guidance are directed at each other in social interaction, these expressions mark a discursive space in which knowledge *of* and obligations *for* each other are fundamentally intertwined. This has explicit normative undertones. Social peers (who know, understand, and care for each other) have to guide and educate other members of the community as best as they can.[33] The linguistic constructions of mutuality as ways of being related to each other (in German, *des Aufeinanderbezogenseins*) introduced here express a fundamental social interrelatedness and reflect a basic sense of living together, interdependently, in relation to each other.

Other, similarly common expressions of mutuality in Swahili, however, are to be grouped around semantic aspects of rivalry and challenge, signifying internal frictions. For this, too, the Swahili coast and its city-states have been well known historically: coastal towns, urban moieties, and subgroups (in town quarters and neighborhoods) have been living in mutual challenge and competition with each other.[34] This is indicated by another set of words characterized by the additional "reciprocal" marker of mutuality. These are, for instance, *-shindana* (to compete with each other), *-jibizana* (to challenge each other, or to tease; literally, "to make each other answer"),[35] and *-pingana* (to oppose, and verbally attack each other). This emphasis on internal competitive challenge complements the earlier one on common obligation—and so we could differentiate two basic forms of mutual relatedness for the Swahili context, an "adverse" and challenging one vis-à-vis an "inclusive" and consolidating one.[36]

We may see the sets of words above as an idiomatic semantic field as well as a kind of discursive resource, as they mark the basic social relationships of mutuality or reciprocity and their corresponding performances while weaving the social and the discursive into each other. This resource is frequently made use of in social interaction, such as when reminding each other to be "good," as part of arguments, altercations, and the negotiation of conflict. Normative reminders or demands of this kind involve religion—here Islam—as a basic framework. Thus the religious is also woven into the basic social fabric, as a constitutive normative basis of common social interaction. The overall web of mutual obligations, then, marks the social group in interaction—through shared space, language, norms, and religion—as a "community" proper.[37]

Moral Obligation and the Normative Shaping of Community

In the scenario of everyday life within the Swahili Muslim community, among the verbal expressions of mutual obligations and demands, there appear some cases of explicit Islamic demands that are formulated and voiced in the same linguistic idiom of mutuality and expressed by means of the linguistic construction as illustrated above. Most prominently this is the case for the general obligation of "commanding right and forbidding wrong" that is already documented in the Qur'an and *hadith*, and which has been discussed as a central ethical principle for Muslim societies across the centuries.[38] The Qur'anic uses of this phrase (e.g., 3: 104; 3: 110; 9: 71) emphasize the unity and (potential) outstanding moral quality of the Muslim community insofar as Muslims adhere to right and wrong and remind others about it. From among the *hadith*, it is added that people should forbid wrong relative to their abilities and the respective situations they are in; they should sensitively consider what can be achieved when confronting ruthless oppressors or violent attackers, for instance, and judge whether they can risk acting up, speaking up, or even just silently condemning and resisting the violators of God's commands (Cook 2003, 3–4).

The equivalent Swahili terms *kuamrishana mema* (to command right to one another) and *kukanyana maovu* (to forbid each other wrong) are often used or invoked rhetorically, by preachers, scholars, teachers, parents, and others, whether in formal Islamic discourse (speeches, lectures, or writings) or among peers in everyday life, to remind others of existent moral and religious duties that have to be followed. Again, we are able to find such phrases and narrative postures in historical precolonial Swahili literature, as well as some anti-colonial literature too, both in the combative *mashairi* and in didactic *utendi* poems.[39] As a historical Swahili genre somewhat emblematic of public educational, moralizing, and admonishing discourse with common religious elements, within the regional Muslim social sphere, the *utendi* may even be said to embody such a moral discursive obligation, namely to pass on knowledge and speak up when necessary.

Thus the sense of a socially specific discursive space within the Swahili Muslim community is shaped and reshaped through specific speech acts, verbal art forms, and social practices. Social and discursive "inter-action" in the community, through word and deed, indicates a mutually deictic "being-with-each-other" (reminiscent of Heidegger's *Mit-Sein* as a human existential).[40] This is true for everyday acts such as greeting each other and praying together, as well as more complex intellectual processes, like the actual negotiation of conflicting views and mutual claims and demands vis-à-vis each other, in debates, and also formalized poetry (which in the Swahili context has clear roots in the spoken word, and for several genres has long continued to be meant to be recited publicly).

The insight that the religious is inherent to a conception of moral community, which again is constituted and constantly reconfirmed by performative acts (including speech) of mutual concern, corresponds to Samira Haj's reflections upon a "modern" Islamic conception of morality. She argues that in an Islamic conceptual framework, "the focus on practice and obligation is argued for and grounded in a set of shared beliefs and understandings, which assumes an individual belonging within the [moral historical] community" (Haj 2009, 29).[41] Haj concludes this point by stating that it is indeed the actual performative response to mutual social obligations vis-à-vis each other that makes individual members of the community achieve their moral status. This matches my observations about the Swahili context. "A Muslim as a member of the community is conceived of as *a self that cannot attain its own good except in and through achieving the good of others and vice versa*" (ibid.; my emphasis). This statement also expresses the common view of moral membership to the Swahili Muslim community.

As expressed in a variety of Swahili discursive idioms (only some of which are explicitly Islamic), it is the performative response to socially recognized and pertinent demands that makes individuals achieve moral recognition in return for good behavior. For instance, the overlapping sets of proverbs ranked around *utu*, the central Swahili concept for goodness (lit., human-ness, with emphasis on being humane), emphasize the social character of human beings and the achievement of morality through performance: *mtu ni utu* (a human being is goodness), *mtu si kitu* (a human being is not a thing), *mtu ni watu* (a human being is people), *utu ni kitendo* (goodness is action).[42] In comparative view across the Muslim world, this links up again with shared ideas about a "public interest" or "common good" (in Arabic, *al-maslaha al-amma*) in society that is realized through mutual social responsibility performed in public interaction (Tripp 2006, 55; Salvatore and Eickelman 2006).

These sets of elaborations on such a social web of mutual obligations, expressed and enacted through words and action, link to the anthropological project of accounting for "ordinary ethics" in everyday interactions, a project that Michael Lambek engages in (2010; 2015). He emphasizes the important point that people, anywhere in the world, in their everyday interactions, often conceive of themselves as consciously ethical agents who seek to do good. This is a perspective that anthropology has until recently neglected, often relying on established conceptual boxes like "politics" and "religion" (Lambek 2010, 1–4).[43] Linking Austin's speech act theory and Rappaport's critical theory of ritual with Arendt's theory of human creativity, Lambek advocates that the ethical is intrinsic to ordinary language and one's performative action or behavior in everyday life. Following Hanna Arendt, he argues that judgment (of one's own and others' social action) is something that is required and necessarily exercised in everyday life by everyone, anywhere in the world. In actual situations in which people have to respond, as they need to behave somehow, in relation to criteria that are already part of their web of social interrelations, as "instantiated through human speech and action"—in this sense, he argues, "Ethics is intrinsic because there are always criteria already in place" (43). We are always already part of an existing social world with norms to be adhered to, and we justify our actions accordingly.[44] This actual necessity for people, of having to make judgments because they have to act within the practical situations they find themselves in, had long before been pointed out by Kant, in a useful essay on what it means to find orientation in one's thinking. In practice and within specific situations, his argument goes, social actors cannot avoid having to position themselves vis-à-vis others, within the already existent norms and pressures of the world they live in. And in positioning themselves, they draw from a reservoir of available normative reference points (that they can adhere to, reject, transgress).[45]

Lambek speaks of a kind of "ordinary ethics" (coined after the example of Austin's ordinary language philosophy) that individuals are enveloped in, as they are "entailed in these performative and practical qualities of speech and action, promising and beginning, forgiveness and acknowledgment" (2010, 53). These are aspects that human beings everywhere recurrently engage in, simply by way of participating in social interaction, in their specifically normatively tuned and semantically structured life-worlds. We may do well to continue thinking with this in mind, and then recall the general Islamic demand of "commanding right and forbidding wrong" (see Cook 2000). Invocations and contestations of this demand are present, visible, and audible in Swahili Muslim publics and in everyday life, and they may also be seen as a regionally specific variant of such "ordinary ethics" inherent in everyday life among Muslims (and not only a label or shorthand for an intended universal and definitive kind of "Islamic ethics" in an emphatic sense).[46] We can see Lambek's point illustrated in Swahili everyday life, too, that ethical demands are always already in place within a (mutually oriented) social community; they are inherent to it, and acts of invoking them publicly reaffirm them as valid, reminding others of the need to keep them in mind when acting, as they will be judged according to them.

These kinds of reminders, invocations, and reaffirmations of norms occur in everyday discourse and practice, as part of disputes or arguments and debates, or as part of educational discourses or moral warnings to others, in different settings, and in various ways of communication. They are formalized in genres of admonishing poetry (like the *utendi*), in Islamic sermons or writings and publications, in parental and educational advice, and in conversations among neighbors and friends.

Such socially embedded debates and discussions are the most common kind of Swahili intellectual practice in everyday life, thus combining sociality, fundamental being-with-each-other (see Heidegger's *Mit-Sein*) or being in communicative relation with each other (-*wasiliana*), with discursive mutuality, the "generic" -*jadiliana* (mutual discussion; teasing; challenging) that expresses mutual discussion and competitive verbal exchange. This is what constantly happens, for instance, at *barazas*, regular social meeting points in front of people's houses (or mosques). Men of the neighborhood meet at *barazas* to discuss the events of the day as well as any other specific matters of interest.[47] These groups assemble before or after evening prayers and can build their discussions on an intimate social knowledge about each other. We might speak of *baraza* settings as traditional emerging publics, or rather semi-public spaces in the Swahili setting: while all social interaction is local and face to face, the rules of participation are partly of the kind of discourse-oriented abstractions that characterize "publics" (the accessibility of a common discursive space; and the reasonability of discursive negotiation).[48] At the same time, the ethical principles of mutual obligation in social interaction continue to hold: educating one's peers, reminding each other of what is right, and warning each other against doing wrong. These are recurring instances at the heart of *baraza* discussions. This happens similarly in other social settings and discursive genres, too.

As already mentioned, we can also turn to classic examples from Swahili poetry. For centuries poetry has been an immensely rich and important field of social discourse comprising many subfields and genres in coastal society, fulfilling roles as political instrument, historical mnemonic device, space for riddles, intellectual challenges, wordplay, religious and worldly education, and private and public expressions.[49] It is striking to see that, with a view to the distinctions made above, we can generally speak of two corresponding generic types of Swahili poetry, which can be characterized as, firstly, educational, moralizing, and admonishing, and thus inclusive and enhancing a sense of unity by stressing mutual obligation within the community (e.g., the *utendi* genre); and secondly, as adverse and challenging, thus expressing rivalry and competition, either internal to the community or vis-à-vis an outside group (e.g., in the *shairi* and *nyimbo* genres). Interestingly, all recitations (i.e., all performances) of these old and common genres of Swahili poetry—that were written in order to be orally performed, and thus have a special mediating and dual status (in some ways comparable to the Qur'an)—constitute the sensitive (aural) formation of a discursive public.

Having experienced, in their upbringing, common forms of joint listening to didactic or historical *tenzi* epics, with their admonishing tone and often tragic content, Swahili native speakers produce a certain attitude of acquired emotionally charged habitus of listening (*Gestimmtheit*). Listening to other kinds of poetry like *nyimbo* or *shairi* can similarly go along with a different kind of habitus, a provocative or daring one, as these genres are often used to challenge, to insult, or to ridicule rivals or opponents, both in private and political contexts (wars; battles; election campaigns).[50] This often happens in the form of riddles or enigmatic language, or for instance popular music, like *taarab*, that is built on the *nyimbo* genre. Moreover, as many studies have shown (especially Askew 2002),[51] the creative ways in which (semi-) public performances of popular songs can be appropriated for private disputes and rivalries (notably about lovers and related jealousies) have no clearly defined limits. Thus publicly uttered words known to all listeners can still be used to mediate private messages in a complex double entendre that nobody but those involved will understand. Such usages of poetry in social interaction point to the duality or double existence of texts that Karin Barber (2007) emphasized, with texts both mediating a message and at the same time (possibly) commenting on the message that is in the process of being transmitted.

Intellectual practice, as much as it is explicitly concerned with Islam—that is, as much as Muslims invoke or refer directly to Islamic knowledge as guidance and to their own religious self-understanding as Muslims—indicates Muslims' "ways of reasoning and reasons for arguing" within the *umma*, from a locally based and transregionally guided perspective (Asad 1986; also Mandaville 2001). It is valuable, then, to study the intricacies of these aspects, and the relationships between ways of reasoning and reasons for arguing, as part of the internal dynamics of the *umma* in its local and transregional varieties. It links knowledge about reflexive processes, arguments, and their expression and presentation within society with awareness about the motivations that trigger disputes, mutual challenges, and contested discursive exchange. Thus in combination, we may be able to acquire a picture of both how and why people think, argue, and express themselves in particular social spheres or (trans)regional settings.[52]

Placing Intellectual Practice within Islam as Discursive Tradition

Apart from being a world religion, Islam can be understood as a discursive tradition.Muslims from the different parts of the world sometimes disagree about what is considered right or wrong, and need to discuss or argue over properly following Islamic rules. Muslims are members of a globally dispersed community, the *umma*, whose accepted authoritative sources about norms and proper behavior are the Qur'an and *hadith*. This is why internal arguments among Muslims usually refer to them. According to Talal Asad (following the moral philosopher Alisdair McIntyre), discursive traditions, and Islam among them, represent historically shaped and dynamically reshaped continuities between past, present, and future that are identifiable by the shared reference points invoked by its members. Research on Islam, Asad argued, had neglected exploring the diverse regional "indigenous discourses" and particular narrative styles that, in their interweaving character, actually constitute "the world of Islam" as a dynamic set of overlapping discursive traditions. His approach sought to do just this, following the internal dynamics of reasoning that involve reference to Qur'an and *hadith*. As a guideline, he said, "the ways of reasoning and the reasons for arguing" among Muslims should be analyzed to understand Muslim communities from within. An internal perspective on society was needed, to be able to follow the specific historical dynamics of discourse and interaction (Asad 1986, 7–11; on *umma* and Qur'an and *hadith*, 14).

Samira Haj has elaborated further upon the dynamic character of "tradition" in her study of key figures of Islamic reform, clarifying that "tradition refers not simply to the past or its repetition but rather to *the pursuit of an ongoing coherence* by making reference to a set of texts, procedures, arguments and practices" (Haj 2009, 5; my emphasis). It is as a result of the intellectual effort put into the flexible production of such coherence in a rapidly changing life-world that we can understand the *ulama* as "custodians of change" (to use the expression by M. Q. Zaman, 2002). Moreover, "a tradition is not simply the recapitulation of previous beliefs and practices; rather, each successive generation confronts its particular problems via an engagement with a set of ongoing arguments" (Haj 2009, 6). Methodologically, then, this indicates the need to combine ethnographic and historical research on the specific forms of the construction of meaning in different contexts of interaction. The forms of intellectual practice involved, such as the negotiation of arguments about right and wrong, "proper behavior," or a "good life," as part of a knowledge-oriented process of reasoning, need to be understood with regard to the particular settings and dimensions of their time.

Strategic forms of reference-making and argued responses to challenges (as explored in subsequent chapters) are indeed expressed and mediated through social practices that are "intellectual" because they are driven and motivated by knowledge and expertise. The engagement with ongoing arguments is a kind of self-positioning that proceeds intellectually (at least in part), and so is the invocation of texts, procedures, and arguments. In each region or social community, this is mediated by (or performed in) particular forms, genres, narrative styles, and rhetoric.

Reason and Tradition, Knowledge and Language

This is true not only for Islam and the global *umma*, but also for other discursive traditions. Similar concerns have been raised and parallel arguments made in African studies debates over a corresponding period of time. This was connected to the fact that African societies, like Muslim societies, had largely been conceptualized as Western societies' other, namely as more "simple" (as opposed to "complex"), "traditional" (i.e., static and fixed, as opposed to "modern"), and "closed" (as opposed to "open"; see also Horton 1970, drawing from Popper), and with a neglect of their historical dynamics, internal debates, and intellectual achievements. African thinkers responded to such simplified images of their societies with a variety of conceptual points and arguments—among them, "how not to compare African traditional thought and Western thought," as Kwasi Wiredu emphasized in a classic essay insisting on the need to respect and stick to proper levels of comparison (Wiredu 1980). Paulin Hountondji, in turn, castigated the "extroverted" nature of Africanist research (by both Western and African researchers) in speaking to the interests of a Western audience of former colonizers and thus deepening existent dependency relationships (1996; 1990). He made clear that reason and tradition are by no means mutually exclusive (Hountondji 1983). On the contrary, "traditions" (originating etymologically from the Latin *tradere*: to transmit or mediate), have always fulfilled a dynamic function of mediating or passing on, to the next generation, ideas and practices that proved valuable and meaningful in society (1983, 139), thus constructing a continuity between past, present, and future (to which Asad in 1986 and Zaman in 2002 refer when looking at Islam). Hountondji also emphasized the need for research to focus on internal criteria for knowledge, and the shifting dynamics of its internal contestation and negotiation in society, by advocating a focus on the historical and scientific dimensions of "endogenous knowledge"[53] (1997), and on the specific varieties of "internal pluralism" (1983, 137; 1996, 168).

Along the same lines of critique, in a scientific discourse he called "Africanism"—parallel to Said's "Orientalism"—V. Y. Mudimbe (1988; 1994) laid out the contours of Western scholarly constructions of "Africa" from ancient Greece to the present. As a constructive demand for future research, Mudimbe coined the much-quoted slogan that studies of knowledge, philosophy, and African intellectual culture more widely need to follow the framework and criteria of "African epistemes" (Mudimbe 1988, viii). Kwasi Wiredu pushed a similar point, by arguing for "the need of conceptual decolonization" in African philosophy (1995; 1996). He called for liberation from the constraints that education and institutional academic practice in the former colonial languages had imposed upon African thinkers, and for a reorientation toward African concepts as central pillars for philosophical reflection, seeking to link up contemporary academic philosophy with "African philosophical traditions" (Wiredu 1996, 113–135). While Wiredu never advocated a radical turn to afrophone literature and philosophy in the way that Hountondji called for (Hountondji 1996, 168) and Ngũgĩ has long practiced,[54] the shared emphasis on the need for linguistic sensitivity, recognizing the value of African languages as intellectual tools and resources, is remarkable. This sensitivity is also shared with Africanist researchers in anthropology, literature, and history who study dynamic traditions of knowledge and their internal contestations, with a focus on language use, rhetoric, and reasoning (e.g., Barber; Vail and White; Askew; Janzen; MacGaffey). My own research here is stimulated by these different interdisciplinary and transregional fields of research, and draws from them as needed. And while the reflection upon postcolonial experience and its ongoing effects, in scholarship and the wider world, unites academic representatives of "postcolonial thought" from Africa, the Middle East, South Asia, and the global south more widely, I also seek to grasp, by ethnographic means, as much of an understanding as possible under the circumstances, of the actual thinking, debating and reasoning processes that take place as efforts of intellectual orientation as part of everyday life within society—what we may call "postcolonial thinking" (on which I shall say more below).

Overall, in this book I look at how specific reasoning and arguing processes are shaped, expressed, and negotiated, and how they make sense in a specific cultural and religious context and a regional language different from Western paradigms. Providing ethnographic-cum-conceptual accounts of particular case studies of intellectual practice gives us valuable insight, not only about society elsewhere, but also about the thinking of society (and the wider world) from that particular elsewhere. Based on this, we may be able to reflect upon conceptual and practical tendencies, implicit to and suggested by such case studies, and clarify their conceptual frameworks, in order to work out and employ them as serious, reasonable alternatives to think with more generally; of thinking the world, and thinking society.

Sociality, Discursive Space, Texts

Intellectual practice refers to social action by means of which knowledge is invoked, acquired, passed on, qualified, or negotiated, and this is most commonly done discursively. In variable forms and genres that relate to social circumstances and situations, from sayings, riddles, and playful teasing to confrontational mocking and serious scholarly research (for instance), and as part of social interaction, the scope of intellectual practice is related to regionally specific types of sociality.[55] Forms of expression and genres of speech and texts correspond to the ways people interrelate in society. As they are being shaped by people in interrelation, these mediators of communication (texts and media) are in turn reshaping the people that use them. I argue that "intellectual practice" refers to the ways in which social actors move conceptually through mediated discursive (or otherwise meaningful) space, as they are concerned about proper orientation for themselves and about the ascription of meaning in society, especially in terms of their own status, prospects, and perspective. These mediated spaces, as much as they are openly accessible for people to engage with and contribute to, constitute kinds of socially specific "publics" in which people interact.[56] Now, as intellectual practice can be described as knowledge-oriented and socially embedded movement through meaningful social space, an empirical focus on it allows us to see more clearly what kinds of social spaces there are specifically, and how social actors actually move through them. In other words, this can also be a useful entry point to the study of society more generally.

In the subsequent chapters, therefore, I introduce the interrelationships between intellectual practice and Swahili Muslim publics on the one hand, and on the other, between intellectual practice and platforms, strategies, and forms of mediation providing the spaces and channels within which the actual seeking of orientation, the provision of guidance, and the struggle of negotiating one's own position vis-à-vis others, individually and socially, take place. In the contexts investigated here, these acts of self-positioning are pronounced through the kind of postcolonial experience (of marginalization) endured by coastal Muslims in Kenya. As part of these reflections, I also touch on the kinds of strategies developed by social actors in response to the challenges that the specific conditions of their postcolonial experience impose upon them. Showing how the spheres of the social, the moral, and the religious are mutually intertwined in social interaction in the Swahili context, this book presents an initial diachronic comparative discussion of Swahili invocations of the general Islamic obligation of "commanding right and forbidding wrong" (Cook 2000) in chapter 2. Then, looking at the ways of how these were employed in three different Swahili Islamic media projects, this is explored in more detail in the chapters that follow (chapters 3, 4 and 5).

Conceptualizations and "Thinking Society"

Looking at the layers that overlap and complement each other in this study, I have sketched out the conceptual trajectories to be pursued here. The task is to gain an understanding of the internal perspectives on the agendas of engaged individuals, for the media platforms they create and shape. The analytic strands here, with their overlapping emphases—on texts, publics, knowledge, rhetoric, reasoning, and mediation processes—were flagged up for their respective value for the exploration of the internal tensions and debates marking the coastal Kenyan Muslim community at different points in time. Above, we have gained an initial sense of how knowledge, language use, and normative obligations are interwoven in social interaction and become constitutive of intellectual practice as a research field. An analytic focus on their interrelationships enables us to better understand the different kinds of mindful interaction (*Sich-Auseinandersetzen*) in society, and the values attributed to different positions. From such a point of analysis, we can approach the conceptual reservoir that the societies we study have to offer, also for possible paradigms to think with more generally, such as in social theory.

Through ethnographic accounts of regional universes of intellectual practice, insight is gained, as I said, not only into society elsewhere, but also about the thinking of society from that particular elsewhere. This may be internally contested but shares a common conceptual framework. Gaining insights into the specific dynamics of society, while looking at the discursive negotiation of self and self-positioning within a strained community under external pressures, cannot be brought about without ethnographic knowledge based on fieldwork with local actors and close readings of their texts (or texts that matter to them). Overall, as I spell out in the concluding chapter, I seek to show that by working with (and not just on) concepts, idioms, and insights from our regions of study, in our ethnographies and close readings, we actively work toward the overcoming of the dominance of Eurocentric frameworks for analysis. The success of this is reliant upon available pathways of thinking society differently, based on accessible regional models from elsewhere (here, the Swahili coast)—and it is our task as researchers, and particularly as anthropologists, to make them accessible.

This is where the current ethnographic and anthropological project links up with and feeds into the bigger questions and concerns of social theory, philosophy, and postcolonial critique. In particular, research on African philosophy has long been calling for the need to (re)write substantial accounts of African traditions of thought and intellectual history on the basis of "African epistemes" (after Mudimbe 1988), as I have mentioned above. This book thus works toward overcoming the ongoing predominance of analytic approaches and frameworks that are molded upon variations of Western epistemes and overcoming the sense of an ongoing extroverted and Eurocentric perspective in the understanding of African thought and intellectual practice.[57]

This also means to adjust and augment the kind of analytic language we use for understanding the world, so that we will gradually overcome a largely monolingual—anglophone—paradigm of study and replace it with a multilingual one. Recently, Ousmane Kane (2012) has made a convincing conceptual argument along these lines, for the study of "non-Europhone intellectuals." Kane is particularly interested in the Islamic arabophone and Ajami library that is an integral part of African intellectual history.[58] He criticizes two of the most established figures in African philosophy, V. Y. Mudimbe and Kwame Anthony Appiah, for confining their focus and interest to Europhone discourse (2012, 1–3). While I do not agree entirely with this critique (as the work of both is important for exploring afrophone intellectual histories), the thrust of Kane's call for more new research efforts, to work thoroughly on intellectual traditions (thinkers, concepts, narratives), is timely and important: Histories of endogenous creative and critical thinking in African languages need to be investigated, from the past into the present. A focus on the respective regional specifics of intellectual practice is necessary for a rich and complex understanding of African intellectual traditions.

Ngũgĩ wa Thiong'o has been arguing for decades, with a sharpness and consistency that we do not often find among African philosophers,[59] that true intellectual liberation for Africa needs to proceed through African languages—and it is hard to see how this could not be so. The cultivation of critical thought through them needs to be pushed and supported, as well as the exploration and documentation of afrophone conceptual frameworks and traditions in historical and contemporary usage. Recently, Ngũgĩ (2013, 162) has challenged African philosophers to philosophize "in African languages directly" and thus "add originality to the wealth of human knowledge."[60]

We may connect these points (more or less closely) to some of the calls of postcolonial critique over the last decades; there is a clear resonance and family resemblance, in terms of a wider project envisaged (or to be envisaged). We can think, for instance, of Ngũgĩ wa Thiong'o's vision of "decolonizing the mind" (Ngũgĩ 1981) that is working toward "moving the centre" (Ngũgĩ 1993) of global thought and intellectual debate, in tandem with Kwasi Wiredu's call for "conceptual decolonization" (1995; 1996) in African philosophical thought. Looking beyond African authors, as we have seen, Chakrabarty's well-known (and controversially discussed) call for "provincializing Europe" (orig. 2000) is another case in point, for putting the West in its place, as one region among others in world history, and in terms of the ways in which this is narrated and human society is conceptualized—and the recent project of establishing "world philology" as a critical intellectual project across languages and regions can be seen as one fruitful pathway in this direction (Pollock et al. 2015).

In his concluding reflections on the project of a critical intellectual "post-Orientalism"—which may be understood as a kind of critical postcolonial critique of postcolonialism—Hamid Dabashi (2009, 272–73) suggests that "changing the interlocutor" can make all the difference for the character and the terms of critical debate. The West should no longer be seen or treated as the "principle interlocutor" of the world, the generic intellectual counterpart to be argued with and to be convinced—which, Dabashi says, the West remained even throughout the postcolonial projects of Edward Said and Gayatri Spivak. This call for a different common interlocutor (or perhaps more appropriately in plural—different interlocutors) from non-Western regions, meaning audiences and engaged intellectuals from postcolonial elsewheres, who may then be critical "listeners" as well as vivid "narrators" of humanity's relevant stories (and histories), is important, as it redirects our perspective. Indeed, seeking to understand the significant guiding role of active narrators and critics in societies elsewhere—in this case, from the Swahili coast—and the potential significance of narratives and critiques from there, is my concern here. This can be done through specific accounts of the complex regional types and paradigms of thinking the world and finding orientation in it. As researchers, we take on the role of both narrators and critical listeners, and we contribute by means of sensitive and critical engagement, according to our specific disciplinary, regional, and personal qualifications, to the wider project of "rethinking the world"—of making possible for others to rethink it according to paradigms and perspectives from elsewhere.

Notes

1. They use Swahili as their primary language in everyday life, and they are usually referred to as "Swahili" or "Arab" (for those of Omani or Hadrami origin) or "Mijikenda" (for people from the coastal hinterland). Members of Muslim groups who immigrated long ago from South Asia but kept a separate religious and social identity that is also marked in everyday life, like the Bohras, Ismailis, Khojas, and Kenyan Somalis, are not included in the way I use this term here, though of course one could say they are Muslims living on the coast.

2. For a related leitmotif in Zanzibari discourse, see Bissel 2011.

3. For historical accounts, see Coupland 1965; Al-Amin Mazrui 1995; Strandes 1961 (1899).

4. See also Triulzi (1981), who has spoken of such a constellation. I am grateful to Roman Loimeier for making me aware of this.

5. During a Ramadhan lecture in Mombasa, in January 1999.

6. For instance, in part of the Lamu *maulidi* sermon quoted below, the speaker characterized the experience of enduring KANU and NARC periods of rule thus (my translation): "This is something that the government should know, that we don't have peace with the government. . . . I said to my friends one day in our discussions about the new constitution, 'If you want to understand the Kenyan governments of KANU and of NARC, just look at an Arabic poem and an aya from the Qur'an'." About the KANU government, the Arab poet says, "Stick to Allah but don't mention him"; "saying his name is forbidden"; "sleep with Allah but don't wake up"; "nobody succeeds today except for the one who sleeps"; "if you are told that your day is night and very dark, and if you are told your honey is bitter, be patient, and you will ultimately win". This was about "our KANU government experience, and about [our] NARC [experience]," the poet says, "You have been given the freedom of speech there, where there is no freedom of speech; but then you did not speak, until you burst/exploded" (Maulidi sermon by Sayyid Aydarus, 2006, circulating on cassette).

7. In this case, Swafaa Mosque. These communal recitations are the main ritual and celebratory event of the *maulidi* festivities, which include lots of other recitations and other performances—some of which are clearly Islamic in character and present and perpetuate a certain ideal of piety, while others emphasize a festive (and almost party-like) character that captures the whole town; some of the latter are performed in the vicinity of main mosques (recitals of ancient poetry to drumming; mock fighting; dancing) and some at the seafront (sailing races; donkey races; board games; swimming competitions). Like in other parts of the Muslim world, *maulidi* celebrations and specific practices and performances within them are rejected as unacceptable "innovations" (*bidaa*) by Salafi- and Wahhabi-oriented reformists. Debates about the propriety of *maulidi* celebrations (in general, and in terms of specific aspects) abound on the Swahili coast.

8. Umefika wakati wa pwani kwa jumla tufikirie suluhisho. Suluhisho lisiwe kwenye kiwango cha madiwani, wala kwa kiwango cha mabunge, wala kwa kiwango cha kupewa mawazo katika serikali. Zote hizi zimedhibitika hazifai. . . . Lazima tupange *strategy* mpya. Tujitambulishe kama wapwani. Na kwamba tuna haya. Tuna karata hizi tunaweza kuzitumia. . . . Wapwani, lazima tufikirie. Lazima tujiwekee mwelekeo mpya wa siasa. Na tuwafahamishe hawa kwamba sisi ni sisi. Tusingojee wao kutufahamisha. Tujitambue tusiongojee kutambuliwa. . . . Mpaka leo kuna shaka ya Ukenya wetu? . . . Mwona matatizo ya taa, mwaka ingia, mwaka toka. Tuko kwenye matatizo hayo. Maji ni shida, barabara

matatizo, kila sampuni zinaingia. Mpaka lini tutabaki kuimbaimba wimbo moja? Wimbo ni huohuo. Na kila mwanasiasa yao yuwatutumia kwa wimbo huo.

9. Sisi hatuwaamini. Msipoteze wakati. Hatuwaamini. Nini tumekipata jamaani, kwenye serikali hizi zinazobadilika, sisi kama wa pwani ama kama waislamu. Jamaa nini mafuta yatakavyo kufukuliwa huku, hayatokuwa kama pesa ngapi zinazoingia Kilindini Mombasa? . . . tujaribuni kufuatilia mambo tujue, ni pesa ngapi za ingia kwa siku pale, kwa siku moja? Iko wapi Kilindini? Iko Mombasa? Nini watu wa Mombasa au watu wa mwambao, wa pwani, wamepata wanaweza kujivunia? . . . Aina ya offisi kuu za Kilindini ziko Nairobi.

10. Mwambie Bwana Waziri tutamwomba Mwenyezi Mungu atupe dua, tuyaombee mkienda mafuta yamekauka.

11. On the *utendi/utenzi* genre and its language, rules, and conventions, see Allen 1971; Noor Shariff 1988; Vierke 2011, 6–95). *Utendi* is the Northern Swahili version (used in Lamu and Mombasa), *utenzi* the Southern one (from Zanzibar and Tanzania), also more common in Standard Swahili.

12. This initial address to the reader is overloaded with references to the "coastal" region and its character, and it reads overloaded (though less clumsy) in the original Swahili too: "*Majimbo* ni kijitabu muongozo cha hamasa cha kumzindua mpwani kuonyesha kukinai kwa mateso, maonevu, unyonge na dhuluma afanyiwazo kwa malengo ya kumfanya mpwani asimame kiupwani kwa ajili ya jimbo lake la pwani na kupata uhuru kamili wa mwambao ama jimbo letu la wapwani. Ahsante. Mwandishi." (Khuchi 2011)

13. The quoted text is the MRC's published English version, which is not an exact translation of the MRC's Swahili version of the manifesto, given here: (p. 2) "Sisi raia wa Pwani hatuna uhusiano na katiba inayoendelea Kenya. Pwani (Mombasa) iko na daraja lake kihalali la kulindwa. Nchi hii (Mombasa) inayochanuka kuanzia Bahari ya Hindi hadi Sultan Hamud, kutoka Lungalunga hadi Kismayu, amabyo inamilikiwa na wenyeji waitwao: 1. Wamijikenda, 2. Wataita, 3. Wapokomo, 4. Wabajuni, 5. Waarabu, 6. Wahindi . . . Nchi hii (Mombasa) imekuwa uwanja wa Wakenya kupora na kujitarisha na raslimali zetu.— MATAKWA YETU: Jamii zenyewe kama tulivyozitaja hapa juu zinataka mabwana watawala wao (Wakenya)."

14. Again, the wording of the MRC's Swahili version differs from the English text: "Tunawaombeni ninyi wenzetu tuungane ili tubadilishe mkataba. Wapwani tuamke ili tufaulu kuyapata haya yote tuliyoyataja ndani ya huu mwongozo, na mengine mengi ambayo hatuwezi kuyapata chini ya huu uongozi mbaya wa kikoloni kutoka Kenya. Na imeelezwa wazi katika mkataba wa tarehe 8/10/1963 ya kuwa serikali ya Kenya imeingiliana majukumu maalum kuhusiana na ulinzi baada ya Kenya kupata uhuru" (2010, 12).

15. Oral communication, Jasmin Mahazi, August 2013; see also Mwakimako and Willis 2016.

16. Note that the trope of "singing along" was also used by President Moi himself (quoted in Ngugi 1981, 63), as well as by Ngugi in his critical and partly satirical novel on the Moi regime in Kenya, *Matigari* (Ngugi 1987).

17. The Kenyan African National Union (KANU) was the ruling party that shaped an increasingly authoritarian one-party state, initially under Jomo Kenyatta (1963–1978) and then under Daniel arap Moi (1978–2002).

18. See Salim 1970; Brennan 2008; also Robertson Report 1960 and report on Lancaster House Conference 1962 (Colonial Office 1960, 1962). This paragraph is also based on a number of personal conversations I had with Sheikh Abdilahi Nassir, then the leader of the *mwambao* movement, between 1998 and 2016.

19. Hornsby 2012; Branch 2011. Other communities have also experienced, in their own particular ways, a sense of living on one of Kenya's postcolonial peripheries.

20. In fact, during a public speech in front of a large crowd on Kenyatta Day (October 20) 1967, Kenyatta threatened (and encouraged) explicitly to have KPU oppositionals exterminated ("killed like snakes") (Kenyatta 1968, 343–44). This period of Kenyatta's rule was also the beginning of systematic governmental propaganda literature that lasted until the end of the Moi period in late 2002 (see, e.g., Kenyatta 1971; Moi 1982; Moi 1986; Godia 1984; Njiru and Kutswa 1997). In response, oppositional pamphlets and gray literature, partly activist, partly academic, raised critique (e.g., UMOJA 1989; KHRC 1998; KHRC n.d.; Rutten and Mazrui 1997; Cohen and Odhiambo 2004).

21. For a historical contextualizing account of the pamphlet, also with a view to more recent postcolonial experience, see my recent article on rereading *"Kenya: Twendapi?"* (Kresse 2016), which also includes an English translation of the pamphlet and a reprint of the Swahili original (Abdalla 2016).

22. I found that linking myself to a hermeneutical take on the anthropology of knowledge (Lambek 1993) enabled me to refer to social processes and practices surrounding the invocation, mediation, and contestation of knowledge, while zooming in on specific (potentially philosophical) instances of conceptual critique or fundamental reflections on society, on being human, or other conceptual foci I came across (see Kresse 2007).

23. This is an expression from Ato Quayson's (2003) critical project of (re-)"reading for the social" in anglophone postcolonial literature—a field that is otherwise constrained by the limitations of europhone conceptions in ways that Swahili and other afrophone thinking is not.

24. See MacGaffey 1983, 1986, and especially 2000. For related Africanist works laying out fundamental aspects of regional intellectual culture in different ways, see, for example, Feierman 1990; Lonsdale 1992b; Peterson 2004; Ricard 2004; and also Hallen 2000; Hallen and J. O. Sodipo 1997; Abiodun 2015; James 1988; and Johnson 1994.

25. Here, Collins builds on the idea of "interaction rituals" as developed by Goffman (1967).

26. Note that this is not a relativist conception. See also: "Intellectual life hinges on face-to-face situations because interaction rituals can take place only on this level. Intellectual sacred objects can be created and sustained only if there are ceremonial gatherings to worship them. This is what lectures, conferences, discussions, and debates do: they gather the intellectual community, focus members' attention on a common object uniquely their own, and build up distinctive emotions around those objects" (R. Collins 1998, 26).

27. Collins illustrates and discusses substantial historical case studies from European philosophy (e.g., German romanticism) and Chinese philosophy by means of an actor-network theory approach, combined with selective readings.

28. They also resonate well with the social networks and knowledge–power configurations (which their experts are said to cultivate and control) that Wyatt MacGaffey (2000) has elaborated upon in the Central African Bakongo region, with a view to *minkisi* and *kindoki* practices (often simplistically translated as "witchcraft"—in Swahili, *uchawi*), which involve processes of healing and harming and, as MacGaffey shows, constitute a regionally distinct "political culture."

29. To be seen also in timeless generalizing expressions like "Zulu thought," "Yoruba ethics" or "Luo aesthetics." On the ethnophilosophy debate, see, for instance, Hountondji (1996), Appiah (1992), Neugebauer (1991), and Oruka (1990).

30. The hyphen at the beginning is the common notation for a verb in Swahili, replacing the initial *"ku"* which otherwise marks the infinitive verb form.

31. See also Gilsenan 2005, 269–273. The specific sub-varieties of verbal and nonverbal aspects could be extended considerably.

32. Indeed, "reciprocity" is a good comparative term here. The kinds of mutual relatedness in verbal and wider social interaction in the Swahili context, including the obligation to respond at least in kind, could have provided material for another regional chapter of Marcel Mauss's fundamental account of reciprocity as a "total social phenomenon" (1967). While a historical study of this with particular view on gift giving (and receiving) is out of reach here, there is some literature dealing with this. Interestingly, during times of much better general economic status of coastal Muslims than today, the notion of conspicuous consumption, and of competing and outgiving (and thus beating) one's social others, encapsulated in the rival group or urban moiety (or town), was common and can still be traced today (see Prestholdt 2008; Strobel 1976 and 1979; Ranger 1975; Askew 2002; Fair 2001).

33. A friend, for instance, is expected to stand up for and responsibly help to resolve any conflicts or pending debts (to others), even after death (Nassir 1979, "*mbasi mwema*").

34. Historical accounts of such challenges between towns and within them (e.g., Mombasa, Lamu, Pate, Faza, and Siyu) document this well (e.g., Tolmacheva et al. 1993; Berg 1968; Prins 1965; el-Zein 1974).

35. Literally, "making each other answer (to each other)"; originally from *–jibu*, to answer. *Kujibizana* is also the term for dialogue-poetry in Swahili (e.g., Samsom 1996; Biersteker 1996). It has a long historical tradition, also as mocking one's opponent before battle, and almost always has a challenging character (e.g., Abdulaziz 1979; Biersteker and Noor Sheriff 1995).

36. Note that these observations resonate with Randall Collins's discussion in his sociology of philosophies. Emphasizing that intellectuals, like all social groups, engage in common constitutive interaction rituals, he flags up a basic dialogical constitution of a group of peers, in which the members share a focus of attention in the mutual awareness of each other's engagement; in the course of an intensifying commitment of attention to their intellectual activity, they experience a sense of group solidarity with felt moral obligations to each other (Collins 1998, 22–23).

37. Notably, all key features constitutive of "community" here are of performative character: they can be acquired, and they are not essentialist features (e.g., of descent) that mark a community as exclusive. This makes sense in the situation of wide-ranging transregional social connectivity that has marked the Swahili coastal ports for many centuries, in economic and religious respects, linking them up with global trade routes (e.g., Horton 1987) and religious networks (e.g., Horton and Middleton 2000).

38. The historical debates by notable Islamic scholars across different orientations and *madhhab* have been comprehensively covered by Michael Cook (2000; more basic in 2003). In my generalizations here, I rely on Cook.

39. See, for example, Allen 1971; Nassir 1977; Nassir 1979; Miehe and Bromber 2002; Biersteker and Noor Shariff 1995; Saavedra Casco 2007.

40. In Heidegger (1963) *Sein und Zeit*.

41. Haj describes Muhammad Abduh's goal as "the moral survival of the [Muslim] community" (2009, 28).

42. See more extensive discussions in Kresse 2007 (139–175) and Kresse 2011.

43. But see the recent trend of substantial commendable research on it, also called an "ethical turn" in anthropology (Fassin 2014); for example, Lambek 2010 and 2015; Laidlaw 2014; and Lambek, Das, Fassin, and Keane 2015.

44. Furthermore, "language is central to the ethical and the ethical to language, both to language in the abstract, in the sense of grammar and semantics (langue), and to acts

of speaking, pragmatics and meta-pragmatics (parole)" (49). He takes "speech to be a subcategory of acts (or, perhaps, acts to be a subcategory of speaking)" (2010, 50).

45. In his essay "Was heisst: sich im Denken orientieren?" Kant (1913) provides us with a useful illustration of the primary role of the "practical" (in contrast to the theoretical) orientation, as it responds to the experience of immediate factual constellations or confrontations—where we must act. In Kant's words, we have to judge because we have to act (*weil wir handeln muessen*).

46. This may be all the more so, as this demand does not refer to a specific understanding or definition of what is "right" or "wrong"; it refers to an already established implicit (or inherent) valid sense of this within the community in which the demand is used—and it remains the work of knowledgeable (scholarly) interpretation to clarify and determine exactly the rightness or wrongness of certain actions.

47. See especially Loimeier 2007; Deutsch 2002. There can be specialized *barazas*, and discussions too can become very specialized. I have discussed *baraza* settings and discussions in more depth elsewhere; see especially Kresse 2007 (chapter 3) and Kresse 2005; for a historical example, satirically portrayed by Sheikh Al-Amin Mazrui, see Kresse 2009a, 580–82; in relation to "wisdom," see Kresse 2009b.

48. See Warner 2005, but also Hirschkind's (2006) critique of Warner's inadequate abstraction and lack of social and historical context. Wedeen (2008), looking at organized khat-chewing sessions that seem similar to Swahili *baraza* groups, calls them "mini-publics," a term that may be considered here too.

49. It is impossible to give an exhaustive list of references here, but some significant overviews and key works are Mulokozi and Sengo 1995; Shariff 1988; and Nassir 1977.

50. See, for instance, Askew 2002; Amidu 1990; Njogu 2004; Biersteker and Shariff 1995; Abdulaziz 1979.

51. See also Biersteker 1996; Shariff 1988.

52. Close interpretations and ethnographic studies of such processes within and between Muslim communities are still quite rare (though see Bowen 1993; Marsden 2005; Masquelier 2009; Reese 2008), and my understanding is that more effort should be invested in this kind of research, so that we gain more adequate and complex accounts of the internal dynamics of the societies we are seeking to understand. An interest in the ways in which people are conceptualizing the world they live in is clearly linked with how they negotiate it and position themselves within it. In short, the intellectual and the political spheres need to be understood in relation to each other, and as we have seen already, the religious underlies them, providing norms and values for orientation.

53. "Endogenous" is meant to qualify knowledge from within a cultural tradition—Hountondji prefers the term to "indigenous," which he regards as yet another label provided by an external Western discourse, in parallel to the way "native" was used before. See also Hountonji 1997, Introduction.

54. Since the late 1970s, when he was detained following his efforts to push the use of African languages in critical and politically sensitive literature. See, for example, Ngũgĩ 1981; 1986; 1987; 1993; 2009; on philosophy, see Ngũgĩ 2013; Rettová 2007; Kane 2012.

55. For a recent discussion of sociality as analytic concept, see Long and Moore (2013); for a specific take on British sociality (rural vis-à-vis urban), see Daniel Miller (2015).

56. See also Warner 2005. I do not seek to claim that all "intellectual practice" is discursive or publicly accessible; for instance, Lambek's and MacGaffey's (and others') studies on spirit possession and afflicting powers show that there are others, and this applies

to other "esoteric" (Brenner 2001) schools of knowledge as well. Using "public" generically here as described (following Warner), I do not see the need here to re-engage fundamentally with Habermas's sociohistorical account of the emerging public sphere in Europe (Habermas 1989). Yet I think transregional and transcultural comparison is possible in this regard, and my Conclusion argues, inter alia, that the discursive "transformational potential" that Habermas reckons with for European social history *only*, can also be present elsewhere.

57. See for instance Wim van Binsbergen, who engages in such a discussion vis-à-vis the work of Mudimbe, in a thoughtful biographical and historically contextualizing essay (2005).

58. See also Diagne 2008, and the extensive bibliographic project initiated by John Hunwick and R. S. O'Fahey on the East African coast. A number of research projects were conducted with Arabic as the main research language; for example, Reese 2008 and Bang 2003 and 2014.

59. But see Hountondji (1996, 168), originally already in 1973. Wiredu argues for conceptual decolonization and, in principle, the practice of African languages in academia, but he has hardly pushed this point or practiced it (though see Chike Jeffers's 2013 collection, with a contribution by Wiredu). Confronted with the resounding effect of Ngũgĩ's parallel project for afrophone literatures, Wiredu seems to regard the potential for African philosophy as too small to be worth pursuing seriously (Wiredu and Kresse 2000: http://them.polylog.org/2/dwk-en.htm).

60. Alena Rettová (2007) has been working comparatively on African philosophical texts in at least four African languages for some time.

2 Muslim Publics, Postcolonial Imaginations, and the Dynamics of Self-Positioning

Publics and Muslim Publics

Publics in general, according to Michael Warner (2005), are constituted through performative communication among an imagined community of people who, on the basis of shared language or origin, or overlapping interests, attitudes, and values, also come to forge common discursive spaces. The ongoing activity of mutual communication among participants first creates and then also sustains these spaces. While Warner's study is largely focused on anglophone print media and countercultures—and was criticized for its lack of attention to the diverse variability of specific social contexts (see Hirschkind 2006)—it is still useful for thinking about the Swahili cases here. As fields of discursive relations among participants who share interests and concerns but may be strangers to each other, publics exist as accessible discursive spaces that are organized by "discourse itself" (Warner 2005, 74, 67). They come into being as relational fields of discursive interaction among a network of people who do not all know each other in person but nevertheless constitute a discursive community. This means publics exist only by virtue of being addressed; that is, through processes of mutually directed attention in speaking or writing, listening or reading. They are constituted through mere attention and cease to exist without ongoing participation (87), as "social spaces created by reflexive discourse" (90) on topics of shared interest, and in relation to the specific historical circumstances in which they come into being. Participants are attracted by means of "shared social space; habitus; topical concerns" as they create their memberships (often emphasizing an egalitarian attitude) through the languages they use (106–8). Publics can be seen as projects of joint world-making—or remaking and reshaping—whose unity is linked to an ideological core (114–17).[1]

This links us to some general conceptions of Muslim publics and the role of (new) media within them. Resonating with my discussion of Swahili sociality in the previous chapter, Eickelman and Anderson argue that a public is discursively constituted "by mutual participation—indeed, by performance" (as attentive social interaction explicitly directed at each other, in the open), while a public sphere emerges "from ways of dealing confidently with others in an expanding social universe of shared communication," as the outcome of an extended and consolidated process of having interacted in several parallel or overlapping publics (2003, 16). On the Swahili coast, the public use of the Swahili language in oral and written forms and genres of social and religious commentary made both worldly and Islamic knowledge more widely accessible and relevant to ordinary Muslims. It also opened up new forms of self-education and intellectual engagement. Sheikh Al-Amin Mazrui, for instance (to be discussed in chapter 3), introduced Swahili language for both Friday sermons and Islamic pamphlets around 1930.[2] This illustrates the shifting internal dynamics of local Muslim publics over time.

In this study, I am looking at the constitution of Swahili Muslim publics, through the use of media (largely print, but also radio) that are employed with a specific Islamic agenda in mind, as part of a wider and historically changing regional public sphere. It has become a common trope in the study of Muslim worlds that the uses of new media (whether books, audio and video devices, or the internet) by Islamic groups seeking change and reform in society have challenged and undermined the existent authorities. For instance, the previously exclusive status of the authority of the *ulama*, and their "repertoires of intellectual techniques and authorities" (Eickelman and Anderson 2003, 11) that defined specific Muslim communities, was being reshaped, amended, and pluralized. However, the *ulama* have also adapted themselves and their traditions to new conditions, seeking and often succeeding to remain the guiding figures in their communities and thus retaining the status of what M. Q. Zaman (2002) has called "custodians of change." Thus on the ground, for ordinary Muslims, a "re-intellectualization of Islamic discourse" (Eickelman and Anderson 2003, 11) has taken place and become established among ordinary believers, in relation to their experiences, goals, and aspirations. Overall, the pluralization of authority and the use of media have made religious knowledge more accessible and less exclusive. A shift to regional languages to negotiate Islamic knowledge plays an important role in these dynamics too. In the Swahili region, like in many regions throughout the Muslim world, Islamic discourse and formal education have become more accessible through vernacularization processes initiated by modernizing reformers, feeding into the relevant reasoning styles and forms of argumentation that are publicly used.

Related aspects to consider for a proper understanding of the dynamic interrelations between media employed, publics created, agendas pursued, and debates performed, concern the kind of mediation and the technologies, techniques, and conditions by means of which public discourse (religious or moral) is performed. The specific internal formation processes of meaning-making that often play out as contested struggles and negotiations within communities also need to be understood. In this regard, Birgit Meyer has advocated a critical revision of Benedict Anderson's (1991) conception of "imagined community" while keeping the idea of a dynamic projective forming of community according to common ideas and self-conceptions in place. She pronounces the importance of taking on board the specific material and aesthetic "styles" of processes of mediation that constitute community formation and reformation, while communities are themselves social "formations" (Meyer 2009, 6–7). This is particularly useful for understanding communities situated in transregional contexts of historical and ongoing social connectivity (as we have on the Swahili coast), and it resonates well with Peter Mandaville's (2001) take on Anderson when using the phrase "re-imagining the *umma*" as a narrative leitmotif for his study on transnational Muslim politics.

From a related angle, the need to consider the specific infrastructural provisions of particular (material and technological) forms of media shapes the character of their mediation, and thereby reshapes the respective public character of religion and the religious community (Larkin 2009; 2015). As Larkin discusses with reference to the Northern Nigerian Salafi-inspired reformist Abubakar Gumi, a change in the use of media may signal a transformation of the understanding of religion and of the religious community itself. Because media "re-order the information they transmit," changes in media use affect our social experience in a fundamental manner, since "the infrastructural conditions that set limits on our experiences and social orders" have themselves been changed (2009, 133–34). Thus, understanding media and the ways they are used for the mediation of meaning in society—and how they are involved in the shaping and reshaping of (the understanding of) religion and the self-understanding of community—is valuable for understanding community and society more generally. Looked at from here, media are part of the framework constituting the conditions and limitations of experience for social actors, and thus fundamental for our understanding of social dynamics more widely.[3]

Community (Re-)Formation and Mediation

Meyer's point about the internal dynamics of religious communities—that it is "the *style* in which they are imagined" that distinguishes communities from each other—is an insight that feeds into her critical reconception of religion as sensual mediation (Meyer 2009, 6). This stance also supports the point I am making here, that knowing the actual ways of conveying a sense of a common framework of expression, mediation, and discussion within a group matters crucially for our understanding of it. Such a common framework is expressed by means of language use, choice of genre, and particular wording or pattern of reasoning used in self-representation. Being able to give concrete accounts of how processes of social formation are being envisaged (imagined) and mediated, in observable forms and by material means, provides an entry point to the understanding of meaning-making in society. Thus, aesthetic style inheres within the directive power of shaping social meaning; it becomes a crucial part of the creation of collective sentiment and operates as a "forming form." Efforts to understand the social dynamics of religion and its internal contestations, then, within a particular community, need to include a view on the forming processes of meaning-making that are accessible to us as observers, by means of material evidence (Meyer 2009, 7–9, 11).

Drawing from this approach to the study of religion can support and sensitize my approach to an anthropology of texts (following Barber and others, as described above). Indeed, texts, whether in sound or in script, are such specific material (and ideational) forms of meaning-making; they are always embedded in concrete social and historical contexts, within which they are couched and interpreted. In following the Swahili Islamic texts introduced below, I seek insight into the respective projects of reshaping and reforming of the coastal Muslim community. I pursue this with a view to the fundamental and normative aspects of the aesthetics involved (e.g., in rhetoric), and to religion, following the respective invocations and interpretations of Islam by social actors, who invoke religion as the kind of fundamental (yet distant) mediating and unifying guiding force just described above. Appeals to Muslim unity, brotherhood, and equality are grounded in this.

Print Cultures

Looked at from the angle of African print cultures, this study explores some key moments in the establishment and cultivation of East African Islamic print culture in Swahili as local Muslims pushed their ideological and educational agendas in pamphlets, booklets, and newspapers from 1930. Swahili-language Islamic print culture entered late into the game, compared to print cultures elsewhere on the continent, and in related Indian Ocean regions.[4] From around 1870 to 1930, printed Arabic Islamic texts were circulating on the East African coast in parallel with manually copied manuscripts (shared among their respective Shafii and Ibadi networks across the Indian Ocean), and by 1940, printed books were the dominant source for the local scholarly class (Bang 2011). Even in upcountry Kenya, the Kikuyu Central Association already had its own monthly publication from 1928, and among the South Asians of Mombasa at that time, morning as well as evening newspapers were circulating, as Sheikh Al-Amin Mazrui commented wistfully from a Swahili Arab perspective in 1931 (Mazrui 2017, 126–27). Arabic had been the established language of communication in print media among the coastal Muslim elite since at least the 1860s in Zanzibar-based publications (Sadgrove 2004; Ghazal 2010a, 2010b). On the mainland, Swahili publications were first initiated by the Germans, around the turn of the century in colonial Tanganyika, both in Christian missionary texts and translations and in government newspapers that disseminated political messages and demands while also providing public platforms for entertainment and participation of readers. Attentive commentaries and bold mutual challenges, for instance, featured in poetry debates and letters to the editor (e.g., Bromber 2006). On the British-administered Kenyan coast, such a swahilophone public infrastructure was not established until much later, and it was up to local Muslims with limited resources to start their own print media on their own initiative.

My ethnographic and historical narrative below begins with an account of Mombasa's (and indeed East Africa's) key figure of Islamic modernism in the 1930s and 1940s, who introduced the Swahili language, print technology, and journalistic prose as new elements for the mediation of religion and the negotiation of Islamic knowledge in the public realm. This was Sheikh Al-Amin Mazrui (1891–1947), who was part of the regional *ulama* network and a trained sheikh, while his writings and projects of reform were inspired by the Cairo-based modernists and the discussions about the Pan-Islamic ideals of his time.[5] In chapter 3, I introduce a selection of his popular essays advocating social reform and arguing for modernization based on Islamic principles (Mazrui 2017). These texts attain a certain role-model character, as their rhetorical figures of reasoning and argument were copied and adopted by regional Islamic reformists after him. A closer look at two such examples will be presented in chapters 4 and 5.

Overall, as we will see, pluralization and contestation of religious knowledge on the Kenyan coast have waxed and waned over the course of the cases discussed here. In order to understand the specific regional processes and outcomes of the social dialectics of challenge, response, and counter-challenge between competing groups, a twofold focus on the processes of mediation is useful: on the mediation and contestation of religious knowledge (as knowledge of Islam, and knowledge building on a certain interpretation of Islam), and on related projected processes of religious meaning-making, of material and other actual mediation processes. These mediation processes take place in public, and indeed in particular publics constituted by specific media (as technologies of mediation) that may be employed programmatically to push certain positions and projects.

As the range of possible readings of Islam to be advocated has multiplied in parallel with the technological means and opportunities afforded to groups and individuals in their advocacy, a certain "marketplace" of competing religious positions has emerged. This applies to very different social environments around the world within which the self-positioning processes of believers take place. A model of "religious economy" has been used to understand these processes, as it reflects the actual dynamics between offers (supply) and needs (demand) by religious actors, who increasingly require guidance, in a world of multiple religious options that have emerged through technological progress (Green 2011, focusing on the Bombay printing press world). In such a scenario, the success of religious groups is indicated by their public presence, and this, one argument goes, can only be achieved through their active embrace of new media technologies. This fundamentally changes religious discourse and practice, and our understanding of such social transformations of religious mediation relies in part also on our ability to understand how exactly they are being shaped, by specific kinds and styles of media usage (Meyer 2009, 18). This includes, by means of ethnographic, textual, and historical study, being able to trace and write regionally specific histories of continuity (and discontinuity) within the wider transformational processes in social history, and the respective (variable) emphasis on religion within them.[6]

Living Dead, a Golden Past, and the Loops of Postcolonial Experience

Consider an example from my long-term fieldwork in Mombasa in 1999, the year after the al-Qaeda bombings of the US embassies in Nairobi and Dar es Salaam shocked East Africa and for the first time brought to bear a fundamental sense of thinking "terror" in relation to Islam in Kenya (Hirsch 2008; Subiri 1999). East African Muslims were already feeling a general air of suspicion and a range of restrictions imposed upon them. "These days we are like corpses" (*Siku hizi sisi ni maiti*), Mwalimu Saggaf told me. He was a former student and confidante of Sheikh Al-Amin Mazrui and had been a highly respected teacher and historian, from a family of Hadrami sharifs and reputable scholars. This was when I first heard this image expressed directly to me, and I have heard it quite a few times since. "We are already dead," he said, "but we have not been prayed for and buried yet" (*Tumeshakufa—lakini hatujaswaliwa wala hatujazikwa*). The "we" here referred to coastal "Arab-Swahili" Muslims (Salim 1976), with a view to their position in the political scenario of postcolonial Kenya. A parallel narrative was offered to me by my neighbor from across the street, a second-generation Shihiri immigrant to Mombasa who owned a small shop with which he tried to make a living by selling and repairing secondhand fridges. He made extensive comments whose core statement can be summarized like this: "We are like zombies—dead already, without a will of our own, and steered by an outside power that is making us work while we are sleeping; it is sucking out our blood." With both these interlocutors, I spent hours of informal conversation and discussion during my long-term fieldwork and consecutive visits.

The image of the living dead and similar creatures as part of narrative (self-) portrayals when positioning particular social groups in colonial and postcolonial contexts is not new and has been worked through by social historians and anthropologists (e.g., MacGaffey 1986; White 2000). Here, I pick up on it only as an entry point for the contextual discussion of how coastal Muslims typically position themselves in the political scenarios of postcolonial Kenya: as powerless and dominated from "upcountry," Nairobi, and elsewhere. I have come across similar characterizations, and often a contrasting comparison was made, to a colonial past in which supposedly things had been much better. Indeed, in conversation with me, Mwalimu Saggaf referred to the British colonial era as a "golden age" (in English, which he rarely used), with respect for coastal people and their culture and religion. In consequence, people had a significant sense of freedom and flexibility that allowed them to pursue educational and religious aspirations (in his case, teaching and missionary activities).[7] From his perspective, coastal Muslims had not benefited in any way from independence. On the contrary, they suffered under a Kenyan upcountry government that, according to him, sought to make them suffer because they were Muslims. (Notably, Mwalimu Saggaf was similarly critical of the colonial regime when it came to specific questions of how it had restricted possibilities of Islamic education or Muslim publics.) In 1999, after the Nairobi (and Dar) bombings by al-Qaeda in August 1998, this was well before the post-9/11 US-led "war on terror" scenario, which then affected Kenyan Muslims more severely in terms of loss of rights, as the Kenyan government collaborated with the United States (Seesemann 2007). However, the kind of outright extrajudicial killings of Muslim suspects, as initiated and executed more recently, over the course of 2014, would have been unthinkable then.[8]

Similar sentiments, emphasizing a stark contrast between colonial past and postcolonial present, and also between coastal and upcountry people (*wapwani* and *wabara*), were expressed by members of the younger generation. Once, when I accompanied a group of Old Town youths to a meeting with town council representatives, I saw how one of them became abusive after stumbling into an obviously poor middle-aged man of apparent upcountry origin, on one of the busy sidewalks in the center of the Old Town. Walking on, he said, loudly enough for people around to hear, that in the past "such people" were not allowed inside the town. This is a point that I came across, too, in some conversations among neighbors and friends: how, in British colonial times, upcountry people (*wabara*), as visible outsiders and assumed social inferiors, had to be out of the Old Town by sunset; and how the Old Town neighborhoods had been much cleaner and safer then. Normally, I did not react to such occasional racially biased comments; sometimes, I expressed surprise and incredulity while asking back, questioning the validity of such statements. Mutual racial prejudices of this kind, between people who call each other "Arabs" and "Africans," while there are no clear criteria for this, have long been, and continue to be, part of the wider range of urban social interactions full of tension, in a region that is historically charged with the experience of slavery, serfdom, and labor dependencies (*utumwa*) that took on different shapes, shades, and forms.[9]

Lingering Historical Tensions: Inequality and Dependency, *Utumwa*

Such tensions over questions of racial difference and social inequality often play out on the surface of everyday interactions, in situations as just described. Yet the invocation of rather clear-cut ethnolinguistic categories vis-à-vis each other, between "Arab," "Swahili," and other local groups, plays out differently in different coastal towns (for Malindi, see McIntosh 2009). They underpin everyday life and may feed into it all the time, as historical layers of meaning linked to the experience of serfdom/slavery (*utumwa*) that have not been fully accepted. The historical experience of *utumwa* constitutes a historically loaded field of social tensions underpinning social reality that social actors need to cope with and balance out in everyday life (for Lamu, see Hillewaert 2016). Historical accounts attest to the factual continuation of dependency relationships that characterized *utumwa*, far beyond the abolition of slavery that was declared in 1907, toward the present (Eastman 1994; Mirza and Strobel 1989; Romero 1997). And the emotionally charged mutual perception, also within the contemporary Muslim community, between hinterland and upcountry people, the so-called Africans and coastal Arabs (see, e.g., Ndzovu 2014), somewhat mirrors and echoes the earlier hostile antagonism between the competing "Swahili" and "Arab" clans in the Old Town community of Mombasa in the late 1920s. In 1929 this led to violence after a provocative and arrogant letter to the editor by an "Arab" community leader by which urban Swahilis felt collectively insulted (Kindy 1972, 31–38). Seventy years later, when I was conducting my doctoral fieldwork in Mombasa, yet another letter to the editor by an "Arab" spokesman, under the heading "Don't incite Kenyans on slavery," lectured readers on coastal history yet again, and demanded that "Africans" should stop misusing this topic for their own agenda: "At the Coast today, the few Africans who keep harping on the subject of slavery have hidden agendas based on politics, religion and racism and fueled by an inferiority complex in some cases. They refuse to be practical or learn the art of forgiveness" (*Daily Nation*, May 28, 1999, p. 7)

After extensive elaboration and berating commentary, he ended, not without self-complacency and in a provocative tone that could have stirred up violent responses once again, "There is no such axe to grind in the matter between us, and, in the interests of unity of the country, the elite should shun such worthless propaganda" (ibid.).

The ongoing social relevance of such invocations of historical dependency narratives in the present perpetuates the conflict potential of historical antagonisms between coastal Muslims and non-Muslims, as well as between coastal "Arab Swahili" and hinterland people. During colonial times, Islamic civilizational narratives cast Muslims as typically mercantile urban patricians (*waungwana*) of superior educational status. Non-Muslims of upcountry origin (*wabara*) were cast as their inferior social other, supposedly uneducated (*wajinga*) and uncivilized (*washenzi*). These derogatory ideological narratives—to be discussed further in subsequent chapters—also resonated with British colonial ones, denouncing Africa as uncivilized and subjecting it to a justified "civilizing mission." Indeed, the theme and argumentative pattern of these narratives resembled that of British "civilizing narratives" in Zanzibar in the early 1890s that justified the need for colonial control over "degenerate" and "despotic" Arab rule there (Bissel 2011, 76). Invocations of such tropes and ideologies come up again and again in the readings that follow in the chapters below. Notably, there exist many varieties of status between the two opposite ends of this dichotomy. In fact, the core groups of coastal urban society in Mombasa, the so-called Twelve Tribes, initially came into town as travelers, merchants, migrants, and, above all, refugees between the seventeenth and eighteenth centuries. Mostly they came from the northern Swahili coast, partly through dependency relationships that are subsumable under the term *utumwa*, as serfdom/slavery. Sometimes (but not always) at the bottom end of social hierarchies, these incomers at least had access to niches and pathways to establish themselves as citizens in their own right over the course of time.[10]

The ongoing presence of these ideological narratives with racial undertones among coastal Muslims is also indicative of their discontent and frustration with their social standing in postcolonial Kenya, lacking a perspective for the future. These statements can also be read as reassertive declarations of self-assurance by vulnerable citizens—who see themselves treated as second-class citizens in their own home region, and who are lacking resources and status within a national political entity dominated by their historical adversaries. When expressing positive sentiments about the colonial past, in contrast to such current realities of the postcolonial present (sometimes even casting the former as a "golden age," as we saw above), coastal Muslims are not uncritically celebrating Western colonialism or longing for it to return. Rather, they hold dear in their memories a recollection of social experience in which their self-presentation vis-à-vis external rulers could be confident and self-assertive.

Postcolonial Experience: Coping, Enduring—Resilience and Resignation

Reflecting upon postcolonial experience in Africa, we can account for ways in which people struggle to cope, survive, and find orientation in their lives. Old certainties have vanished, and new ones have not yet been secured. It makes sense, then, to focus on the specific "local strategies of resilience" (de Boeck 1996, 99) that are created and employed by ordinary people in such adverse and pressing circumstances. Such reflection yields insights into the ways in which social tensions and ambivalences play out, and internalized dichotomies are mediated. Looking at forms of changing ritual practice, Filip de Boeck's work on Zaire/Congo brings into view the constructive potential of social forms of mediation, as they offer spaces of possible resistance and opportunities for negotiating tensions (also de Boeck and Plissart 2004). His ethnography explores an important, locally specific (and not necessarily discursive but also performative) reservoir of creative ways "in which sense can be made of the multi-leveled contradictions of the post-colonial universe" (1996, 100). This reservoir is then drawn from and used in public performances of rituals or other practices, when seeking to challenge or transform, or to reconfirm or adjust to the respective forms of authority (which are themselves in flux). These practices, as forms of resilience, both represent and reflect the current social crisis, and beyond that they also offer "the possibility of generating an innovative response to the need for new, mediating identities and forms of governance and of political, moral and social authority" (1996, 101). Such new and creative forms of political commentary (if not critique), generated by people in the midst of adverse experiences, are remarkable as they indicate the possibility of active participation despite the (often desperate) situation people are in.

This focus is reminiscent of Achille Mbembe's emphasis on aspects of creative agency and critical resistance by ordinary people in postcolonial Africa (1992, 2001). It also resonates with my own observations about "skills to navigate the world" that people develop (*Weltgewandtheit*), even and especially under adverse circumstances. Drawing from their available resources of knowledge and experience, people form coping strategies to deal with their challenging realities—as a kind of a creative potential of cosmopolitan attitude of moving flexibly in the world, using practical and discursive skills that combine religious and worldly knowledge to address and tackle issues and confrontations in the here and now (see Kresse 2012; 2013). Here, too, endurance and resilience feed into a pool of possible creative (and possibly critical) responses that some engaged individuals manage to develop and express, and then circulate more widely. On the Swahili coast, often, these responses include wake-up calls to stir fellow Muslims into action, those who did not become engaged (yet) because they could not muster the necessary emotional and intellectual energy to do so, under social and political conditions that seem to dismiss them and write them off.

One important point is to convey a sense of the precarious present that coastal Muslims feel they have been living in,[11] at different points in time during the postcolonial era, and to discuss how they have responded to it, for example by negotiating their position in terms of "endurance" or "resilience." We can look at the early 1990s in Mombasa, for instance, a time when the Islamic Party of Kenya (IPK), which was never accepted to be properly registered by the government, was nevertheless powerful and so influential as to be able to effectively "shut down" the city (Nassir 2008; Oded 1996). The general attitude of coastal Muslims was characterized by one researcher as one of "coping with Christians"

(Cruise O'Brien 1995), both in terms of facing a new demographic majority of incoming Christian outsiders in their home area and of facing external rule by an upcountry government that was seen to present itself as Christian. As quoted above already, while the state proclaimed itself to be secular, it was perceived to be Christian.

In parallel, what we consider further in the chapters that follow is how coastal Muslims have given up, become dispirited and disillusioned, under such circumstances, and how they shaped and facilitated their own publics as discursive spheres in which endurance and resilience were cultivated. In this way, the expression "past present continuous" captures the sense of a common mode of experience in which social actors are enveloped. As coastal Muslims struggle to reorient and reassert themselves, in the kinds of postcolonial publics that allow them to do so, they engage, overall, in processes of self-positioning that proceed relationally, mediating between knowledge and social experience. This leads, and responds to, expressions of a (religiously shaped) sense of self that is negotiated within the (internally diverse) coastal Muslim community, in the kinds of local media I shall portray and discuss in the subsequent chapters.

Self-Positioning and Reassuring Oneself (*Selbstvergewisserung*)

Underpinning these processes of self-positioning (*Selbstverortung*) are further internal processes on which "positioning" is based. The German term *Selbstvergewisserung* (literally a process of reassuring oneself of oneself) is useful to think with here, as the variety of connotations that this term evokes and expresses addresses a range of related layers of meaning that resonate well here. *Vergewisserung* denotes a gradual and conscious process of gaining "certainty" (*Gewissheit*). It implies a careful consideration of the circumstances in question, and it is often used in the sense of "making sure" (also in practical matters, such as whether all windows are closed, etc.). Applied to the "self" as in *Selbst-Vergewisserung*, it refers to the processes people can engage in to double-check on themselves, as a kind of conscious and thorough reflexive inventory, "taking stock" of what one's own self consists of, what its current state and status is, and how it relates to and should position itself vis-à-vis its significant other reference points. *Selbstvergewisserung* is needed in situations and periods of fundamental crisis, uncertainty, and insecurity—yet often, it cannot be had or achieved. And it is on the basis of completed processes of *Selbstvergewisserung*, according to common assumption, that one can position oneself better within one's life-world, with a better knowledge of oneself and the surrounding influencing circumstances. Thus, *Selbstvergewisserung* leads to a better self-positioning or self-localization (*Selbstverortung*) in society. It is an ongoing process of introspection in relation to social contexts and the wider world, yet never fully achieved. Finally, *Vergewisserung* also has the connotation of *Gewissen* (conscience), thus referring to fundamental ethical dimensions that are involved here as well. As a process concerning also (and especially) a normative perspective upon oneself in society, being engaged in *Selbstvergewisserung* is understood as part of an ultimately morally driven project (becoming a better person), not a strategic one (e.g., economic success). In the Swahili publics discussed below, such processes are being played out and worked through in the respective media as mediating facilitators.

The chapters of this book, then, focus on different points in time in Kenyan postcolonial (and colonial) history, by working ethnographically on internal debates among coastal Muslims, as they feature in local Islamic media initiatives and attempt to provide guidance for personal and communal self-positioning in this scenario. Pamphlets and newspapers as well as lectures, speeches, and radio discussions are studied, and by combining close readings and ethnographic contextualization—socially, historically, and within national politics—the struggles of self-positioning are explored and analyzed. This is done both with a view to Muslims vis-à-vis each other and vis-à-vis the state and the external rule by Christian upcountry people (*wabara*), the historical adversaries of Muslim coastals (*wapwani*). In this way, this book critically maps out the ways in which topics representative of their postcolonial experience are tackled and negotiated within the coastal Muslim community at specific points in time. Ordinary Muslims as well as scholars evoke images and imaginary memories of coastal society under colonial rule (and sometimes, prophetic futures of postcolonial rule), in the face of decline and desperation. Overall, the dynamics of self-positioning can be seen to be shaped (to a significant extent) by performances of intellectual practice.

It is helpful to keep these connotations in mind to understand the processes of public discussion among coastal Muslims in postcolonial Kenya that are to be discussed here. Normative stock-taking is going on as part of the contested local, national, and transregional politics that Muslims are engaged in, and moral goals are clarified and negotiated as part of (and next to) political and religious discussions within the community. We can see this happening in the brief critical essays published by Sheikh Al-Amin Mazrui in Mombasa in the 1930s (chapter 3), as well as in the subsequent commentaries and discussions assembled in the Islamic newspaper *Sauti ya Haki* in the 1970s (chapter 4) and the more recent discussions on Radio Rahma, Mombasa's first postcolonial Islamic radio station, between 2005 and 2007 (chapter 5). As differently initiated and oriented projects of internal debate among coastal Muslims in these (in each case) new and specifically shaped Swahili Muslim publics, they each present differently pitched processes of self-reassurance (*Selbstvergewisserung)* and self-positioning (*Selbstverortung)* in the particular postcolonial society on Kenya's coast. As the respective Islamic media and Swahili Muslim publics treated and discussed in each chapter constitute case studies (representative to an extent that remains to be determined), each chapter opens up the view on such processes at a specific point in time. These cases are discussed through close readings of texts in context. But there is no intention of presenting the chapters as a sequence attempting a comprehensive historical coverage of the postcolonial era or coastal Muslims' experience of it. They are specific instances only, with a certain illustrative value.[12]

The Critical Study of Postcolonial Experience

This book combines an ethnography of postcolonial experience with an anthropological view of Muslim politics on the Kenyan coast focusing on Swahili Islamic texts and Muslim publics as part of dynamic internal debates. Each chapter zooms in, analyzes, and takes issue with a particular "window of social experience," a particular Swahili Muslim public in a specific form at a particular point in time. Thus exploring their complexity as socially meaningful discursive spaces provides us with "maps of experience." This term was once used by Vail and White (1991) to characterize their readings of southern African praise poetry that also reflected forms and dynamics of social critique in relation to ongoing political processes. It is useful here for my emphasis on the specific regional grounding of the accounts that themselves become perspectives on society. Overall, my narrative draws from and in turn responds to calls for substantial ethnographies and related discussions on postcolonial Africa; and it complements recent studies of locally grounded and translocally oriented Muslim perspectives on social and religious reform in Africa.[13]

What emerges, I suggest, is essentially a critical study of social experience that is closely linked to local actors, as it has drawn from, and engaged with, texts and internal debates, and thus the dynamic negotiation of meanings, positions, and arguments within the community itself. It is fruitful here to draw from an understanding of a "critical" investigation as one in which we look at "the conditions of possibility of experience"—how certain kinds of experiences could come into being and are made possible through the kinds of contexts and conditions they are part of.[14] Making sure, as anthropologists or social scientists more widely, to be in the know about the framework of empirical conditions for the possibilities of specific experiences of the social actors we are seeking to understand is crucial to our project of understanding.

This is based, as Johannes Fabian has worked out, on the long-term experience of "shared time and space" of the researcher and the people he or she studies, acquired during lengthy periods of fieldwork in the respective community and cultivating personal relationships with its members. Mutual trust between researcher and interlocutors is a key feature too, as anthropological research builds on personal interactions. For Fabian, such criteria of a "critical anthropology" have emerged out of his fundamental critique of anthropology (1983) as it was typically practiced then, casting the people it sought to understand as socially inferior and under-complex "others."[15] One of Fabian's recurrent leitmotifs of ethnographic research lends itself to the interpretation of postcolonial experience as a seemingly recurring past present continuous. "Remembering" processes between past and present are self-enveloping dynamics whereby people are entangled (and sometimes, liberated) in loops of their own projective and experiential imagination. My own ethnographic portrayals, readings, narratives, and interpretations that are presented here have grown out of a long period of interaction with a variety of coastal Muslim interlocutors in Kenya, and a long-term concern to understand the complexities of internal debate and the framing and presentation of the respective arguments concerned. Critical anthropology for me also entails ongoing interaction (as much as possible) with the interlocutors whom I portray or write about (with their informed consent), and to convey a sense of the relevance that the issues I discuss have for them, as central to my research while not being uncritical of their opinions and attitudes.

Complementarily, it has to be kept in mind that working with unspecified and generic conceptions of colonial (or postcolonial) experience is counterproductive, as it simplifies the complex social contexts and historical processes we should be seeking to understand. What is needed above all is attention to the specific ways in which human practices unfold over time, in particular regions and linguistic contexts, thus shaping a sense of "critical history" (Cooper 2005, 12). This is strengthened by exploring and following the meanings of indigenous categories and conceptual frameworks, after first having freed oneself of the constraints of Western categories and analytic concepts (ibid., 11, 32). Such considerations link up well with Karin Barber's reminder that for those seeking to explore the "postcolonial condition" in a certain region, there is no alternative to working through the available sources in the relevant regional languages. There is also no substitute for the laborious analysis of specific texts, with firsthand knowledge of the authors and the social context within which they were living and writing (if such knowledge is at all available), so that an appropriate contextualizing understanding is possible.[16] It is such kind of work that I am seeking to provide in the following three chapters, each devoted to a specific case study. Before that, I provide a preliminary comparative discussion as an outlook, in order to build a sense of shared themes and discursive motifs among them.

Swahili Islamic Media as Platforms for "Commanding Right and Forbidding Wrong"

There is always more than one way as to how reality can be understood, and how orientation is sought and provided (grounded, formulated, mediated) in society, both by those who seek it and by those who seek to provide it. People draw from a range of interpretations of social reality, to make sense of situations and statements they are confronted with or concerned by (Laidlaw 2014, 189–90). Based on their experience, social actors reckon with diversity and position themselves within a wider "internal pluralism" (Hountondji 1996, 168) in society, in which they seek to find their way. Yet, in normative terms, there is commonly a consensus about norms (that have to be adhered to) and obligations (that have to be fulfilled), about what is "right" and "wrong"—and we have already gained a sense of how religious dimensions are involved here.

Coastal Muslims in Kenya commonly submit to a general obligation to remind their fellow Muslims about the right path, and this again can become a key motivation for (and justification of) personal engagement in public moral discourse and publication activities. While the dissemination of knowledge and guidance has taken different forms and genres over time—from didactic poetry to radio programs and websites—all of these draw from a shared pool of authoritative references (in Qur'an and *hadith*) and rhetorical devices. Comparing these usages concretely across time can provide windows on the respective social experience, allowing us to gain a sense of continuities (and differences), and about how the status of certain kinds of knowledge may change (indicated by changes in the ways of invoking them).

At three different points in time, the texts discussed here employ or invoke the very same "divinely imposed obligation" (Cook 2000, 9) vis-à-vis their respective audiences. The Swahili Muslim publics to be discussed here were all launched from Mombasa, by engaged individuals, to campaign for social reform, toward a "better" society—more educated and more just.

In these three Islamic media projects, overlapping commonalities and differences, continuities and breaks are to be found. These concern styles of addressing and engaging fellow Muslims, as well as idioms, reasoning patterns, and rhetoric employed. But also particular doctrinal concerns, about how to behave and present oneself in certain situations, as a member of one particular subgroup of Muslims vis-à-vis others (e.g., in how to praise the Prophet; whether and how to pray for the deceased; what to wear and how)—these are clad in particular established arguments and criticisms, as part of ongoing ideological debates. Notable and reoccurring in public discourse and personal conversations are discursive references to the divine obligation of "commanding right" (*kuamrishana mwema*) and "forbidding wrong" (*kukanyana maovu*) to each other as religious peers. Reminding others about right and wrong, whenever one sees possible transgressions and violations arising, is demanded from all Muslims. Social responsibility to share one's knowledge and, above all, to hinder others from doing wrong—which often also means hindering them from what they think is right—is thus discursively enacted. As "commanding right, forbidding wrong" expresses the basic demand for good moral behavior, this formula also lends itself to invocation and citation in public discussion. Indeed, it is used in everyday discussions and also found throughout the Swahili Islamic media projects explored here.

The three examples discussed here (and in more detail in the following chapters) represent three different types of uses: firstly, an authoritarian one, whereby a superior author is verbally pushing and pressing the audience to comply by employing what we could call a "rhetoric of fear" (see also Hirschkind 2006); secondly, an overbearing academic one, in which the writer turns his wealth of (secular and religious) knowledge artistically against his ideological opponents by what we could call a "rhetoric of shaming"; and thirdly (and quite differently), a kind of "open-access" usage, whereby the idea of providing all members of the community the possibility of appealing (i.e., commanding and forbidding) is, as a principle, embodied in the medium itself, a live radio broadcast inviting all its listeners to phone in and raise the points they regard as necessary. Now the discussion of these three cases will focus on selected quotations, to which I will partly return in subsequent chapters, in order to discuss them in more detail and with more context.

Sahifa—Sheikh Al-Amin Mazrui

The earliest of these cases is from August 1931, written by Sheikh Al-Amin bin Ali Mazrui (1891–1947) of Mombasa, introduced already as a major regional Islamic scholar and the initiator of local Islamic publications in Swahili. We first look at the concluding passage of an article called "How to Refrain from Forbidden Acts" (*Ndia ya kuzuilia maasiya*), published in his weekly pamphlet *Sahifa* ("Page"), which had a print run of only one hundred copies. The sentences quoted below reiterate and lay out in strict terms that all are obligated to command right and forbid wrong. Even under difficult circumstances, in changing and unreliable times, everyone needs to comply, for otherwise society may collapse. All those who are known to commit bad deeds must be warned and cautioned, he says; otherwise, those who neglect doing so will have to face blame and take responsibility on the divine judgment day in the aftermath:

> When we stop *commanding right and forbidding wrong*, and also when we respect an evil person who does not pray, and when we give them preference in our gatherings and meetings, and we make drunkards our friends, and we chat and laugh with those who commit bad deeds, then we have disobeyed the commands of Almighty God, and on top of it, we have created reasons for increasing bad deeds and for accepting what is wrong. And these brothers of ours will come and blame us, tomorrow in the Hereafter, because we saw them doing wrong, and then we left them alone, we did not forbid them, while we have been commanded to make them avoid hell-fire, and to make them avoid hell-fire is to make them avoid the evils which are the reasons for entering hell-fire.
>
> *Tutakapowata* kuamrishana mema na kukatazana *maovu, tena tukalihishimu jitu lisilo sali na kulitanguliza katika baraza yetu, na walevi wakawa ndio marafiki zetu, na wenye vitendo vibaya tukasema nae na kuteka nao,*

tutakuwa tumevunda amri ya Mwenye-ezi-Mngu, tena tumefanya sababu ya kuzidi maasiya na kudhihiria munkari. Na hawa ndugu zetu watakuja tulaumu Kesho Akhera kuwaona katika maasiya tukawawata tusiwakataze, nalhali sisi tumeamrishwa kuwaepusha na Moto, na kuwaepusha na Moto, ni kuwaepusha na maasiya ambayo ndio sababu ya kungia motoni (Uwongozi 20; Mazrui 2017, 142–45; my emphasis).[17]

We can understand this paragraph as a rigid and extensive elaboration upon the call to do right, presented by a community leader of superior intellectual status, motivated by grave paternal concern. In reflecting upon the obligation to forbid wrong, and in response to the need to honor this obligation, the text reiterates, perpetuates, and enforces the moral call. By reinvoking the obligation, at the same time it reaffirms its validity [like Lambek (2010) argued, with a view to "ordinary ethics"]. The pamphlet, as medium here, is used as a public platform of rhetorical affirmation of this call—which, as the implicit underlining argument goes, needs to be upheld, as otherwise the idea of community (as people living in mutual reference to each other) would be undermined, and society could collapse.

Thus in this text, notably unlike in many others of the same genre by Sheikh Al-Amin (which are often witty and humorous while also sharp in their social critique), a rhetorical strategy of warning by inducing fear is employed. The relevant reasoning process is about providing a complete account of the responsibility that individuals have in responding to the demand, and that noncompliance (not warning others) will have punitive repercussions. This message seems to correspond to the social situation it addresses, one in which sins and wrongdoing are being committed, and witnessed by others without interference. Just like the topic it covers, the text employs drastic means while discussing a scenario of social decay and emergency. Overall, it presents an argument for the necessity of taking responsibility and adhering to this Islamic obligation, as otherwise the community and indeed society itself may disintegrate, and the ideas of "right" and "wrong," when no longer upheld, may lose their meaning.

Sauti ya Haki, "Voice of Justice" (1972–82)—Sheikh Muhammad Kasim Mazrui

The second text works quite differently, in its strategies of reasoning and rhetoric with the "forbidding wrong" quote in this case. It is from *Sauti ya Haki* (Voice of Justice), an Islamic newspaper that ran quarterly between 1972 and 1982, had eight pages and a print run of 500 to 5,000 copies. It was edited by Sheikh Al-Amin's closest student, his nephew and son-in-law, Sheikh Muhammad Kasim Mazrui (1912–82). In November 1974, the lead article, entitled "*Haki juu!*" (Justice up!—or Long live justice!), was written in celebration of its third year of publication. However, a main motivation for the article was to respond to accusations that had been raised by *Sauti ya Haki*'s adversaries, the Hadrami Alawiyya *masharifu*, who were said to have claimed that by publicly raising matters of internal Muslim differences, *Sauti ya Haki* had undermined the Muslim community and played into the hands of Western "enemies of Islam." In response, the editor here presented an extensive argument about the "importance of forbidding each other" (*umuhimu wa kukanyana*). Stating that nothing bad could really result out of forbidding wrong (which we know is not always true), and nothing good out of failing to do so, he pointed at prominent figures in Islamic history known for forbidding wrong to others: Ibn Taymiyah, Muhammad Abdul-Wahhab, and Muhammad Abduh—and, more recent and closer to home, Abul-A'la Mawdudi from Pakistan (whose writings, translated into Swahili, are circulating in East Africa), and Sheikh Al-Amin Mazrui (p. 1).[18]

Responding to the reproach of causing disunity among local Muslims, the article clarifies that information about disunity had already reached those Western outsiders—the potential "enemies of Islam," as they are called in the text—independently of *Sauti ya Haki*. The editor even refers to and quotes from some recent academic anglophone publications on Islam in East Africa at the time, including Spencer Trimingham's *Islam in East Africa* (1964), Jan Knappert's *Swahili Islamic Poetry* (1971), and John Mbiti's *African Religions and Philosophy* (1969). He points out how these authors gathered their own observations during visits in the region, and how their publications concur in portraying popular Muslim practices as a kind of "mixture" with local customary practices and traditional religion, referring to spirit possession healing rituals (*uganga*), the use of amulets (*hirizi*), the worship of saints (*walii*), and related phenomena. He argues: "Saying that enemies of Islam did not know about shameful behavior of Muslims up until the time these were criticized in SYH is completely untrue. The enemies of Islam go around on their own in Muslim towns in order to trace our shameful behavior and then write about them in their books."

Such observations by foreign researchers were not wrong, the editor commented, and to simply deny them would be not only wrong but also inappropriate. Instead, Muslims should warn each other and forbid (or prevent) each other (*kuonyana na kukanyana*) from participating in such actions, and thus creating the impression of "shameful behavior" in the first place. Those who have become corrupted are they, as Muslims and fallible human beings, not Islam itself (*walioharibika ni Waislamu tu si Uislamu wenyewe*) (SYH Nov. 1974, 6f).

Here, the remarkable familiarity of *Sauti ya Haki*'s editor with current academic books on regional Islam at the time becomes substantial strategic knowledge that is employed for a knockout counterargument against their opponents, set to convince readers of *Sauti ya Haki*'s integrity while responding to the accusers in a way that makes them look foolish: ill-equipped, misinformed, and out of touch. This is a very different use of the newspaper's discursive space for reflexive and critical engagement from the one sketched out above.

Sheikh Muhammad Kasim's well-informed comments on the current research on Islam in East Africa at the time, and his awareness about fieldwork being conducted by foreign researchers in Swahili towns, should not really surprise us. After all, his nephew, Ali Mazrui (d. 2014), was already an established professor of political science at Makerere University in Uganda at the time, and his own two sons were, at the time, already active in academia and undergoing further higher education abroad.[19] However, such a kind of critical reading and direct engagement with anglophone academic texts, commenting on current fields of research (as produced here in a local publication by him) is something that the scholarly community commonly does not reckon with. Yet actually seeking, initiating, and facilitating such critical dialogue between experts of different kinds would surely be beneficial to regional research (particularly this kind, on regional religious practice and self-understanding), and at the same time, to Islamic scholars and Muslims from the area as well. Such matters about (unexpected, but not at all unexpectable) transregional flows of knowledge that may mutually inform and fundamentally shape or reshape one's knowledge of social others and their worlds should be kept in mind as this book progresses.

Radio Rahma; *"Elimika na Stambuli"* (Get Educated with Stambuli), 2005–07

Finally, we look at a popular weekly discussion program of a local Islamic radio station—called "Get Educated with Stambuli" and broadcast from March 2005 onward. Using the idiomatic expressions of mutual concern discussed above (e.g., reminding, educating, understanding; i.e., *kumbushana, elimishana, fahamiana*), including that of "commanding right and forbidding wrong," was frequent, by presenters and moderators as well as studio guests (often local scholars, notables, or public figures), and also by many of the listeners who called in to participate in discussion. The maiden broadcast in March 2005 had the character of an informal introductory brainstorming session, eliciting many ideas and gaining many active callers in response. As the two producers said, this program was all about the creation of an openly accessible discursive space, to be used as a platform to facilitate mutual education and frank critical discussion of important topics among local Muslims. The audience was asked to suggest topics and issues to be addressed, which it did, and subsequent broadcasts took these up. This particular program became a bit of a local institution, also with its critical edge vis-à-vis both the state and the established Muslim elites. The topics covered included the problem of drug abuse, proper dress in public and when attending mosque, the history of Islam in East Africa, the coastal independence movement, water supply in Mombasa, misuse of *waqf* funds, schooling and education, discrimination against Muslims by the state, and many more. Each time, Stambuli started off the broadcast with a brief introductory discussion. He was always well prepared and brought along any available documentary evidence (which much impressed his listeners and gave him a fine reputation). He was also able to address sensitive questions clearly and head-on, in a measured tone and with thoughtfulness and respect.

An appreciation of the program for its mediating qualities was once highlighted on the program itself (in July 2005), by studio guest and visiting speaker Prof. Mohamed Hyder, a highly regarded elderly Muslim activist, long engaged in projects of civic education. He had just taken part in the program's discussion on "terrorism" (*ugaidi*), and at the end of this intense and sensitive session, Prof. Hyder concluded his remarks with emphatic praise of the radio program's active role in enabling and mediating discussion among coastal Muslims on such sensitive topics.

> And we, in our ongoing discussions with each other, if God wishes, by discussing more and more amongst ourselves about matters such as those [covered today], Radio Rahma has given people a chance to be able to exchange (and possibly change each other's) thoughts about such matters. And I would like to congratulate you. I am very happy to have been able to be with you here today.
>
> *Na sisi inshallah katika kujadiliana, na kujadiliana zaidi, kuhusu mambo kama haya, Radio Rahma imewapa watu nafasi ya kuweza kubadilishana fikra kwa mambo kama haya. Na napenda kuwapa pongezi, nafurahi sana kuweza kuwa pamoja na nanyi siku ya leo.*

By making it possible within the community to discuss such matters among themselves, Prof. Hyder emphasized, Radio Rahma gave local Muslims the opportunity to develop and build their thoughts on important social matters, through open interaction with others. From his perspective, the actual provision of an openly accessible discursive space making such fruitful exchange (and a potential change of mind) possible for people in the first place is marked as a crucial achievement here (which is discussed further in chapter 5).

Comparative Reflections

As we have seen, the invocation of the same obligation here does not mean actually demanding the same, and perhaps not even understanding the obligation in the same way. In these textual examples, three different readings can be seen to be at work. Sheikh Al-Amin's text performed a reading of "forbidding wrong" that rotates around the necessity for individuals to take on responsibility and speak out when witnessing wrongdoing in their midst. If they do not respond, the argument goes, they are to be blamed as well, as they are participating in the moral erosion of society itself. If this text is representative of how the Mombasa Muslim community understood itself in 1930—following the assumption that texts are representative of a common self-understanding in society (Barber 2007, 5)—we can observe the existence of an unquestioned, strict hierarchy between the superior knowledgeable and authoritative sheikh, who is also the public speaker on behalf of his community, and the ordinary Muslims with little knowledge as his (largely passive) audience, expected to heed given directives and advice.

In *Sauti ya Haki*, Sheikh Muhammad Kasim portrays "forbidding wrong" as a matter of moral conscience. His well-reasoned defense is designed to convince his audience of his superior knowledge in both worldly and Islamic matters. Through his argument and rhetoric, Sheikh Muhammad aims at embarrassing his opponents (the Hadrami *masharifu* of Riyadha Mosque in Lamu), in making them appear as rather ignorant accusers. In a situation of fundamental rivalry, the argumentative and rhetorical struggle is about winning over the wider public as followers, using the newspaper as a platform.

Finally, the radio discussion show highlights very different aspects. This was all about access and the possibility of active participation for everyone in shaping their own community. While mutual "self-education" rather than commanding or forbidding, strictly speaking, was at the center here, "speaking up" (by calling in, via telephone) against abuses of power was encouraged and became prominent, as the radio program built a dedicated community of listeners (a diverse range of people) who, as callers, were also regular contributors. Thus we have an egalitarian character emphasized here, among fellow Muslims. This was "forbidding wrong" from below (by the people, for the people, so to say)—for which, as was pointed out, the existence of an accessible discursive space for public interaction was crucial.[20]

With their shared focus on one common obligation that is invoked by these different local Muslim reformers in their respective publics, at different points in time yet in the same place, these cases show how knowledge (of religion, or the world), language and speech acts, social practice, and religion are intrinsically interwoven in specific settings and normative discussions. They also point to a sense of the appreciation and status that certain kinds of knowledge convey upon individuals, which at the same time bind and oblige them socially. As we could see here already, the same idiomatic reference point addressed can well be used with different intentions and meanings in mind, and its invocation can be made to push for different things. More reflections on this will be raised later on. What I wish to create a sense of, for now, is an awareness of the presence of these multiple and complementary aspects that feed into each other and need to be considered, when we seek to understand social action and interaction that declares itself to be religiously oriented and motivated, and "valid" (or true) because of the assumed authority of a certain status of knowledge that is invoked. These overlapping and interweaving dynamics mark intellectual practice as a wider research field, in which aspects of context, process, agency, and performance of knowledge-oriented social practice are highlighted in analysis.

Reflection upon the cases touched upon here generates a cluster of questions about the features and kinds of Muslim publics seen at work here, and these will be pursued in the following chapters. The analysis will proceed by looking closely at the variety of empirical details that constitute meaningful social context here, and by presenting close readings of selected texts in context, with a view to the genres, idioms, and rhetoric employed.[21] Overall, a larger complex picture is emerging, one of overlapping fields of language use and social practice that have to be investigated more closely, and which in their interrelationships create and constitute something like a regional universe of intellectual practice.

Notes

1. In this, they may also have a destructive character and direction, pursuing the goal of "unmaking" and destroying. I use the term "world-making" here in the way that Nelson Goodman (1978) and, before him, Ernst Cassirer (1944), framed the active and creative processes of the constitution of meaning by human beings in their life-worlds, as basic human activity.

2. The introduction of Swahili for topical sections of the Friday sermons is mentioned by Alamin Mazrui and Hammad Muhammad Kasim Mazrui (2017).

3. While I agree with this insight, I admit that as my own work here focuses mostly on the motivations for and patterns of reasoning and arguing, venturing into a deeper analysis of the specific material infrastructure of the media discussed here goes beyond the limits of this study.

4. See, for example, Peterson 2004; Barber 2012; Mokoena 2011; Hofmeyr 2013; Peterson, Hunter, and Newell 2015; Brennan 2011; Hofmeyr, Kaarsholm, and Frederiksen 2011. On Indian Ocean South Asia, see, for example, Green 2011; Robinson 1993.

5. See, for example, the works by Amr Ryad (2008) and Dyala Hamzah (2013) on Rashid Rida and *al-Manar*, and Sajid (2015) and Cleveland (1985) on Shakib Arslan. On East Africa within such transregional debates spanning the Arabic-speaking Muslim world, see Ghazal (2010a; 2010b); Bang (2003; 2014). On Sheikh Al-Amin Mazrui, see Pouwels (1981); Matthews (2013); and my own recent introductory essay (Kresse 2017).

6. While this goes beyond what I shall be able to achieve here, in my case studies of religious mediation and negotiation in the colonial and postcolonial periods, these are big questions of a wider scenario that my research here also speaks to. If my case studies convey a good sense of the internal dynamics of religious discourse, how its contestations and negotiations are embedded in social history, and how the creative use of media shapes, changes, or even transforms the community of Swahili-speaking coastal Muslims, through the kind of specific textual and ethnographic study that I sketched out here, this will have been a successful endeavor—even though questions about specific infrastructures and the workings of technological effects will necessarily remain open.

7. Also, the lands historically possessed by his family were not endangered—unlike later on, when a decade-long court case took much of that, and his confidence in Kenya's legal system, from him.

8. See *Friday Bulletin*, November 14, 2014 (issue no. 602); see also related discussions there, as in issues no. 578, 587, 631, and 636. See also the investigative TV documentations by Al-Jazeera (http://interactive.aljazeera.com/aje/KenyaDeathSquads/); and KTN's "Jicho Pevu," by Kenyan journalist Mohamed Ali (https://www.youtube.com /watch?v=GMERO18jUsw).

9. For different historical accounts on coastal slavery/serfdom and its transformation in the late colonial and postcolonial era, see, for example, Cooper 1980; Mirza and Strobel 1989; Eastman 1994; Glassman 1995; MacMahon 2013.

10. Summarized in Kresse 2007, 45–55. See Parkin 1991; Willis 1993; Ranger 1975; Berg 1968; Berg 1971.

11. Earlier literature on this includes Beckerleg 1995; Ali Mazrui 1993.

12. There are more and other instances that could just as well have been chosen for chapter-length discussions, had the same kind of rich primary source materials been available. For instance, it would be interesting to analyze the IPK (Islamic Party of Kenya). This was an important and politically influential initiative during the early years of multi-party democracy under Moi in the 1990s, about which little has been published (Cruise O'Brien 1995; Oded 1996; Oded 2000; see also Ndzovu 2014; see also the activist newspapers *The Message* and *The Milestone*). Other possible topics include Islamic sermons and speeches that address and discuss issues of national politics directly, in front of local Muslim audiences and by means of oral rhetorical performances that demand particular attention in their own right. I do include some discussion of these two mentioned aspects in the chapters here, based on the materials I have had access to, but further research would be welcome.

13. On postcolonial Africa, see Werbner 1996; 1998; 2000; Mbembe 1992; 2001; Bayart 2000; Chabal and Daloz 1999; Chabal 2009; de Boeck and Plissart 2004. On Muslim perspectives, see Soares 2005; Tayob 2007; Reese 2008; Masquelier 2009; Schulz 2007; 2012.

14. Even if this reproduces the language of Kant's critical philosophy that was focused on the "conditions of possibility of experience" (*die Bedingungen der Moeglichkeit von Erfahrung*), the interest here is fundamentally different from Kant's, for whom this phrase was part of a wholly conceptual and meta-epistemological project of *Erkenntniskritik* that he developed it, in his *Kritik der reinen Vernunft* (Kant 1930), according to an intellectual project whose guidelines he clearly spelled out programmatically in his *Prolegomena* (Kant 1988).

15. Fabian's work since *Time and the Other* (1983) can be read as variable pathways and possibilities of research that illustrate clearly that he also practices what he preaches. His foci of research—such as on performance, deep knowledge of language, critical readings of historical sources, and the interactive dynamics of social remembering—have been carefully selected to this end, and his publications are explicitly linked back to his critique as a point of departure (see, e.g., Fabian 1986; 1990; 1996; 2000; 2001). He sees such critique as a feature of an overarching approach, and not as a new kind of subdiscipline or subfield of anthropology (2001, vii). For related examples in a wider range of critical anthropology, we can also look at the works of James Ferguson, Akhil Gupta, Liisa Malkki, Michael Lambek, Michael Jackson, Edward Simpson, and others.

16. See Barber 2007, 224–25; Mbembe 2001, 7–9 See also Sheldon Pollock's (2015) program of a "critical philology," which can be understood along related lines.

17. Those who did wrong are not alone to be held responsible for their sins; all those who knew about them without seeking to intervene need to take part of the blame, as they associated with wrongdoers (against better knowledge), condoning wrong and in turn perpetuating it—thus ultimately acting against the actual needs of their mistaken peers (who would have needed reproach).

18. *Sauti ya Haki* (SYH) rejects the reproach that it had caused any disunity among local Muslims. Rather, it argues that it had taken the role of "forbidding wrong" seriously, just like its historical role models, and was now receiving (some) angry responses in return. The article reiterates that all Muslims must act upon violations by their peers and forbid one another doing wrong (*kukanyana maovu*). This was not to be taken lightly, and no one ignoring it could be called a good Muslim. In fact, SYH itself justifies its own existence with reference to this phrase, as it seeks to speak up as the "voice of justice," forbidding wrong whenever this seemed necessary.

19. His two sons are Alamin Mazrui, who became a writer and professor of linguistics and literature and went into exile after being imprisoned by the Moi regime in 1982, and Hammad M. K. Mazrui, who studied in Nigeria, Iraq, and Mecca and became Chief Kadhi of Kenya (between 2002 and 2010). Personal communication.

20. Cook also noted such an egalitarian (and even "democratic") character (2000, 584). Cook also speaks about the debates around the obligation as an "intellectual tradition" that he seeks to explore within the society where it flourished, also to see what difference it may have made in the streets (2000, xiii).

21. Rhetoric needs to be looked at more closely, as the invocation of knowledge and certainties in sermons and pamphlets is often an instrumental strategy pushing for an ideological position (Kresse 2008).

PART II
READINGS

3 Colonial Experience and Future Anticipations

Sheikh Al-Amin Mazrui and Swahili Islamic Pamphlets, 1930–32

As we have seen laid out already, coastal Muslims in postcolonial Kenya often seem enveloped in loops of memory that keep them linked to, and even trapped within, patterns of thought and action that, in part, already characterized social life in the colonial past. We need to turn to the colonial period itself in order to capture how the present, postcolonial sense of self came to grow and build upon past experiences, as coastal Muslims have felt marginalized by successive Christian governments from "upcountry" (*bara*). Especially during the period of Daniel arap Moi's rule (1978–2002), when he combined his frequent church attendance with giving political speeches, the impression for Muslims was that the state that proclaimed to be secular was actually Christian, and thus biased against them. They saw themselves losing out in political, economic, and educational terms, and they were subsequently seen as lagging behind "upcountry" Kenya. Throughout the postindependence period, frustration and resentment have continued to brew, and at different times these sentiments were either expressed or kept in check (according to the situation). In the perception of many coastals, such external domination took on features that they characterized as "colonial rule," as the exemplary statements from the introductory chapter illustrated—public statements by Muslim representatives, private commentaries among individuals, or statements in political pamphlets in the early or late postcolonial periods.

These claims express a deep and wide-ranging frustration of coastal Muslim citizens with consecutive Kenyan governments, about the neglect they received. In other words, the point about claims that the present postcolonial experience was similar to the experience of British colonial administration (between 1895 and 1963) is that people on the coast did not see substantial benefits and fruits of independence coming their way, while at the same time they saw the Christian upcountry rulers and their communities and allies prosper and dominate (and even exploit coast-generated wealth, like port revenues). This further increased the economic and political gap between the two groups, alienating coastal Muslims from the state.[1]

But as much as this study seeks to understand case studies of coastal Muslim experience in their specificity and from sources that provide internal points of view, the coastal Muslim case is not exceptional in the sense that common features of postcolonial rule in Africa are at work throughout Kenya's postcolonial history: the "politics of the belly" (Bayart 2000); a "centralized despotism" (Mamdani 1996); and the use of "disorder as a political instrument" by those in power (Chabal and Daloz 1999) to guard and consolidate their status, through a system of governmentality that was ranked around the central figure of the ruling autocrat (Mbembe 2001) as a kind of supreme political being whose will was paramount (Oruka 1997). These were overarching features of postcolonial experience that coastal Muslims in Kenya shared with a number of other marginalized groups that were not sufficiently tapped into the decisive networks of dominant political power and thus had to live with the consequences.

The essays by Sheikh Al-Amin bin Ali Mazrui (1891–1947) discussed in this chapter show, among other things, that by that time already there was an anticipatory sense within the coastal Muslim community that they were going to be losing out, politically, as Kenya was being transformed into a "modern" colonial supplier state that expanded economically and technologically. Here I track and trace specific narratives and commentaries on these dynamics, as provided by Sheikh Al-Amin Mazrui, an Islamic scholar of elite Omani background, and a *kadhi*, engaged writer and social critic, who published the first regular series of Islamic newspaper pamphlets in Swahili, called *Sahifa* (The Page), from October 1930. A selection of these writings was preserved in a reprinted collection with the title of *Uwongozi* (Guidance), first published in 1944, and the twenty-six essays contained therein provide the main source material for this chapter.[2]

The claim that "the rethinking of political community is largely a result of Muslims living in translocal spaces which are themselves the product of wider migratory and globalizing processes" has been made with a view to translocal Muslim politics in the postcolonial era (Mandaville 2001, 191). However, it may already apply to the kind of late colonial settings we find in Mombasa, too. This statement, which summarizes the translocal dynamics of "reimagining the *umma*" and drives processes of internal reform of a Muslim community, is a useful starting point to sketch out the coastal Muslim community of Mombasa at the time when Sheikh Al-Amin Mazrui engaged in reformist activities, seeking to improve coastal society, and published his Swahili Islamic pamphlets, calling upon people to wake up and participate.[3] At this time, when the concept of a global Muslim *umma* was just emerging as an actively re-coined Islamic term vis-à-vis the politically dominant Western colonialism (Mandaville 2001, 189; Kurzman 2002), Mombasa was clearly a significant translocal space that had been shaped by wider processes of migration and movement over many centuries, as part of wide-ranging Indian Ocean trade networks of regionally independent city states until the early sixteenth century. Then it became subject first to Portuguese rule (between about 1500 and 1700) and then Omani rule (under Mazrui governors, until 1837, when the al-Busaidi Sultanate of Zanzibar was being established). It was under Zanzibari rule until the formalization of British colonial "protection" in 1895, and Kenyan Independence in December 1963.

As a crucial port in the region, Mombasa's Muslim urban constituency consisted of a wide range of people from connected littorals in the Gulf, South Asia, Europe, South Africa, North America, and elsewhere—sailors, traders, refugees, laborers—who had come to settle here for longer or shorter terms, depending on opportunities and their promise. The immense technological innovations during the British colonial period, including the railway line to Uganda (completed in 1901) and a new deep-sea port at Kilindini (built in the 1920s), added numerous streams of incoming laborers, especially from South Asia and upcountry Kenya, so that the existent previous demographic mix was shaken up and new urban planning projects were initiated. Other legal and administrative measures by the colonial government, like a new Land Ordinance Act (1908) and the final prohibition of slavery locally (1907), also contributed to a fundamental sense of insecurity among patrician Arab and Swahili coastal urbanites about their status and self-positioning in society.[4] The world as they knew it was in the process of completely transforming itself.

Sheikh Al-Amin and the Mazrui in Mombasa

Sheikh Al-Amin's family, the renowned Mazrui clan from Oman, had come to East Africa from the mid-seventeenth century onward, when the forces of the Yarubi imam of Oman joined with East African coastal Muslims in order to fight and drive out the Portuguese. Then already, members of the clan were involved in crucial military and administrative positions, and after a final successful battle, a Mazrui became governor (*liwali*) of Mombasa on behalf of the imam in 1698— namely, Nasir bin Abdullah Mazrui (Mazrui 1995, 21). This position was passed on within the family until 1837, when the new ruler of Oman, Sayyid Said, on his way to establishing Zanzibar as the second leg of the Busaidi sultanate, quashed Mazrui resistance and took over the town by force (and by treachery, according to the Mazrui account).[5] The Mazrui were initially persecuted and never fully regained their political power, but they retained strong influence in regional politics, and grave tensions and rivalries remained between the Mazrui and Busaidi families from then on.

The Mazrui clan also had an established tradition of Islamic scholarship, and among the ancestors of Sheikh Al-Amin were reputable Ibadi *ulama*. Notably his father, Sheikh Ali bin Nafi, had become a leading first-generation convert to the East African Shafii community. He had fled East Africa in 1836 with his father, to avoid Busaidi persecution (as Mazrui clan members were being imprisoned and killed), and he returned after a decade of studies with Shafii scholars in Mecca, where he had changed his doctrinal affiliation to the Shafii *madhhab*. From the 1860s on he was active as a Shafii missionary and gifted public speaker and as such attracted the anger of Sultan Barghash (d. 1888), who had initiated a campaign of Ibadi revivalism from Zanzibar and who demanded religious adherence by his subjects. Sheikh Ali was incarcerated after preaching in Pemba in 1886 and only released by Sultan Barghash's successor after the sultan's death in 1888[6] Sheikh Ali's missionary activities on the East African coast fed into a wider process of integration of (previously Ibadi) Omanis into the Sunni-Shafii community; this was also facilitated through intermarriage[7] and participation in common rituals and festivals. Thus, Sheikh Al-Amin's father, as an influential Islamic scholar who had studied in the Hijaz and who traveled a lot along the coast, was already an important mediator who contributed much toward forging the kind of wider coastal Muslim community that Sheikh Al-Amin would address three decades later. Both worked actively to extend the membership (and internal diversity) of Sunni Shafii Islam on the Swahili coast, and both employed the Swahili language as a major tool. Sheikh Al-Amin became famous for his writings, while his father was well known for his speeches.

The heterogeneous Muslim community of Mombasa in the colonial era, then, provides a good example of a translocal unity, "constituted by a variety of migratory and colonial flows," to use a phrase characterizing the emerging global *umma* at the time (Mandaville 2001, 188). Sheikh Al-Amin's main teachers in their day had been "travelling Muslims"[8] like his father, spending years acquiring knowledge and expertise in the centers of Islamic learning at the time. Their thinking as mature scholars had been shaped by their experiences elsewhere in the Muslim world and the specific "new peoples and bodies of theory" with whom they had come in contact, "Muslim and non-Muslim alike" (2001, 184).

When Sheikh Al-Amin was four, his father died, and he lived with his uncle, Sheikh Sulaiman bin Ali bin Khamis Mazrui, a renowned scholar who became his foster father and teacher. After completing his basic studies with Sheikh Sulaiman, Sheikh Al-Amin went to Zanzibar in regular intervals to study with the two most highly regarded *ulama* of the time, Sayyid Ahmed bin Sumayt (from the Comoros, d. 1925) and Sheikh Abdallah Bakathir (from Lamu, d. 1925). Both were close friends and had traveled and studied in the Hadramaut and Mecca and Medina. Sayyid Ahmed also spent a year in Istanbul, while Sheikh Abdallah spent some time teaching in Java and visited Egypt, Cape Town, Uganda, the Comoros, and Barawa (Farsy 1972, 68–69; 46–49; see also Bang 2003).

Drawing from the teachings of these scholars of highest reputation while confining his own travels to the East African region where he shaped and nurtured his own networks, Sheikh Al-Amin was influenced by further Islamic writers who were not commonly read in Mombasa at the time. Next to the three well-known modernists Jamal al-Din al-Afghani, Muhammad Abduh, and Rashid Rida, his students also mention Ibn Taimiyah and Muhammad Abdul Wahhab (M. K. Mazrui 1980, ix). Sheikh Al-Amin was influenced by the Pan-Islamic, Pan-Arab, and anticolonial ideas that were discussed in the flourishing newspaper debates of his time, in newspapers and journals like *al-Manar*, *al-Fath*, and others.[9] As an Islamic scholar, Sheikh Al-Amin was greatly concerned about the growing threat that two rival religious groups posed to the Muslim community: the Christian missionaries who were supported by the Western colonial powers, and the Ahmadiyya group, which had a strong presence in East Africa but was not acceptable as "Muslim" to him (and many major *ulama* worldwide). His concerns were proven right, as both groups pushed their cause and produced Swahili translations of the Qur'an (the Christians in 1923, the Ahmadiyya in 1953) well before any regional Muslim scholar was able to complete and publish one.[10] This had been one of Sheikh Al-Amin's own big projects, but his translation, which sought to refute what he saw as misreadings of the Christian translation, was never completed, and it was his student and protégée Sheikh Abdalla Saleh Farsy who achieved this task in 1969, with a translation that also responded to Ahmadiyya misrepresentations (Farsy 1969). Some parts of Sheikh Al-Amin's translation were published posthumously (Mazrui 1980; 1981), and his pamphlets addressing the Christian and Ahmadiyya threats were published during and after his lifetime (e.g., Mazrui 1939; 1950).

Sheikh Al-Amin's thinking questioned habits and practices that were common among coastal Muslims at the time, often among the Sufi-oriented Hadrami Alawiyya networks (with the Riyadha Mosque in Lamu as their main base).[11] For instance, he criticized the repetitive learning of the Qur'an by heart that was not linked to the development of an understanding of the text, but made students repeat it "like parrots" (*kama kasuku*; *Uwongozi* 12); he rejected the aura of superiority with which some *masharifu* presented themselves in public (*Uwongozi* 5); he opposed some of the performances of their common ritual practices (like *khitma*, *tahlil*, and *dhikr*) as unacceptable religious innovations (*bidaa*); and he spoke out against unreasonable and lavish spending during *maulidi* celebrations in honor of Prophet Muhammad's birthday, for which many families ran themselves into heavy debt (*Uwongozi* 15; *Uwongozi* 16).

Such public critique, commentary, and forms of communal self-questioning were raised in the *Sahifa* pamphlets he wrote between 1930 and 1932. The kinds of arguments that he put forward, and his reasons for arguing against certain established habits, preferences, and trends in social behavior among local Muslims, provide a rich resource of themes and points for discussion and analysis. They feed into his agenda of social and religious reform in the region, an agenda that he shaped and coined through his publishing activities that also took over

and adapted anticolonial and Pan-Islamic leitmotifs from contemporary publications in the Arab world. Among reform-oriented Muslims in East Africa,
Sheikh Al-Amin Mazrui became the leading role model, with a view to religious
lines of argument as well as with a view to calls for modernization and social
change. His texts and some of their striking quotes were frequently picked up and
employed even in more recent internal debates (see chapters 4 and 5). In other
words, Sheikh Al-Amin Mazrui's short essays for *Sahifa* covered many topics of
concern, but they also provided a range of forms and patterns of argument to be
raised in later debates within the coastal Muslim community.

Sheikh Al-Amin's own way of rethinking political community, of reimagining the *umma* in Mombasa, was shaped by specific influences, not least by
the observation and experience of British colonial rule; but also by the Islamic
scholarship he had been exposed to, through highly regarded and widely traveled
ulama like Sayyid Ahmed bin Sumayt and Sheikh Abdalla Bakathir. In addition,
the scope and depth of Sheikh Al-Amin's reading, scholarly and journalistic,
Islamic and worldly, is said to have gone well beyond the established local canon.
And so, even though he did not travel extensively beyond East Africa (apart from
haj in 1932; see Tamim 2006, 60), as an active reader and lucid observer who
sought stimulation from elsewhere, he integrated and adapted new thoughts that
he came across as part of his critical engagement with his own community, with
a view to the needs and possibilities for reform from within. The term "critical
Islam" has been used as a label for scholars pursuing such pathways in similar
postcolonial circumstances (Mandaville 2001, 185, 190–91), and one could apply
this term here too, with a view to the essays discussed. Yet these only represent a
minor proportion of Sheikh Al-Amin's writings overall, which also included,
among others, partial Swahili translations from the Qur'an (*juzuu*; 1980; 1981);[12]
a collection of 130 *hadith* translated into Swahili;[13] a history of the Mazrui in East
Africa (1995) and a booklet on basic Islamic education for children (Mazrui n.d.),
both written in Arabic; and a number of general educational pamphlets: about
the proper legal procedures on marriage and divorce (*ndoa na talaka*); in praise
of Islam and Prophet Muhammad (using quotations from the bible on the one
hand and by famous Westerners on the other); and yet others, on practical matters like the potential for using *zakat* in East Africa, or simply listing the Arab
and Swahili names of animals that are *halal* to eat according to Shafii law.[14] A
small but significant body of scholarship on Sheikh Al-Amin Mazrui exists, yet
until now his texts have hardly been subjected to close readings, and they need to
be explored much further.[15]

The *Sahifa* Pamphlets

In Swahili, *sahifa* is an alternative term for "page," next to the more common
ukarasa. It is a loanword from Arabic, and its Arabic meanings feed into the

richer sense of Sheikh Al-Amin's agenda. Originally referring to "a surface for writing" that could be of different materials, in early Islamic history it commonly meant broadsheets of important messages that were to be read out to the community and implemented, thus having clear practical intent.[16] The *Sahifa* pamphlets were published as double-sided sheets of paper covering a particular topic each Monday between October 1930 and February 1932. After that, Sheikh Al-Amin published a longer (eight-page) bilingual Swahili–Arabic sequel called *al-Islah* (Reform) between 1932 and 1933.[17] This followed the same agenda and also included letters to the editor, a dialogical form, within the medium itself. Arguably, these two pamphlets of his have provided the two main prototypes for both the form and the agenda of subsequent Islamic pamphlets in East Africa until today. Particularly the eight-page format has frequently been used, by the Mombasa-based Swahili *Sauti ya Haki* quarterly (1972–82), the bilingual English–Swahili newspapers of the Islamic Party of Kenya (IPK), the *Message* and the *Muslim Voice* in the early 1990s, the popular Tanzanian Swahili Islamic weekly *An-Nuur* (available all over East Africa since the mid-1990s), and the main weekly publication of the Kenyan Muslim community, the English *Friday Bulletin,* edited and published from Jamia Mosque in Nairobi around the same time.[18]

Sheikh Al-Amin Mazrui's journalistic writings, his critical essays for *Sahifa* (reprinted in *Uwongozi*), and later for *al-Islah,* are illuminating to read, as historical documents but also much more. In them, we find a highly educated Islamic scholar acting as a well-informed and engaged social commentator, critical of Western colonialism and drawing from the lively Pan-Islamic Arabophone discussions at the time, inspired by the "Salafi" and "neo-Salafi" reformers operating largely from Cairo (after Schulze 2000, 18, 95). These Arab intellectuals were voicing discontent about the state of the Muslim world in contemporary global politics and engaged in rebuilding social networks and political discourse among Muslims based on the principles of early Islam and taking the Prophet's companions as pious forefathers (*al-salaf al-salih*) and role models to develop a vision of concurrent modernization and Islamization.[19] It is for this kind of effort that we can see Sheikh Al-Amin Mazrui argue in his writings, with a clear sense for local specifics. As a descendant of an elite Omani family and an integral member of the urban community of coastal Muslims, consisting of the Swahili *waungwana* (patricians; freeborn citizens), the Swahili-speaking Arabs (of both Omani and Hadrami background), and further residents and laborers of middle and lower status, he was able to directly address these groups who constituted the primary audience for his essays. He did not hesitate to criticize fellow Muslims, and he employed his rich vocabulary and rhetorical skills in Swahili to present sharp and fundamental points of internal critique (sometimes in a humorous manner) that were meant to make them wake up to the adverse realities they had to face. His language in the essays was therefore clear and accessible, following an oral narrative mode loosely based on the Mombasa dialect (Kimvita). In this way, he reached out to an audience from a wider demographic spectrum beyond that of local scholars and intellectuals only. His essays sought to educate people along worldly and religious lines—as the subtitle of the *Uwongozi* collection states, *katika dini na dunia*, "in religion and the world")—and to instigate them to engage in practical ways to improve their community, their social status in colonial society, and their moral status as Muslims.

As author and editor of *Sahifa*, Sheikh Al-Amin was the initiator of Swahili Islamic print media in East Africa in February 1930. This was late compared to Arabic publications from Zanzibar, which began in the 1870s (Ghazal 2010b), and to colonial Swahili newspapers, which the Germans launched in the early 1900s in Tanganyika (Bromber 2006, 68–69). It also followed the established presence of local Indian newspapers (see *Uwongozi* No. 17). *Sahifa* was handwritten by Sheikh Al-Amin in Arabic script (also called *Ajami*) and then copied in "cyclostyle" to be distributed every Monday in a print run of only one hundred copies (M. K. Mazrui 1980, ix). These critical essays upset and offended part of the community, as Sheikh Al-Amin's closest student, Sheikh Muhammad Kasim Mazrui, noted (M. K. Mazrui 1995, 2–3), while the frankness of his talk and the sting of his internal critique was much appreciated by others. Contested topics addressed in public here included appeals for more and better education (secular and Islamic) for a wider spectrum of people (including women); the status of women; patriotism; proper economic spending; and the dangers of imitating others, especially Westerners.

Popular demand led to a selection of the *Sahifa* texts being reprinted, in 1944, under the title *Uwongozi*, or "Guidance" (Mazrui 1944, foreword; Mazrui 2017, 42–43). When Sheikh Al-Amin wrote these essays, he was admonishing his fellow coastal Muslims, whom he addressed as *wapwani* ("coastals"), and at the same time encouraging them to do the right thing. At that point in time, the *wapwani* were in the process of losing their privileged status, of being recognized as the East African "civilizational other" by the British colonialists. This was in contrast to upcountry Africans (*wabara*, literally "mainlanders"), for whom things had only recently started to change, after Nairobi became the center of colonial rule (1907), and upcountry laborers were proving themselves as a mobile and flexible labor force that was needed for further modernizing and industrial projects. In Mombasa, these were the new deep-sea port at Kilindini and its infrastructure—and similarly (before that) the railways, and also new technologies like the telephone, the telegraph, electricity, and radio technology (*Uwongozi* 4, 18).[20]

Sheikh Al-Amin, as a respected Islamic scholar, a committed Salafi-oriented modernist reformer, and a Pan-Islamic critic of colonialism, became the leading public voice for social and religious reform among coastal Kenyan Muslims. In retrospect, his publishing activities, with their critique of lavish spending during *maulidi* or wedding celebrations (chapter 13), or of traditional divination practices (chapter 11), have to some extent been locally understood as marking the beginning phase of two major, formally opposed groups of coastal Muslims: the "modernists" following and continuing Sheikh Al-Amin's project, and the Sufi-oriented followers of the Alawiyya based in Lamu at Riyadha. However, Sheikh Al-Amin himself had amicable personal relationships with a number of Alawiyya scholars, as teachers, students, and peers, not least the founder of Riyadha Mosque, Sayyid Habib Saleh (d. 1935) himself, and his son Ahmad, as well as its subsequent leader, Sayyid Ali Badawy (d. 1988).[21] Sheikh Al-Amin is seen, on the one hand, as active and traveling missionary, the initiator and figurehead of social and religious reform among coastal Muslims (Farsy 1972, 42–43), leading to increased and more pronounced internal tensions and oppositions. On the other hand, Sheikh Al-Amin is also remembered as a committed mediator in religious disputes and personal rivalries, a humble person despite his superior knowledge and education, showing respect for scholars with different doctrinal standpoints and Islamic interpretations, while sharply rejecting the Ahmadiyya (Tamim 2006, 48–60).

Transregional Perspectives and Mediations

One way to introduce the mindset and world of ideas that Sheikh Al-Amin Mazrui worked to disseminate among East African Muslims is to have a closer look at an arabophone writer who was inspirational to Sheikh Al-Amin: Shakib Arslan. As we know, Sheikh Al-Amin was a regular reader not only of *al-Manar*, but also other influential Pan-Islamic, Pan-Arab, and other Arabic journals circulating at the time, like *al-Fath* and *al-Zahra* (both published by Muhibb al-Din al-Khatib's Salafiyya Press), or *al-Liwa, al-Mu'ayyad,* and *al-Hilal*.[22] In November 1930, a month before Sheikh Al-Amin published his first issue of *Sahifa*, an extended essay on the "decline" of the Muslim world was published in *al-Manar.* It was written by one of the most prominent Arabic writers for the cause of Pan-Islamism, Shakib Arslan, the so-called Prince of Eloquence.[23] Arslan's essay addressed many of the topics that Sheikh Al-Amin also covered, from the angle of the specific situation in East Africa under British colonial rule (or, more precisely, "protection," as the Coastal Strip was a protectorate leased from the sultan of Zanzibar).

Many of the key conceptual terms and rhetorical phrases used in Arslan's text (which I read in English translation) also underlie the arguments for social reform and a renewal of religious consciousness in the Swahili texts by Sheikh Al-Amin. There is a clear emphasis on performance and the need for action in order for progress to come, as "dedication," "striving," and "zeal" are called for, for

Muslims to make proper headway in the right direction. The conclusion flags up the need to sacrifice in order to progress (118–20) and indeed speaks of a "science of 'sacrifice'" as "the greatest science," one that includes striving by bodily means and material wealth (119). "Action" and "work" are held up high as performances upon which "honor" and "fame" can be built, in relation to the resulting achievements. Arslan emphasized the need for solidarity and "unity" among Muslims, while Muslims were also presented as their own worst enemies (30); Arslan even claimed that many Muslims had ceased to be *muslim* (those who submit to Allah) and instead had become *mustalim* (those who surrender to the enemy) (45). Islam, according to Arslan, used to be a motor for progress in the early history of Islam and now needed to be renewed as such. This was to be achieved through the proper use and dissemination of "knowledge" of both worldly and religious nature (e.g., 91–92; 95–96) so that the state of "ignorance" (*jahiliyya*), with its destructive effects (laziness, fatalism, fear, idleness, self-delusion), could be overcome and left behind. Arslan pointed to the beginnings of a current powerful "Muslim awakening" that Western powers were monitoring closely (2), a reform process for which the Prophet's companions (*salaf*) were invoked as role models (68–71). He characterized the representatives of such reform as thoughtful modernizers who integrate a sense of regional cultural traditions into their program of social change. Such a balance is necessary, he wrote, as currently "the sophisticated 'ultra-moderns' [who blindly imitate Western secularism] and the conservative conventionalists [who follow religion as a binding custom] are ruining Islam between themselves" (50). The former destroy and disown Muslim societies' historical traditions and religious identity, while the latter are against any kind of change at all. He was critical of Western culture (and well placed to be, having spent thirteen years in Europe) and considered Japan as an exemplary nation that managed to retain its cultural traditions while modernizing successfully.

Shakib Arslan was a central figure of Pan-Islamism and a celebrated journalist in the Arab world. Looking at his text as a background to the writings of Sheikh Al-Amin, we obtain a sense of a widely shared transregional agenda of reform that could be applied across social and cultural divides by Muslims in different regions with a sense of common purpose. While the similarities here are striking, I do not seek to suggest that Sheikh Al-Amin was not an original thinker—but it is important to be aware of the specific aspects of common agendas and their corresponding overlapping or shared vocabularies for social change and reformative action.

In my discussions of the *Sahifa* essays here, I focus first on Sheikh Al-Amin's characterizations of Mombasa's urban community, and in relation to that, I subsequently flag up some of Sheikh Al-Amin's points of critique. Thus I recount the state of affairs that he reports to his readers, before going into the specifics of his discontent and his suggestions for improvement. These social commentaries reflect upon coastal society in connection to global politics, with a perspective on the moral conduct, practical knowledge, and religious education of the coastal Muslim community. The essays raise internal social critique, and by providing guidance and intellectual orientation, they seek to address how best to deal with issues such as the ever-increasing economic hardships, the coastal people's ongoing loss of status within the colonial system, and related matters. My readings illustrate and substantiate these points, discussing them in their social and historical context, with attention to the texts and contexts, their wording, and the rhetorical strategies involved.

Mombasa in the *Sahifa* Essays

Mombasa, here commonly called by its old name Mvita—often rendered as a city of war, most famously in the poetry of Muyaka (Abdulaziz 1979, 18–21)—is cast as a town that represents the coastal Muslim community in decline and decay, in contrast to its recent growth and the developments that transformed its urban character: the completion of the new deep-sea port at Kilindini, and of the Uganda railways, built by thousands of laborers from South Asia and upcountry Kenya. These references are largely left implicit in the texts themselves, but they provide important contexts for his audience at the time. The old coastal port town had become a colonial city that continued to accommodate a large influx of labor migrants from upcountry Kenya, colonial India, Shihir, and elsewhere. Sheikh Al-Amin estimated that out of 75,000 inhabitants (about half of whom were Muslim), the historical coastal urban "Swahili Arab" population consisted of about 12,000 (*Uwongozi* 26). Writing with an acute sense of the community's minority status and other detrimental dynamics, Sheikh Al-Amin here built a commentary voice that combined harsh criticism with a sense of solidarity and understanding, as he pushed for modernist reform in religious practice and social life.

Muslims in Mombasa, according to Sheikh Al-Amin, were "poor in everything," lacking knowledge, wealth, and leadership—and still they demanded equal status with Indians while unwilling to contribute in the same way to the community (*Uwongozi* 26). A common comment about Mombasa's urban community, "In Mvita nothing gets done" (*Mvita haifanyiki jambo*) (*Uwongozi* 17), reflected, as Sheikh Al-Amin identified, a lack of "zeal" (*ghera*), of disciplined effort and determination among coastal Muslims, who had been deluding themselves on different levels (*Uwongozi* 5). Because of this, he said, there were no future prospects to be identified for the community. Elsewhere, in a *Sahifa* edition that was reprinted in the Islamic newspaper *Sauti ya Haki* some decades later and under the headline "Truth in a Joke" (*ukweli katika mzaha*), Sheikh Al-Amin provided a biting satirical depiction of a group of coastal Muslim elders (*wazee*) in an imaginary conversation as representative of "the people of Mombasa." The

old men he portrayed there seemed a bit ridiculous, as hard-headed traditionalists lacking worldly outlook and religious knowledge, suspicious of others and
the outside world, and reluctant to consider new ideas (*Sauti ya Haki*, July 1978;
translated in Kresse 2009a).

Readings in *Self-Positioning*: Coastal Muslims and Their Others

Like reform-oriented modernist writers in others parts of the Muslim world,[24]
Sheikh Al-Amin found fault with his people's habit of thoughtlessly imitating
European ways (*Uwongozi* 18; *Uwongozi* 24). How come, he asked, we seem to
copy only the bad habits and sinful ways from the British (*Uwongozi* 4)? What is
wrong with us, what makes us do this? In consequence, he posed an anticipatory
question: "What will happen to us [should we continue to conduct ourselves in
this way]?" As an acute observer of global developments and colonial politics,
he referred to that time as a period of fundamental social transformation. He
raised the possibility of an inversion of social status of coastal people vis-à-vis
upcountry people, in reflections that also announced, almost prophetically, a
"Black Peril" (*khatari nyeusi*). This was the vision of a future in which the self-
disciplined, educated, and technologically trained upcountry people, *watu wa
bara*, were to become administrators and rulers over the coastal *wapwani*, who
were largely uninterested in modern education and seemed increasingly unquali-
fied in comparison. While many coastal Muslims seemed enveloped in what
Sheikh Al-Amin called a "deep slumber" (*Uwongozi* 18; *Uwongozi* 5), inactive and
unmotivated to take any initiative, African laborers from upcountry had migrated
to Mombasa, where they were dominating the labor force at the docks and in the
colonial homes. They were also engaged in qualifying themselves further, to work
for the railways and other modern industries (telephone and telegraph services,
electrical appliances, and other specialized skills and crafts that were in demand).
As flexible and progressive laborers who were ready to do any jobs required, those
in this group seemed determined to continue their self-education as a pathway to
a better and more independent life in the future (*Uwongozi* 18).

The term "Black Peril" (*khatari nyeusi*) was inspired by the trope of the "Yellow Peril" coined by Western writers and journalists for the Japanese and Chinese
in the early 1900s, casting them as emerging—and frightening—world powers on
the modern global stage.[25] Seen as a diligent and disciplined labor force that was
undergoing programmatic modernization after years of isolation, they were perceived as a major threat to Western political and economic hegemony (this was
closely followed in the Pan-Islamic Arabic press at the time). Coastal Muslims,
according to Sheikh Al-Amin, needed to work hard to guard and keep their historically superior social status vis-à-vis the incoming *wabara*, as this hierarchy
was now becoming ever more fragile. It had been based on a civilizational narrative of superiority over all "upcountry folk" (*wabara*), who were portrayed as

largely uncivilized people (*washenzi*), servants and former slaves (*watumwa*) and others in dependency relationships with the coastal urban patricians (*waung-wana*). The latter deemed themselves superior on the basis of their religion, their literacy and education, and the historical transregional networks they engaged in. In Sheikh Al-Amin's text here (as well as in others, until today), this narrative is tinged with racial undertones, pitting a narrative "us" of originally superior "Arab-Swahili" coastals against the "threat" or "danger" (*khatari*) of supposedly inferior "blacks." In turn, such assumptions are, of course, hotly contested and rejected by members of groups who feel discriminated against, from the coastal hinterland and upcountry regions. The historical tensions expressed in such language have not been resolved until today, and they continue to burden social relationships within the wider Muslim community as well as the Kenyan nation (e.g., McIntosh 2009; Mwakimako 2010; Ndzovu 2014).

In the recent postcolonial present, however, this narrative has often been used in an inverted manner, and it is people from upcountry, from Nairobi or central Kenya, who comment (sometimes with pity, more often with antipathy) on the supposed "backwardness" of coastal people, educationally and economically. Thus this opposition remains an important rhetorical reference point and a discursive trope in public discourse. Coastals and other Kenyans continue to use these oppositions in ways that either resonate with or invert the historical perspective that underpins Sheikh Al-Amin's writings. And while Sheikh Al-Amin, as the leading modernist reformer among coastal Muslims, publicly questioned the sense of these discursive oppositions within a life-world that was radically changing, some of his coastal Muslim peers have continued to invoke these oppositions as affirmations of their supposed civilizational superiority.

Overall, in his characterizations of groups of social others in Mombasa as they appear in the *Uwongozi/Sahifa* texts, Sheikh Al-Amin presented their engagements and achievements in comparison to his own group, the urban *wap-wani*, whom he urged to wake up from their deluding slumber and take charge of their own situation. He advocated practical initiatives that would improve the social, economic, and educational status of their community, so that it could advance and come to terms with the changing realities of the modern world and British colonial rule. At this point in time, self-conceptualizations of Muslim urbanites as more civilized and superior to others were becoming more and more baseless but were still very much in people's heads.

Reading "Obligations of Muslims Today" (*Uwongozi* 26)

"It cannot be hidden that the state of affairs of Muslims these days is one of decline and weakness and degradation, [and] all these would not have befallen them if they had not abandoned their religion that *commands* them great things and *for-bids* them degrading things."[26] This opening sentence of the essay called "The

Obligations of Muslims Today" (no. 26 of the *Uwongozi* collection) sets a scene for discussion. It introduced, or restated, a common perspective on the decline of the Muslim community at the time—locally and globally—and it flagged up the need to return to a "proper" understanding of Islam to redress this situation. The sentence also reiterated a central inherent theme in Islam, by pointing to Muslims' perpetual obligation of commanding right and forbidding wrong, which applied locally as much as anywhere in the global *umma*.

After commenting that Muslims were currently in such a bad state that "even their enemies" felt sorry for them,[27] Sheikh Al-Amin introduced the scenario of Mombasa that I have already described above. According to Sheikh Al-Amin, the coastal Arabs and Swahili were the weakest of all groups, as they lacked the leadership, knowledge, and wealth that could help them improve their situation. This image was a clear inversion of the common historical (self-) portrayal of East African urban Muslims, who presented themselves, and are presented in academic literature, as wealthy traders who acted as cunning mediators between bigger external political and economic powers, forming, over the centuries, a veritable "middle-men society" (Middleton 1992) of traders, scholars, patricians, and freeborn noblemen (*waungwana*), well-connected to others but also dependent on alliances with them.

In comparison, Sheikh Al-Amin pointed to the wealthy Hindu community (*Mabanyani*) in Mombasa, "who are among the smallest groups, yet they own two daily newspapers"[28]—which exemplified their social power and influence. Such an example of diligence should be emulated. Sheikh Al-Amin regarded newspapers as unique among "modern" things, reaching people's hearts and teaching good ways and new ideas "so that people may prosper and progress" (*Uwongozi*, "Preface"; Mazrui 2017, 42–43). Newspapers disseminate knowledge and information swiftly and widely, and as such are good mediation platforms for the agenda of social change. Sheikh Al-Amin praised the Hindus' ability of modern, forward-looking self-organization, as they kept alive and in public view (in newspapers) their internal debates about their goals for the community's development. This was not an automatic outcome of the wealth of Mombasa's Hindus but an achievement that coastal Muslims should also aspire to and seek to attain for themselves, even if on a smaller and more humble scale, due to their lesser economic resources.

Providing knowledge and insight into worldly matters and religious affairs was important to Sheikh Al-Amin. He rejected imitation as a form of education—even in learning the Qur'an, which was commonly recited to be learned by heart—as in his view, this did not lead to a true understanding of its meaning. "It saddens me a lot," Sheikh Al-Amin wrote (Mazrui 2017, 168–69),

> that the Goans have their own schools, and we have no school at all in all our
> towns, except these Qur'anic schools (*vyuo*) which a child attends from the

age of seven and leaves when approaching puberty, at a point when they do not know anything except reciting the Qur'an, and even the Qur'an is not read how it is supposed to be read; nor do they know the meaning therein; nor even the meaning of sura FATIHA which they recite again and again in their prayers day and night.

> *Yanihuzunisha sana kuwa Magoa wana school yao khasa, na sisi kutokuwa na school yoyote katika miji yetu yote, illa hivi vyuo ambavyo hungiya kijana na umri wake ni myaka 7 akatoka nalhali amekurubia kubaleghe na yeye hajui illa kusoma Kur'ani tu, na hio Kur'ani haisomi kama vilivyo, wala hajui maana yaliyomo, hatta maana ya sura ya FATIHA ambayo yuwasoma mara kwa mara katika sala yake mtana na usiku.*

This speaks to a main point of his agenda—namely, the campaign for good and proper education for local Muslims (male and female), an education that facilitated the exercise of religion as an informed (i.e., knowledgeable) and self-confident practice—not an imitative (and thus ignorant) one, as he saw it practiced around him. Thus he appealed to people to invest into the building of proper local schools for coastal Muslims, similar to the ways that Goan Christians had already achieved this. However, he strongly rejected the thought of educating young Muslims in Christian institutions, regarding this as one of the worst things parents could do (indeed, driving their children into the hands of the "enemy"). Pointing to the obligation of all community members to contribute to the improvement of the state of affairs, he proposed a commitment to a small financial investment to be made by everyone in order to achieve a fundamental improvement (Mazrui 2017, 170–71):

> If we oblige each of us to donate 3 shillings per year, we shall be able to collect 36,000 Kenyan shillings in one year, and this is enough to run the *madrasa* we like, and we will be able to educate our children in everything they need to know in the disciplines of knowledge about religion and the world, to benefit them here in the world and tomorrow in the Afterlife.
>
> *Tutakapo jilazimisha killa mtu katika sisi kutowa Shs. 3/- kwa mwaka twaweza kukusanya katika mwaka mmoja Shs. 36,000 na hizi zatosha kupele-kea Madrasa kama hiyo tutakayo, na kuweza kuwasomesha watoto wetu killa wahitajialo katika Ilmu za Dini na za Dunia za kuwafaa hapa ulimwenguni na Kesho Akhera.*

The independent realization of such projects, as part of self-reliant efforts from within the community itself (and not as a "given" supplied by the government), was important to him. He gave practical advice and appealed to his peers to be actively engaged in things that matter, and to take on responsibility as part of their personal contribution to improve things. Only when they did so, he argued, did they deserve respect, and to be treated on an equal level with the South Asian communities by the government, as they have been demanding (Mazrui 2017, 170–71).[29]

We complain every day that our skills and knowledge are diminishing, and it is completely absurd to expect that the government will uplift us, while we ourselves are stingy with our own wealth. . . . We always ask the government to treat us equally with the Indians (*Wahindi*). So! Have we thought even for a day to make ourselves equal with them in what they donate to educate their children?

Sisi twashitaki killa siku yakuwa taalimu yetu yenda tini, na ni upuzi kabisa kuitaka Sirkali iinue taalimu yetu, nalhali sisi tumabahili wa mali. . . . Sisi twataka Sirkali daima itufanye sawa-sawa na Wahindi. Jee! tumefikiri hatta siku moja kujifanya sawa na wao katika watowacho kuwafunzisha watoto wao?

Sheikh Al-Amin insisted that one had the obligation to put in proper effort toward one's goals, to work for their realization. Only after one has tried everything to the best of one's ability can requests or demands be made—and then they must be made on good grounds. The rhetorical question in the quote above marks a key feature of Sheikh Al-Amin's style of arguing in these essays, as he appealed to his peers, again and again, to truly engage in the improvement of their own affairs, and to invest the resources at their disposal.

His essays are full of rhetorical question marks, ostentatiously demanding answers while implicitly supplying them already. As stylistic means, we may regard them as "questioning marks" to his community. They are public signs of an investigative iterative process of social self-questioning that Sheikh Al-Amin, as publicist and scholar, engaged in on behalf of his people. His questions addressed soft spots and weaknesses within the community that had an adverse effect (such as examples of neglect); they demanded accountability and responsibility from the group. These questioning marks were integral building blocks of Sheikh Al-Amin's way of raising the social consciousness of his community, to encourage a critical rethinking of their efforts, and to counter communal lethargy, which he saw at the root of the perpetuation of social decline among coastal Muslims.

Next to such questions, other rhetorical figures employed by Sheikh Al-Amin include pronounced references to other groups of urban coresidents whom he singled out for comparison. They were beneficial to look at, as they had devised successful strategies for coping with problems and issues. "Look at them!" his texts appealed to readers, again and again. "These people have a point here. Look how they do this, and learn from them!" For instance, an essay called "Zeal, People . . . ! !" (*Ghera jamani . . . ! !*) points to an example from a remote elsewhere that is instructive to think about (as we have already seen). This is Japan, which from the late nineteenth century was making a prominent and much publicized rise to the stage of global politics; Sheik Al-Amin commented upon this, with a view to knowledge and education (Mazrui 2017, 126–27).

Look at the Japanese; when they saw the Europeans advancing in knowledge and the arts, their zeal did not allow them to accept to be left behind. . . . They embarked on teaching themselves the scientific knowledge of the Europeans as well as their arts with dedication and effort, until now they have become one of the largest powers that are feared even by the Europeans themselves, to such an extent that today Tokyo competes with London and Paris and New York in matters of knowledge and prosperity.

> *Tazamani Wajapani, walipo waona watu wa Ulaya wamekwenda mbele kwa ilimu na sanaa, haikuwakubalia ghera yao kuridhia kuwa nyuma, [...] Hapo waliingia kujifunza ilmu za watu wa Ulaya na sanaa zao kwa himma na jitihadi, hatta leo wamekuwa ni katika dola kubwa zinazo ogopewa hatta na watu wa Ulaya nafsi zao, imekuwa Tokyo hivi leo yashindana na London na Paris na New York kwa ilimu na kazi za ufanifu.*

He took the Japanese example of zeal and determination and connected it to the exemplary attitude that he saw among South Asians in Mombasa, an attitude of commitment that led to their building a modern infrastructure of education, health, and information that they also generously shared with others (ibid.):

We see the prosperity of the Indians (*Wahindi*) in their many shops and their big businesses and their very good schools and libraries filled with books of all disciplines, and their (own) newspapers which appear in the mornings and evenings, and their hospitals which assist us with free medication. With all their prosperity, any person who comes to Mombasa today will think that it is the Indians who are the indigenous community (*wenyeji*), and we who *are* the natives (*wenyewe*) are the strangers; they have reached the top and we have become worthless people because of our ignorance (*ujinga*).

> *Twaona ufanifu wa Wahindi kwa maduka yao mengi na biashara zao kubwa na school zao njema njema na ma-library yaliyo jaa vitabu vya killa fanni, na magazeti yao ni haya tuyaonayo asubuhi na jioni, na hospital zao ni hizi zitusaidiazo kwa dawa za bure, hatta, kwa ufanifu wao, amekuwa mtu angiyae Mombasa leo, huona Wahindi ndio wanyeji na sisi wenyewe kama kwamba ni wageni, waliokuja kwa juu, tumekuwa sisi ni watu duni kwa ujinga wetu.*

Ignorance, as lack of knowledge, and a lethargic or lazy attitude, as lack of engagement, were flagged up as two indicators of an unworthy community here. Again and again, Sheikh Al-Amin implored his readers to take the improvement of their lives into their own hands, and to act in responsible ways to pursue their own group interests in public (ibid.).

What is it that prevents us from opening our own shops, so that we stop our money flowing into the hands of others? Why don't we have our own schools? Or what is it that stops us from having a library like them, to make it easier for us to acquire knowledge? What is preventing us from having our own newspaper that guides our communities and show them the way and our interests?

> *Ni lipi lituzuialo kufanya maduka yetu, takakhitari mapesa yetu kwenda katika mikono ya watu wengine? Kwani hatuwi na ma-school yetu wenyewe? Au ni jambo gani litupingalo tusiwe na Library kama wao tukajisahilishia ndia ya kupata ilimu? Ni lipi lituwasalo tusiwe na gazeti ya kuongoza jamaa zetu na kuwaonesha ndia na maslaha yetu?*

Again, a string of rhetorical questions is used to drive home a point to the readers, before this same point is reiterated in positive language and constructive terms (ibid., 126–28):

> There is not one thing that can stop us from all this, except that we lack zeal. . . . We are not saying that we should establish the same that the Indians have; no, but we should do this in relation to our . . . ability. . . . If we want to move forward in comparison to other people, this [being active] is the only way that will make us reach our goals. Or if we aspire for things just by desire and without actions, we will permanently continue to apply this bad saying of ours, that in "in Mvita [Mombasa] nothing ever gets done."
>
> *Hapana moja la kutuzuilia na yote hayo illa ni kuwa hatuna ghera. . . . Hatusemi tufanye maduka kama walionayo Wahindi sawa sawa; la, lakini natufanye kwa mnasaba wa sisi na wao. . . . Tukipenda kwenda mbele na kulingana na watu, hii ndiyo ndia ya kutufikiliza katika muradi wetu. Amma tukiwa twataka mambo kwa matamanio pasi na vitendo, tukadumu na kushikamana na tamko letu la ukorofi, na kusema "Mvita haifanyiki jambo."*

That the phrase "nothing gets done" could attain a kind of proverbial status to be attributed to Mombasa seems emblematic of the lethargy that Sheikh Al-Amin sought to combat. He was convinced that coastal Muslims needed to overcome their passive behavior and go beyond customary patterns, thinking creatively about how their difficulties in life could actually be addressed and improved by means of active initiatives and ideas. In conclusion, he appealed to coastal Muslims to organize themselves and actually do something, for "aspiring for things just by desire and without action," as he argued, would only lead to self-destruction.

Patterns of Imitation

In those essays where Sheikh Al-Amin commented on coastal Muslims vis-à-vis the British colonials, he criticized their blind imitation of the powerful foreigners in many of their ways, even with regard to leisure and fashion. There is no acceptable justification for this, he argued in his two essays "Why Are We Imitating the Europeans?" (*Uwongozi* 4) and "Why Do We Wear Western Hats?" (*Uwongozi* 24). For instance, he qualified Western hats as decisively "un-Islamic" items of clothing that are characteristic of non-Muslims (apparently drawing from a recent public *fatwa* on this topic). Notably, he was hereby taking position in a lively and ongoing transregional debate among Muslims, with a stance that was opposite to that of the "global mufti" of his time, Shaykh Muhammad Abduh, in his well-known so-called Transvaal *fatwa* (responding to a query from South Africa in 1903) who took no issue with this habit.[30]

Sheikh Al-Amin warned of group pressures among the urban youth to wear such hats, as young people in particular wished to associate themselves more closely with Western culture, to be closer to power and success. Yet in doing so, he said, they separated themselves more and more from their own customs and religion, "leaning very much towards the Europeans, and lessening their love for their own country," especially if they were not well educated. Such people enjoyed being close to foreigners and thereby alienated themselves from their community. While "avoiding their brothers in meetings, they like to speak English and drop their own language, in contrast to other people who wear their own clothes" (Mazrui 2017, 158–61).[31] This, he wrote, had been shown in recent research in "Sociology" (though he gave no specific reference), and he urged readers to look at illustrations at hand in Mombasa: "As evidence of this, *look at the Indians*, and you will see that everyone who wears their (Indian) clothes has much love for their country (. . .); and those who wear western clothes and caps, you will see that their preference is mostly for Europeans" (ibid., 160–61, my emphasis).[32]

He concluded this text with reference to the two most celebrated Indian role models, kept in the highest regard by Western countries—namely, Gandhi and Tagore, neither of whom succumbed to Western fashions but instead wore their indigenous Indian clothes as cultural symbols of strength and self-reliance (ibid.):

> *Look at Gandhi.* Recently he went to Europe wearing his nappy clothing (*ubinda*) that was not even covering his knees,[33] and his scarf and his sandals. And Tagore visited the whole of Europe in his red mantle (*kanzu*) and his scarf; please tell me, who amongst the Easterners (Orientals) was respected in the cities of Europe like Gandhi and Tagore? [My emphasis.]
>
> *Mtazameni Gandhi, juzi amekwenda Ulaya na ubinda wake haufiniki magoti, na mtandio wake na viatu vyake vya kanda. Na Tagore ametembea katika Ulaya yote, na kanzu yake nyekundu na mtandio wake; tafadhalini nambiyani nnani katika watu wa Mashuriki walio pata hishima katika miji ya Ulaya kama allivyo pata Gandhi na Tagore?*

"No one," of course, is the answer to this rhetorical question here. Dressing in public in shorts as short as the traditional *dhoti* worn by Mahatma Gandhi was inconceivable for any coastal Muslim male. However, Sheikh Al-Amin drew attention to the fact that it was because of Gandhi's sincere and committed attitude—linking up his thinking and acting so convincingly in the way he dressed, in his public self-representation—that Gandhi deserved admiration and respect.

Sheikh Al-Amin concluded by saying that his Muslim peers should know that, according to a legal opinion (*fatwa*) that he did not specify further, the wearing of Western hats was un-Islamic. Moreover, for Sheikh Al-Amin the psychological ill effects of copying dressing habits had been scientifically proven by sociological research. Together, these two strands of reasoning—following the *sharia* and science—brought home an overarching point—namely, that "the greatness of a person is through his *knowledge* and his *work*, and not through decoration."[34] According to Sheikh Al-Amin, knowledge and work, education and effort, conviction and personal commitment in one's actions are what make people respectable, both within their own communities and around the world. His emphasis on knowledge (*elimu*) and work (*kazi*) goes along with the thrust of a main argument running across the essays.

The point is about, firstly, improving one's knowledge, of religion and of the world (*dini na dunia*), and to pass it on in educating one's peers: making them more aware of how the world works, and more adept in moving appropriately within it. Secondly, it is about one's own work, the specific effort that one puts into the performance of one's actions (*vitendo*)—and it is indeed this aspect of a sincerely committed performance of their actions that made Gandhi and Tagore, in their respective ways, iconic and universally respectable. In this essay, they stood for a culturally independent and politically self-confident India facing the Western colonial oppressor, and so they provided a possible role model for East African Muslims. For Sheikh Al-Amin and within Swahili moral discourse more widely, the conceptual pair of knowledge (*elimu*) and work (*kazi*) or also action (*kitendo*) is important, as it emphasizes the social obligation and practical relevance of acquiring knowledge and putting it to good use, through performance in practice: on the one hand informing one's own actions and thus guiding one's behavior; on the other hand, passing it on to others, educating them and providing moral guidance.

Another text that is centrally concerned with the dangers of ignorance by imitating others, asks, through its title, "Why Are We Imitating the Europeans?" (*Namna gani twawaigiza Wazungu?*) Sheikh Al-Amin explains that all peoples in the world have their own ways of doing things, as specific customs and traditions that they follow. These provide reassurance and confidence to members of a group, and it seems reasonable for them to stick to their customs, as otherwise, they may become disoriented, not quite knowing how to behave (ibid., 60–61):

> Intelligent people in every community will, in everything they are about to do, hold on tight to their traditions and customs in order to avoid becoming like the crow who let go of his own ways and imitated the ways of the weaver-bird, and when he had lost his own ways and not attained those of the weaver-bird, he was stuck somewhere neither here nor there.
>
> *Wenye akili katika kila kab[i]la huwa wao ni wa kushikamana muo na milla yao na ada zao kwa sababu ya kuchelea wasije wakawa kama Ghurabu aliyawata mwendo wake akaigiza mwendo wa Shomoro, khal[a]fu akawa wake umempotea na wa shomoro asiupate, akawa hako huku wala huku.*

Nobody wants to be stuck somewhere in midair, neither here nor there. Yet when it came to social interactions in the real world, Sheikh Al-Amin pointed out that actually many coastal Muslims did just that, losing their own identity without acquiring a new one, as they blindly imitated the Europeans whenever they could, copying the bad habits rather than good ones, to their own disadvantage (ibid.):

> We are continuing every day to imitate the Europeans (*wazungu*); and then, we don't imitate them except in useless matters for which there is no need, or in bad ways which even they themselves regard as bad!
>
> We wanted to imitate them in their customs, but we succeeded in nothing except drinking alcohol and wearing Western hats. But other good customs of theirs, like their ways of speaking and their meetings, and their love for their countrymen and for their communities, and other such things: for us, these things are not worth imitating!
>
> *Sisi twendelea killa siku katika kuwaigiza Wazungu, tena hatuwaigizi illa katika mambo yasiyokuwa na haja, au katika mabaya hatta kwa wao wenyiwe piya!*
>
> *Tumetaka kuwaigiza katika ada zao, hatuna tuliloshika illa kunwa mvinyu na kuvaa vyepeu; ama ada nzuri katika mazungumzo yao na mikutano yao na kupenda Watani wao na jamaa zao na mengine kama hayo; hayo kwetu si kitu cha kufaa kuwaigiza!*

Coastal Muslims, as he observed it, were doing exactly the opposite of what they should be doing when copying other people's bad habits. This again had to do with their lack of knowledge and education, and their need for more zeal and self-discipline. "Poor people of Mombasa!" he exclaimed (*Uwongozi* 4), commenting on the way they parroted English words because they could not distinguish properly between education and language. Like the crow mentioned above, neither here nor there, they were stuck in midair, having lost any sense of their own customs and traditions, and not having acquired a sense of judging those of others. He ended on a critical note, expressing a strong sense of disapproval and even disgust with the ways in which his fellow Muslims were behaving. Not understanding what is right and what is wrong, they cultivated a completely misguided sense of direction, and they had become stuck in a paralyzing and self-destructive cycle. At this point, in conclusion of the essay, Sheikh Al-Amin implored divine mercy so that they might get back onto the right path (ibid., 62–63):

> Glory be to God! Don't we see any things to imitate from the Europeans except for bad ones only? I think that we have become like flies: we do not descend and settle anywhere except in open sores. Or like those beetles who are turned off by pleasant scent, and instead attracted by stench, and rolling up all kinds of impure things.
>
> *Subhanal-Lah! Hatuoni mambo ya kuwaigiza Wazungu illa mabaya tu? Naona kana kwamba tumekuwakana nzi, hatutengi illa katika vidonda; au kama madundu hukirihika kwa harufu njema, na kufurahishwa niuvundo, na kuzingirisha najisi.*

Following this evocative and revolting image of coastal Muslims who are intui-
tively attracted by the worst kind of stench and dirt, he ended with a desperate
prayer, asking for divine guidance for his disoriented peers (ibid.):

> I beg you, Lord! Show us what is right, and guide us so that we may follow it;
> and show us what is deceitful, and guide us so that we may avoid it. Amen.
>   *Nukuomba Ya Rabbi! Utuoneshe Hakki, utujaalie niwenyi kuifuata, utu-*
> *oneshe la batili, utujaalie ni wenye kuliwata.*

Again, knowledge about right and wrong, and guidance about ways of fulfilling one's moral obligation, to do what is right and avoid doing wrong, and in
extension (as we saw earlier) to be able to command right and forbid wrong from
others, are fundamentally at the heart of the agenda of Sheikh Al-Amin's educational texts. Seeing members of his community going badly astray, he sought
to convey the necessary knowledge and guidance to help resolve this social crisis through his writings, as his response to his own moral obligation given his
knowledge about Islam and the world (*dini na dunia*) and having critical insider
awareness about the poor state of coastal society.

Social Experience and Anticipation

If this text, then, can be read as a verbal illustration of the culmination of social
crisis in colonial Mombasa, witnessing a severe loss of the sense of self (socially
and individually), Sheikh Al-Amin's essays also include corresponding texts that
speak to such a culmination from a different angle, and with an almost prophetic
voice. These are texts in which past and present social experience is reconsid-
ered, reflected upon, and projectively thought forward, toward a future that is
based upon, or at least builds on, current conditions. Concisely, past experiences shape anticipations about the future—and, based on his knowledge and
sensitivity about these shared experiences, Sheikh Al-Amin was in a position
to express such anticipations in public, as social critic and (at the same time)
respected leader commenting on his community; and he did so from the perspective of his own social group, with their interests and worries in mind. As discursive consolidations of worries or concerns about the community, or hopes for it,
such anticipatory comments then could themselves become part of the project
of internal social critique and guidance that Sheikh Al-Amin was engaged in
through his essays. This project is contested, however, and as such reflects an
ongoing internal tug-of-war between competing (and mutually contradictory)
ideological positions.

This is what is dramatically played through in the essay "The Black Peril!"
(*Khatari Nyeusi!*), already commented on above. This essay opens with reference to the notion of an East Asian "Yellow Peril" as it was commonly projected
and commented upon by Western media and, consecutively, the influential and

globally circulating Arab press at the time. Japan's and China's investments in modernization, militarization, and economic competition were seen to endanger the economic and political predominance of the West, and a derogatory and racist discourse around this term ensued, as a public means to fight back against such tendencies (Schmidt-Glintzer 2014). Building upon the term "Yellow Peril" comparatively while using Japanese modernization as a reference point, this article describes a supposed East African parallel, the "black danger" posed to coastal Muslims by the disciplined and educated upcountry African labor migrants. They are portrayed as dedicated and hardworking people who have become skilled and educated due to their own effort. In contrast, says Sheikh Al-Amin, coastal Muslims were out of touch with the realities of the rapidly changing modern world, and had moved far away from their self-image of superior status as patrician noblemen (*waungwana*).

A bold rhetorical statement from this text exhibits an almost prophetic character as it anticipates a negative future, based on the experience of a dispiriting present at the time of writing, a time of fundamental change. This statement addresses the potential scenario of inverted social hierarchies between the passive *waungwana* and the diligent *wabara*. It raises the hypothetical prospect of a return of slavery, now with the coastal former slaveholders being subject to the upcountry people, in a reversal of historical power relations, a reversal that would (to a lesser degree, of course) actually happen after Independence.

Sheikh Al-Amin reproaches his coastal peers for being in "deep slumber" while the *wabara* laborers in town were doing all the laborious jobs that none of the urban coastals would take on. After completing their daily tasks, the *wabara* would also, as Sheikh Al-Amin recounts with admiration, even take evening classes and use every spare minute to further their education (Mazrui 2017, 130–33).

> And the kinds of employment performed by the upcountry people who are here, is mostly as servants (*u-boy*) and cooks and sweepers, and these jobs do not leave anybody with any bit of time. Despite this, you will see that a sweeper who gets a little chance will put his broom aside, he will take out his book and read; likewise, you will *not* see a cook who, once he is has covered his pot, will *not* go outside with his slate and write; nor will you see a servant ("boy") who does *not* have a book in his pocket wherever he goes.
>
> *Na utumishi wa watu wa bara waliomo humu, ghalibu ni u-boy na upishi na kufyagia, na kazi hizi si za kumpa mtu nafasi hatta kidogo, na pamoja na hayo utamuona mfyagiaji akipata nafasi kidogo hutupa ufyagio wake, akafuna kibuku chake akasoma; wala humuoni mpishi illa akishafinika chungu chake hutoka nde na sleti yake akaandika; wala humoni boy illa killa endapo.*

Mazrui saw fundamental social changes being brought about by the new technologies and new media of the time (the telegraph, the telephone, the steam engine), changes that would affect not only living and working habits in everyday life, but also social hierarchies and power relationships on a national scale. If people did not keep up with those developments, they would lose out in practical terms when it came to redesigning the labor landscape and social hierarchies. Some of the upcountry groups had organized their communities well in their home region, as Sheikh Al-Amin commented, with reference to the Alliance High School project that had been initiated by an alliance of local protestant churches in the Kikuyu area in 1926 (and became a success story). If the coastals would not quickly pursue such initiatives as well, he said, they would lose out, and due to their lack of knowledge about the modern world, they would have to become the new servant class. As Sheikh Al-Amin put it, building his appeal to the following culminating rhetorical statement (ibid., 132–33),

> Understand that what I described will inevitably happen, because people with such kinds of knowledge and skills [as the *wabara* have now acquired] will not agree to be sweepers or street-cleaners [anymore]! But these kinds of work will always be for the ignorant people, and this time the ignorant (*wajinga*) will be us coastal people (*sisi wapwani*). And if ever slavery were to return, well it would be us who would be sold by the Kikuyu and bought by the Kavirondo!
>
> This is indeed the *Black Danger* that I fear, and there is no way to avoid this fear other than first to get rid of arrogance and hatred in our hearts, and of the ways in which we obstruct each other from matters of common interest.
>
> *Fahamuni haya hayana budi yatakuwa, kwa sababu watu wenye ilimu kama hizi si wenye kukubali kabisa kuwa ni wafyagiyaji wala kuwa ni mato-pasi! kazi hizi zitakua ni za watu wajinga, na wakati huwo watakuwa watu wajinga ni sisi watu wa pwani. Na lau kama utumwa utarudi, basi tungeuzwa ni Wakikuyu tukanunuliwa ni Wakavirondo!*
>
> *Hii ndio khatari nyeusi ambayo naiogopa, wala hapana la kutuvua na khatari hii illa kwanza ni kuondoa bughudha katika nyoyo, na kushikiana kinyume katika mambo ya maslah.*

Though Sheikh Al-Amin was still thinking about his community in racialized terms and within the horizon of a colonial framework (under British rule), it was clear to him that for the future, the acquisition of new kinds of knowledge, skills, and expertise would lead to respectable jobs and positions in society, and to a more secure economic and social status altogether. Thus, he outlined an agenda for coastal Muslims to pursue, in order not to lose out in the future. For in the society that he saw emerging, well-qualified, educated, and trained people would be needed; only their jobs would be safe and their future promising. Yet this attitude was in stark contrast to that of many coastal Muslims, who continued to invoke notions of cultural superiority that were now clearly passé. Sheikh Al-Amin feared that his coastal peers might lock themselves up in a static imagined past, while times were actually changing fast. They were in danger of positioning themselves outside developments in society, and of depriving themselves of shaping their own future. Thus the real danger to them here was their own ignorance, and their lack of interest in constructively confronting the challenges they faced.

In texts like *Khatari Nyeusi!*, Sheikh Al-Amin acts as a harsh critic of his own community. It is intriguing to see how his focus on the importance of knowledge and education as means to assist in running society reckons with, builds on, and emphasizes the importance of performative ideas of "action," "work," "dedication," "zeal," and so on. It is to these key terms that we need to pay attention, if we want to understand and lay out the conceptual framework of Sheikh Al-Amin's thinking, also as a potential role model for others. It seems promising to explore further the semantic potential around the shared connotations, here, of performance and "work." These are, indeed, aspects and meanings that underline Sheikh Al-Amin's earlier point about the relevance of "knowledge" (*elimu*) and "work" (*kazi*) as performative processes that people are engaged in. In addition, the Swahili terms *kitendo* (action), *ghera* (zeal), *fahari* (fame/reputation), and others evoke the understanding that the performance by a person, and the attitude of the performer, should be what matters most when it comes to addressing questions about deserving a certain position in society. This is a fundamental conceptual step that Sheikh Al-Amin is pushing for (against resistance from his community), away from what we might call a "traditionalist" descent- and status-centered view to the idea of a merit-oriented one focusing on qualification, ability, and achievement. While doing so, however, he is himself still partly entrenched in the biased conceptual framework that he pushes his community to overcome.

We should note that Sheikh Al-Amin ended this harshly critical essay with a constructive and mediating appeal, "to dispel arrogance and hatred in our hearts," advising his people to rid themselves of what caused difference and disunity between them and others. According to him, this was the only way to avoid future isolation and domination by those others, and contribute to a common future in which decisions may be guided by "matters of common interest" (*maslaha ya umma*), as is advisable. Here again, his argumentation and choice of words reflected a conceptual affinity with the Egyptian modernists who inspired his agenda.

Before concluding this discussion of Sheikh Al-Amin's project to reform and indeed reshape his community by using basic print technology to create a new Swahili Muslim public, a discursive space in which his authoritative voice reflected upon communal challenges and prospects, we still need to consider the status of language. We must also address historical consciousness-building as part of the agenda to be pursued. Swahili was the chosen language for this first Swahili Islamic newspaper on the Kenyan coast, because it was the first language of most coastals and the dominant everyday language and long-established lingua franca for the region, among Muslims and non-Muslims. No other language could have spoken to a similarly large and diverse audience of first-, second-, and even third-language speakers. While Arabic was the undisputed religious language for all Muslims, the creation of a more widely accessible platform for general religious education and social critique in Swahili supported the egalitarian character that Sheikh Al-Amin's reform agenda had, not least through its emphasis on performance. Using Swahili also fed into a missionary agenda, of attracting recent converts or non-Muslim Africans to Islam. That, according to Sheikh Al-Amin's students, was an important goal, too (M. K. Mazrui 1980, x).

The *Sahifa* newspaper project spearheaded the agenda of establishing a new public space in which Swahili, in an accessible form of conversational everyday language, was used to initiate and conduct a wider, more generally accessible public debate about Islam and society among local Muslims. This was done despite the reservations of a significant part of the Muslim community—the Alawiyya, who rarely participated in published debates.[35] However, next to the importance of Swahili for building such new publics and enabling an open debate, Sheikh Al-Amin also insisted on the continuing relevance of Arabic. One of Sheikh Al-Amin's *Sahifa* essays (*Sahifa* 12), "The Arabic Language and Us Muslims," pushes the point that all Muslims need to put effort into learning Arabic, as their proper religious language. Only fluency in Arabic could assure Muslims of proper rational knowledge of Islam and its main texts, and such knowledge was needed for people so as not to become dependent on others. With this in mind, Sheikh Al-Amin argued that his Swahili-language publications were meant to serve only for a transitional period (as necessary temporary crutches, so to say) and could be dropped once fluency in Arabic was commonly achieved—though whether or not he really believed in this vision is hard to say. Thus overall, despite the fact that he sensibly used Swahili as a means to disseminate education and information toward social change, he also insisted publicly on the obligation for each and every Muslim individually to learn Arabic properly so as to ensure that he or she could act as a conscious and independent believer.

Finally, historical consciousness and knowledge about the history of Islam were important to Sheikh Al-Amin, in the light of British educational politics. Sheikh Al-Amin commented on the demands of the school curricula and pointed out that pupils had to learn the colonial versions of European history, while information about the basic history of Islam and its achievements did not feature in class (in contrast to Christianity, which was actively taught and pushed). Muslim pupils did not even know the name of the famous classic Arab poet al-Muttanabi, he said, but they had to learn Shakespeare's sonnets and other texts by heart (*Sahifa* 12). Bearing witness and raising critique of these processes of "colonizing the minds" of young coastal Muslims through education is a central part of Sheikh Al-Amin's agenda. And as further response to this, Sheikh Al-Amin and his followers later set out to write a wide-ranging series of Swahili educational booklets on Islamic history for local readers, including a string of life histories, of Prophet Muhammad (Farsy 1942) as well as the four *khalifas* (M. K. Mazrui 1958; 1960; 1962; 1965) and even Imam Hassan and Hussein (Farsy 1999a; 1999b). These again caused controversies as they sometimes combined their historical accounts with a critique of the *masharifu.*

In terms of language politics, Sheikh Al-Amin here, in a colonial context, anticipated and pushed a point made later by Ngũgĩ wa Thiong'o in an emphatic postcolonial tone: that one needs to build and cultivate one's perspective on the world in one's own language; and that one should be taught one's own history, to instill knowledge and pride about where one comes from, as well as a sense of where to go and what to aim for in life. Employing one's own language and decolonizing one's mind, then, becomes a rich resource for liberation and empowerment on other fronts.[36]

As part of his reflections on coastal society and its decline, Sheikh Al-Amin also provided an argument against the common emphasis on status-thinking among coastal Muslims. According to him, this culminated in the mistaken but rarely questioned equation of "civilization" (*ustaarabu*) with "Arabness" (*U-Arabu*)—which, he said, is self-delusion (*Uwongozi* 5). Pushing for an egalitarian stance and performative focus as described above, he argued that people err when assuming that being an Arab by descent means that they can claim *ustaarabu* for themselves. Rather, one's *ustaarabu* has to be shown and proven in one's conduct and performance; it is a quality that people may achieve individually (or not), within their community, which alone is able to recognize and honor such behavior—and the social community should continue to cultivate this sense, despite the colonial condition that largely pressed for different values and attitudes. Sheikh Al-Amin's insistence on the understanding of *ustaarabu* as a performance-related quality is important, with a view to internal conceptual debates about the term, and about the (diverse possibilities of) interpretation of related common terms, norms, and values more widely.

A Swahili Muslim Public: Media, Language, and Self-Positioning

The *Sahifa* texts were the first regularly circulating printed Swahili Islamic prose texts on the Kenyan Swahili coast, in 1930, and some reflection is in order on the kind of public that was created and opened up here, and with which goals in mind. A first answer can be found in Sheikh Al-Amin's foreword to the *Uwongozi* collection of *Sahifa* reprints, where he reflected upon the beneficial effects of shaping community that are brought about by the newspaper media. As he said, "Among all the modern things that show people good ways, and that bring good thoughts into their minds and wake up their hearts, so that they will get up and move forward, there is nothing like the newspaper" (*Kitangulizi*).[37] These days all groups had their own newspapers, he explained, and the idea was to inform one's community about all kinds of good things they could benefit from, and to warn them about any kind of evil so that they might avoid it. This is essentially what he saw himself doing in his pamphlets: passing on moral knowledge to his coastal peers, engaging in "commanding right and forbidding wrong" (see Cook 2000), and bringing new ideas to their attention, in order to wake them up and stir them into action—all this by means of a "little newspaper" (*kigazeti*), as he referred to the two-sided pamphlet *Sahifa*.

With their critical stance, the *Sahifa* texts at the time sparked off some lively reactions among urban Muslims and provided a new, publicly accessible reference point for internal debate. Sheikh Al-Amin had, after all, been inspired by local observations and discussions in the first place—and many of his essays convey a vivid sense of the currency and urgency of themes for the community at the time. His public expressions of doubt about the community, and his critique of the ways in which people presented themselves, were appreciated by at least part of the readership, as the demand for reprints of the *Sahifa* essays showed (Mazrui 1944, preface).[38] Readers who enjoyed the texts did so most likely for their entertaining language, the questioning of established traditions, and the frank critique of misguided people and their actions—or a combination of these. Others reacted angrily and felt offended (M. K. Mazrui 1995, 2). And while these contrasting reactions point to a possible polarization of the urban community, they also show that the essays managed to touch the nerve of truly important issues in society. Sheikh Al-Amin expressed impatience and discontent with the state of affairs in his own community, as a member of the social elite who himself was critical of elitism (while not completely innocent of it). He used his vivid, appealing, and (mostly) well-argued essays—which, as we have seen, had much in common with similar reformist publications around the Muslim world at the time—to break up attitudes and patterns of behavior that he regarded as traditionalist and dogmatic, and to wake up those whom he saw having succumbed to them.

Conclusion: Colonial Critic—"Colonial Thinker"—Ambivalence

If Sheikh Al-Amin was outright critical of his social peers and their lack of engagement, he was, as we have seen, also critical of colonialism and its specific impositions upon social life in Mombasa—whether this concerned the lack (or even denial) of religious teaching for Muslim children in colonial schools,[39] or the negative role model of European codes of dress and behavior that many locals imitated. These were common aspects of critique for Islamic reformist thinkers across the Muslim world at the time, from the late nineteenth century onward, such as Jamal al-Din al-Afghani, and then Muhammad Abduh, Rashid Rida, and others, who became categorized as "Salafi."[40] As we have seen, Sheikh Al-Amin was also wary of the technological development and modernization that came along with and was implemented under colonial rule, thus also creating opportunities, for instance of swifter and easier communication, travel, and possibilities of trade across vast distances.[41]

To portray Sheikh Al-Amin as an "anticolonial" thinker in a pronounced way is not quite adequate, even though he was critical and decisively suspicious of British colonial attitudes and policies, and also of Christian missionary activities that he saw threatening to undermine Islam and Muslim communities.[42] However, being integrated into the colonial administrative system, as appointed *kadhi* of Mombasa (1932–37) and later as chief *kadhi* of the whole Kenyan Coastal Strip (1937–47), his position was ambivalent. As social commentator in these essays, he pointed his readers to both the virtues and vices of Europeans, identifying their discipline and patriotism as well as their pursuit of science and technology on the good side, and indecent behavior, dancing, and alcohol consumption on the other. He identified and warned against the dangers of cultural and religious impositions that came with colonialism—not dissimilar to what was later commonly discussed as "cultural imperialism" in the Cold War period—yet his essays did not include any outright critiques of colonial oppression or calls for anticolonial resistance. He commented upon the social world around him as an internal critic, like a "scholar-journalist" (Zaman 2012, 11) concerned about coastal Muslims in their shortcomings and daily struggles. He did not seek outright confrontation with the colonial system—though he may not have shied away from that, had the situation arisen.

What seems to have mattered most to Sheikh Al-Amin was the well-being of his community, and he was concerned about any potential negative effects upon it. As we have seen, his writings call upon the dispirited and discontented coastal Muslims to engage with the current social and political transformations, as he felt they needed to take a stand. Worried about the future position of coastal Muslims in a rapidly changing society, a main function of his writings was to spread awareness and sensitivity about these concerns. However, being integrated into the colonial system himself, as an appointed judge, he was also in part representing and facilitating the colonial administration of his own community.

This reflects well the kind of ambivalence (or even double bind) that he and other colonial subjects were situated in. Individually, people could benefit from certain positions or ways of participating in the colonial system, while overall still being part of the dominated subjects under colonial rule. It is with a view to these ways of individuals pragmatically coming to grips with or taking on a role or position—these acts of self-positioning, or being positioned, within the colonial (and later, similarly, postcolonial) sphere—that we can usefully think about the forms that people's strategies of endurance of and resilience to) colonial rule took. People were developing ways of bearing the situation they were in, coping with it, and adjusting to it. These were ways of "arranging" oneself with reality, forms of "arrangement," as Filip de Boeck (1996) has called it for Zaire/Congo, with a view to building one's own strategies of resilience within everyday life as it had become, under the conditions of one's postcolonial experience.

Not unlike the colonial situation that Sheikh Al-Amin was commenting upon, the uncertainties for coastal Muslims about their political membership in the postcolonial state had (or continued to have) paralyzing effects. Not only was there a lack of status within the new political system; there was also a lack of knowledge, confidence, and orientation about how to deal with this—and these dynamics increased disillusion and discontent with the postindependence situation. Coastal Muslims in the postcolonial period have been similarly uncertain and disoriented about their place, their role, and their marginalized position in Kenya, and similarly in need of guidance. As we shall see in more concrete terms in the following two chapters, they felt disempowered, discouraged, and destabilized within the workings of national politics. Through this experience, and an enduring lack of perspective, a kind of vicious circle of political passiveness (a mixture of docility, indecision, and frustration) was set in motion, with its origins in the colonial period. Docility, read as tacit approval of governmental politics, was encouraged, and then taken advantage of, by consecutive upcountry governments, to the extent that the quiet submission of coastal Muslims was almost taken for granted, especially during the long years of Moi's one-party rule (i.e., until 1992). This is exemplified in commonly made comments by Shariff Nassir, who was President Moi's right hand and coastal KANU leader for almost his entire period of rule (1978–2002). Like President Moi himself, Shariff Nassir is remembered, on public occasions, regularly advising the coastal community, telling them to "stay as you are" (*wabakie hivyo hivyo*)—namely, quiet, docile, and causing no problems. Of course, among Kenyans it was known that this phrase included a silent intimidating threat of "or else" completing the remark.[43] This may, in some ways, be read as further perpetuation of the colonial condition that was, at least in part, taken up and described by Sheikh Al-Amin.[44]

Sheikh Al-Amin's Legacy

Reflecting upon Sheikh Al-Amin Mazrui and his writings presents us with a starting point for understanding the dynamics of transregionally inspired yet locally embedded critical thinking in coastal East Africa, and possibly beyond. His thinking has, in turn, come to represent a foundation, a resource, and a guideline for the following generations of coastal Muslims. Especially his students sought to engage critically and in public with their Muslim opponents as well as their own self-positioning in the postcolonial scenario, as we shall see in the next chapter. They were able to build on his work, and to use him as a role model and source of inspiration, in their own use of print media for their cause. Following his stance, they too created new Swahili Muslim publics through pamphlets, newspapers, and lectures, and they kept in play a critical internal debate within the coastal Muslim community. The strategies and patterns of Sheikh Al-Amin's arguments in his public engagements provided explicit and implicit reference points for them, as they were seeking to clarify, for themselves, the relationship between Islam and the contemporary world, in order to (re)position themselves within the wider Muslim community and the postcolonial state.

In this sense, this chapter on Mombasa's most important public intellectual in the colonial period and his project of social critique feeds into the understanding of Muslim actors in postcolonial society, in Kenya and beyond. They are dealing with similar (and, one could say, "inherited") structures, within their community and vis-à-vis the state. If Sheikh Al-Amin's critical social essays that we discussed here were foundational and inspiring for later critics, they also provided guidance and models for how to raise and phrase critique. This would be used and developed further by his students, and passed on to a much wider and more open public during the following generation. We can summarize Sheikh Al-Amin's main points about social reform with three mutually related appeals to the community. Firstly, the call to "wake up" and become aware of one's situation (and one's strengths and weaknesses); secondly, a call to "educate yourselves," both in religious and worldly terms, so as to be aware of one's obligations (as Muslim and as citizen) and as well-informed as possible; and thirdly, in consequence, to "do what you are obliged to do," contributing to the common good and well-being of one's community, following a generally accepted social obligation and divine command.[45]

Picking up on an understanding of "postcolonial critique" as established within the academy over the last decades, it may be useful to think of Sheikh Al-Amin's efforts and writings discussed here as an exercise in "colonial critique." It is a critique of coastal Muslims by a social peer and contemporary who is disappointed about what they have allowed themselves to become, within the (admittedly adverse) conditions of the kind of colonial world they live in. From here, Sheikh Al-Amin may be seen as an "enabling critic," seeking to strengthen and reform his community into a more knowledgeable and socially active force, more awake and wary about what is going on in terms of global politics, colonial strategies, and debates about Islam and the *umma*, as all these aspects have effects upon the (actual and imagined) well-being of the community, upon coastal Muslims' self-perception and also their sense of self-positioning in the world. We could conceive of Sheikh Al-Amin's intellectual and social agenda as a form of critical and liberating "colonial thinking" (with some anticolonial features)—that may already point to a related "postcolonial thinking" in the future. While he was completely embedded in the colonial world, his critical engagement with it, and his concern about the place of his community within it, was already oriented beyond it. He anticipated an upcoming new era that was likely to bring new challenges and worries but also potential opportunities for coastal Muslims—if they could get their act together.

From another perspective, it is important to keep in mind that Sheikh Al-Amin, as Mombasa's most famous and most prominent scholar and community leader of Omani Arab origin, has continued to be a contested iconic representative of the (Omani) "coastal Arab culture" that is resented by many (Muslims and Christians) of the Mijikenda communities, against the background of social inequality in the region. They rejected what they saw as an unfair and ongoing Arab dominance of the *kadhi* office (of the Islamic judge) on the coast, extending from the colonial into the postcolonial era. This, to them, seemed to illustrate undue collusion with the (external) state. In their view, the fact that such positions, and especially the position of chief *kadhi*, were being given to members of the Mazrui clan all too often reflected an ongoing and unfair racial bias (see Mwakimako 2010; Ndzovu 2014).

Social Ambivalence and the Lack of Resilience

Thinking about Sheikh Al-Amin's social commentaries on his own community presents us with an example of discourses of "modernist Islam" and Islamic reform elsewhere in the Muslim world at the time, beyond a Middle Eastern, Arabocentric perspective and the famous Cairo-based figures (see Kurzman 2002; Mandaville 2001; also Baldauf 2001). The transregional references in Sheikh Al-Amin's writings can also connect us to wider reflections on the Indian Ocean region and the character of East African coastal society as one that spans across the ocean, representing influences from its own specific interregionally connected or internalized elsewheres (for Mombasa, prominently the Hadramaut, Oman, Kutch, and Gujarat).[46] Here, groups of social actors shaped by their communal transoceanic histories and ideologies of belonging, negotiate and take on, collectively and individually, their own particular spaces of meaningful social membership vis-à-vis other, similarly situated groups or individuals, who are internal social companions (peer-residents) and adversaries at the same time.[47]

With internal tensions and social ambivalence as features characteristic of coastal East African urban society, both among people generally and between translocal groups of people especially—a situation that was pronounced in the colonial scenario—the issue of finding ways of seeking and negotiating equivalence between social groups becomes another important focus for understanding society. Sheikh Al-Amin writes about Mombasa's coresidential groups of social others, comparing them with his own group, in ways that run counter to alternative possible ways of local public discourse—namely, to let each community mind its own business. Sheikh Al-Amin obviously transcends such a directive, as he draws from other groups' examples to alert his social peers to what to do better, and how. He uses references to other groups as illustrations of positive initiatives or dispositions that coastal Muslims could adopt for themselves—the "zeal" of the Indians, the thirst for knowledge and the self-discipline of upcountry Africans, or the strategic mind of the European colonials, as we have seen. And he ventures so far as to point at weaknesses and mistakes among them as well, as when talking about the meaningless and potentially harmful character of British leisurely activities (gambling, sports, dance, drink).

Thus Sheikh Al-Amin's writings introduce a comparative perspective into public discourse that makes deliberations about solutions to problems affecting the urban coastal community overall, on the basis of reflecting upon approaches, strategies, and actions of the different resident social groups within it, in relation to each other. From this point, the groups view each other as potential equals, and learning from each other becomes a real possibility. At the same time, recognizing members of other groups as social equals as well as rival contenders for social status (jobs, roles, positions in society), becomes part of more complex and difficult social reality. As Sheikh Al-Amin advocated, coastal Muslims have to put in at least as much time and effort into (self-)education as upcountry Africans (or anybody else), if they want to stand a chance to be eligible for any respectable jobs in the future. It is this sense of negotiating social equivalence in terms of abilities and skills that are openly accessible, to be acquired by all and no more linked to origin, ethnicity, or community, that Sheikh Al-Amin introduced into the coastal Muslim community, as their leading Islamic scholar, their critical and demanding educator, and—through his writings—their public voice and representative.

At a time when Swahili littoral society was confronted with influences of all kinds, and when, as part of these influences, the effects of technological modernization and colonial rule on coastal society and its people could not be contained or controlled from within, Sheikh Al-Amin made his readers aware of these interrelated dependencies. He wrote from a perspective that cast the other neighboring urban social groups as different but equal, as human peers to learn from, and thus sought to create a discursive scenario in which learning from each other, as part of serious interaction with each other, became possible. This perspective began to question the previously assumed clear social hierarchies between groups—which the white colonials initially took over, used for their purposes, and then transformed.

The guidance that Sheikh Al-Amin sought to provide for coastal Muslims was intended to make them more knowledgeable and self-reliant, able to tackle and negotiate the challenges of their rapidly modernizing and externally governed life-world for themselves. Being "knowledgeable" here means having acquired a certain amount of religious and secular education as well as worldly judgment that would enable people to become more independent social actors. The idea was that this should feed into the shaping of a better future (or at least fending off a worse one), for a community that was undergoing a testing period of ongoing loss of social status and political influence.

Looking at how matters progressed from the colonial past to the postcolonial present—with the most recent reiterations of coastal marginalization by upcountry governments being expressed by coastal politicians during regional election campaigns in early 2016—one might be tempted to say that Sheikh Al-Amin's initiative of waking up and liberating coastal Muslims politically has had no lasting effect. On the whole, there is a sense that coastal Muslims have not managed to represent their interests successfully within the wider polity—by means of "knowledge" (*elimu*) and "work" (*kazi*), as he said they should—neither vis-à-vis the British colonial nor the Kenyan postcolonial government. Judging from the research literature, historical accounts, and my own observations over the years, coastal Muslims have experienced a continuous phase of frustration and disillusion with the state over the postcolonial decades. This experience, similar to that of other marginalized groups in Kenya, has shaped the consciousness of coastal Muslims in very specific ways.

Analytically, this can be captured by somewhat ambivalent expressions like "coping" (Cruise O'Brien 1995) or "endurance," through which a burdensome character of the experience is conveyed, while a creative potential for future change can still be reckoned with (or accounted for). Similarly, "resilience," as a keyword for the paradigmatic postcolonial attitude of enduring and continuing to hope while creatively making do with one's adverse experiences and limited possibilities, makes sense (de Boeck 1996; de Boeck and Plissart 2004). The term here refers to people's dynamic ability to flexibly adapt and adjust to impositions of power while still, at a basic level, being able to pursue an agenda of their own. It may be possible, in reflection, to connect this to the kind of attitude that Sheikh Al-Amin demanded from his fellow coastal Muslims, to act as dedicated, engaged, and well-informed social actors in a difficult present for the improvement of their society and living conditions.

Thus we begin to see here, in different ways, resonances, traces, and parallels emerging between the early 1930s and the late postcolonial period, in Sheikh Al-Amin Mazrui's important "internal criticism" (Zaman 2012) of his fellow Muslims. Such comparative thoughts are expanded further below (chapter 5), as I interrogate case studies from the postcolonial period, and look at similar internal criticism of the regional Muslim community by self-educated and engaged laymen of the younger generation.

Sheikh Al-Amin, well-read as he was on matters of global politics and Islamic religion and the sciences, used his considerable reservoirs of knowledge and information as resources to provide guidance (*uwongozi*) in worldly and religious matters to his readers, during a period of social transformation and external rule, with the ultimate goal of reshaping and reforming coastal society in response. And if providing guidance was one characteristic feature of the essays, a second one was social critique: reminding people of what they should be doing, and reprimanding them for not doing so.

But the public that came into being here through the circulation of the *Sahifa* texts was initiated in a strictly hierarchical top-down approach, and the essays ultimately represented the views and opinions of only Sheikh Al-Amin. So even if he was, as people say, without equal in breadth and depth of knowledge (worldly or Islamic), there was no plurality of coastal voices or opinions to be found here. The readers were provided with commentaries by an apparently almost omniscient narrator, who berated and informed, directed and advised them, urging them to change themselves and become engaged in facilitating social change. While the "little newspaper" (*kigazeti*) he created was bringing a new Swahili Muslim public into being, created exclusively by the writings of Sheikh Al-Amin, it did not really provide a common platform for mutual exchange within the coastal Muslim community—though it may have provoked such exchange. Rather, Sheikh Al-Amin created a platform for the dissemination of his own views, his own reflections, and his own advice, even if he did this on behalf of his fellow coastal Muslims and with their common interest in mind. And because the topics he chose were meaningful to others, because he was knowledgeable, witty, and humorous and combined his advice with new and interesting facts for the readers, he can be said to have been successful with *Sahifa*. Other measures of success are that he offended part of the community with his internal criticism, while another part was inspired and eager to read more.

Still, as writer, editor, and publisher rolled into one, Sheikh Al-Amin was so dominant here that no real exchange or mutual engagement on an equal or dialogical level was possible in this new medium itself, even if much social debate was ignited. This began to change in Sheikh Al-Amin's subsequent publication, the eight-page-long bilingual journal *al-Islah* ("Reform"), published between 1932 and 1933, which also integrated some readers' letters,[48] and things were going to be quite different for subsequent Swahili Muslim publics, as the following chapters will show. In any case, Sheikh Al-Amin Mazrui did raise challenging ideas here that were new to the coastal East African Muslim community, concerning social and religious reform, Pan-Islamism, and a critical perspective on colonialism and Western society. These were similarly raised and disseminated elsewhere in the Muslim world at the time, especially in the thriving arabophone press that he followed and drew from. Often, these ideas went against established views and conventions in his community. Thus as a reformer, he was voicing discontent with the way things were and raising discomfort for those who had arranged themselves with the state of affairs, as he sought to pass his messages on to the minds of his readers.

Notes

1. The recent calls of the MRC (Mombasa Republican Council) between 2010 and 2013, that *pwani si Kenya* (the coast is not Kenya) illustrates this well too.

2. There is a steadily growing secondary literature on Sheikh Al-Amin and his works; see, for example, Pouwels 1981; S. Salim 1985; A. I. Salim 1987; el-Masri 1987; Soghayroun 2001; Mraja 2011; Caruso 2012; Matthews 2013; Kresse 2017. Sociohistorical contexts of Mombasa at the time are recounted in Kindy 1972; Hirji 2012; A. I. Salim 1973; Strobel 1979; Pouwels 1987. The last three authors also make use of the *Sahifa/Uwongozi* essays as a source.

3. It is intriguing to see how this quotation, written with a view largely to media use and globalization processes at the end of the twentieth century, is appropriate also as a qualification of the dynamics that characterized Sheikh Al-Amin's attempts of reforming the Swahili-speaking Muslim community of Mombasa in the 1930s.

4. Carmichael 1997; Cooper 1980, 233–72; Cooper 1987, 26–41; Janmohamed 1978; Stren 1977.

5. Remarkably, the only internal account of the Mazrui history was written by Sheikh Al-Amin himself, in Arabic, in the 1930s (Mazrui 1995).

6. See Farsy 1972; Tamim 2006; Tamim 2013. Farsy recounts a story that was circulating in the region, about how Sheikh Ali condemned Sultan Barghash for doing this; in response, Barghash told him he would not be released as long as he himself (Barghash) was alive, after which Sheikh Ali responded boldly that this would only be a short while ahead (Farsy 1972, 9–11).

7. Of course, this had its own severe difficulties in the conception of *kafaa* from the viewpoint of coastal Arabs. A superior status to (even well-established *waungwana*) Waswahili and Africans was commonly assumed by Omani as well as *ashraf* families (often Hadrami); see Kindy 1972; A. I. Salim 1973. For recent discussions of the relevance and conceptual scope of *kafaa*, see Matthews (2013) and especially Limbert (2014).

8. As Mandaville describes, building on Edward Said's motif of traveling theory (Said 1984).

9. Interview, Sayyid Abdulrahman Saggaf Alawy (Mwalimu Saggaf), June 2014. See also Martin 1971; Ghazal 2010a; Ghazal 2010b.

10. Reverend Godfrey Dale, based in Zanzibar, published his translation in 1923 with the Christian Missionary Society (Dale 1923). The Hadrami Alawiyya scholars remained opposed to a written translation/commentary (*tafsir*) of the Qur'an. See the careful comparative study by Lacunza Balda (1997).

11. The Riyadha Mosque in Lamu was founded around 1890 by Sayyid Salih bin Alawy Jamal al-Layl (d. 1935), following the role model of its namesake in Seyoun, Hadramaut, which was founded in 1879 by Ali al-Hibshi, whose *maulidi* celebrations Habib Saleh took over and introduced to East Africa (see Bang 2003; el-Zein 1974; Lienhardt 1959).

12. The *juzuu* were selected core Qur'anic quotes used for basic Islamic education; the two volumes include Sheikh Al-Amin's completed translations and commentaries of suras of the Qur'an: al-Fatiha and al-Baqarah (1980); and al-Imraan and an-Nisaa (1981).

13. Mazrui n.d.

14. Mazrui n.d.; Mazrui 1939; Mazrui 1946; Mazrui 1944.

15. Pouwels (1981; 1987) and Lacunza Balda (1990; 1997) have thus far worked most closely with his texts; Strobel (1979) and A. I. Salim (1973) regarded them as an important resource. See also the hagiographic biography, Tamim 2006.

16. See "Sahifa," *Encyclopedia of Islam* (Ghedira 2012). I am also grateful to Saud al-Zaid for explanations.

17. Matthews (2013) provides an excellent overview and discussion of the *al-Islah* project, which followed the same programmatic features as *Sahifa*. *Al-Islah* is commonly translated as "Reform," particularly with a view to the Arab modernists (Abu Khalil and Haddad 2016) who inspired Sheikh Al-Amin Mazrui.

18. The double-sided one-page format was used, for example, between 2003 and 2004 by the Muslim Civic Education Trust (MCET) in Mombasa, for well over 200 pamphlets of a series under the name *Kenya: Waislamu waitakavyo* (Kenya: The Way the Muslims Want It).

19. For recent discussions on this term, see Lauziere (2010) and Sajid (2015, 30–35). For a thorough African contextualization in contemporary Ethiopia, see Ostebo 2012.

20. On the sociopolitical contexts at the time, see Carmichael 1997; Janmohamed 1978.

21. See Tamim 2006; this was also conveyed in one of the Ramadhan lectures given by Sheikh Abdilahi Nassir that I attended in Mombasa, in December 1998 through January 1999.

22. See Martin (1971, 535). Arslan was pointed out to me as a reference point for Sheikh Al-Amin by Mwalimu Saggaf, who partly grew up in the house of Sheikh Al-Amin. He was a student and confidant of his who also picked up his journal subscriptions from the post office for him; interviews with Mwalimu Saggaf, Mombasa, July 2012 and June 2014. On Arslan, see Cleveland 1985; Sajid 2015.

23. Arslan 2004; Rashid Rida uses this well-known praise-name for him in his foreword (Arslan 2004, xx). This long essay was written in response to a query about the causes for the weakness of Muslims in the contemporary world on the one hand and the material progress of the Western powers and Japan on the other. The query had been sent to *al-Manar* by a former student of Rashid Rida's, Shaykh Muhammad Bisyooni Umran, from West Borneo.

24. For Western Asia, see Baldauf 2001.

25. See, for example, Schmidt-Glintzer 2014. According to Mwalimu Saggaf, Sheikh Al-Amin had been inspired to borrow from the trope of the "Yellow Peril" after reading a translated article by a European scholar who wrote about it in an Arab newspaper (unfortunately, he did not remember the names more specifically). Interview, July 2012.

26. Swahili original: *"Hayafitamani mambo yaliyo wapata Wa-islamu hivi leo ya kwenda tini na udhalili na utwevu, na haya yasingewapata illa ni kwa kuiwata Dini yao iwaamrishayo mambo matukufu na kuwakataza mambo matwevu"* (Mazrui 1955, 45).

27. Swahili original: *"hali ya kusikitikiwa hatta ni maaduwi zao"* (ibid.).

28. Swahili original: *"Mabaniyani katika Mombasa—nao ndio katika watu wachache, wana Magazeti mawili ya killa siku"* (ibid., 46).

29. The colonial divisions based on racial lines, between "Asians," "Arabs," and "Africans," increased and emphasized existing tensions within a coastal Muslim community where such divisions in everyday life were often (not always) blurred and sometimes hardly visible. On internal debates about "native" and "non-native" categorizations, see Kindy 1972; Salim 1976.

30. See Voll 1996; Sedgwick 2010.

31. Swahili originals of both quotes: *"hupondokea sana kwa Wazungu, na mapenzi ya Wataniwao huwapungukia katika nyoyo zao"*; *"watu hao wapenda kutangamana na Wazungu na kuwaepuka ndugu zao katika mikutano, na kupenda kusema Kizungu na kuiwata lugha yao."*

32. Swahili original: *"Na dalili watizameni Wahindi mutawaona killa wavaao nguo zao wana mapenzi zaidi ya Watani wao na Jamaa zao, na wavaao nguo za kizungu na vyepeu mutawaona mapondokeo yao sana ni kwa Wazungu."*

33. He is referring here to the *dhoti*, a simple folded loincloth worn by Hindu laborers that Gandhi came to wear during the times of his anticolonial campaigns.

34. *"wafahamu yakuwa utukufu wa mtu ni kwa Ilmu yake na kazi yake, la si kwa na pambo."*

35. See also Topan on "Swahili as a Religious Language" (1992). Alawiyya's avoidance of media and public debate with opponents is also a feature of later publication projects by reformers, who often publicly addressed them and invited them to participate (see chapter 4). There are some few exceptions to the media avoidance, as the verbal attacks on Sheikh Muhammad Kasim Mazrui and Sheikh Abdalla Saleh Farsy respectively fed into a couple of pamphlets, after the former had integrated criticism of the behavior of some *masharifu* within a booklet on the life of Imam Ali (M. K. Mazrui 1965; see Badawy 1966), and after the latter had published his Swahili translation/commentary of the Qur'an (Farsy 1969; see Badawy 1970).

36. See, for example, Ngũgĩ 1981; Ngũgĩ 1986; Ngũgĩ 1997; Ngũgĩ 2009.

37. "*Katika mambo ya kisasa yanayoonesha watu ndia nzuri, na kuwatia fikira njema katika akili zao, na kuziamsha nyoyo zao, hata wakainuka wakenda mbele, hapana kama Gazeti.*"

38. They, in a sense, may have become silent recruits or anonymous or outright supporters of the reform agenda.

39. See *Sahifa* text "*Dini na skuli*" (Religion and School), in appendix of *Uwongozi* translation (Mazrui/Kresse 2016).

40. See Lauziere (2010) for a fine summary discussion of history and difficulties of the use of this label.

41. See Gelvin and Green 2014; for East Africa particularly, see Reese 2004 and Reese 2015.

42. It was due to such concerns, too, that he first embarked upon the project of translating the Qur'an into Swahili, in response to a Swahili translation published in 1923 in Zanzibar by Father Dale of the CMS (Church Mission Society), a work that Sheikh Al-Amin regarded as full of mistakes and distortions. But wary of the gravity of his response to Dale's work, he never completed his own translation beyond the four suras *al-Fatiha, al-Baqarah, al-Imraan,* and *an-Nisaa* (Mazrui 1980; Mazrui 1981; see M. K. Mazrui 1980, xi).

43. See the (unpublished) public lecture by Sheikh Abdilahi Nassir at ZMO, in July 2008 (Nassir 2008).

44. It was only with the appearance of the IPK in the early 1990s, as part of multiparty democracy campaigns, that such a stereotype was clearly shaken off and countered, with an emphasis on Islamic values and Muslim unity against the authoritarian state. What matters most is to gain focus, through these texts, on the internal debates within the community, in terms of the "what" and "how" of such debates.

45. There are some obvious conceptual and rhetorical similarities with common Enlightenment motifs and phrases, especially if we think of Kant's definitions of enlightenment as the "liberation from self-inflicted nonage" (*Befreiung aus der selbstverschuldeten Unmuendigkeit*); or as being awakened from a "dogmatic slumber"; or, simply, the ability to think for oneself (*die Faehigkeit, selbst zu denken*). There is a wider academic discussion on related comparative motifs, and the possibility of speaking of an "Islamic Enlightenment" (esp. Schulze 1996). In regionally specific terms, I have reflected earlier on the activities of Sheikh Al-Amin's students as a reform movement with features of a kind of "Swahili Enlightenment" (Kresse 2003).

46. Coined as "maritime culture" (Prins 1965) or, with a similar thrust, "littoral society" (Pearson 2006).

47. See also Ho 2006.

48. On *al-Islah*, see Matthews 2013. Though this term is commonly translated as "reform," this view is not shared by everyone (I am grateful to Ridder Samsom for pointing this out). It is beyond my expertise, however, to cover such conceptual contestations here.

Figure 1. "PWANI SI KENYA" (The coast does not belong to/is not part of Kenya), graffiti with the signature call of the MRC, in Old Town Mombasa, 2012. Photograph by the author.

Figure 2. The two coastal Kenyan Mwambao representatives Abdilahi Nassir and Omar Basaddiq (in the center, from left to right), at the Lancaster House Conference in London in 1962. From the archives of Sheikh Abdilahi Nassir, with kind permission.

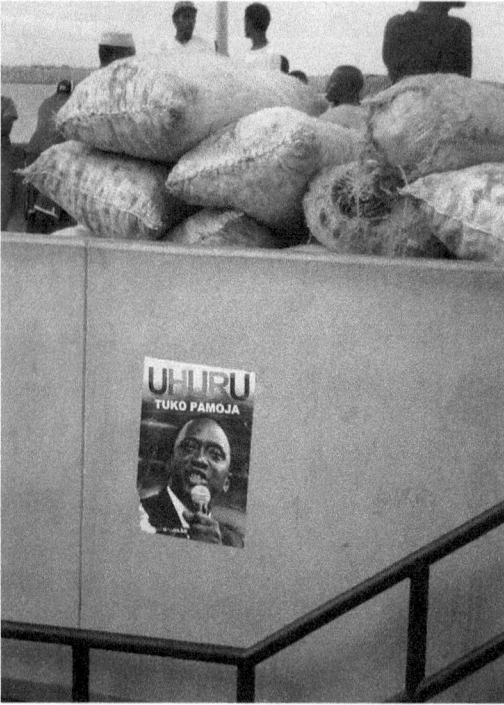

Figure 3. "UHURU—tuko pamoja" (Uhuru—we are together), Uhuru Kenyatta election poster at Lamu Port, 2012. Photograph by the author.

Figure 4. Crowd at Lamu Fort, waiting for Uhuru Kenyatta to speak, 2012. Photograph by the author.

Figure 5. Picture of Sheikh Al-Amin Mazrui, from the Saggaf Alawy Library, with permission. With permission also by Alamin Mazrui.

Figure 6. Abubakar Amin in the Radio Rahma studio during a broadcast. Mombasa, 2005. Photograph by the author (with permission by A. Amin).

Figure 7. "UKIMWI upo!" (AIDS is here!), Radio Rahma poster in central Mombasa, 2010. Photograph by the author.

Figure 8. "Drugs kill!" Radio Rahma poster in central Mombasa (in front of post office), 2010. Photograph by the author.

Figure 9. Stambuli and his father, Sheikh Abdilahi Nassir, in a café in Mombasa, 2006. Photograph by the author.

Figure 10. Painted container used by Radio Rahma for charity events, placed permanently at Makadara Grounds, central Mombasa, 2007. Photograph by the author.

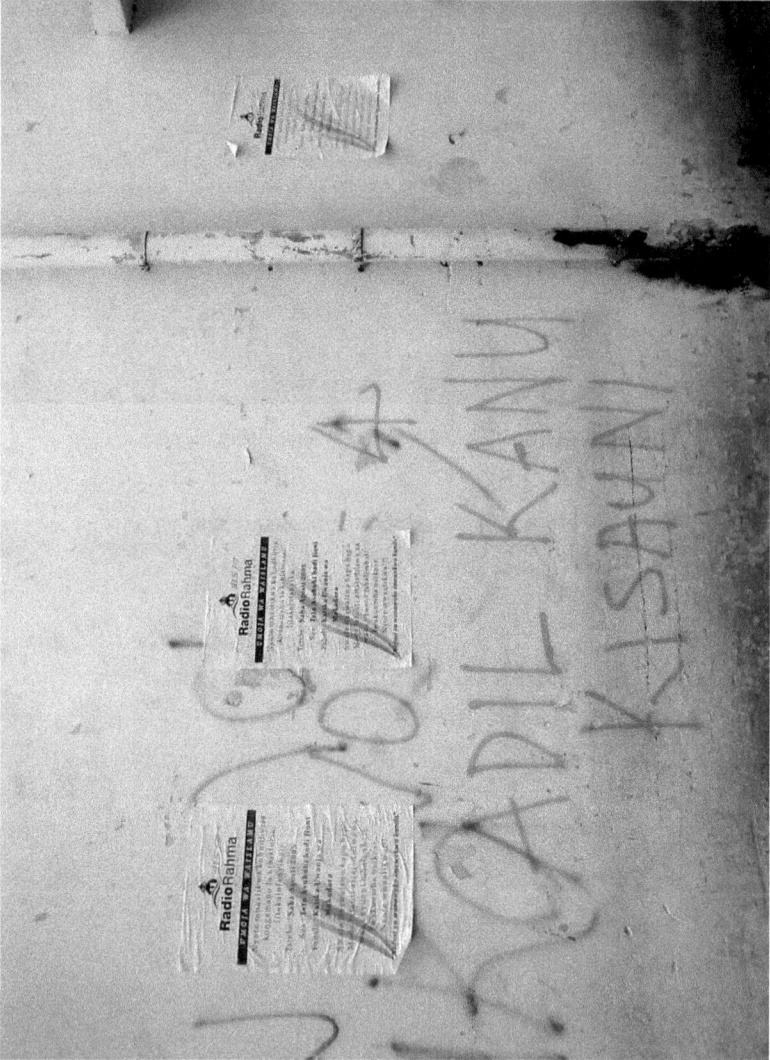

Figure 11. Posters on wall in Mombasa Old Town announcing public meeting on "Muslim unity" at Makadara Grounds for August 2005. Mombasa, 2005. Photograph by the author.

4 The Voice of Justice

An Islamic Newspaper in Postcolonial Kenya, 1972–82

THIS CHAPTER EXPLORES the discursive dimensions and thematic threads of a reform-oriented modernist Swahili Islamic newspaper, *Sauti ya Haki* (Voice of Justice), published in Mombasa between 1972 and 1982 by the two most renowned students and followers of Sheikh Al-Amin Mazrui. Sheikh Muhammad Kasim Mazrui (1912–82), a nephew of Sheikh Al-Amin Mazrui, was its editor-in-chief, and his peer and age-mate, Sheikh Abdallah Saleh Farsy (1912–82), acted as *Sauti ya Haki*'s mufti, the authoritative Muslim scholar answering questions about Islamic law that came up in the newspaper's regular "*fatawa*" section. Farsy had come to Mombasa from post-revolutionary Zanzibar in 1968, following an invitation by the Kenyan government to become chief *kadhi* of Kenya (on the request of Sheikh Muhammad Kasim, the former chief *kadhi*) after a *haj* pilgrimage and an extended visit to Mecca earlier that year (Loimeier 2009, 393–400). This appointment of an incoming Zanzibari ally of Sheikh Muhammad Kasim to the position of highest authority aggrieved the Lamu-based Alawiyya *masharifu*, who had been keen for one of their scholars to have this position. These tensions accentuated those of doctrinal difference, marking an uneasy relationship between Lamu Alawiyya and Sheikh Farsy from the beginning of his stay in Kenya.

As former students of Sheikh Al-Amin Mazrui, Sheikh Farsy and Sheikh Muhammad Kasim Mazrui were among the most reputable scholars of their generation. Together with their students and allies, they continued Sheikh Al-Amin's agenda of reform, educating their readers about matters of Islamic knowledge and proper conduct while also raising critique of improper or unacceptable behavior in religious or practical terms. Like him, they expressed social critique and provided guidance through educational writings in *Sauti ya Haki*, in addition to their immense publication output of books and pamphlets on basic Islamic education (how to pray, how to fast, etc.) and common Muslim practices they opposed as *bidaa* (unacceptable innovations in religion), along with biographies of Prophet Muhammad, the four caliphs, Sultan Sayyid Said, and other prominent historical personalities.

Sauti ya Haki was ostensibly published in Kimvita, the Mombasa dialect of Kiswahili, at a time when coastal Muslims were consciously resenting the adverse effects that the colonial language policies and their imposition of so-called Standard Swahili had, with its secularizing or "de-Islamisizing" tendencies. Indeed, Sheikh Al-Amin Mazrui had already warned his followers about this in the 1930s (A. Mazrui 2007, 98), when writing about the educational status and the identity of coastal Muslims. Now, for Sheikh Muhammad Kasim as editor, it seemed important to use Kimvita not only as the appropriate local form for a journal published in Mombasa, but also, as his son commented, as a more genuine Islamic idiom of Swahili, lending itself to Islamic discourse (A. Mazrui 2007, 102). In this chapter, I focus on the arguments and internal debates that were facilitated within the regional Muslim community, by means of this newly founded newspaper that was introduced as a platform for public Islamic discourse, presenting itself also as the mouthpiece and "tongue" of the local Muslim community (*ulimi wa umma*). Yet as we shall see, representing a common consensus was a rather strong claim within a contested field of Islamic debates about how Muslims should position themselves in society.

In the texts of *Sauti ya Haki*, we encounter a pronounced sense of an internal dual opposition within the regional Muslim community, between representatives of the next generation of modernist reformers and the leaders of the Alawiyya networks of Hadrami *masharifu* scholars and their families who largely resisted the calls for modernist reform (for instance, rejecting secular education, especially for girls). This opposition had already come into being during the times of Sheikh Al-Amin, and it was reflected in some of his article discussed above. The oppositional characterization of "modernists" against "traditionalists" is, in some ways, a simplifying shorthand for more complex realities on the ground. Both groups invoke relevant discursive traditions of Islam for their cause in mutual challenges to each other, and both defend their social position in the here-and-now of the contemporary world. Nevertheless, this opposition characterizes the division between these two major groups quite adequately, for an initial description that gets us into the frame of an internal perspective—which can then be developed in a more complex manner.[1] The largely Mombasa-based modernists emphasize rationalism as a socially liberating force and the compatibility of the Qur'an and modern science, while the largely Lamu-based *masharifu* stress the need to follow the spiritual pathway of their grandfather Salih bin Alawy Jamal al-Layn, commonly called Habib Saleh (who was an important social reformer in his time, coming to Lamu from the Comoros).[2] The oppositional difference is perhaps most palpable with a view to social hierarchies: While one side emphasizes performative features of ability and achievement as the criteria that distinguish people within the model of a largely egalitarian Muslim community, the other side stresses the ongoing social significance of descent lines as creating a divinely sanctioned social hierarchy of the Muslim community. Indeed, while attitudes toward the performance of Sufi-oriented ritual practices (like *maulidi*, *dhikr, khitma, tahlil*, and *hawl*)[3] mark stark lines of difference between these two groups, mutual opposition seems most pronounced when the nature of social hierarchies is invoked. Still, both groups have descendants of the historically privileged groups of coastal Arabs as leading figures. The Salafi-oriented modernist reformers linked to the Omani Arab (and formerly largely Ibadi) elite around the Mazrui are facing the Sufi-oriented Hadrami Alawiyya *masharifu* led by descendants of the Jamal-al-Layl in their rivalry for a dominant form of Islam in the region.

In *Sauti ya Haki*, the heritage of Sheikh Al-Amin Mazrui's agenda is visible not only in continuing themes of debate, but also in the structural backbones of the publication project, in its regular strands and subsections. The rich reservoir of Sheikh Al-Amin's writings was used to provide authoritative sources for education and discussion: over the years, his Swahili translations of 130 *hadith* were reprinted (1972–78); his popular booklet on educating the youth (*Hidayatul Atfal*, written in Arabic), widely known and used across the region for teaching children,[4] was fully reprinted in a serial Swahili translation. Other series and thematic strands completed the core of each issue, all of them organized, in combination, to argue for social change and modernist reform[5] on the Kenyan coast and in East Africa more widely.

Sauti ya Haki had its own agenda of reform and social critique, and it sought to attract followers and convince readers, with an emphasis on the importance of knowledge and education (*elimu*). The idea that Islam itself demands the acquisition and cultivation of worldly and religious knowledge was crucial to the project; also, that proper Islamic conduct includes the obligation to pass on one's knowledge to one's social peers, and that one needs to act upon one's knowledge when interacting with others. As we have seen already, the insistence on putting knowledge into action (*kitendo*) follows the thinking of Sheikh Al-Amin Mazrui and a tradition within Swahili thought that emphasizes the obligation to actual performance of knowledge and goodness as a moral demand of members of the community. The proverb "*utu ni kitendo*" (humanity/goodness is action), for instance, one of several mutually overlapping and complementary proverbs on *utu*, illustrates this. It makes the point that the actual good-ness of goodness (being humane) is in the doing of a good action (its performance), not in saying or invoking it.[6] Here we have an instance of what we can describe as an intertwining of a knowledge economy with a kind of Islamic moral economy in social interaction within the community.[7] Normative expectations, demands, obligations, and duties are invoked and negotiated, in relation to the kinds of experiences that people have and the kinds and channels of knowledge they have access to; this happens in everyday life as well as in public discourse.

This chapter proceeds by discussing illustrative readings that reflect narratives of self-positioning by coastal Muslims, in wider social, political, and historical contexts, as the newspaper claims to speak up for the Muslim community, advertising itself as "the tongue of the *umma*" (*ulimi wa umma*), as well as, of course, the "Voice of Justice" (*Sauti ya Haki*). In fact, while *haki* commonly means "justice" or also "right/rights" in Swahili, the linguistic roots of *haki* in the Arabic *haqiqa* invoke "truth" as a second major connotation, so that *Sauti ya Haki* can be associated with what is right, true, and just. Here, I read the newspaper texts themselves as meaningful historical and ethnographic accounts of past social experience of coastal Muslims in the early postcolonial period that continues to shape and influence the present.

Reading *Sauti ya Haki* provides access to the vivid social universe on the Swahili coast that it reflects and comments upon for a good decade, during a period of political transition, from the first to the second Kenyan president (in 1978). Diverse concerns, wishes, and aspirations among local Muslims become visible, in their relation to everyday life (through queries, commentaries, and letters). On the one hand, these feed into and shape the main internal opposition of regional Swahili-speaking Shafii Muslims, between Mombasa-based reformists led by students of Sheikh Al-Amin Mazrui (d. 1947), and Lamu-based followers of the Alawiyya, led by the descendants of the founder of Riyadha Mosque, Habib Saleh (d. 1935). On the other hand, concrete worries, challenges, and rivalries, as they play out in everyday life for people individually, are visible in the publications as well: for example, how to assure proper marriage or burial procedures; what to wear, and what not; and how to behave, in specific situations of need or emergency. As a way to make Islamic discourse more accessible to ordinary Muslims, the reformists also pushed for the lecture parts of the Friday sermons (*khutba*) to be held in Swahili—this was rejected by the Alawiyya *masharifu*, which led to mutual standoffs and actual fights in mosques between followers of the two groups.[8]

Sauti ya Haki—Summary and Overview

Before Sheikh Muhammad Kasim Mazrui launched *Sauti ya Haki* in August 1972, he had already been following the example of his teacher and mentor, Sheikh Al-Amin, writing pamphlets for the reformist cause that he circulated as numbered "papers" (*karatasi*) in biweekly intervals. They had been reprinted and published locally in three volumes of *Hukumu za Sharia* (judgments of Islamic law; 1970–72), and *Sauti ya Haki* integrated several of the trademark features of these papers into its own profile.[9] As editor, Sheikh Muhammad collaborated closely with Sheikh Abdallah Saleh Farsy, his successor as chief *kadhi* who became *Sauti ya Haki*'s mufti, responsible for giving authoritative legal opinions (*fatawa*) on any readers' queries. In general, *Sauti ya Haki*'s articles emphasized a rationalist understanding of Islam, along with its compatibility with modern science, and they flagged up the need to safeguard proper Islamic teachings and practices against unacceptable innovations (*bidaa*). Along these lines, a major goal of *Sauti ya Haki* was to represent the *umma* to itself from a reform-oriented modernist point of view, and to provide a platform for the exchange and dissemination of information and opinions on education, social critique, and social change among East African Muslims.

The newspaper was published between three and four times a year, until 1982, when Sheikh Muhammad Kasim Mazrui died (on April 5); his longtime companion in the agenda, Sheikh Abdallah Farsy, died later the same year (November 8) in Muscat, Oman, where he had just moved to retire and join his family. The last two issues of *Sauti ya Haki*, from May 1982 and November 1982, commemorated these influential scholars and proponents of Swahili Islamic reform who followed in the footsteps of Sheikh Al-Amin and expanded the impact of his project. Not knowing how and under whose leadership best to continue after their demise, the publication project stalled and was never taken up again.

Each of the issues of *Sauti ya Haki* consisted of eight pages, and apart from a main thematic article written by the editor, it included the following regular sections: commented selections of translated *hadith*; *fatawa* in which the mufti answered concise questions very briefly; a serialized Swahili translation of Sheikh Al-Amin's Arabic book *Hidayatul Atfal* (On Educating the Youth); and, from 1977, a serialized discussion section on "Science and the Quran." The last page, called "*mkia wa dhahabu*" (literally, "the golden tail"), offered space for brief and often humorous readers' comments and observations, with responses by the editors, and for public announcements to the community (deaths, upcoming events, or important visits). Frequent longer letters to the editors by concerned Muslims from all over East Africa were given space under the heading "*barua*" (letter), and these often led to discussions that carried on over several issues;[10] often, additional articles with a special focus written by regional Islamic scholars were included (e.g., on divorce, on *maulidi*, on the neglect or misuse of mosques, on human equality, etc.).

A remarkable new element of *Sauti ya Haki* as a Muslim public was that it incorporated real dialogical dimensions within its printed discussions of Islamic matters: readers' queries or reactions and letters to the editors were published and integrated into the journal's structure in increasingly regular intervals. These features were sometimes used by the editors to restate public challenges to their opponents of the Alawiyya *masharifu*, even individually and by name, to justify their positions on specific practices that the authors considered *bidaa*. For instance, the three issues of 1978 pursued the challenge to Sharif Mohamed el-Beidh and Sharif Khitamy, two leading Alawiyya scholars and representatives, to justify, with evidence from Qur'an or *hadith*, the practice of *hawl* (annual communal prayers in memory of a deceased, usually a sharif), which they culti-vated and had defended in sermons (April 1978, 8; July 1978, 8; October 1978, 8).

The paper's print run consisted of 500 copies initially and went up to 5,000 copies per issue later on. While the newspaper was printed in Mombasa, by the City Bookshop, the costs were carried by the Nairobi-based Anjuman Himayat Islam community. The group was founded by South Asian Sunnis and included Muslims from "upcountry," among them the chairman at the time by the name of Maulidi Jasho.[11] Copies were sent throughout East Africa in exchange for post-age stamps sent in by subscribers, and letters to the editor were received from neighboring countries including Uganda, Tanzania, Burundi, and the Comoros, apart from Kenya itself. This illustrates the wide-ranging web of swahilophone Islamic connections in the wider East African region. The newspaper advertised itself within its own pages, wooing for readership among Swahili-speaking Mus-lims with the following lines (e.g., Aug. and Nov. 1972, 2), which also appeared in abbreviated versions:

Voice of Justice

1. is the tongue of the Muslim *umma*
2. will provide you with important teachings
   (in your religion which are beyond doubt)
3. will supply you with translations of the Hadith of your Prophet
   (that will explain many things in religion, and will teach you good Islamic behavior)
4. if you read this journal regularly, you will become a true Muslim (an hon-orable representative of your religion, and someone who does not agree to be fooled by the treacherous tricks of the devil)

It comes out every three months[12]
Don't miss out on reading it![13]

This blurb pushes an overarching bold claim to speak out for the regional Muslim community as its communicative organ—"the tongue." It also reiterates the rel-evance of knowledge and education in order to become a "true" and good Mus-lim, while pointing to an internal antagonism in the local community, in which un-Islamic challenges and temptations by "the devil" still had to be mastered and overcome. These features characterize the project overall.

Beginnings and Agenda: Contesting Knowledge . . .

The first issue of *Sauti ya Haki* was published in August 1972, announcing itself on the front page under the heading "*Bishara ya kheri*" (blessed good news) and offering thanks to God and to the worldly providers of the funding to publish this newspaper. The editor expressed hope that in future *Sauti ya Haki* might be published in monthly, and then weekly, intervals, and ultimately even daily.

Already, its impact would be more beneficial than a normal quarterly newspaper, he argued, "because it will provide the opportunity to tell each other a lot more; to answer questions that have been asked, and also to be used as a weapon to protect oneself against attacks by the enemies of Islam" (p. 1). Thus its merits are envisaged to lie in the facilitation of internal dialogue among Muslims in the region, and the mediation and management of conflict. Who the "enemies of Islam" are is left open here, but over the course of the years of publication, the term is used for Christian missionaries and Western intruders, the Ahmadiyya, and for Muslim adversaries following competing ideologies of Islam.

The debates in *Sauti ya Haki* are largely framed as a contest over knowledge (*ujuzi; elimu*), truth (*ukweli*), and justice (*haki*) that is internal to the Muslim community. This is enacted in rhetorical narratives in which one's own knowledge and education (*elimu*) is pitted against the ignorance (*ujinga*) of others (the ideological rivals), who in turn may respond with counter-claims and arguments—not unlike earlier public forms of cultivated rivalry in the Swahili region (between moieties or city states) such as *kujibizana* poetry, which often includes trading mocking and mutual insults.[14] In the essays of *Sauti ya Haki*, a civilizational grand narrative that characterizes Swahili society on the whole, with its opposition between Muslim patrician *waungwana* and low-status and less educated or ignorant people (*wajinga*), is adapted and used, casting a narrative "we" of knowledgeable and open-minded actors vis-à-vis lesser-educated others. As the contest over knowledge is fought out within the Muslim community, *Sauti ya Haki* can be understood as a communicative platform, a public that is dedicated to continuing Sheikh Al-Amin Mazrui's concern to provide proper guidance to a wide scope of ordinary Muslims. Hereby, knowledgeable experts like religious scholars and scientists are seen to have an obligation to inform and lead their (less-knowledgeable) fellows.

From a wider comparative perspective on the Muslim world, we can say that a classic rhetorical motif is at work here, of presenting Islam as the creed informed by proper knowledge and a monotheism that stands for civilization, against pre-Islamic customary practices that are blindly followed in ignorance (*ujinga*) and thus determining a veritable sphere of ignorance (*jahiliyya*). This motif is to be found in recurrent phases of renewal and reform in Islamic history. At the time of *Sauti ya Haki*, the writings of the two Islamic thinkers using this rhetorical motif, Sayyid Qutb from Egypt and Abu al-Ala Mawdudi from Pakistan, were popular and influential among Sunni reformist groups in East Africa and elsewhere.[15]

The maiden issue of *Sauti ya Haki* opened with a programmatic article called "*Fitina ya dini*" (Religious Discord), which focused on how disunity and uncertainty had spread among Muslims. The author explained that the current decline of Muslims in the contemporary world was due to their suspicions about modern technologies, viewing them as irreconcilable with religion and proper piety. This, however, was unjustified, since human beings as the makers of modern technologies and machines were themselves created by God, who had supplied them with the abilities to create such new things. There was no fundamental opposition between technology and religion as such, nor any reason to assume a clear division between worldly and otherworldly glory (*utukufu wa akhera*). A conceptual characterization of "worldly glory" (*utukufu wa ulimwengu*), of social progress and economic success, is put forward, arguing that it was to be achieved through a well-balanced mediation of three constitutive aspects—namely social unity (*umoja*), knowledge (*elimu*), and wealth (*utajiri*). No nation in the world could prosper without a proper balance between these three (Aug. 1972, 4). Bringing these aspects into balance had been demanded by Islam from its beginnings, the article pointed out, with quotations from the Qur'an. This was in contrast to Christianity, which forbids its followers mundane wealth, as the article argues with reference to the Bible (Matthew, chapters 6 and 9). It goes on to say that those who had brought progress to the non-Muslim world were not pious Christians but nonbelievers who thought of religion as backward. Thus readers should be aware that Christians had not progressed because of following their religion, but on the contrary, "they progressed by following the teachings of the religion of Islam" (*wamekwenda mbele kwa kufuata mafunzo ya dini ya Kiislam*; p. 5). Realizing this, Muslims should find their way back to proper Islam and feel strengthened in their religious adherence.

This argument, like many brought forward in *Sauti ya Haki*, echoes the thinking of Sheikh Al-Amin Mazrui, the editor's teacher and mentor.[16] The conceptual triangle underpinning the argument here reiterates the centrality of socially informed knowledge for an envisaged "good" society, virtuous and at the same time economically thriving. Wealth is conceived of as a good thing, as long as it is spent in ways that are guided by knowledge that has the common interest of the community in mind. In this way, enhancing social unity (*umoja*), wealth is seen as a good and necessary resource to improve living conditions for all. Here, as in related arguments, we see the conceptual relevance of the idea of a common good, or public interest (*maslah* in Arabic; *maslaha ya umma* in Swahili), which had been taken up by Sheikh Al-Amin Mazrui from Muhammad Abduh and Rashid Rida.[17]

The concluding passages of the article sketch out the social ills of the rule of ignorance that the coastal Muslim community is currently suffering from:

> Because there is a lack of order of religious expertise in our towns, and a lack of religious schools (*madrasa*) agreeable to all Muslims, our Islamic community has been entered by a disease of sheikhs who are not known for the degree of their education in religion. So much so that anyone having a shawl, a

board and a piece of chalk can call himself "sheikh" and pose to have religious knowledge (Aug. 1972, 5–6).

Kwa sababu kukosekana mipango ya taalim ya dini katika miji yetu, na kukosekana Madaris yenye kukubaliwa na Waislamu wote umma wetu wa Kiislamu umeweza kuingiliwa na ugonjwa wa kupatikana mashekhe wasioju-likana kadri ya elimu yao katika dini. Hata imekuwa killa mwenye kumiliki kashida, kizibao na jubba, huweza kujiita "shekhe!" na akadai ujuzi wa dini.

This "disease" that the Muslim community brought upon itself made Muslim youths turn away from their religion, the author says, and he urged people to make sure that they could distinguish between truly knowledgeable leaders and false pretenders. Thereby, they should keep in mind that Islam and its proper teachings were always compatible and never in contradiction with facts (Aug. 1972, 6). That Islam is never in contradiction with facts can also be rephrased into saying that it is always compatible with science—and this is another prominent thematic sub-strand in *Sauti ya Haki* that is developed during its years of publication. A series on science and the Qur'an was launched in May 1977, with a front-page article, "Science in the Mirror of the Qur'an" (*Sayansi katika kioo cha Qur'an*). Mohamed Hyder, a professor of zoology at the University of Nairobi, with origins in Mombasa (and a PhD in marine biology from the University of St Andrews), introduced the topic with a biographically toned article on the Qur'an's compatibility with modern scientific knowledge. He explains how he had had the chance to think seriously about this, during a recent sabbatical, in stimulating discussion sessions with Sheikh Abdalla Saleh Farsy in Mombasa. Turning to *Sauti ya Haki*, Prof. Hyder followed the advice of his father, a well-connected community leader (see Kindy 1972) who insisted that such insights should be made accessible and popularized, and the journal agreed to publish a series of articles on science in relation to the Qur'an (May 1977, 1–2). The series ran regularly in every issue until January 1982, also featuring guest contributions and letters to the editor. While this first article discussed the scientific notion of the earth's atmosphere, with its constituent parts of molecules and the ozone layers that constituted important protection for human beings—protection that scientists saw as coincidental yet believers regarded as a divine design—later articles covered a wide spread of topical matters while using references to the Qur'an to illustrate its capacity to anticipate themes and insights of modern science.

Again, we can understand this thematic strand as part of a continuation of a larger project advocating modernist reform for the coastal Muslim community, as it had been conceived from 1930 onward by Sheikh Al-Amin Mazrui. His legacy also comes out in other regular strands and series that constituted the core of this newspaper. A number of his earlier articles were prominently reprinted, as they still resonated well with current issues that the editor sought to address, with their respective critiques of a narrow-minded traditionalist attitude, as a humorous sketch, in July 1978 (*Mazungumzo . . .*); of the (mistaken) obsession for building new mosques (and adorning them lavishly), in October 1978 (*Misikiti . . .*); of divination practices, in January 1980 (*Kutizamia . . .*); and of local burial customs, in September 1980 (*Ada zetu . . .*). These themes were all frequently covered in the sections of the newspaper throughout its existence, as part of commentaries, articles, or letters to the editor.

On the whole, the spectrum of Sheikh Al-Amin's texts involved here alone already reflects a sense of the ongoing internal conflicts that shaped (and reshaped) the regional Muslim community. As already mentioned, two regular sections in *Sauti ya Haki* drew directly from Sheikh al Amin's work and were part of each issue from the beginning. Firstly, 130 selected *ahadith* with commentaries in Swahili translation[18] appeared until October 1978. Secondly, his popular book on "educating the youth" about Islam, *Hidayatul-Atfal*, appeared in a complete serial translation that ran from the maiden issue until May 1981. In January 1982, the well-known "forty collected *ahadith*" by the famous Shafii scholar Imam al-Nawawi[19] (1233–77) followed, as the new *hadith* series in translation. In these ways *Sauti ya Haki* disseminated commentaries on the Qur'an and the *hadith* (the two sources that all Muslims must follow), making them accessible to a wider swahilophone public as general normative knowledge.

Reading 1: Knowledge and Experts (and the Legacy of Sheikh Al-Amin Mazrui)

That true and proper Islamic knowledge needs to be cultivated and disseminated within the Muslim community remained an ongoing key theme for *Sauti ya Haki*, and its second issue continued the argument in an article called "Knowledge and Experts" (*Elimu na wataalamu*). Two kinds of knowledge were differentiated: Islamic (what concerns Muslims "as Muslims") and general "worldly" education, like healing, mathematics, biology, or geography (Nov. 1972, 1). It is claimed that "worldly" education can be understood as part of religious knowledge more widely, as it is needed to practice religious duties and it feeds into a wider consciousness of the world as a divinely created unity. Criticizing the neglect of knowledge within the Muslim community, also by means of a humorous illustrative example of a prototypical "ignorant sheikh" (see below), this article continued to praise Sheikh Al-Amin Mazrui as someone who pushed for education in all fields of knowledge. He was praised as "the first" proper role model "in our towns" and an example to be emulated (November 1972, 2). Sheikh Al-Amin is remembered as the first scholar who used his knowledge to free himself from the bondage (*kamba*, lit. "rope") of those who went before him. He did so by being critical in his readings, and by passing on to his students books that were avoided or condemned by local scholars. Keen on translating *hadith* and Qur'an into Swahili, he began to make his own selections and translations, and he used them for religious education.[20] "He himself did not bind himself with the rope of his teachers, nor did he bind his own students with his opinions" (2). As a result, "this attitude brought him war from those bigots (*washupavu*) among his fellow sheikhs, and they attacked him, his classes, his books and also his students," to the point that they called him an unbeliever and made it difficult for people to study with him. To top it all, the article says, some of the adversaries came to him to study what they could not learn elsewhere, and then they continued their war against him. In the years to follow, the article went on to say, people's resolve to progress through education was broken, and ordinary Muslims were intimidated by their sheikhs and feared reading any books with opinions that differed from theirs. At that point, "their education ended, just like the books of their sheikhs, and *their thinking lacked Freedom*' (my emphasis)[21] (no. 2, 2).

This is the state of affairs that the *Sauti ya Haki* editor addressed as his present social environment. In such a community, in which striving for knowledge had ceased, ordinary people took on a belief that scholars were never wrong, and thus followed them "like the blind following the seeing" (no. 2, 5). This belief, the article goes on, was encouraged by a group of sheikhs who deemed themselves superior to other human beings, and who pushed communal divisions, intending "to bring about subgroups and separation in religion and make themselves the rulers of those groups" (5); they are said to have employed colonial "divide and rule" politics for their own purposes. Readers were reminded that no sheikh, no matter the extent of his knowledge, effort, and sense of justice, will ever exceed the boundaries of being human (*u-wanadamu*). Even the Prophet, the closest to a perfect example of a human being, can be seen to have shown doubts and weaknesses (5). The lack of proper attitude to follow religious guidance through one's knowledge of Qur'an and *hadith* is said to have led to the dominance of such leaders, who make strategic use of their half-knowledge to build and protect their own status. Unity among Muslims has become undermined, and when people criticize needless overspending by these sheikhs (for instance), they are denounced as "Wahhabi" (5).[22] However, the article concludes, it is good to see among local youths a growing interest in changing things: "They have begun to wake up and to cut the ropes of religion that had been tied for a long time" (5). An era of proper, knowledgeable orientation is envisaged, overcoming the current oppression of free thinking by such "colonialists of religion" (*wakoloni wa dini*), who lack humility and knowledge.

In hindsight, and on the basis of my own fieldwork in the coastal Muslim community about twenty-six years after these quotations from *Sauti ya Haki* were written, it is intriguing to see how much the rhetorical patterns of mutual attack by representatives of local groups on each other seem to resemble each other. The reproach of causing disunity within the community is a common one, one that I have also come across many times—it is a rhetorical warning that others seek to take over the community by means of *fitna* (causing disunity). Calling someone a colonialist (*mkoloni*) of religion—that is, someone who first divides and then rules a community (in which he ultimately does not belong) by unjust and oppressive means—follows similar lines.[23] As long and as much as representatives of one group cast themselves as protectors of communal unity, knowledge, and true religion, they will cast their adversaries as ignorant or misinformed dividers, and as a danger to religion. This applies similarly for other regions of the Muslim world. Thus, to give us a better sense of regional specificity in the course of this study, it is useful to focus on the (shared) rhetorical patterns and idioms of argumentation and self-presentation in the Swahili examples here, across time.

A Story (*Kisa*) . . .

One way to bring in common local elements of oral rhetoric for the presentation of an argument to local readers is to use narratives that have a personal and anecdotal character as some kind of didactic master narrative, telling them as if they were part of an oral sermon or lecture in front of one's local peers. We can find this, from time to time, in the articles and commentaries of *Sauti ya Haki*, and I am now turning to one such narration used in this particular article ("*Elimu na watalaamu*" ["Knowledge and Experts"], *Sauti ya Haki*, Nov. 1972, 2). The subheading used to mark the beginning of this narrative here is *kisa*, indeed the common name for "story" (usually orally presented). I am presenting the whole story in translation below, and we should keep in mind that, while it is something of a complete didactic narrative in itself, it is also positioned in the middle of the article just discussed, and thus it is surely also meant to exemplify central aspects of it. The narrator here is a well-educated local Islamic scholar, familiar with "modernist Islam" and its proponents. Indeed, we can take the narrative "I" here to be the editor of *Sauti ya Haki* himself, Sheikh Muhammad Kasim Mazrui, who passes on this account of his (real or fictional) encounter with a local sheikh who had never before heard of Rashid Rida's journal *al-Manar* (The Lighthouse), nor of the so-called Commentary of Manar (the Qur'anic *tafsir* by Muhammad Abduh, the teacher and mentor of Rashid Rida), but is quick to judge:

> One day I was somewhere in our coastal towns, when I heard a local scholar as he was talking badly about the *Tafsir of Manar*. He said it was a terrible *tafsir* and presented some great dangers to Muslims. So I asked him: "Sheikh, have you seen this *tafsir*?" He said, "No, I have not yet seen it, but I have heard that this man *Manar* is a really major unbeliever. In this *tafsir* he attacks (warns of) many things that are agreed upon by Muslims." Then he asked me, "And you, have you seen it?" I answered him, "Yes, I have seen it and I have read it; but I did not see those things you are talking about." Then I explained to him that *Manar* is not the name of a person, but the name of a newspaper which was produced by Sayyid Muhammad Rashid Ridha in Egypt. This man wrote

down the *tafsir* of the Quran by his sheikh, Muhammad Abdo [sic]. Then he publicised it in his newspaper. That is why it is called *Tafsir of Manar* or Tafsir of Sheikh Muhammad Abdo. When I told this to the sheikh, it was obvious that all this I told him was strange (news) to him. I thought he might like to see it, but he did not say a thing.

Some time later, this sheikh was my guest at home. At about ten o'clock in the morning he wanted to rest a bit, he lay down on a bed and he asked me to give him any book that he could look at until falling asleep. I gave him the *Tafsir of Manar.* When it was about 12 o'clock, I went to wake him up, and I found him sitting on the bed and reading the book with great interest! When he saw me, he said, "What a surprise, this *Tafsir of Manar*! From starting to read this until now I have not seen anything bad, but instead I have benefitted a lot, more than from any other *tafsir.* The differences in [the ideas in the book] are no more than those between other scholars!"

Therefore, many of those who criticize scholars and do so on the basis of what they have heard or read in the books of the enemies of those scholars, without having read themselves the books of those who are criticized, should better make sure whether what they have been told is true or not (Nov. 1972, 2).

As we can see, the author presents his readers with a humorous anecdote about local prejudice and ignorance, here embodied by someone who has the status of being knowledgeable, and who should have the capacity to lead and guide others. Instead, his example of uncritical behavior, in terms of simply passing on a prejudice that he was told (without double-checking its truth), undermines the common (or communal) sense of what is true (*kweli*) and what is right (*haki*), and thus needlessly endangers the unity of the local community—and all of this because of a lack of knowledge as well as a deceptive self-conceit about one's knowledge and capacities. On the surface, this is a satirical critique of the common local perception of (meaning: ignorance about) the famous Cairo-based Islamic newspaper *al-Manar,* published and edited by Rashid Rida, scholar, journalist, and editor, whose newspaper connected the Muslim world, who advocated social and technological reforms, who was for modernization but against westernization, for self-determination and against colonialism. More fundamentally, the story is a demolition of the naïve, ignorant, and careless attitude that the anonymous "local sheikh" here represents—a figure that does not in any way come across as evil, but simply clueless, something which, in a position of responsibility, might be just as dangerous.

As part of the kind of Islamic newspaper that *Sauti ya Haki* represents—reform-oriented and "modernist"—this is a powerful story, a narrative that ridicules this sheikh as a prototype of traditionalism in local Islam, as naïve, ignorant, and stubborn though well-meaning and teachable (reformable) in the end. This anecdote reflects a rhetorical strategy of using humor and irony to criticize opponents. Knowledge as a reference point is picked up and played through here, on two levels of meaning: supposed "knowledge" that people ("experts") publicly claim to have while ultimately being ignorant; and true knowledge and real status as a proper expert. Overall, of course, this feeds in to *Sauti ya Haki*'s wider rhetorical strategy of exposing its opponents as somewhat deluded, self-conceited, and undereducated traditionalists.

On second thought, there is another kind of critical question emerging that is perhaps no less fundamental. Assuming this anecdote is based on real experience (which is not unlikely), how come our author here responds to the trust and frankness offered to him by the sheikh (who in private conceded his ignorance about *al-Manar*) by publicly ridiculing him? Moreover, the local sheikh is surely identifiable within the rather small Muslim community where people know each other well. Thus such a narrative portrayal can also be understood, to some extent at least, as a morally reproachable act, as it misuses trust to make a point in a public ideological battle. And if the anecdote was fictitious, is such a way of using it not a little mischievous too? I shall get back to such questions about moral status in the concluding discussion.

The *Fatawa* Section (on Legal Opinions)

If, as I argued above, my readings and (re)contextualizations of texts, events, and social dynamics in these chapters do provide windows of social experience, or "maps of experience" as Vail and White argued (1991), conducive to the understanding of society through local texts (Barber 2007), this becomes particularly palpable with a view to a reading of regional *fatwa* literature. Performed in similar ways all over the Muslim world as an "interactive genre" (Gräf 2010, 75), following the simple pattern of (usually) brief questions and answers on practical matters that carry with them a degree of legal uncertainty, these texts in each case follow the specific intentions of individuals in particular situations and living conditions. In combination, as collections of local *fatwa* texts in each issue, they mediate a characteristic image of a regional Muslim community at a specific point in time. Not only do we, as readers, obtain a sense of the common concerns and worries that people in specific communities see themselves facing, and the hopes they have for themselves or family members. We also see how questions are asked, by means of which words, vocabularies, and rhetorical gestures—and the same is true for the replies, given by a designated mufti, a qualified Islamic scholar with the authority to provide his considered opinions. These have to be legally justified with reference to the pathway of interpretation, but these do not all have to be laid out to the questioner. In *Sauti ya Haki*, the answers were usually as short as the questions, but in some exceptional cases the replies do lay out and cover the ground of their approach and progression explicitly, and they provide references to the holy scriptures to justify themselves.

Topically, a large proportion of questions were concerned with the clarification of status with regard to life-cycle events (marriage and divorce; death and subsequent customs, rituals, and practices, and inheritance issues) and the propriety of ritual practices, above all *maulidi*, but also special kinds of prayer and recitation sessions and visits to graves (*khitma, tahlil, hawl*, and *ziyara*) as locally practiced. People were concerned about what was acceptable, or recommendable, or obligatory according to (proper interpretation of) Islamic law, often with the intention to find justification and assurance for what they were doing. Common questions have to do with matters of death and bereavement and subsequent proper burial practices and inheritance rights; or with prospective marriage (about the suitability or advisability of envisaged partners) or divorce, always seeking to make sure that one does not inadvertently do wrong. As *fatwa* judgments are not legally binding "verdicts" (in the sense of Western law) but only legal opinions—defined by the processes of interpretation they are embedded in—public *fatwa* fora (in newspapers, on websites, or elsewhere) are also kinds of marketplaces in which Muslim believers can shop around for opinions that enable them to proceed with what they were doing (or hoping to do).[24]

Apart from matters of personal concern, the central and most controversial matter of common concern to the whole coastal Kenyan Muslim community has been about *maulidi* practice, how to honor and praise Prophet Muhammad—with variations of largely mutually exclusive opinions being favored by the two main competing groups. On the East African coast, *maulidi* celebrations, and their ritualized recitations in (and outside of) mosques, have been historically important: as public communal events and unique annually reconstituted Muslim public festivals, *maulidi* have been shaping regional Muslim identity (e.g., Boyd 1981) and have been interpreted as reaffirmations of Muslim unity (Parkin 1984); similarly, controversies about *maulidi* have been reshaping it (e.g., Kresse 2006). The practice of *maulidi* has been fundamentally contested within the Muslim world for a long time, , and a large body of theological and ideological arguments exists for and against the general practice and its specific sub-aspects.[25] The latter include intonation and vocalization, accompanying instruments, bodily posture and the movement of performers, its spatial organization, and other aspects. Discussions of these are invoked as a publicly accessible resource to draw from, by *maulidi* supporters and opponents and by scholars and laymen alike, to support their case and contest that of others. *Maulidi* celebrations (to be precise, certain kinds and ways of praising Prophet Muhammad in word and ritual action, in Arabic or Swahili) are considered as not only admissible but recommendable by some, but at the same time as inadmissible and forbidden by others, as undue innovations (*bidaa*) after the Prophet had already perfected religion. For instance, some ways of praising the Prophet are seen by critics to be ascribing divine qualities to Muhammad, the human being; and some ways of performing communal recitations are seen to desecrate religious space (e.g., when using drums within a mosque). Thus a long and dynamic history of regional debates about the kinds of acceptable and recommendable *maulidi* practices has been ongoing in the region, in relation to the transregional networks concerned.

Laying out all the different forms (texts, performances), adherents, and networks of *maulidi* that have been present, discussing the controversies about them in detail, and accounting for the kinds of mediation processes to achieve compromise—and thus reestablish Muslim unity—cannot be achieved here, as that would represent a book-length study in itself. What should be clear by now, with a view to the editors of *Sauti ya Haki* (a Muslim public forum for discussion), is that their coverage of the controversies about *maulidi* was inevitable, in relation to all these aspects and the substantial presence of local supporters and opponents. And it was likely that this coverage (with all its aspects) would be a kind of litmus test for the newspaper and its makers. Would they be able to address the realities of both enthusiasm about and opposition to *maulidi* among coastal Muslims, covering events and controversies taking place and providing guidance about the principles of judging these practices? And would they, at the same time, also be able to push their own agenda of a critical reform of *maulidi* practices, without alienating a sizable (or even major) part of their readership, and their constituency? Indeed, these constitute the *umma* that they were claiming to represent, with this newspaper as their "tongue" (*ulimi*), and literally, as "voice of truth and justice" (*sauti ya haki*). And so, comments, discussions, and (largely critical) arguments about *maulidi* celebrations can be found in *Sauti ya Haki*, not only in the *fatawa* section (where such queries occur but are not dominant) but everywhere: in front-page articles and editorial leads, in letters to the editor, in special temporary topical subsections (spanning over several issues), or as part of public announcements, humorous anecdotes, or critical commentaries.

The *fatawa* section, as one of the constant features in each of the issues, responded to real questions sent in by readers from all over East Africa, including countries like Tanzania, Uganda, Zambia, and Burundi, and from places as far away from Mombasa as Ujiji, Tabora, Nairobi, Lamu, Dar es Salaam, Lushoto, Mwanza, Arusha, Pemba, and Kasese, while also including many queries from Mombasa itself. The queries were always preceded by the name and location of the person seeking clarification (often with proper postal address), except for a few cases where no name was given (anonymization was possible upon request). The *fatawa* section was an important and highly visible instrument for the cause of reform, as a means to build and improve (or steer and direct) common knowledge about religious directives and constraints, and to rectify positions that would be seen by the editors as common misconceptions. Usually about a page or so in length was used for these purposes, and as question and answer were kept to a concise minimum of two or three lines, up to ten queries or so could be clarified in each issue. In this way, a sizable resource of authoritative answers was steadily built up as a kind of regional reference encyclopedia in subsequent issues. The published questions and answers represent an overview of concerns common to Swahili-speaking Muslims in the wider East African region, for whom *Sauti ya Haki* then was the dominant (and probably the only) dedicated Islamic newspaper. The main opponents of *Sauti ya Haki*, the Lamu-based *masharifu* faction of the Hadrami Alawiyya, who were also those usually targeted by its rhetorical attacks, did not publish their own newspaper, and they avoided engaging directly with *Sauti ya Haki*, whether publishing in it or writing letters to it. In many cases, though, indirect quotes and summaries of comments and criticism by *masharifu* sheikhs and leaders are given and then used as indicators and starting points for an explicit discussion between the two camps.

The *masharifu* were not silent about conflicting opinions about common practices, or competing interpretations of Qur'an and *hadith*. But they preferred direct interaction with their followers, in oral lectures and the *khutbas* or Friday sermons as their media of discussion and contestation. These were also their preferred media for disseminating knowledge and reasserting positions within their own group.[26] Thus as observers here, we cannot witness the same kind of a "religious economy" with many competing print media by competing groups, as described for Bombay from the 1840s till 1914 (Green 2011).[27] But the discussions among East African Muslims, and the rhetorical pushes and pulls of their (much smaller) religious market, are hardly less vivid or intense, even if in terms of local Islamic print media, *Sauti ya Haki* was the only newspaper and thus may have seemed unchallenged in public. But the channels of challenges worked differently, largely through oral transmission within the networks of supporters. As I lay out, the main features of mutual critique in the (often fierce) debates between these two rival groups vying for regional hegemony can be seen in *Sauti ya Haki*, even though the newspaper was never just a simple platform for, but rather a partial participant in, the debates it was publishing. A more thorough historical ethnography of the wider regional debates in the 1970s than we can provide here could yield a rich and fascinating picture, of which *Sauti ya Haki* constitutes only one significant sub-perspective.

Before January 1982, all *fatwa* judgments were made by Sheikh Abdallah Saleh Farsy, who was also chief *kadhi* (1968–81). When Farsy left to retire in Oman, the new chief *kadhi*, Sheikh Nassor Nahdy (1982–2002), took over as the so-called mufti for *Sauti ya Haki*. To provide a more concrete taste and overview about what was going on in the *fatawa* section, here is a brief collection of queries and responses that were posted in *Sauti ya Haki* in 1973 and 1982, as sample years (involving both muftis) from the initial and final phase of the paper (I provide brief indications of most answers in brackets):

How and when are divorces properly pronounced and valid? How is inheritance distributed? If the death of someone is uncertain, can inheritance be initiated? [No.] (Nov. 1972). Is it okay for women to use birth control? [Yes.] Does anyone who calls himself a "Muslim" have to be washed and buried according to Islamic rites after death, even if he hardly went to mosque? [Yes.] Was *tahlil* (the repetitive exclamation of the *shahada* in a rhythmic tune) a *sunna* of the Prophet? [No.] Should *surat talkin* be read to the deceased (by a "professional" reader)? [No.] Did the Prophet read *khitma* to the deceased? [No.] Is it acceptable that in Ramadhan many vices can be seen practiced (at night), like card games, meeting up between lovers in public (gardens)? [No, but common.] Is it okay to have a blood infusion? [Yes.] It is not okay to wear clothes that do not show one's affiliation to one's religion [but a veil, which is also worn by Christian nuns, is okay] (February 1973).

Why are dogs and pigs considered unclean? Is using non-Muslims' things not prohibited, if it is not done simply to imitate? [Yes.] Is it forbidden to publish a translation or commentary of the Qur'an without the Qur'an itself? [No.] Which *sura* should a groom read to his bride? [Given.] How should "eda" be conducted? Which are proper healing *duas*? [Nonexistent.] (May 1973.)

Should Muslims believe that Jesus's blood was spilled for them? [No.] Why is Muhammad not mentioned in Christian and Jewish books? [He is, in the book of Barnabas, but that is usually obstructed from view.] Must one pray two *raka* before joint Friday prayers? What is good and what bad *bidaa*? [Religious innovations are all bad; nonreligious ones depend on their effect.] Is it fine for *muadhin* to call out other than the call for prayer? [No.] How does one make up for missed prayers? How can all different Muslims be united? [Through the Qur'an only.] What is the proper recitation when burying someone? After an argument, people must not refrain from greeting and talking to each other for longer than three days. (August 1973.)

Does *maulidi* have the status of *ibada*? [No.] And is its performance obligatory for Muslims? [No.] Is it true that Muhammad was created out of light? [No.] Is going to the cinema *haram*? [No, not per se.] Is it all right to take out a life insurance policy? [No.] Does a woman have to wear a *buibui*? [No, but she needs to be properly covered.] If a death occurs when traveling, can a corpse be brought home for burial? [No, should not.] In Ramadhan, is it proper to start and break the fast together with the Egypt/Mecca time zone? [Yes.] What is the correct way of washing oneself during Ramadhan? [Given.] People who occupy themselves with *uganga* (traditional healing), can they be called "*kafir*" (unbelievers)? [Only if they know that doing this actually constitutes acts of unbelief.] (November 1973).

Is it all right not to recite the *shahada* before burial? [Yes.] Should one pay an *alim* to read verses on behalf of the deceased? [No.] Is it all right for a fasting person to eat during travel? [Yes.] Are people allowed to refrain from participating in *dhikr*? [Yes.] Is it fine to pay a sheikh 1,500 Shilling to read *tahlil* for the deceased? [No.] Is Muhammad's urine medicine? [No.] Is it all right to give one's child to a Qur'anic school where the teacher teaches *maulidi* only (the recitation and drumming), and not the Qur'an? [No.] Is there a status difference between recent converts to Islam and old (born) Muslims? [No.] Does the (newly wedded) wife have a right to insist they live with her parents? [No.] (May 1982).

The spectrum of topics and concerns seen here, while covering common general themes such as marriage and divorce rights as well as burial rules and requirements, represents a regional profile of contested Islam. It points to insecurity (and a corresponding awareness) about different opinions on ritual practices and undue innovation (*bidaa*), with a view to *maulidi* and other practices like *tahlil*, *khitma*, and *dhikri*. Controversies over these practices reflect a central rift or split between Sufi-minded adherents and reform-oriented critics within the regional Muslim community, along the thematic lines of the queries listed above. And the presentation of the legal opinions (*fatawa*) here clearly rejects special mediatory practices, like praying for others (by *masharifu* or sheikhs), and seeks to assure and maximize individual believers' direct access to knowledge, for them to act more independently and take their own matters into their own hands. So the collected queries and opinions above can be read, indirectly at least, as programmatic statements positioning the reform-minded faction of Muslims led by the editor and the mufti of *Sauti ya Haki* (Sheikh Muhammad Kasim Mazrui and Sheikh Abdallah Saleh Farsy) within a wider field of locally raised questions and concerns vis-à-vis a range of customs and ritual practices that were commonly favored by the Riyadha Alawiyya faction.

Reading 2: Forbidding Wrong . . . (*Kukanyana Maovu*)

In November 1974, the lead article, entitled "*Haki juu!*" (Justice up!—or Long live justice!), was written ostensibly to celebrate the completion of *Sauti ya Haki*'s third year of publication. However, as the introduction made clear, a deeper reason for the article seemed to lie in the need to respond publicly to accusations that were raised and spread by the newspaper's adversaries—namely, that *Sauti ya Haki* was splitting the local Muslim community and thereby playing into the hands of the "enemies of Islam" (e.g., Christian missionaries, Western outsiders). And so the editor used this article for a wide-ranging and calculated response. He appealed to the lesser-educated Muslim readers, who may have become confused and needed a proper explanation in order to understand *Sauti ya Haki*'s stance (p. 1). His argument hinged on the "importance of forbidding each other" (*umuhimu wa kukanyana*), as a subheading indicates. Stating, rather sweepingly (and mistakenly, as we know), that nothing bad could come out of forbidding wrong and nothing good out of failing to do so, he named several prominent figures in Islamic history known for speaking out and forbidding others from doing what (they thought) was wrong, and who suffered repercussions in response: Ibn Taymiyah, Muhammad Abdul-Wahhab, and Muhammad Abduh were flagged up; three prominent revivalist scholars at different points in time and with largely divergent agendas. More recently and closer to home, the author mentioned Abul-A'la Mawdudi from Pakistan, and the founding father of regional Islamic modernism, his teacher, Sheikh Al-Amin Mazrui (p. 1). Thus, the author concluded, the disunity among local Muslims could not have been caused by *Sauti ya Haki*. Rather, taking "forbidding wrong" seriously as an obligation, as these historical figures did, leads to angry responses by those identified as doing wrong who are being called to task for it.

The article addressed four accusations that *Sauti ya Haki* faced by its opponents, summarized by the following claims, introduced by "it is said" (*yasemwa*) (p. 2):

(a) that differences between religious leaders always (as a rule) bring about war and hatred between them and their groups (*yasemwa: khitilafu baina ya viongozi wa dini huleta vita na chuki baina yao*),

implying that the pronouncement of differences should be avoided.

(b) if everyone were to be left to do as he likes in matters of religion, there would be peace for everyone (*yasemwa: lau kama kila mtu angeatiliwa kufanya alionalo katika itikadi yake, ingepatikana amani*),

implying that all Muslim subgroups should keep to their own business, and be left to do so.

(c) if religious leaders differ, those who are not educated will fail to know the right way (*yasemwa: viongozi wa dini wakikhitalifiana, wasiosoma hushindwa kujua ndia ya sawa*),

implying that public religious disputes will create confusion among the less knowledgeable within the community.

(d) naming, or passing on, any bad things that Muslims have done is to pass weapons to the enemies (*yasemwa: kutaja maovu wayafanyayo waislamu ni kuwapa maadui silaha*),

implying that criticizing one's Muslim peers (meaning other Muslims) in public may lead to the destruction of the whole community.

While in each case a violation of an assumed code of peaceful cohabitation among Muslims is implied, the points are, one by one, responded to in the following ways:

a) The existence of different *madhhab* in Islam need not necessarily lead to war and hatred; indeed, internal difference has historically been part of an overarching Muslim unity that can be handled peacefully.

b) An attitude of letting everything pass is not acceptable and cannot work within Islam; if all were to be left to their own standards and criteria of religion, there would be no way of calling violators of basic standards to account.

c) Indeed, public discussion between religious parties or subgroups may lead to confusion for the lesser-educated Muslims; yet this problem cannot be surmounted "until all Muslims do learn their religion very well, as they have been commanded to do" (p. 2)

d) Speaking out in public against wrong deeds is a moral and religious obligation, not a matter of choice or negotiation; disunity is not a result of the act of "speaking out" (i.e., forbidding wrong), but rather, doing wrong is the cause for speaking out in the first place.

The editor centers his article around the fact that it is an obligation for all Muslims not only to put effort into studying their religion carefully, and to act according to their best knowledge, but also that all Muslims must act upon violations by their peers and forbid one another doing wrong (*kukanyana maovu*). This was not to be taken lightly but is a real obligation, and people who ignore it cannot rightfully call themselves good Muslims. Indeed, *Sauti ya Haki* itself, in a way, justified its own existence with reference to this phrase, as it sought to speak up as the "voice of justice," forbidding people from wrong whenever this seemed possible, imminent, or already happening.

On the point of reporting and discussing matters of Muslim disunity in its pages, he said, *Sauti ya Haki* had not disclosed any sensitive or improper information to outsiders; rather, it had spoken up against wrongdoing it witnessed; in other words, it was following its obligation of "forbidding wrong." The editor clarified that information about disunity had already reached outsiders before the potential "enemies of Islam"—independently of *Sauti ya Haki*. He even referred to recent anglophone academic publications on Islam in East Africa at the time, and quoted from them to make his point:

> Saying that enemies of Islam did not know about shameful behavior of Muslims up until the time these were criticized in *Sauti ya Haki* is completely untrue. The enemies of Islam go around on their own in Muslim towns in order to trace our shameful behavior and then write about them in their books. If you do not know this, read "Islam in East Africa" by Trimingham, and you will see how he mixes Islamic religion and primitive traditions and finally stirs them into one. Knappert has done this too, in his book which is called "Swahili Islamic Poetry," and Cunning in his book which is called "Islam in Tropical Africa."[28] And here we present to you briefly some words expressed by Reverend John Mbiti in his book "African Religions and Philosophy" published in 1968 . . .[29]

These external researchers had been visiting the coastal towns for themselves and observed some of the practices that *Sauti ya Haki* had been criticizing: the worship of "saints" (*walii*), pilgrimages to graves (*ziyara*), spirit possession rituals (*uganga*), the use of amulets (*hirizi*), and altogether, an emphatic focus on ritual celebrations that was indeed unacceptable (in the editor's view). The editor quoted from Mbiti's classic book commenting on such practices as diffusing Islam in the region, through activities of *maulidi,* healing cults (*ngoma*), and witchcraft (*uchawi*), often supported by the involvement of *masharifu* leaders. The example of Mbiti thus showed how "Islamic and traditional religion [or traditionalist faith] have become mixed"[30] and that Islam was growing in the region; but this growth was due to popular ritual activities that resonated with, or were similar to, local customary practices—not because of successful Islamic teachings. Local Islamic teachers were described by Mbiti as rather inept when it came to dealing with the modern world (here retranslated into English): "Even though they have good knowledge of the Qur'an and *sheria,* this knowledge is not enough to make them able to justify [or explain; lit. *eleza*] their religion in the modern world"[31] (Nov. 1974, p. 3).

The editor pointed out that these observations by foreign researchers were not wrong, and to simply deny them would not be appropriate for local Muslims. Instead, they should warn each other and forbid each other (*kuonyana na kukanyana*), "in their efforts to bring Islam back to its pure self." Even in this state of destruction, they should know that those who have become corrupted are Muslims (i.e., fallible human beings) and not Islam itself (*walioharibika ni Waislamu tu si Uislamu wenyewe*).

The article then responded to the argument that popular practices associated with *maulidi* (involving musical and dance-like performances) should be deemed acceptable even if they were, strictly speaking, *bidaa* (religious innovation), considering that they attract many people to Islam and lead to new converts. However, this kind of trade-off calculation is rejected, pointing to the fact that one could make a similar case for witchcraft (*uchawi*) and popular dances (*mabeni, ngoma*) attracting people to the local Muslim community, yet certainly not in the name of Islam. Ultimately, he argued, the number of Muslims was not most important for Islam, but the firmness of belief and practice. As an illustration, the editor narrated the example of a Giriama couple that once came to him in his capacity as *kadhi*; being very ill, the wife converted to Islam with the approval of her husband, in the hope of becoming well. After this did not happen, the couple returned to him, seeking her release from Islam.[32] Sheikh Muhammad explained that such instrumental kinds of conversions that lacked the basis of belief were inadmissible in Islam.

The article concluded with a critique of the Muslim community, as seen in the national political context. As Muslims were factually under Christian rule and domination, Sheikh Muhammad remarked, they had become quiet and kept still, accustomed to concede to the powers that be and the demands and circumstances brought upon them. He compared them to corpses waiting for the day of resurrection. This powerful image expresses immense frustration about the contemporary state of affairs for Muslims in Kenya, their declined status since independence, and their passive attitude: "Muslims in this country are under the foot of Christianity; they are not active; they are quiet like water in a pot, and they are not able to stir up anything that has quieted down. They are corpses who have no expectations to be revived up until the day of resurrection of all dead!"[33]

We can, I think, read an implicit demand into this statement—namely, that Muslims should actually resist any submission to external forces, and they should rid themselves from paralyzing inactivity. Instead, they should stand up for their rights, even and especially under such adverse conditions—but all this is not explicitly said.

In conclusion, the editor repeated that all Muslims must continue to obey God's commands to warn each other and to forbid each other from doing wrong. They must value Islamic knowledge, become educated, and educate each other. He recounted a story from the Qur'an[34] that narrated how people turned into monkeys because they did not warn each other and keep each other from sinning; and he invoked this story as a prophetic omen that now seemed to apply to East African Muslims, who were behaving like monkeys, simply imitating others, without reason: "Monkeys are contemptible animals, cowardly, stupid, and they love to imitate. And all these features are what we Muslims have these days. And there is no reason for this except for this same one, having violated God's commandment of forbidding wrong."[35]

This quotation expresses the editor's immense frustration with his Muslim peers, the state of Muslim disunity, and (in combination with the previous quote) the inferior status of Muslims as citizens on a national scale. Yet the emphatic image of the imitating monkeys representing coastal Muslims is not simply an insult to the Muslim opponents and rivals (though this is part of the story)— it also expresses a critical perspective on the community as a whole. The article attempted to connect all the relevant topics discussed into a larger whole. It connected the focus on doctrinal disagreements with the larger perspective on culture and religion, and ultimately (even if rather indirectly) a wider political perspective toward the possibility of resistance, critique, and liberation. The implicit point seems to be that resistance can only happen when based on unity; that unity needs to be achieved through conscious and proper education; and that within this education process, the kinds of Islam-diluting processes that *Sauti ya Haki*'s opponents engage in will only be counterproductive. Overall, the role of *Sauti ya Haki* was presented as a moral and educational one based on the principle of *kukanyana maovu* (forbidding wrong) that applies to all Muslims, as individuals and as a group.

Ultimately, this wide-ranging article returned the initial reproach of the Muslim opponents back to them. The message, then, was not that *Sauti ya*

Haki played into the hands of the external "enemies of Islam" (Christians and Westerners), but rather that their opponents' activities did so, due to their lack of proper knowledge, critical engagement, and moral commitment. It was thus almost inevitable that Muslims would be trapped in a postcolonial vicious circle of national power dynamics.

Reading 3: Muslims, National Politics, and the State

The *Sauti ya Haki* publication period from 1972 to 1982, for coastal Muslims in Kenya, was also marked by political self-positionings and attempts to arrange oneself with the KANU government in terms of national politics. KANU had established itself as Kenya's one and only party soon after independence, first in 1964 (merging with KADU), and finally in 1968 (quashing the rebelling KPU) (Hornsby 2012, 95, 215), and it was in complete control of Kenya as a one-party state until multi-party elections in 1992. The post-Independence "Africanization" policies also worked against coastal Muslims, as a group that was often collectively dismissed as "Arab" outsiders. This was a rhetorical motif casting fundamental suspicion on coastal Muslims, which was recurrently employed by successive Kenyan governments. In particular, relations to the all-powerful presidential figures of Jomo Kenyatta (1963–78) and Daniel arap Moi (1978–2002)—both autocratic rulers—had to be carefully balanced and maintained (e.g., Dumila 1971; Dumila 1978). The media at the time were "self-censoring" and understood well that "the government allowed little criticism" (Hornsby 2012, 310). For the editors of an Islamic print media, this meant taking care to show the expected public allegiance to the president and his national political agenda, while also keeping enough distance so as not to be seen (by one's Muslim constituency) as too close to the government and its policies.

Thus *Sauti ya Haki*'s references to national politics, the president, and the government may be read to carry implicit signs as well as explicit indications of endorsement and support (that all media had to show during KANU's single-party rule). Like other media or speakers on public occasions, *Sauti ya Haki* used the common and informal honorific title for the president, "*Baba wa taifa*" ("Father of the Nation"), in its writings. In an article called "The Father of the Nation Wakes Up the Nation" (October 1975), *Sauti ya Haki* commented on a recent speech by President Kenyatta given during a visit to Mombasa. Kenyatta spoke of the project of unity for the young Kenyan nation, and *Sauti ya Haki* applauded the president's explicit recognition of Islam as the second major religion in the country. It also latched on to the president's speech to bring home a point about egality in Islam, emphasizing that speaking of Arabs as the "original," "better," or "superior" Muslims vis-à-vis lesser African ones did not make any sense, just as Europeans (*Wazungu*) were not per se better Christians than Africans (pp. 1–2). The first point of Kenyatta's speech indicated his government's public endorsement of peaceful coexistence and cooperation between Christians and Muslims—indeed, he not only acknowledged Islam but also demanded the communities to interact in "brotherhood and love" (*undugu na mapenzi*). This could be read as an encouraging step forward in mutual relations, from previous positions of distrust. The second point was linked to Kenyatta's anticolonial argument against the myth of Arab superiority and their claim to be the rightful and natural leaders of Islam; this, the article said, was a myth constructed by the former colonials to sow disunity and division among the ruled.

In actual fact, the article reported, there was no basis for these divisive qualifications (not in appearance, nor in clothing, food habits, language, religious expertise, or other features). Within the coastal urban population, it was the colonial Europeans who stood out as clearly distinguishable and separate, while otherwise the population had grown together and blended into each other over centuries. Yet through their power and their *fitna*, the white colonials had succeeded in inserting hatred into the hearts of Muslim and non-Muslim Africans, pitting them against each other ("*wamefaulu kuzijaza chuki nyoyo za Waafrika*"; p. 2). The colonials had also succeeded in fostering, in the minds of many Muslims, the acceptance of an inferiority complex based on the prejudice that Islam stood against development and modernization—a statement that the author rejected completely, pointing to the modernist assumption of the compatibility of Islam with modern science and technology.

This article is altogether remarkable in that it shows through which rhetorical strategies both parties sought to formulate and shape a common platform of interest for Muslims and Christians as Kenyan citizens. One such strategy is through an emphatic anticolonial stance. Through the projection and acceptance of the white colonials as the cause of disunity and inequality between "Africans" (of different faiths, ethnic origins, and regional backgrounds), both sides decreased their respective burden of interpreting the past, for themselves and the others, and in turn gained more rhetorical maneuvering space for the negotiation of "national unity." As a bottom line, Kenyatta's speech offered an olive branch signalizing reconciliation to the Muslim community. *Sauti ya Haki* responded by offering praise for the government in return. All of this was expressed through somewhat vague and all-embracing statements (of quasi-diplomatic character), on a level of public discourse through which, potentially, foundations for specific instances or projects of future cooperation might be secured further.

Along these lines we find further references to and invocations of the government in the issues of *Sauti ya Haki*. In 1977 the newspaper published a vote of thanks to "Father of the Nation" Jomo Kenyatta for agreeing to keep the jurisdiction in family law (including marriage and inheritance) in the hands of Muslim judges within the general reform moves of the judicial system in Kenya, and it also expressed gratitude for creating the position of a *kadhi* of Nairobi, which had been demanded by Muslims ("*Shukrani kubwa kwa Baba wa Taifa*," January 1977, p. 6).[36] Reference to the government is sometimes also used for framing comments to shape internal discussions within the Muslim community. In a subsequent note, Attorney General Charles Njonjo was congratulated for initiating a "Miraa Prohibition Act" in Parliament that would make both the sale and consumption of *miraa* (also known as *mairungi* or *khat*) illegal in Kenya. This decision clarified its legal status within the realm of secular politics, while its status from an Islamic point of view repeatedly appeared uncertain in the pages of *Sauti ya Haki*. In response to a reader's query, for instance, a proper consideration of this was promised, making clear that such legal interpretation was not a straightforward matter but would have to be researched (Nov. 1974, 8).

In May 1974, the concluding section for letters and editorial comments, "*Mkia wa dhahabu*" (lit., The Golden Tail), reported that during a recent *maulidi* event, the speaker had publicly asserted that the opponents of *maulidi* were also opponents of the government, as it was common for the government to be praised during *maulidi* celebrations. In response, the editor conceded their critical stance on *maulidi* celebrations, yet responded by asking back whether the government should be praised only during *maulidi* ("*Je, Rais na Serikali yake hawafai kuombewa ila katika maulidi tu?*" p. 8). He referred to many meetings having taken place since Independence in which the government and Muslim representatives (also from *Sauti ya Haki*'s side) had engaged in constructive talks to consolidate relations further, and he asked why others never participated in any of them if they were truly interested in supporting the government in the name of the Muslim community.

Despite such declarations of support, some critical comments were also expressed on national politics and particular politicians who were seen to be failing expectations.[37] Remarkably, the editors also used their space for the political education of Kenyan Muslims within the given democratic system, seeking to enhance their influence as active, engaged, and responsible voters and citizens. For instance, they cautioned readers with a warning (*onyo*) not to give their vote to a candidate for any other reason than out of conviction that this person will have the best interest of the *umma* at heart, and would represent the *umma* well and responsibly in all actions. Otherwise (if they voted for someone out of different motives) God would punish them for their neglect (August 1974; see also May 1979).

In a brief comment on the same issue (again in the final section of editorial notes), corrupt politicians were criticized as enemies of the people, indeed as "thieves of the community" (*mwivi wa umma*) who should be punished harshly, and here an explicit rhetorical reference to the severe punishment of thieves according to the *sharia* is made (Aug. 1974, p. 8). Much frustration was expressed here, about corruption and the misuse of influential positions by people who should be working to improve regional standards of living (through educational or economic programs), as the corrupt, self-interested, and greedy politician began to emerge as a common new stereotype in postcolonial Kenya, making for a bleak perspective with a view to social improvement on the political front.

On the same page there was a reply to the question whether the president should be welcomed on his visit to the coast with Islamic *samai* recitals (accompanied by flutes). The editor did not advise against it but cautioned that it might be more appropriate and better appreciated if one made sure the songs were in Swahili rather than in Arabic. A similar issue was covered a year later, concerning the problematic use of *maulidi* in politics (July 1975, p. 8). Under the heading "*Maulidi* and Politics' (*Maulidi na siasa*), the editor commented on a report from Nairobi about a *maulidi* having been celebrated in support of a non-Muslim politician who was himself present in the mosque on the occasion. The whole event obviously seemed part of an election campaign. The editor condemned such activities as gross violations of Islamic practice, since only the Prophet himself should be honored by the praises. He appealed not to let Islam and *maulidi* be misused for the sake of "propaganda" (English in the original; ibid.). Another article demanded that politicians in general and the president in particular face the challenge and responsibility to act as a God-fearing person (*mchaji wa Mungu*) in order to be properly respected (May 1979, p. 8). This generically religious (rather than Islamic) term might well have been chosen for its usefulness in interfaith situations such as here, where the respective person of whom adherence to adequate moral values were demanded was not Muslim—but should be God-fearing to be respectable and acceptable.

On the death of President Jomo Kenyatta in 1978, *Sauti ya Haki* appropriately dedicated its front page to the loss of the "Father of the Nation," invoking God from beginning to end in an article written like a glorious praise poem. Addressing God already in its headline ('*Ewe Mola!*'), it recalled how God's divine powers had given Kenyatta the force to overcome colonialism, and how God had brought him to become the leader of the nation for the last fifteen years (Oct. 1978, p. 1). It praised him as a good leader but also pointed out that death is indeed at the end of every human being's life, without exception (perhaps alluding to the all-powerful status that Kenyatta had attained).[38] The article ended with a prayer-like plea to God, to help the incoming President Moi to be a good guide for the people so that Kenya could develop further (October 1978, p. 1, p. 8).

Under the rule of the new President Moi, the editors picked up on several occasions to congratulate Moi on his opinions or decisions. For instance, they approved of his public critique of belief in "witchcraft" (*uchawi*) among Lamu residents, which Moi had expressed in a speech during a visit (Jan. 1980, p. 1).[39] They also endorsed his campaign to stop and suppress the sale and consumption of coconut wine (*tembo*) on all publicly accessible premises, discos, and nightclubs

("clubs" in the Swahili original) in and around Mombasa. This practice had resulted in significantly destructive effects on everyday life for all residents of the areas (January 1981, p. 3). An interesting editorial strategy was employed in the first case, which also referred back to the genealogy of *Sauti ya Haki* itself: The main article incorporated (or led over to) and reprinted an older one by Sheikh Al-Amin Mazrui, thus invoking the undisputed authority of the East African master of Islamic reform for these themes. Such techniques of collage and quotation were also used in other issues for befitting topics; for instance, in a humorous critique of a naïve and uninformed narrow-mindedness, a traditionalist attitude that Sheikh Al-Amin had seen as representative of the people of Mombasa, and criticized for it, almost forty years before (July 1978, p.1; translation in Kresse 2009, 80–81).

The previous pages have given us bits and pieces of information, as they appeared in *Sauti ya Haki*, about the ways in which coastal Muslims related to the postcolonial Kenyan state in the 1970s and early 1980s and presented themselves as good and law-abiding citizens who used opportunities to praise the government when its actions coincided with *Sauti ya Haki*'s goals, such as in curbing drug use (locally brewed alcohol, *miraa*, etc.) and beliefs and practices related to "witchcraft" (*uchawi*), like spirit possession or the use of amulets. However, a respectful distance to (and largely, silence on) state authorities was kept, while Muslims' democratic engagement within the state, as responsible voters and citizens, was strongly encouraged. If this constitutes one side of the "double axis" on which Kenya Muslims had to act, vis-à-vis the *umma* and vis-à-vis the state, on the other side, too, a few prominent examples of reported events within the global *umma* should be mentioned.

For instance, the assassination of King Faisal of Saudi Arabia was reported in a front-page article (July 1975). A report on an international Islamic conference on *da'awa* missionary activities (Feb. 12–17, 1977), in which many well-known *ulama* took part, among them Sheikh Yusuf Qaradawi and Sheikh Abdulaziz bin Baz, was provided by a Swahili-speaking participant, Jaabir Yusuf (May 1977, 6). Also, a *fatwa* by Sheikh Abdulaziz bin Baz, then director of the University of Medina, against the practice of *maulidi*, from April 1973, was published in Swahili translation in February 1974 (p. 2, p. 7). This *fatwa* hinged on the point that Prophet Muhammad had perfected (*kuikamilisha*) Islam and thus all attempts at additional innovations were pointless and even threatening to religion. An editorial paragraph introduced Sheikh bin Baz as part of those who regarded *maulidi* as wrong and harmful religious innovation (*bidaa*) and thus *haramu*—in contrast to another school of thought, which regarded it as harmless celebration and thus acceptable. The editor's focus on an existent diversity of opinions is remarkable, and the subsequent edition of *Sauti ya Haki* featured a lead article on the discussion of *bidaa*. This clarified, in a fictional dialogue between a student and a sheikh, that distinctions between "good" and "bad" *bidaa* could only sensibly be made about worldly items (such as innovations in technology or dress), not in religious matters, where there were no "good" *bidaa*. The editor admonished readers to follow properly documented scholarly opinions in their deliberations (May 1974, 1, 6).

An ongoing social debate over *maulidi* continued to be covered in the newspaper every now and then, reflecting its importance for many Muslims in the region and reporting on a variety of celebrations and controversies about them, including a range of arguments for and against permissible ways of practicing *maulidi*. And while the editor took a critical stance on particular (e.g., wasteful or impious) ways in which *maulidi* were celebrated, he did not reject the practice completely but instead facilitated public debate over it, as part of the educational process that *Sauti ya Haki* was supposed to provide. Remarkable in this regard is an account from August 1973 about Sheikh Farsy and others experimenting to introduce "a new way of celebrating *maulidi*" (*maulidi ya namna mpya*) that would continue to honor the occasion without violating any Islamic principles. Sheikh Farsy had presided over a *maulidi* celebration held at Muslim Hall, Mombasa, for the National Union of Kenyan Muslims, in May. He had given a speech praising the features and deeds of Prophet Muhammad, and no standardized or ritualized versions of praises had been "read" or recited. The editor commented that this way of performing *maulidi* was drawing from some very old Islamic traditions in Syria and Egypt, where one or several sheikhs take turns to speak out in public, commemorating different aspects of the Prophet's achievements—as thus the critique of unacceptable innovation (*bidaa*) did not apply. *Sauti ya Haki* suggested this procedure as a possible pathway for *maulidi* celebrations in East Africa in the future, in which all Muslims could participate with good conscience, and it invited readers' opinions on this suggestion.[40] There was no proper follow-up discussion on this idea as such, but similar reports and commentaries on the issue continued.

In general, the discussions in *Sauti ya Haki*, on this and other topics, turned angry or bitter in tone whenever claims to superior rights over other Muslims that were attributed to local *masharifu* were mentioned. These were matters that kept the two main groups apart.

Sheikh Abdallah Saleh Farsy as Contested Figure

In *Sauti ya Haki*'s debates, different ideas about privileges and social hierarchies, as much as different interpretations of Islam, kept the *masharifu* and the modernist factions apart. The *Sauti ya Haki* readings also show us how differences between them manifested themselves publicly in controversies over Sheikh Abdalla Saleh Farsy, who had been successful in attracting many Muslim youths to the reformist cause. Moreover, he had also criticized the *masharifu* and their insistence on a superior social status over others, and he sought to overcome the perpetuation of dependencies that went along with it, by means of educational campaigns.[41] Most controversially to the *masharifu*, he had completed and published a Swahili translation of the Qur'an in 1969 (responding to a Swahili translation that the regionally influential Ahmadiyya had published, in 1956). Leaders of the *masharifu* faction rejected this, denying the need and value for any written translation. In response, some of them passionately criticized Sheikh Farsy in their classes and public lectures, as well as in a rare pamphlet.[42] They cast him as lacking knowledge, and also as *mgeni*, "outsider," picking on his Zanzibari origin—a recurring motif commented upon in the pages of *Sauti ya Haki* (see also Bakari 1995). Such controversies, which can be linked back to issues about access to knowledge of the Qur'an (with *ulama* enabling or controlling it), were flourishing during *Sauti ya Haki*'s years of activity.

The *masharifu* faction complained that the reformists were given support by the government, which had reaffirmed the status and public standing of Sheikh Farsy as chief *kadhi*. The newspaper carried recurrent reports and commentaries on verbal attacks on Farsy by the *masharifu* faction, who intended to undermine his authority. One case is reported about a certain sheikh from Lamu who was upset about Sheikh Farsy's opposition to the custom of reading sura *talqin* for a recently deceased person. He is said to have come to Mombasa, gathered Bajuni youth around himself and encouraged them to disrespect Sheikh Farsy, casting him as an outsider who did not deserve to be followed (Jan. 1976, 8). On the same page, the editors announced that a previous agreement between scholars of both factions to refrain from attacking each other (*ilikubaliwa kuwa isiweko tena kushabuliana katika mikutano na majukwaa*) was no more valid. The idea had been to have all matters of concern raised and aired through the public platform and mediatory "tongue" (*ulimi*) of *Sauti ya Haki*. This had been announced in *Sauti ya Haki* (no. 3), but it was said that the peace agreement had not been honored by the opponents. The editors announced that *Sauti ya Haki* would respond in kind.

These tensions continued. In late 1976, Farsy resigned from his position as chief *kadhi* (saying he wanted to retire and live with his children in Oman), but after the government requested him to continue, *Sauti ya Haki* announced with gratitude that he had accepted to be reinstated (January 1977, 8). In January 1978, *Sauti ya Haki* published a celebratory article on Farsy's Swahili Qur'an translation and commentary (*tafsir*), by a scholar who had the reputation of being very critical of Farsy, Sheikh Ali Seneda (Gunda). Yet this article went overboard with praise, claiming that Sheikh Farsy had achieved a veritable "revolution" (*mapinduzi*) with this work. In particular, he appreciated how Farsy had managed to capture the aspects related to *tauhid* (the doctrine of God's unity), also by spelling out how inattention to them could lead to instances of undue innovation in religion (*bidaa*), whose common forms he identified to make people aware. Sheikh

Gunda (Jan. 1978, 1–2, 8) also praised Farsy for managing to reemphasize the egal-ity (*usawa*) of all Muslims, against what he called a "superiority complex" (English in the original) of the *masharifu*; and against the "inferiority complex" of others, who acted as blind followers of the former and accepted their claims. Farsy was said to fight these attitudes and to seek to bring people back "to respect[ing] each other without discriminating against each other" (*kuheshimiana kati yao bila ya kubaguwana*), so that they could unite again. In advocating the divine command that people "should desist from insulting each other, and resist being treated with contempt" (*waache kudharauliyana na wasikubali kudharauliwa*), Sheikh Farsy was pushing for social egality—and that is why people from these two groups (with inferiority and superiority complexes) disliked and attacked him so much (p. 2), as he forced them to rethink the world they lived in.[43]

This pattern of social critique of the opponents in combination with a defense of Sheikh Farsy was repeated in an article in January 1981 (pp. 1–3). Here, the opponents of Sheikh Farsy were scolded for not accepting the authority of the chief *kadhi* whom the government appointed on their behalf, and who was well qualified through his Islamic knowledge. Indeed, the article insisted, knowl-edge about Islam must be the decisive factor for worldly and religious guidance for Muslims, because it is this knowledge alone that can assure them to be on the right path (not going against God's will). This also meant that the obligation to forbid each other (*kukanyana*) should be taken seriously, when one witnesses one's peers about to do wrong—a wrong that one can identify based on one's knowledge. It was not permissible to let others practice Islam as they liked, if this contradicted one's knowledge about what is right (Jan. 1981, 3). The community was thought to disintegrate if the principle of "forbidding wrong" was not fol-lowed, and if, as had recently happened, Muslims turned to the police and asked them to resolve their conflicts for them (in one case, about drums being used in a mosque). How should these secular powers ever provide an authoritative answer and proper guidance for internal disagreements among Muslims?

While Sheikh Farsy was cast as a pillar of knowledge (*elimu*), social egality (*usawa*), and unity (*umoja*) by *Sauti ya Haki*, opponents took him as a rhetorical reference point to represent adversity within East African Islam, an oppositional figure and "outsider" (*mgeni*), whose position (as chief *kadhi*, and as modernizer) was also seen as partly sanctioned and guarded by the government.[44] Thus strong and effective rhetorical motifs of a power struggle were inserted into a debate that on the surface was about knowledge as a basis for proper behavior and agree-able ritual practice. Use of polemics seemed inevitable between two oppositional groups here, yet for individual believers who sought orientation, this made things more confusing.[45] The social effects of this remain visible until a later historical point in time, as the presence of polemics in the public negotiation of knowl-edge increased further (see chapter 5). At the end of 1981, however, Sheikh Farsy announced his final leave from the office of chief *kadhi* (Jan. 1982, 5) and was given a grateful farewell by *Sauti ya Haki*, in an extensive article that described his overarching achievement on behalf of all Kenyan Muslims, including the recognition of Idd-el-Fitri as a public holiday by the government (p. 8).

The Death of Sheikh Muhammad Kasim and the End of *Sauti ya Haki*

Sauti ya Haki came to a sudden end when Sheikh Muhammad Kasim Mazrui died in Mombasa on April 5, 1982. In *Sauti ya Haki*'s obituary, he is remembered as a "light of Islam in East Africa" (*alikuwa taa ya islamu katika Afrika ya Mashariki*; May 1982, p. 1), a leading figure who followed in the footsteps of his famous teacher, Sheikh Al-Amin Mazrui, by "releasing people from the bad effects of ignorance and bringing them into light." He is portrayed as not being content with just faith (*imani*) in God, reminding people again and again that it was the intellect (*akili*)—the faculty of reasoning—that differentiated human beings from animals (p. 2).[46] In his view, it was sinful not to use this properly, and he is said to have advocated that "not employing the human intellect for cleaning and ordering one's faith was against the way God had created human beings" (*kutoipalilia imani na akili tuliopewa ni kwenda kinyume na maumbile ya binadamu*; p. 2). Following previous reformers, like Sheikh Al-Amin Mazrui and Sheikh Ali bin Nafi Mazrui (d. 1894), his activities had been geared toward bringing about a "revolution of thought" (*mapinduzi ya fikra*) in his own community, a revolution that aimed at social change, and toward the overcoming of ignorance and traditionalism to achieve a more just society.[47]

Through his work on *Sauti ya Haki*, the obituary goes on, Sheikh Muhammad Kasim sought to provide Muslims with some sense of being able to measure and assess, for themselves, and with a critical mind (lit. "eyes of intelligence": *macho ya akili*), the sorry state their own society was in, and work toward change. To the extent that *Sauti ya Haki* was successful in this—as the obituary says—it was Sheikh Muhammad Kasim who succeeded in pursuing these aims. The obituary ends in citing his most important publications (among them, biographical pamphlets on the first four caliphs, and a brief history of slavery in Islam), noting in conclusion that he had also been busy with his own Swahili translation of the Qur'an.[48]

Despite Sheikh Muhammad Kasim's death, it was intended to continue *Sauti ya Haki*. Sheikh Abdilahi Nassir was announced to take over as editor. He was a former politician and managing editor (with Oxford University Press) and publisher based in Nairobi, as well as a former student and confidant of the deceased.[49] Yet the only issue that Sheikh Abdilahi would actually oversee in publication happened to be the next and final one, in November 1982. Coincidentally, this covered the death of Sheikh Abdallah Saleh Farsy (on Nov. 8, 1982), who only that January had retired from being chief *kadhi* of Kenya and returned to his family home in Oman (where he was said to be missing his Swahili environment dearly). This final issue carried the headline "And I Have Died!" (*Na mimi nime-fariki!*), an exclamation made by Sheikh Farsy when he heard about the death of his friend Sheikh Muhammad Kasim.

The editorial obituary on Sheikh Farsy emphasized the immeasurable loss to the East African Muslim community caused by the death of these two scholars. Yet it also appealed to the readers not to despair, but to continue with their agenda in their spirit, and to look forward with confidence. Sheikh Farsy was praised for his vast knowledge and his skillful writing. His leading position as an influential Islamic writer in Kiswahili, following the example of Sheikh Al-Amin, was highlighted for recognition (he published over forty Islamic pamphlets, next to his popular Swahili translation of the Qur'an from 1969). But the most endearing impression is brought across when the author emphasizes Sheikh Farsy's ability to share his knowledge generously, with all kinds of people, whether in the mosque, the street, or the marketplace. As the author put it, celebrating his generosity, Sheikh Farsy was "Sheikh Give, not Sheikh Bring" (*sheikh toa, si sheikh lete*), a giving, not a taking (demanding) sheikh. This applied not only to the knowledge and advice he gave but also to material wealth: He gave away to the needy whatever he earned, and he died without any properties or riches.

After the death of these two regional leaders of Islamic reform, it was hard to keep the momentum going, of continued publishing for this cause, without any appropriate person able to take over. The designated editor, Sheikh Abdilahi Nassir, was not to continue, for practical reasons (as he was based in Nairobi and the newspaper in Mombasa). Later in the 1980s, he turned to Shiism, and he became a central figure for the growing community of Swahili and African Shii converts in East Africa.[50]

The end of *Sauti ya Haki*, following the death of the two editors, can also be seen as the end of the project of maintaining a common discursive medium for public Islamic discussions among the wider constituency of Swahili-speaking Shafii Muslims on the Kenyan coast and beyond, at least for some time to come.[51] What became visible and more and more dominant during the 1980s and into the 1990s were somewhat "directive" influences of transnational Islam in the region, as Swahili Islamic pamphlets have frequently been externally funded by ideological missionary networks (especially from Saudi Arabia, Iran, and Pakistan). In translation or as commissioned works by associated East African scholars, these directly represented the ideological standpoints and agendas of these groups. Thus the internal divisions among the subgroups of East African Muslims also become reshaped along the lines of such transnational influences and activities (see also Bakari 1995), and the regional Muslim constituency inadvertently witnessed ideological battles with mutual attacks and veritable mud-slinging that took place in Swahili translations of "missionary" pamphlets commissioned, financed, and distributed in the thousands by the networks of the two rival Islamic superpowers, Saudi Arabia and Iran, vying for adherents in what they saw as the East African periphery of the Muslim world (see Kresse 2009, 84–86).

In terms of print media, *Sauti ya Haki* represented the last common discursive platform for public Islamic debates among the coastal Kenyan Muslim community for a long time, until the *Friday Bulletin*, which covered the whole of Kenya, began publication in Nairobi during the mid-1990s; its form and topical structure can be seen to follow *Sauti ya Haki* as a role model. Later, after the end of the Moi era (from 2003), it was Mombasa's newly emerging Islamic radio stations, *Radio Rahma* and *Radio Salaam* (initiated between 2004 and 2006), that again provided common discursive bases for public debate, at a time when the sharp ideological attacks of local Salafi-oriented groups (e.g., Ansaar Sunna, Ahlul Sunna, "Muslim youth"), commonly called "Wahhabi" by everyone else, on local Sufi and Shii adherents had toned down somewhat.

Concluding Reflections

Reflecting upon the impact and relevance of *Sauti ya Haki* leads to a focus on strong internal tensions between its normative reformist demands and its actual effects upon the community. The Islamic demand of "forbidding wrong" to each other (*kukanyana maovu*) that the paper followed not only represents a general obligation among all Muslims. Its basic motif of being mutually alert and conscientious in one's awareness vis-à-vis each other can be understood as rooted in common social interaction more generally (greetings, conversations, *baraza* discussions, didactic poetry, speeches, and lectures), as I laid out earlier on. On this basis, *Sauti ya Haki* responded to—and at the same time expressed and discursively performed the demand of—"forbidding wrong," which itself was also a justification for its publication.

Vis-à-vis its readers, *Sauti ya Haki* makes an exclusive claim to possessing correct and proper (i.e., divinely sanctioned) knowledge that needs to be heeded for people to be "good Muslims." While the arguments in its articles are largely well worked out and convincing, the opponents' position is often ridiculed, satirized, or otherwise described as unworthy. This is problematic, since while claiming to act as a unifying "tongue of the *umma*"—on behalf of all Muslims of the region—this is part of a specific doctrinal agenda, which in practice ultimately divides the regional community between its followers and dissenters. We can find this underlying many articles in *Sauti ya Haki*. Under the mantle of the need to create Muslim unity, also vis-à-vis the "upcountry Christian government," a discursive terrain is mapped out where ultimately the opposing Muslims seem to be left only with the choice of either becoming an integral part of the reform project or being cast as "enemies" of the good cause of "justice" (*haki*) that *Sauti ya Haki* is the voice of. Ultimately, the normative terms that could shape Muslim unity here seem quite fixed and unquestionable after all.

This rereading of Sheikh Muhammad Kasim is somewhat in contrast with my earlier work on him and his related writings that preceded and fed into *Sauti ya Haki* publications (Kresse 2003). There, I highlighted his rationalist stance and its liberating intent, and an inherent dialectic turn to the dogmatic as part of his far-reaching critique of supposedly wrong or misguided practices. At the same time, I also pointed to the understanding of him as a moderate reformist who makes a point of mediating (and adjusting) his reformist messages for his East African audience, and also expressing understanding for people's attachment to ritual practices that he, as a reformist of a stricter kind, would have to reject. What we see in the writings of Sheikh Muhammad (and his close collaborator, Sheikh A. S. Farsy) is a particular East African, Swahili form of Islamic reformism, casting itself as a rationalism that seeks to liberate (and empower) the underprivileged and lesser-educated Muslims by providing more direct access to the knowledge and education they need for their personal guidance. It is publicly critical of what it sees as wrong (misconceived or innovative) practices by local Muslims, due to a lack of proper knowledge and education, but it is nevertheless tolerant of a range of local customs and understandings (particularly with a view to *maulidi*). However, this is just one side of the story.

A related and perhaps no less powerful effect of *Sauti ya Haki*'s articles may well have been one of accentuating existent divisions within the Muslim community. The question arises whether this double bind—proclaiming unity while perpetuating disunity—is the inevitable outcome of an agenda of reform that pushes for knowledge and education along certain lines and particular convictions of critique, and a vision of Islam that cannot be shared by all Muslims in the region. After all, it is a vision of Islam that is in opposition to that practiced by many local Muslims, thus also negating what they stand for. Highlighting difference and fundamental internal tensions obstructs it from the possibility of achieving communal unity (as advocacy of unity on one's own terms indeed will not yield unity). Understanding the reform project of *Sauti ya Haki* in its wider social-historical context and timeline leads us back to the idea of dialectic as a useful leitmotif to think with after all.[52] For it is through negation, and the consecutive negation of negation, of certain crucial beliefs and practices within the community, that change and social transformation is achieved. Yet the kind of change actually achieved rarely ever matches the extent of change aimed for.

As we have seen, *Sauti ya Haki*'s dual role, of providing a public platform for education and debate among regional Muslims, as well as pushing a reformist agenda that defined itself in contrast to a large part of the regional Muslim constituency, accentuated internal tensions that could not be balanced out. Nevertheless, by making accessible to a wide audience of ordinary Muslims the relevant textual sources, of Qur'an and *hadith*, in the regional language (through translations and reprints), and by adding a sizable collection of *fatawa* and articles addressing topics of concern for East African Muslims in the here and now, the Swahili Islamic discursive tradition was greatly substantiated. The texts of *Sauti ya Haki* and the related educational publications and Swahili translations constitute a large resource of authoritative reference points that provided guidance to many ordinary Muslims. They were enabled to access this resource on their own, and they became less dependent on local sheikhs making selective interpretations on their behalf (and sometimes for their own benefit, as *Sauti ya Haki* criticized). Having access, they themselves could engage in the defining processes of negotiating and determining their own position in a wider field of options and possibilities, by picking up on the reasoning and arguing patterns offered in *Sauti ya Haki* in their own intellectual practice.

To conclude with a view to the relevant features of intellectual practice in *Sauti ya Haki* and the kind of public that it constituted, looking at the negotiation of knowledge and the exchange of arguments performed here, three perspectives stand out (which I will only briefly point out here and pick up again in the concluding chapter).

Firstly, we have seen that particular figures and personalities were crucial points of reference, in articles and debates. Largely, these were Sheikh Al-Amin Mazrui, Sheikh Muhammad Kasim Mazrui, and Sheikh Abdalla Saleh Farsy, the key figures of regional Islamic modernism (while their opponents featured only indirectly, and contributing authors, like Prof. Hyder, have to be kept in mind). They mattered as authors (who were cited or countered), as role models or their opposite (like Sheikh Farsy for his opponents), or as social activists; and their intellectual biographies, doctrinal orientation, and ethnic and family backgrounds mattered as well.

Secondly, we could observe common patterns of reasoning being employed, in the kinds of arguments and critiques presented. For instance, there was frequent use of the emphatic mutual attention expressed by the Swahili verb ending -ana, most prominently perhaps *kukanyana* (to forbid each other) and *kuheshimiana* (to respect each other). Grammatically, it expresses mutual causation and implies moral obligations within the community. These stylistic forms of moral speech were also used rhetorically, as I discussed, to make one's point and push one's position in a situation of social competition and ideological rivalries. In such discursive disputes, an overlap, and even a blurring into each other, of the fields of knowledge and rhetoric is often observable (see Kresse 2008).

Thirdly, Swahili key concepts to think with, in the engagement for an envisaged future society to be proud of, were also presented and discussed. *Usawa*, for instance, denoting social equality, was central for *Sauti ya Haki*'s critique of unjustified social hierarchies and dependencies, and its engagement for a more open and more just society. *Haki*, meaning "justice" in Swahili but also having connotations of "truth" (as an Arabic loanword), is a central programmatic term for the reform agenda pursued here and features prominently in the journal's title; finally, *haki* also means "right(s)" and is often cited in political slogans. And *elimu* has been a central term throughout the whole process of this reform agenda. It is on the basis of the knowledge and education (both *elimu*) of the reformist leading figures here that these pursued the agenda of spreading *elimu* so that it could be acquired and employed by ordinary Muslims independently for their own orientation and liberation, thus ultimately for their realization of a more just (*ya haki*) and equal (*ya usawa*) society.

These three ways of framing arguments and making points vis-à-vis each other in public debate constitute important conceptual pathways through which we can reflect more on the contrasts and similarities between regional Muslim actors here, and the (historical and linguistic) continuities of intellectual practice.

As for the workings of *Sauti ya Haki* as a specific Muslim public and media platform, we can summarize and highlight some main aspects in relation to Sheikh Al-Amin's pamphlets of a generation before that were discussed above. While this print publication is partisan and involved in pushing a modernist agenda of reform, the local Islamic voices it opposes, resists and responds to, as ideological opponents and rivals, become audible here too, even if indirectly and by means of reports by *Sauti ya Haki* authors. As rivals, these other knowledge specialists are also central to—yet remarkably absent from—the discursive negotiations in the newspaper itself. As mentioned, *Sauti ya Haki* did include readers' letters to the editor in each issue, yet these were never truly controversial and mostly providing supplementary points and aspects for a previous editorial or article. The scope of residences from which these writers sent their letters was admirably wide-ranging and included relatively faraway places like the Comoros, the Hadramaut, Burundi, and Uganda. However, their letters largely complemented rather than challenged *Sauti ya Haki*'s agenda. Thus, while multiple voices and authors became publicly visible and were seen to participate in a public discursive negotiation of Islam in the newspaper—in notable contrast to the sole and authoritarian leadership and authorship performed by Sheikh Al-Amin in his publications—this, as it featured, did not constitute a true and direct debate of mutual engagements and challenges, as the positions and arguments of the opponents' side were only ever indirectly reported and summarized. Thus the public perception of these opponents in the newspaper remained reliant upon *Sauti ya Haki*'s reformist writers. Their agenda and the selection of topics covered continued to follow the role model of their deceased teacher, Sheikh Al-Amin.

In comparison to Sheikh Al-Amin's pamphlets, noting an emerging multiplicity of Muslim voices in public is important here, even if this does not (yet) indicate a pluralism of competing agendas of reform. Still, a sense of multiple audible voices and positions in these debates does open up opportunities for more actual pluralization later on. The contributions to *Sauti ya Haki* were written, selected, and edited to fit its cause and push its agenda. What we can see manifesting itself more and more over the decade of *Sauti ya Haki*'s publication is the coordinated effort to gradually establish the editor's understanding of a specific purifying agenda of reforming the local Muslim community, following the footprints of Sheikh Al-Amin Mazrui, as the dominant public Islamic discourse of the region. From that point, Sheikh Muhammad Kasim and his followers are seeking to overcome the strong and socially embedded Sufi traditions that include a variety of performances they regard as *bidaa*. Dominating the local print-based public discourse on Islam, also due to a remarkable reluctance by Sufi rivals to employ print media to engage in discussion, may well have given the modernist reformists an edge of superior presence in public discourse overall. At the same time—as we can anticipate from reading *Sauti ya Haki* (and as I was assured by interlocutors)—the field of oral discourse, in sermons, lectures, and *baraza* discussions, will have been more evenly and hotly contested.

Notes

1. We should keep the qualifications of flexibility to "tradition" in mind, as discussed in the introduction (using, e.g., Asad 1986, Haj 2009, Hountondji 1983). For the other group, as we have already seen (chapter 3), the term "modernist" also conveys an adequate initial sense of the self-understanding of its members, who advocate modernization on Islamic terms and reject imitative Westernization. Considering specific details, about individual figures who do not fit well into such a simple grid, a more complex and ultimately more adequate perspective can then be gradually developed. For instance, Said Omar Abdalla (d. 1988), who ran the Muslim Academy in Zanzibar, studied in London, and later lived in Paris and the Comoros, was embedded in Alawiyya Sufi traditions while also engaged in secular studies and open to modernist influences (Bakari 2006). Also, the pathways of two grand-sons of Habib Saleh in Lamu, Sayyid Hassan Badawy and Mzee Mwenye, who broke with their brothers at Riyadha Mosque and founded the Shia-oriented Swafaa Mosque in the 1980s (which now has a populous following), point to specific and complex trajectories yet to be studied and understood in context. Finally, some of the recent Salafi-oriented reformists in Kenya can be traced back not to the Mombasa-based faction but to Ustadh Harith Swaleh, who shaped his own reformist critique before and after studying in Sudan (initially in the Bajuni area) (Swaleh 2012). He taught people such as the influential Sheikh Ahmed Msallam, a long-term translator for the Saudi Arabian embassy who openly endorsed "Wahhabism," by publishing a booklet with the title *Huo ndiyo Uwahhabi* (*This Is Wahhabism*).
  2. See el-Zein 1974; Bang 2003.
  3. These terms were explained in the introduction.
  4. See Kindy (1972, 119); M. K. Mazrui (1980, ix; 1995, 2).
  5. As Kurzmann (2002) and others have argued, the Islamic modernists advocated social and technological modernization on Islamic terms (that they had to work out and define) but

not Westernization, which they decried as simple copying of practices and processes of social organization. See also Hourani 1983.

6. For a longer commentary on the proverb, and on *utu*, see Kresse 2007, chapter 5.

7. See Kresse 2009; Lambek 1990; Lonsdale 1992b; also Tripp 2006, after Scott 1976.

8. Interview with Munir Mazrui, July 2010.

9. Kresse 2003; n.d.

10. We know that, generally, letters to the editor have often been used by editors to push their own cause further (by means of amendments, manipulations, fabrications, and so on; see, e.g., Bromber 2009, for colonial British Swahili war press, WWII). Here too, the section may have been used in this way, though the names and addresses of letter writers were provided. I have not been able to verify this either way.

11. Interview with Munir Mazrui, July 2010.

12. Actually, it almost always came out every four months.

13. Swahili original: "*Sauti ya Haki: 1. Ni Ulimi wa Umma wa Kiislam; 2. Itakupa Mafunzo muhimu na yaliyosahihi katika dini yako; 3.* Itakupa tafsiri ya Hadith za Mtume Wako za kukufahamisha mengi katika Dini, na kukufunza tabia njema za Kiislam; *4. Ukisoma gazeti hili killa linapotoka, utakuwa Mwislam wa Kweli, Mwenye Ghera ya Dini Yako, na asiyekubali kudanganywa na vibaraka vya shetani.—Linatoka kila miezi mitatu. USIKOSE KULISOMA!*" (from No. 4, May 1973; p. 8).

14. This has widely been covered; for example, by Biersteker (1996) and Samsom (1996).

15. See the Swahili translations of Maududi (e.g., 1974), funded and printed by the UK-based Islamic Foundation with a branch in Nairobi. See also Calvert 2010. Interview, Sheikh Ustadh Harith, July 1999. Interview, Sheikh Abdilahi Nassir, November 1998; June 2005.

16. In an essay titled "*Mali, ilmu na tabia njema*" (orig. August 1931), Sheikh Al-Amin had argued that wealth (*mali*), knowledge (*ilmu*), and good character (*tabia njema*) had to be well balanced vis-à-vis each other so that agreeable social and economic progress could be achieved (*Uwongozi* no. 21).

17. For explicit usages, see, for example, *Uwongozi* no. 8, 19, 21, 25. For a commentary essay on the shifts of meaning in the use of this concept in Rashid Rida's writing, see Hamza 2013. More generally, Salvatore and Eickelman (2006); Khadduri's (2007) entry on "*maslah,*" in the *Encyclopedia of Islam*.

18. This had first been published as a book, probably in the late 1930s, but there is no date of publication given with the edition that I had access to: *Hadithi zilizochguliwa* (Selected *Hadith*), selected and translated by Sheikh Al-Amin Mazrrui, edited by Sheikh Muhammad Kasim Mazrui, Mombasa.

19. His name is spelled like this in *Sauti ya Haki*: Yahya bin Sharafudin Nawawy.

20. *Juzuu ya umma* (Mazrui 2001), still used and available in Islamic bookshops. On his response to the challenge of Christian missionary and Ahmadiyya translation projects of the Qur'an, see chapter 3. On Swahili Qur'an translations/commentaries, see Lacunza Balda 1997.

21. Swahili original: *Elimu zao zikakoma pale vilipokoma vitabu vya masheikh wao, na fikiri zao zikakosa Uhuru.*

22. We can observe the common use of "Wahhabi" as an insult word in East Africa. In response, some East African scholars have adopted it as a positive self-identifying label (e.g., Muhammad Kasim Mazrui 1971; see concluding chapter below). See also Kresse 2008.

23. In the same way as the insult is used here, against Hadrami Alawiyya *masharifu* as, ultimately, destroyers and oppressors, I have witnessed this argument being used against so-called Wahhabi reformists.

24. My understanding of *fatwa* literature in this section is informed by Gräf 2010 (esp. 41–75) and Messick 1993 (136–140, 149–150). The point of viewing *fatwa* literature as a particularly illustrative entry point to the understanding of Muslim communities, as their "marketplaces" for testing ideas, was emphasized by Werner Ende, personal communication, Berlin, April 2016. Building on Messick (1993) and others, M. Q. Zaman (2002, 31–37) has highlighted that the Western colonial period brought about a paradigm shift as to how a flexible and processual understanding of *sharia* (Islamic law) has switched to a more static and content-focused one.

25. See Fuchs, de Jong, and Knappert (2007), entry on *"mawlid"* in the *Encyclopedia of Islam 2*.

26. Vgl. Bang 2003; 2014.

27. On Indian Ocean print cultures, see also Hofmeyr et al. 2011, and for a case study on Gandhi's consciousness-building popular printing press project in South Africa, see Hofmeyr 2013. On the impact of print on Islam in South Asia, see Robinson 1993.

28. This would be the book edited by I. M Lewis (former professor of social anthropology at LSE, University of London), published in London in 1966. Titles and author names of the other two books are (almost) correct (Knappert, Leiden 1971; Trimingham, Oxford 1964; Mbiti, London 1969).

29. *Muradi na maneno haya ni kusema kwamba maadui wa dini ya Islam hawajui aibu za Waislamu ila wakati zikanywapo katika Sauti ya Haki. Hili si sawa kabisa. Maadui wa Islamu huzunguka wenyewe katika miji ya kiislamu kutafuta aibu zetu kisha wakaziandika katika vitabu vyao. Kama hujui haya soma "Islam in East Africa" cha Trimingham uone jinsi alivyoitangamanisha dini ya Islam na mila ya kishenzi kisha akaikoroga pamoja—Na kama haya ameyafanya KNAPPERT mwenye kitabu kiitwacho SWAHILI ISLAMIC POETRY na CUNNING katika kitabu kiitawacho ISLAM IN TROPICAL AFRICA. Na hapa twakuletea kwa ufupi maneno aliyosema Rev. John Mbiti katika kitabu chake AFRICAN RELIGIOUS (sic) AND PHILOSOPHY kilichochapishwa 1968.*

30. *"Inaonesha wazi kuwa itikadi za Kiislamu zimetanganywa na zile za dini za Kiasli."*

31. *"Ijapokuwa wana ujuzi mzuri wa Kur'an na sharia lakini ujuzi huu hautoshi kuwawezesha wao kuieleza dini yao katika ulimwengu wa kisasa."*

32. The same kind of conversion narratives and dilemmas seemingly enforced by Muslim spirits upon Giriama Mijikenda has been documented and discussed by Janet McIntosh (2009; also 2004).

33. *"Waislam katika jimbo hili wako tini ya guu la Ukristo hawataharraki, wametulia kama maji ya mtungini wala hawatukutishi kilichotulia. Ni maiti wasiotarajiwa kufufuka mpaka siku ya kufufuliwa wafu!"*

34. A reference is not provided here.

35. Swahili original: *"Manyani ni nyama madhalili, waoga, wajinga na wapendao kuigiza. Na sifa hizi zote tunazo sisi Waislamu hivi leo. Na hapana sababu illa ileile ya kuvunda amri ya Mwenyezi Mungu ya Kukanyana maovu."* This critical take on a passive habit of imitating others can be compared to a similar piece by Sheikh Al-Amin, written in 1930 for *Sahifa*, criticizing the mindless imitation of the bad habits of the British, which again resonates with similar Pan-Islamic writings in Arabic at the time (*Uwongozi* no. 4, 'Namna gani twaigiza wazungu?' Mazrui 1955, 6–8; cf. Arslan 1930); see chapter 3.

36. This is said to be the outcome of a meeting that Chief *Kadhi* Sheikh Abdallah Saleh Farsy had with the president on December 15, 1976. The editor expressed relief on behalf

of Kenyan Muslims that a previously envisaged change of law was not implemented, due
to the president's generosity and mercy (*huruma*). Said law would have fundamentally
disenfranchised Muslims from running their own legal family affairs in their accustomed
ways (which before Independence had also been assured in writing, by Kenyatta, to all
subjects of the sultan of Zanzibar living in the Coastal Strip; see also appendix in Kindy 1972).

37. Critique of the government itself would have to be clad in general (and thus sufficiently
vague) expressions, or to be written in special Swahili idioms and metaphors that concealed
the target or the character of the criticism to outsiders.

38. Indeed, this reminder of human temporality resonates a lot with Abdilatif Abdalla's
famous poem *Mamba* on Kenyatta, written in prison where he was put after criticizing Kenyatta
as dictator in November 1968. The poem describes an old and sly and all-powerful crocodile
(*mamba*) yet reminds people that this creature too will have to die someday (Abdalla 1973).

39. President Moi was there during election campaigns for the regional MP, and he
addressed a recent tragic local shipping accident, in which over thirty young women had
drowned during a celebratory daylong campaign trip. The article commented on some
disturbing reactions by local political rivals, who apparently initially rejoiced upon hearing
the news. This accident has also been remembered in an *utendi* poem "*Ajali iliyotokea*,"
performed by Mohamed Kadara, recordings of which are still circulating in Lamu.

40. It is possible that these celebrations became the precursor to the now common joint
public *maulidi* celebrations in Mombasa, conducted together by all Islamic groups based in
the town, where groups of Qur'anic schools take turns to recite praises, after speeches given
by senior representatives, but no joint public ritual activity is performed.

41. See Lacunza Balda 1990; Loimeier 2009, 375–400; Kresse 2003; Kresse 2008.

42. *Fimbo ya Musa* (1970), by Sayyid Ahmed Ahmed Badawy ("Mwenye Baba").
Interlocutors from Lamu remembered the oral attacks.

43. Another oral public discussion about Sheikh Farsy's Qur'an translation was reported
on in January 1980 (p. 8). One opponent was said to have insisted that one should cut the *tu*
(only) out of the translation of the *sura fatiha*—leading to amusement in response, as this
would be violating the central principle of *tawhid*.

44. Apparently the Alawiyya leaders were offended that Farsy came to Kenya upon
the direct offer of the highly coveted position of chief *kadhi* by the government, on the
instigation and recommendation of Sheikh Muhammad Kasim, who was the previous chief
kadhi (Loimeier 2009, 395–400). These kinds of struggles about prestigious positions between
the rival groups were prominent in the colonial era (Mwakimako 2010) and continued in the
postcolonial period. Thus the ways in which strategic or pragmatic alliances with the state
and its power could be made useful for the standing and impact of the reformist project need
to be kept in view.

45. This is also an impression I received from many conversations with local Muslims.
It seems that the 1980s (and 1990s) were a period of accentuation and radicalization of such
existent oppositions and rhetorical battles between regional "Wahhabis" and Sufis and
modernists (in which later, gradually, Shii Ithnashari converts became a force to reckon
with). For a historical sketch and the relevance of rhetoric in the negotiation of knowledge,
see also Kresse 2008.

46. "*Na hapa ndipo tuwezapo kufahamu umuhimu wa al-marhum kwa umma wa Islamu
wa hapa kwetu. Kwani al-marhum hatosheki kwa imani tu. Alikuwa akisisitiza kuwa jambo
limtafautishalo binadamu na nyama ni akili*" (p. 2).

47. *Kwa kufuata za watalaamu kama Sheikh Al-Amin, Ali bin Nafi, na wengineyo basi, Sheikh al-marhum Muhammad Kasim alikuwa na lengo ya kuleta mapinduzi ya kifikra katika jumuiya yake, mapinduzi yatakayowakomboa na pinga za ujinga na taasubi zilizowakabili ili wajibidiishe kuleta mabaliko yatakayoona na ndia ya haki.*

48. *Historia ya watumwa katika Uislamu na dini nyingine* (M. Mazrui 1970).

49. His publishing house Shungwaya Publishers published the completed sections of Sheikh Al-Amin Mazrui's translation of the Qur'an (1980; 1981).

50. Interview, July 2010. Nassir 2003a; 2003b; 1989a; 1989b; 1990; see also Kresse 2007, chapter 6.

51. In the early 1990s, the *Message* and the *Muslim Voice*, two bilingual English/Swahili newspapers close to the Islamic Party of Kenya (IPK), which were published irregularly, took over such a function, and from the mid-1990s, the Tanzania-based *An-Nuur* (in Swahili) was commonly read in Kenya as well. From the late 1990s, the weekly anglophone eight-page *Friday Bulletin*, published from Jamia Mosque in Nairobi, took over the role of a national representative weekly newspaper for Kenya's Sunni Muslims.

52. See Kresse 2003.

5 "Get Educated with Stambuli!"

An Open Discussion Platform on Local Islamic Radio, 2005–07

A New Space and Time: Radio in the Hopeful Post-Moi Era

This chapter turns to the more recent past, and to the spoken word creating and sustaining a public, as we look at vivid debates on a Mombasan Islamic radio station, concerning issues in the contemporary self-understanding of coastal Muslims in postcolonial Kenya. The debates looked at and analyzed in this chapter were initiated and moderated in 2005, by two engaged young laymen, Stambuli and Abubakar, who will be introduced in more detail below.[1] They were neither *ulama* nor returnees from educational institutions in the Middle East. They broadcast their show on the new Islamic radio station in Mombasa called Radio Rahma, which advertised itself as *Sauti ya Ruhuma* in Swahili, and the "Voice of Mercy" in English. This was a time of new hopes and beginnings, as the long-awaited "post-Moi" era in Kenyan politics had recently begun, after the general elections of December 2002. Across the country Kenyans were looking forward to a period beyond authoritarian politics and with more meaningful participation in national politics. This was also the period of public debates about a new constitution, ultimately put in force in 2010. Yet these hopes could not always be realized, and they often ended in disappointment.

Mwai Kibaki, a former vice president under President Moi, became Moi's successor in December 2002. He had won the elections against Moi's protégé, Uhuru Kenyatta, the son of Kenya's first president, Jomo Kenyatta, in whose "footsteps" (*nyayo*) Moi had followed during his autocratic rule that spanned a period of almost twenty-five years. Moi ruled between 1978 and late 2002 under the banner of what he called "*nyayo* politics." In an ideological treatise written after reshaping Kenya into a *de jure* one-party state (in response to a coup attempt in 1982), Moi described *nyayo* politics as framed by the motto of "peace, love and unity" as commanded by a strict and paternal president (Moi 1986; see Ngũgĩ 1987). Moi did not run for president again in 2002, as he had negotiated "golden handshake" agreements (including legal amnesty) in return for his retirement. He stuck to the newly implemented constitutional limit of two terms in office, and he endorsed Kenyatta's son Uhuru (who became president in 2013) as presidential candidate.

Many Kenyans had high hopes for political change in the Kibaki-led post-Moi era (2003–13). But this did not come to much due to the close entanglements of the old and new regimes. As a recent historical account put it, "Moi's men of the future helped keep Kenya stuck in the past" (Branch 2011, 245). The continuous involvement of the same major political players in the same old issues—corruption and ethnic rivalry—soon led to much frustration among ordinary Kenyans throughout the country. As a church leader and critic of the government, Timothy Njoya, wryly commented in 2005 (when the courting period of the new Kibaki government was over) on the spelling of the governing National Rainbow Coalition, it was now clear that NARC really stood for "Nothing Actually Really Changes" (Branch 2011, 258). This expression would stick and often be quoted in public, to characterize the period of the first Kibaki presidency, with corruption being the most emphatic but not the exclusive reference (see also Wrong 2009).

Radio Rahma

Radio Rahma was started in Ramadhan 2004 by Abdulswamad Shariff Nassir, the son of KANU's and President Moi's former main man on the coast, Shariff Nassir (d. 2005). No private radio stations were allowed until the final phase of Moi's rule. However, Islamic programs, and educational and poetry sections of the colonial coastal Swahili radio program *Sauti ya Mvita* based in Mombasa, were very popular among coastal Muslims, not least due to the popular poet, speaker, and moderator Abu Sulaiman (Brennan 2015). Here, I discuss how Radio Rahma, the first private Islamic radio station in Mombasa, was used as a communal discursive platform to address common concerns, to build unity by negotiating internal divisions. Christian radio stations were already sprouting around the country, picking up on the opportunity of more relaxed media laws early on (Branch 2011, 234). All this was set in the ongoing post-9/11 politics with Kenya's participatory role in the US-led "war on terror," which amplified the sense of an ongoing opposition between a Christian upcountry government allied with Western (Christian) powers against its increasingly disenfranchised and discontented Muslim constituency. Muslims had come to be seen and treated more and more generally as potential terrorist suspects or supporters by the government, which collaborated with the United States to the extent of informally handing over Kenyan citizens for interrogation by the Americans, in violation of international law and human rights (Prestholdt 2011). Having come under systematic surveillance after the al-Qaeda terrorist bomb attacks on the US embassies in Nairobi and Dar es Salaam in August 1998 and subsequent terrorist attacks on Israeli tourists in and near Mombasa in November 2002,[2] coastal Muslims had again become, like in the early post-Independence period, a vulnerable minority that was publicly suspect. They needed to prove their allegiance to the state, and their membership in it, in more demanding terms than other Kenyans. Among the most commonly cited examples for this are difficulties in the acquisition of national ID cards and passports: Muslims complained about facing an often clearly impossible task, in having to submit original birth certificates of both sets of parents and grandparents as well as their own, whereas non-Muslim Kenyans only had to show their own birth certificates (e.g., Nassir 2008; see below).

In this context, what was remarkable about the efforts of the radio programs discussed here was the dedication with which they used local Islamic radio as a creative means for opening up public debate within the *umma*—in potentially unifying but also controversial ways. This was not dissimilar to how *Sauti ya Haki* engaged in facilitating debates among Muslims in the 1970s (though that was part of a clearly defined reformist agenda). Here, however, the more accessible discursive space and more flexible ways of direct communication that the radio offered as a medium were taken advantage of, to initiate and cultivate open discussions, also on socially sensitive and contested topics. In doing so, this program was not alone but rather one among a few program initiatives and activities on Radio Rahma (and other stations). A Muslim "women's forum" program, *Ukumbi wa Mamama*, for instance, followed a similar impetus with similar success (Alidou 2013, 145–70). That program used the discursive space they shaped in innovative ways, by interrogating "power relations within the patriarchal Muslim community" and, at the same time, by challenging "the hegemony of the non-Muslim majority" (Alidou 2013, 169). By doing so, important public debates about topics that were not usually addressed in public were generated (e.g., on AIDS, sexuality, women's rights, and reforms of legislation of rape), and this had an empowering effect on the participating and wide-ranging audience of listeners and speakers of different age, gender, status, and ethnic background. Thus in terms of a perspective on the internal dynamics of the community, again, constructive processes of "re-imagining the *umma*" (Mandaville 2001) can be observed, and agendas of social "re-formations" (Meyer 2009) can be analyzed, with a view to the active role that coastal Muslims could and should play, both as members of the Muslim *umma* and as Kenyan citizens.[3]

With the new Kibaki government at the turn of 2002–03, media law relaxations that were begun at the end of the Moi era were formally consolidated, and thus opened up a secure long-term perspective for private media channels in Kenya for the first time. Abdulswamad S. Nassir, the son of the well-known coastal politician Shariff Nassir (d. 2005), who had been KANU's leading representative on the coast as well as Moi's "right hand" and one of his close followers since the 1970s, was granted a license to open a small Islamic radio station based in Mombasa, to broadcast locally. He set up offices for Radio Rahma just across Nyali Bridge, on the northern side of the channel, facing the Old Town area of Mombasa Island. The station began by broadcasting recitations of the Qur'an and religious poetry during the month of Ramadhan in 2004. This was well received within the Muslim community, and the owner felt encouraged to establish a complete time-filling program, consisting of news bulletins, discussions, and phone-ins, as well as educational broadcasts, a women's program, quiz shows on Islamic or Swahili knowledge, and brief advertisements by local businesses, apart from the ongoing element of religious recitations and Islamic music. This included religious (missionary) songs in Swahili, Arabic, and English.

One of Radio Rahma's popular talk radio programs, and the one on which I focus this chapter, was called *Elimika na Stambuli!* (Get Educated with Stambuli!). Its makers were two local men in their late thirties or early forties. They had managed to build up a reputation for their program by successfully engaging a regular and active audience, men and women of different ages who called in or sent text messages to contribute their questions and comments. The two men were Stambuli Abdilahi Nassir, whom I knew well from my previous fieldwork, and Abubakar Amin, who was one of the few full-time employees of the radio station whom I also got to know well. Stambuli, whom I have known for over fifteen years now, provided me with a selection of digital recordings of this weekly live broadcast discussion program, some of which I had also listened to live.

The show was popular with locals, and it seemed to attract a wide demographic spectrum of listeners, as confirmed by my informal conversations with friends and acquaintances and from looking at numbers and profiles of callers and senders. This included a large proportion of women callers (perhaps up to 40 percent) as well as elderly people and even children, all with considered opinions. Indeed, a young boy had called in during the maiden broadcast, telling a personal story to remind people about the need for good neighborhood relations (*ujirani*) and calling upon them to jointly resist against unjust demands and pressures from the local housing authorities. He was often cited and referred to in subsequent broadcasts as a remarkable case of responsible engagement by a child. In terms of circumference, people called in from Mombasa and the surrounding area, up to about Malindi in the north and Ukunda in the south, the towns that roughly marked the endpoints of Radio Rahma's limited reach (unlike today, where it reaches Lamu in the north and Tanga in the south).[4]

The communicative skills of most callers were remarkable, as they were at ease and spoke clearly and confidently when raising their respective issues, comments, and questions (none of the stage fright phenomena we might often encounter in Western contexts, with people conscious of being "live on air"). The tone was much like in a normal social situation in which people were already familiar with each other, like in *baraza* settings, for instance. A sense of openness, frankness (including possible confrontation), and common purpose was cultivated by the moderators, who constructed a kind of "virtual *baraza*" here, with regular attendance of many silent listeners from afar, some of whom would call in now and then and were recognized by others. People sometimes gave themselves names, like one *Mzee wa kawaida* (Ordinary Old Man), though the moderators asked for and preferred their real ones. Callers often spoke up or commented as representative voices of a certain town or neighborhood or age group from particular locations and perspectives.

"Educating Yourself through Others"—the Project and Its Makers

The maiden broadcast of the *"Elimika na Stambuli!"* program in March 2005 introduced the idea and conception of this new public space for open debate. In principle, this was exciting, as the program promised to address a wider audience of ordinary Muslims and take on their concerns, and to discuss them in thematic sessions where people could participate by calling in or writing SMS text messages. So the first broadcast consisted mostly of an extended session of Stambuli and Abubakar brainstorming with the audience, after a brief introduction of the basic idea of the program. The goal was, they said, to educate oneself (*kujielimisha*) by participating, as the title itself already marked: "Get Educated with Stambuli"—*Elimika na Stambuli!* This includes the idea of mutually educating each other (*-elimishana*) among all participants, between moderators and makers on the one side and the listeners on the other, all of them together constituting this new public platform. Saying they would be interested in taking up any suggestions for important topics from their audience, Stambuli and Abubakar encouraged everyone to call in and provide ideas and starting points for discussion. Discussions could touch upon any relevant social, historical, political, or economic matters, and the idea was to inform and educate each other in an ongoing mutual and respectful dialogue. *Elimishana, juzana, pashana,* as common set expressions for educating each other and informing each other, were significant keywords that the moderator Abubakar flagged up in his introduction. Also, the common normative obligation of "commanding right and forbidding wrong" was invoked by some callers, and also by the moderators themselves (e.g., "Brief History of Islam in EA," 29:00; see also chapter 2).

The show was scheduled to be broadcast every Saturday morning between 8:00 and 9:00 for an hour, and during this first show, the two moderators were eager to get ideas from the audience and encouraged all listeners to call. People responded well and called in immediately. Among the first suggestions for discussion was a request by a female caller to address the problem of drug addiction in the community (8:23–9:03). This was an issue that had been causing much grief and worries for many years, throughout the years of Moi's government, she said. Many families were affected, and addictions of local youths had already torn many families apart. And since politicians obviously continued to be reluctant to take up this matter, she urged community members to address this problem together "as Muslims" (*kama Waislamu*). She proceeded to urge listeners to participate in consecutive steps of doing so in joint discursive efforts, from talking with each other (*tuzungumze*), to discussing with each other (*tujadiliane*), toward a joint assessment of a quick solution (*tuangalie suluhisho moja kwa moja*) to see how this problem could be eradicated (*tuone tutalitatoa vipi*). The woman had hoped that now, in the new post-Moi era, things would improve and the government would show more interest and initiate sensible policies, but nothing of the sort was visible. Another female caller expressed concern about the recent spread (or, perhaps, return) of *shirk* practices (*ushirikiana*) in the community (e.g., ritual or healing practices that were interpreted as committing polytheism), and she wanted this to be discussed. And a (probably middle-aged) man requested that a session should address the issue of proper behavior and dress code for men when going to mosque for prayers—he condemned young men wearing football shirts as showing contempt toward their religion.

The moderators responded with appreciation and encouragement, and they promised to pick up these points in subsequent sessions. Stambuli pointed out that there was a saying that in order to rule people, one had to know and use their history. He also touched on the need to understand the history of (school) education on the coast and pointed to earlier local projects of Muslim schools that people were not aware of anymore. For instance, the Mombasa Institute of Muslim Education (MIOME) was initiated in 1951 on Mombasa Island in Tudor with funds largely raised through the various local Muslim communities and donations by wealthy Muslim philanthropists.[5] After Independence, this became the Polytechnic College that was frequented largely by students from upcountry, who usually had better secondary school education and higher final grades than the coastal students. So, on different social fronts, as the two explained, there was an increasing sense of loss of status within national politics among coastal Muslims. With this in mind, the cultivation of a common historical consciousness and a self-confident sense of belonging here, of having indubitable rights as residents and citizens, was also envisaged.

They announced that their broadcast would not accept racist language or a focus on "tribal" divisions (*ukabila*), as it was dedicated to working for the benefit of the local Muslim community on the whole, and thereby to strengthen its unity (*umoja*). They wanted the audience to support this goal, but unlike others, they thought it crucial to openly address issues of concern in order to achieve this unity. They saw themselves engaging in internal critique, for the better of society in the long run. Stambuli pointed out, counting himself in as part of the community he was addressing and critiquing (in a common rhetorical manner), "We are still sleeping" (*bado twalala*; 56:00). In other broadcasts, he would employ this theme and call upon his fellow Muslims to "wake up" (*Amkeni, ndugu zangu!*; Feb. 4, 2006, 21:19). As we have seen before with Sheikh Al-Amin Mazrui using such expressions—and again, his students a generation later—this motif, of the community being in slumber and in need to be woken up, is a reoccurring feature of a certain kind of rhetorical self-positioning by local reformers over time. It is an image that has been used and passed on among them. This can also be seen, for instance, in Sheikh A. S. Farsy's history of regional Shafii *ulama*, where he remembers Sheikh Al-Amin as the one "who uncovered our eyes and who opened our mouths" (Farsy 1972, 45).

The *"Elimika"* maiden broadcast succeeded in stimulating immediate interest in its idea of facilitating a community-wide, self-reflexive discussion, and it did provoke a flow of callers to participate spontaneously, addressing issues and concerns that they seemed to have held for some time. Thus the possibility, provided here by the show (an easily accessible public space of interaction), to express oneself, formulate one's wishes and ideas, and assert one's rights and status in public, already provided an important channel of self-realization. As I witnessed over time, while listening to a number of subsequent broadcasts, some of the topics requested in the maiden broadcast were covered by extended discussions in programs later on. This was appreciated and seen as encouraging, within a community that, on the whole, was rather dispirited and thus far had low confidence in the media representing their opinions correctly, in anyone claiming to be their spokesperson and representing their interests, as local politicians and the Muslim elite had long let them down.[6]

Wake-Up Calls, Social Critique, and Practical Tips

Abubakar was one of the two or three main moderators employed by Radio Rahma, and he was on air during early morning, afternoon, or evening hours, depending on the broadcasting schedule. Apart from the joint program with Stambuli, he also moderated quiz shows and advertising phone-ins, and he ran an evening show discussing social issues concerning the Muslim community. He gave voice to representatives of local youth initiatives one time, and he interrogated a local politician on his record another. Abubakar was well educated in Islamic and secular matters and spoke Arabic and English apart from Kiswahili. Originating from the coast, near Mombasa, he had moved to Nairobi, where he completed media training courses and worked for Kenya's first Islamic radio station, Iqra Radio, broadcasting in English and Swahili, before joining the Radio Rahma team.

Abubakar was also Radio Rahma's front man when it came to public events that the radio organized for the community. For instance, he hosted and moderated an Islamic educational day (that I attended) sponsored by Radio Rahma, where speeches were given by Islamic scholars from Mombasa and the region (some of whom had studied at Islamic universities abroad) at Makadara Grounds, the traditional meeting place for the Muslim community just outside of the Old Town area. On that occasion, the speakers were addressing a sizable but by no means huge crowd (considering Mombasa's potential), which was organized in neatly divided gendered seating sections where groups of women and men sat on mats laid out on the grass. The scholars lectured the community on issues such as self-discipline, time management, the value of work and education, and related matters. A few Qur'an and *qasida* recitations by Qur'anic schools created pauses for quiet reflection and meditation in between. This event can be understood to underline and represent the goals and aspirations of Radio Rahma within the region: It sought to bring together, speak out for, and educate local Muslims. This resonates with the earlier claim of *Sauti ya Haki* that we saw above, to be "the tongue of the *umma*" (*ulimi wa umma*). Radio Rahma also started activities of food provision and the collection of secondhand clothes for the needy; it had approachable contact offices in the center of town, where its well-designed advertisements hung prominently on lantern masts, bearing variable succinct reminders to Muslims, to do good and avoid evil, to command right and forbid wrong.

Yet while there were claims and efforts of bringing Muslims together, creating and shaping a common platform of debate for the *umma*, there were also reservations among local Muslims about the radio station being dominated by certain ideological interests and possibly being steered from the outside. Some thought it wanted to lead (or even push) Muslims along the path of a Salafi-oriented Islamic reformism—locally commonly called "Wahhabi"—with the intent to "purify" and reground Islamic practice in the example of the early Muslim community, rather than provide the facilities for constructive discursive engagement between different interpretations of Islam. They would see indications for this in the kinds of scholars who were prominently linked to the station, granted airtime, or thought to be influential in guiding and directing its programs, but also in those who were missing in the public gatherings or excluded (as it seemed) from the airwaves of the "Voice of Mercy." In this matter, things were altogether rather complicated and ambivalent. Sometimes strategies of exclusion of certain local scholars could reasonably be suspected; sometimes they were obvious, as when a scholar's presence at the event described above was first advertised on air and afterward his invitation was withdrawn. There were conflicting signals, and pulls and pushes in different ideological directions connected to Radio Rahma and its makers.

Once, for instance, at the end of *maulidi* celebrations in a town outside of Mombasa, I watched a group of elderly men who had participated enthusiastically in the procession and recitations. I witnessed them take issue with Abubakar from Radio Rahma (who was there in private but had identified himself to them). They dismissed the radio station as being run by "Wahhabis" who were intolerant to *maulidi* processions (and other performances they held dearly) and had a destructive effect on the Muslim community. They claimed these "Wahhabis" used incorrect interpretations and arguments and presented as "Islamic" what was actually against Islam. Their gripe with Radio Rahma—and here with

Abubakar as its representative—was that it facilitated and disseminated what they called "propaganda," privileging the wrong kind of Islam without giving the right one even the chance to present its case to the listeners. Radio Rahma was, they implied, partial to a dogmatic and intolerant attitude, and they put the challenge to Abubakar that they wanted a public discussion live on air between their own scholars and those others, to prove to the *umma* who possessed the true knowledge of Islam. Indeed, they said, it was a matter of proper knowledge of Islam to find the right guidance and overcome unjustified opinions. They demanded to be given the chance for such an open debate, and were not quite content when Abubakar responded that it was not up to him (and certainly not him alone) as a mere presenter, to decide this matter, but he would pass on this demand to his superiors. He also responded that they were wrong in thinking the radio station was dominated or run by "Wahhabis," and he did not regard himself as such. Had he not come, after all, to attend and participate in this *maulidi* of his hometown? He went on to say that initially (and somewhat ironically, as it seemed now) he had intended to broadcast these celebrations live on Radio Rahma, but organizational and technical difficulties had made this impossible. The old men grumpily reiterated, while starting to make a move for their late-night homeward transportation to Mombasa (eventually providing me with a lift), that they wanted to have a contest of minds between the two parties broadcast live on air, in order to show that their position was superior and based on the true knowledge of Islam—but that never happened.

This scene that I witnessed (having accompanied Abubakar to the *maulidi*) was just a little side event at the very end of the peaceful and dedicated *maulidi* celebrations that had filled the evening and much of the night. Yet what it illustrates well is the ambivalence and complexity of specific social situations that may occur suddenly in the everyday, in which arguments over certain practices (or even institutions) as properly "Islamic" are situated. Concretely, this example also underscores the ambivalence within the combined forces that together are meant to construct a unified popular image of a particular radio station as "Islamic." But these forces are diverse, as Abubakar with his doctrinal orientation is differently positioned from a certain scholar associated with the radio station that both of them, in a way, represent to others. Still, in terms of self-presentation and advertising, it nevertheless presented itself as unified. Assuming the kind of social consensus that it was seeking (and at the same time claiming) to represent, it was, one could argue, a bit like the *umma* itself. It constituted a Muslim public and sought to attract more individual believers as audience by counting them in, through the use of sufficiently vague and general rhetoric. After all, who would not want to feel included as part of the community of the "Voice of Mercy"? Radio Rahma was indeed very popular with local Muslims of different ages and genders before it had to stretch itself to compete with its main (and more recent) rival Islamic radio station, Radio Salaam, which was much more generously funded and based in the center of town (whereas Radio Rahma lay across the Bridge in Nyali). The new rival had, I was told, copied the successful programming strategies initially used by Radio Rahma (use of music, quizzes, etc.), and it followed a somewhat more restrictive interpretation of Islam. While, with the advent of Radio Salaam, Radio Rahma's days of being the only communal coastal Muslim radio station were clearly over and rival tensions were due to influence both programs and airwaves, I shall not be following this rivalry in my discussion but instead will continue to zoom in on the specific "*Elimika na Stambuli!*" program here.

The Makers: Stambuli and Abubakar

When listening to the discussions in Stambuli's program during my annual visits between 2005 and 2007, I witnessed a vibrant and steady participation from listeners, with men and women of different age groups (and a range of educational backgrounds) contributing engaged comments and questions, complaints and suggestions to carry further the queries and discussion initiated by the makers of Radio Rahma. Abubakar contributed to the initial success story of Radio Rahma in no mean way, it seems to me. His rare and well-balanced combination of abilities qualified him perfectly for the job as moderator in a radio station that was Islamic but also worldly in outlook, and that wanted to be in touch with the thoughts and feelings of ordinary Muslims in their everyday lives. Apart from linguistic and scholarly expertise, as mentioned above, he was truly gifted in the art of relating to people, with an air of politeness, seriousness, and respect. Yet he was also flexible and able to adjust, when need be, to create a sense of sincere encouragement for callers for whom it was hard to talk and express themselves, or to assert an authoritative position vis-à-vis people who were either taking too long or violating the rules of politeness and proper expression. He had a pleasant voice and carried himself somewhere between statesman and sportsman, between journalist and scholar, as everyone's potential friend and interview partner.

Abubakar's co-moderator and the initiator of the show was Stambuli, after whom the show was called ("*Elimika na Stambuli!*"). He had no previous radio experience or media training before going on air together with Abubakar, but he too brought in a mixed background of qualities that contributed much to the interest and positive feedback that their program then generated. As a former musician, he was used to performing in front of audiences. He was a good speaker who employed simple rhetorical skills to much effect, speaking slowly and clearly in short sentences, able to focus on a few keywords that would stick in the minds of the audience. He was known within the Muslim community for his initiative to start a kind of independent social consciousness movement among young Muslims a few years back. Then, as a religious layman with a critical mind and a sizeable proportion of insider knowledge and documentary evidence, he had given regular public speeches in local mosques, criticizing the Muslim establishment for not showing engagement and solidarity with their disadvantaged ordinary peers (Kresse 2007, 214–18).[7] But he also criticized these same ordinary Muslims for not standing up for themselves and trying to improve their own circumstances. His contributions to the radio program were inspired along such lines of social and political engagement. Stambuli had also traveled extensively in East Africa and had lived in dire straits among poor, desperate, and hungry people. Based on these experiences, he knew how to address and speak out for the disadvantaged, pointing at social problems that otherwise were often veiled in public discourse. Over time Stambuli had built up his reputation among local Muslims by speaking and acting emphatically beyond established social divisions of tribalism (*ukabila*) and religion (especially *madhhab*) that he saw as obstructing social progress.

Stambuli became a popular figure in Mombasa through this weekly show. He started each show with a prepared speech on the chosen topic, of about ten minutes, after which the listeners were invited to contribute by asking questions or airing their views. Practical topics I listened to included, for instance, a critical look at the Mombasa City Council for letting the existent water hydrant system deteriorate, leaving hydrant locations unmarked and broken water pipes in a state of disrepair. Stambuli drew attention to the fact that such neglect caused serious health risks and unnecessary problems when the hydrants were needed in an emergency. In this case, people phoned in to provide concrete information about where in the area repairs needed to be done and demarcation renewed. This seemed to have an almost immediate effect, I thought, when a day or two after that broadcast, I saw city council workers marking hydrant locations in bright yellow paint at different locations in the Old Town.

Over time, Stambuli and Abubakar tackled a number of controversial topics in their phone-in discussions, stirring up, reigniting, or picking up on public interest. Among such topics were, to name a few examples, a critical look at the economy (*uchumi*) and economic potential of the Kenyan coast and how, in their eyes it had been exploited by the upcountry government (e.g., in taking the port revenues, and by restricting fishing and the mangrove wood trade); the still sensitive historical question of how and why the Mwambao coastal Independence movement had failed, a topic that was discussed in the presence of one of the representatives from 1961; and a look at how social life and educational awareness on the Kenyan coast compared to other Muslim regions in the world (discussed with a Kenyan Swahili Muslim professor living in Turkey, Professor Mohamed Bakari).

The *"Elimika"* program, like Radio Rahma on the whole, became something of an institution within the Muslim community of Mombasa, with many tuning in regularly and contributing to on-air discussions by calling in or sending SMS messages. A number of initiatives on matters of local politics and social well-being were sparked off through them, and both hosts, but especially Stambuli, were regularly approached by local politicians, businessmen, and functionaries for further advice. Stambuli made it clear from the beginning that he would be able to back up any statement he made with documentary evidence, and indeed he did so, for instance when reading (in Swahili translation) from a formal letter written to Jomo Kenyatta on behalf of the sultan of Zanzibar confirming the Kenyan takeover of the Coastal Strip and repeating the agreed conditions. People found such reliability in the provision of evidence very impressive and reassuring—in stark contrast to the many pledges, pleas, and broken promises they had heard from politicians over the years—and this increased his reputation further.

Guests and Topics of Discussion

While the makers of *"Elimika na Stambuli!"* drew from a pool of topics requested by their audience for the choice of themes they covered from week to week, they regularly invited suitably qualified or experienced speakers as guests to their show. Often, these were scholars or local dignitaries, and their respective knowledge and expertise would feed into or underpin the discussion of the announced topic. As three illustrations to be discussed in more detail below, they invited

- Sheikh Abdilahi Nassir, the former leader of the coastal Independence movement Mwambao in the late colonial era from the early 1960s, who responded to questions on the historical situation and his involvement back then;
- Najib Balala, then minister for tourism and cultural heritage, who spoke about the place of coastal culture and heritage for Kenyan national identity, and about recurrent issues of marginalization and discontent among coastal Muslims; as a coastal Muslim representative of what was commonly seen as the "upcountry (Christian) government," he had a sensitive job to do in addressing current difficulties and tensions; and
- Prof. Mohamed Hyder, a retired professor and civil activist, who was invited by Stambuli and Abubakar to attend a discussion about "terrorism" (*ugaidi*) and whether it could be justified as *jihad*.

Listening closely to these broadcasts, as I show here, gives us a sense not only of the diverse and complementary topical dimensions of internal discourse they sought to cover, with a view to the consciousness-building agenda of the program. This concerned the historical underpinnings of postcolonial experience for coastal Muslims, and attempts at addressing and mediating internal tensions within the Muslim community. We also gain a sense of how important and socially sensitive matters are raised and discussed in public.

A proper and respectful form of discussion was important to both Stambuli and Abubakar, and every once in a while they spelled out for their listeners a brief catalog of rules of engagement in discussion, to make sure that these rules were adhered to. Adhering to them should be understood, they said, also as performative expression of proper (i.e., Islamicly informed) conduct: interacting respectfully with one's peers. Core points here included respectful tone, form of address, and vocabulary when speaking to others; not to invoke matters of ethnic or racial origin (*ukabila*), and not to mention the names of one's adversaries on air; to present one's contributions clearly, and to provide arguments and (as much as possible) evidence when engaging in discussion. Insulting language was not acceptable—also and especially not when talking about social others (Christians, Hindus, etc.) or the Kenyan state and its representatives. From time to time, the moderators would interrupt callers who were violating these rules, or they would use breaks in the program to remind people about them. In this way, they could be seen to attribute as much importance to the proper recommendable form of discussion as to the actual topics of discussion themselves.

Historical Consciousness and *Mwambao* Anxieties: Sheikh Abdilahi Nassir

Next to raising the kind of practical issues concerning the organization of everyday life as mentioned above, raising a politically sensitive historical consciousness among coastal Muslims was another goal of Stambuli's program. He had done this already years before, when he operated as a self-declared activist and public speaker in mosques and *madrasas* in Mombasa and Malindi. Here, he invoked the importance of the knowledge of history for political liberation and progress of Muslims in a national arena, and he dedicated several broadcasts to historical topics, one of them on the history of Islam in East Africa. He pushed the point that Islam had been present on the coast since the eighth century, citing proper archaeological research as evidence.[8]

Another discussion of history was on the coastal independence movement, which in the late colonial period had represented the hopes of coastal citizens for an independent postcolonial future (Brennan 2008; A. I. Salim 1970). Its aspiration had been, as its leader, Sheikh Abdilahi Nassir once put it, to be able to interact and negotiate as equals with Kenyatta, as "the prime minister of a neighboring country" (Sheikh Abdilahi, interview). Many coastals feared difficulties and suppressive or violent repercussions from the upcountry government, as aftereffects of a long history of opposition and mutual suspicion. Indeed, statements to such effect had been made back then, in campaigns by politicians like Tom Mboya when rallying for *wabara* votes (Prestholdt 2014). Two Mwambao representatives had participated in the political decision-making process about independence at the Lancaster House Conference in London in April 1962, but they remained unsuccessful in changing the prearranged agreement between the British government, the envisaged KANU government for Kenya (under Kenyatta), and the sultan of Zanzibar, who until then legally was the nominal political head over the Kenyan Coastal Strip Protectorate of the Sultanate. The two Mwambao representatives, Omar Basaddiq and Sheikh Abdilahi Nassir, had refused to sign the agreement, not wanting to endorse a formal decision that ran against their expressed interest (and this is noted in the report of the conference).[9] However, in the coastal community, due to deep disappointment about this decision, rumors spread that the two had "sold" Mwambao to the new upcountry rulers and become "traitors" to the coastal cause.[10] Stambuli and Abubakar now invited Sheikh Abdilahi Nassir as a visitor to the broadcast in order to publicly address the Mwambao episode in social memory, to clarify the baselessness of such rumors, and to reorient discussion in the community toward the current situation and for the best interest of coastal Muslims at present. Stambuli was not impartial, however, as Sheikh Abdilahi was also his father. While this was not explicitly mentioned in the broadcast, many listeners will have been aware of this fact. The decisive matter, from Stambuli's perspective and the *"Elimika"* show, however, must have been to create and use an occasion where the lingering rumors could be publicly addressed and disproved. Only then, it seems, matters could be aired and clarified, and after they were addressed in public, the community would be able to progress under different circumstances and with different possibilities.

Because of Sheikh Abdilahi's biography, the broadcast, when it happened, also had to take another sensitive matter on board. He had become, over the last two decades, a figurehead of Twelver Shiism in East Africa and its growing constituency of Swahili and African converts. Having become Shii in the 1980s, as an Islamic scholar of Salafi reformist orientation at the time, Sheikh Abdilahi published a string of leaflets defending Shiism against recent attacks launched by Saudi-funded publications (Bakari 1995; Kresse 2007; Kresse 2008). For this reason, too, he had been verbally attacked by local Sunnis, and (for a while) ostracized socially. Thus from being a local political hero in the late 1950s when he became the MP in the pre-Independence Parliament for Mvita district at a very young age, to the current state of ambivalence (between being respected, adored, and feared—as a public speaker), a lot of socially meaningful contestations and changes of fundamental issues for the coastal community had happened in which Sheikh Abdilahi was involved. A few months before the broadcast with Sheikh Abdilahi, the makers of Radio Rahma had announced that they had invited him to a public discussion with other local Islamic scholars on the topic of globalization—and later they disinvited him. This had been embarrassing for the station, and allowing Stambuli and Abubakar the space to broadcast a program with him on Mwambao in June 2005 also sought to make up for the bad handling of matters then. Thus, for many in the coastal Muslim community, this was a special broadcast event that merited attention, and the air will have been loaded with expectations of different kinds.

When the broadcast finally happened, all these sensitive points were indeed raised and touched upon, by different callers from a variety of angles. And while the anticipated calls came asking Sheikh Abdilahi about Mwambao and his religious conviction, it was surprising that overall the program became a broadcast of reconciliation, with some historical anecdotes (e.g., of discussions with Jomo Kenyatta) being shared. About half the callers were of the older generation who knew Sheikh Abdilahi in person and used the occasion to reconnect and wish him well—one caller praised him as "my sheikh" and "a source of inspiration"; another one due to his extensive knowledge, called him "a college in himself." Most of the older generation here reconnected and reconfirmed their relationship with someone whom they remembered from the past, as a determined politician, formidable speaker, and knowledgeable scholar, providing guidance to some and food for thought to others. This was in marked contrast to some of the other, younger callers, who sought to cause unease through confrontational questions about his Mwambao experience ("Did you sell Mwambao?") and his turn to Shiism ("Did you become Shii?"). Sheikh Abdilahi calmly responded no to the first (explaining the circumstances) and plainly yes to the second question.

The show ended with a sense of increased familiarity and understanding of this historical person, who, in a way, had been reintroduced to the wider local public by means of this specific communally oriented program that, due to its accessibility and openness (anyone could call in and say anything) created the impression of facilitating an egalitarian discourse of sorts among coastal Muslims. It was a platform that was ready to critique the existing hierarchies within the community, criticize Muslim elites, and wake up Muslim commoners to stand up and take charge of their lives—despite the adverse political circumstances they had to endure. Thus, next to a clarification of rumors about historical processes, the program achieved a better understanding of a past major political representative of the community. A consciousness about the historical developments leading to people's experience in the present was also increased through this discussion, marking the existent dynamics of internal diversity among coastal Muslims.

Political Membership and Coastal Heritage: Minister Najib Balala

One program involved the popular coastal politician Najib Balala, a former mayor of Mombasa and minister for culture and heritage at the time. They invited Balala to discuss Muslim citizens' problems in obtaining IDs and passports. Given the circumstances, Balala had to perform a difficult split, balancing between his position within the government and his identity as coastal Muslim, with solidarity for his peers. He resolved to attempt to reinvigorate a proud and positive coastal Muslim identity as part of Kenya, based on the term *ustaarabu,* denoting coastal nineteenth-century "civilization" during the Busaidi Sultanate period. He highlighted it as a distinct qualification of East African coastal civilization that means "going forward, progressing" (*ustaarabu ni kwendelea mbele*) and one not to be equated with "Arabness" or "being Arab" (*uArabu*). Here, he put his finger on a continuing sore spot in social relations, on the coast itself and concerning relations with the whole country: the racially defined and differently pitched tensions between the partly interrelated and partly competing groups of coastal Arabs (*waArabu*), Swahili patricians (*waungwana*), lower-class urban Swahili, coastal hinterland Mijikenda, and upcountry people (*wabara*). Throughout long parts of the history of the Northern Swahili coast, these precarious tensions were negotiated, also through channels of opportunity and integration (el-Zein 1974; Ranger 1975; Parkin 1991; Willis 1993). These tensions and ideologies of difference had been pronounced and accentuated by British colonial policies that distinguished "native" from "non-native" citizens and categorized people along tribal and racial lines that were not necessarily the predominant markers of identity for the people themselves (Kindy 1972; A. I. Salim 1976). These tensions have continued to dominate political discourse and rhetoric in the postcolonial era, and Balala, as a national politician from the coast, had to address and handle it very carefully.

When Balala said, "*Ustaarabu si uArabu* (civilization is not Arabness)," he was consciously or unconsciously echoing Sheikh Al-Amin Mazrui's words of seventy-five years ago that we discussed above (May 7, 2005; 1:01; chapter 3). Such a pronounced public self-positioning of coastal Muslims as "Africans" and not "Arabs" (a term with which other Kenyans often insult and exclude them), and as representing a coastal African civilization that is not qualified by "Arabness"—contrary to one common strand of public opinion and ideology—pursues a proven strategy[11] of marking and reclaiming one's citizenship within the field of national political discourse, one that has often invoked rhetorical "politics of the soil" against coastal interests (Prestholdt 2014). In practice, Muslims are often denied equal recognition as Kenyans. They have been experiencing severe difficulties and delays in obtaining passports or identity cards (IDs), and even when they have them, sometimes authorities refuse to accept their documents as genuine (e.g., police who claim to be looking for terrorist suspects).[12] Callers repeatedly brought up this issue in a number of *"Elimika"* broadcasts. Balala advocated that the government nowadays was committed to the swift provision of ID cards and passports to Muslims (like all citizens) as their right (*haki*); he agreed with people's complaints about this matter and promised improvement. He argued for a fundamental reassertion of coastal Muslims within the state, and thus connected to other relevant fields of discussion—education, for instance, as Balala elaborated: "Civilization (*ustaarabu*) began here at the coast (i.e., on African home soil, not in Arabia), and there was education here before any university was founded upcountry." So, seeking to mobilize history for coastal people's interests, he argued for the historical precedence of the coast, expressing and invoking coastal Muslims' pride in the history of Islamic education. However, he did so at a time when coastals were trying to catch up with the *wabara* and fill the ever-growing gap in terms of quantity and quality of educational facilities. Vivid discussions were under way about initiatives to finally start a university in Mombasa, after so many had been founded upcountry already—but yet again, until then, they had come to nothing.[13]

Listening In: Vicious Circles—Debating Terrorism (*Ugaidi*) and *Jihad*

Probably the most sensitive and courageous program that Stambuli and Abubakar presented together was a topical double bill on the discussion of terrorism (*ugaidi*), in two consecutive broadcasts in July 2005. This program was designed to revolve around the discussion of the (not uncommon) claim that terrorist attacks could be justified as *jihad* and thus acceptable acts of revenge against Western military aggression, an argument that invoked the support of Islam (Qur'an and *hadith*) for the killing of unarmed civilians. Stambuli and Abubakar, and many among the callers and contributors, insisted that there was no way in which the violent agenda of killing defenseless victims (especially children and women) could be acceptable in Islam. However, some callers (both men and women) expressed principal sympathy for such acts, out of solidarity with suffering Muslims in places like Iraq and Palestine. These callers cast such violence as justified defensive reaction to brutal oppression and waves of ongoing military attacks and arbitrary killings committed above all by the armed forces and special agents of the United States and Israel as part of the so-called war on terror launched by the US Bush regime. They saw these actions as aimed at humiliating the Muslim world, and as part of a long ongoing history of aggressive, combative, and strategic Western politics led by the USA.[14]

My interest in following this specific topic particularly closely here lies not in what some may assume to be a spectacular nature of discussion. Rather, I have pursued it (initially somewhat uneasily) in the conviction that listening in to, seeking to understand, and trying to catch even an ethnographic glimpse of the internal ambivalence and complexity of such a debate is important, on a topic as divisive, sensitive, and contested as this one—as it is negotiated within a community whose members are often simplistically cast by external commentators as suspects prone to commit violence. It is of benefit to observe and follow the ways in which the moral dilemmas that come up for the social actors whom we try to understand are addressed, as part of decision-making and self-positioning processes negotiated by them as individuals (with their particular life experiences).

The point is to take seriously the difficulty and seriousness of the internal contestation of such violence within a community which is itself under pressure (oppressed, or under threat of violence), and whose members can (potentially) relate to the victims as well as the perpetrators of such actions, based on the range of recent historical experiences in their midst.[15] My interest here is along the lines of exploring the contents and dynamics of such communicative interaction here as guided and safeguarded by Stambuli, the initiator of this particular public discussion about it, thereby also confronting (and irritating) his listeners on a Saturday morning.

I see Stambuli here as an initiator and facilitator of social debates that need to be had within the community because of the dilemmatic situation people are in. We can think of this as part of engaging in wider processes of consciousness-building (or even "democratization"), where Muslims in particular regions are thinking through and formulating their own meaningful ways of achieving more, better, and fairer political participation, for instance, while still being critical of Western hegemonical explanatory schemes (for Indonesia, see Hefner 2000). Such specific engagement, embedded in regional complexities of political discourse and debate, needs to be understood better (and studied without simplistic paradigms) in Muslim and non-Western contexts. And if this concerns the lines of political participation, the view to the actual moral dilemmas that community members face, it is no less important to look at the moral dimensions of obligation and responsibility as well. Here, for Stambuli and his fellow Muslims, there is the unavoidable task of having to respond somehow, by word or deed (or in refraining therefrom), to claims voiced around them, that (in this case) violent attacks on civilians are justifiable (or even commanded) by Islam. These are claims that cannot be ignored or taken lightly. They present an obvious dilemma that needs to be addressed, as the suggested action violates the accepted parameters of social interaction.

Stambuli, in these broadcasts, pursued the agenda of facilitating such painful discussions within the community because it was important for all—who are, in any case, affected—to consider the situation and build their own judgement, so as not to blindly follow calls to violence in the name of Islam, which may lead not only to regrettable destruction and loss of life but also personal sin. Thus the public claims and calls for terrorist violence as part of "Islamic" (i.e., religiously obligated) resistance, from Stambuli's perspective, needed to be addressed and critically discussed in public too, as difficult as this is. The calls to a political "Islamic" agenda need to be balanced against existent and agreed-upon moral demands and obligations that clearly are positively Islamic—like, for instance, the accepted divine command and obligation for all Muslims to "command right and forbid wrong" (Cook 2000). Stambuli made a sensitive but necessary public discussion possible, in response to a strong sense of moral obligation. Initiating the discussion had nothing to do with an apologetic stance for violence. On the contrary, it was itself a performative act of "forbidding wrong" by Stambuli, for as he stated and argued in the program, such violence (in all the ways he could see) was forbidden by Islam. People needed to clear their minds to see this and make sure, firstly, not to participate in such violence, and secondly, to make sure to stop everyone in their vicinity from being pushed or seduced into participating in it.

Listening now to Stambuli and Abubakar—or engaging in a verbally mediated reconstructive "re-listening" of them—conducting these sensitive and contentious discussions, and the diverse ways in which callers contributed and conducted themselves, avails us the opportunity to witness the meaningfulness, for the participants, of such an open internal discussion. Here now, in public and live on air (and without possibilities of "filtering" callers or controlling what they would say), this highly contested issue was taken on, a topic that would usually be discussed among groups of trusted equals, in *baraza* groups or in private conversations. Facilitating a live discussion on this topic, which was loaded with tensions and could erupt in confrontations on air, was daring. As Stambuli explained to me retrospectively, he felt the obligation for his program to publicly address and discount this point that was commonly brought forward by some Muslims, that terror (*ugaidi*) was justifiable as *jihad* (effort).[16] His own efforts to make this particular discussion happen were aimed at making sure that public debates on fundamentally contentious and divisive matters such as this one could and would be held in the Muslim community. Stambuli was driven to challenge those who sympathized with terrorist attacks, as he thought they had not considered the matter properly, nor their own position and responsibilities in relation to it. In his introductory speech to the second part of the discussion, he rephrased his questions to his audience in the following way:

> My question is, what do you [listeners] out there think? Is it okay for anyone to come and fight with others, whether he is Muslim or non-Muslim, to come into Kenya and destroy [things and people] and then leave while people are dying? Those who remain behind, it's up to them, they will know what to do. Do you agree with that? . . . Do we divide ourselves so that, if Abubakar and his people are not mine, and if it were up to ourselves, I would crush and pulverize Abubakar[17] if he didn't help me? Well, if that happened to Abubakar, would you help him? Why such bloody attacks, my elders, my mothers, my siblings?

Let's speak on the phone, let's discuss these matters, according to religious criteria. I agree, and I think my brother Abubakar has already grown used to it. He has already died in his heart and in his head. Even if you want to insult and accuse us, also call us! This is the fortress [a safe and protected space] of the radio. Call if you want to insult us, make us look like fools! Please call, for your own sake! Whether you are a Muslim, or no Muslim: call! Whether you are Chinese, African or European, call, for your own sake! Tell us your opinion on what we are discussing.[18]

Stambuli ended his introduction with such appeals to call in and engage openly with what had been said thus far. These appeals underpinned the inclusive conception of the program: that anybody out there who could understand the discussion and felt concerned was invited to participate, even outsiders. Engaged discussion about such matters was needed in a community that had to reassert itself and that had to be seen (and see itself) as an integral part of the nation, of a wider unity across divisive tribal, racial, and religious categories. These appeals implored the coastals to wake up and stand up for their own rights—as Stambuli reiterated in other broadcasts (e.g., on February 4, 2006, "*Amkeni ndugu zangu*"; 21:19). This rhetoric, employed when addressing his own community through a discussion of national and global challenges in a rapidly changing world in which coastal Muslims experienced increasing marginality in their own country, echoes the writings of Sheikh Al-Amin (chapter 3).

Stambuli was aware of the vulnerability of his own position in this endeavor, as became clear from his behavior in the exchanges over the course of these two broadcasts. In his introduction to the second session, he cautioned people that even if they disliked (literally "hated") him, they had no right to simply dismiss him as an unbeliever (*mkafiri*) for what he said, only because he contradicted what they thought, or what their sheikh said. He too considered himself a faithful and sincere believer who had the right to speak and to be listened to with respect, just like he had listened to others and heard them out, over the course of discussion the previous day: "You, my friend, as a human being you have the right to think I am in the wrong—and I don't deny that; as I said yesterday, I respect your opinions. But just like you understand religion in a certain way, grant me the same right in the way I understand that religion—even if you hate me for how I understand this religion. It may be that you beat me (i.e., you are in the right), or it may be that I beat you (I am in the right)" (13:04).[19]

Stambuli wanted his fellow local Muslims to take on responsibility and address directly their internal differences about fundamentals of Islam vis-a-vis each other, on the basis of the religious bond that ultimately held them together, as a Muslim community.

In these live discussions, Stambuli expressed concern that even under the current circumstances (in 2005) of discrimination and mistreatment of Muslims

in Kenya, there was far too little solidarity among them. The rich and powerful among them continued to benefit, while the poor and needy struggled. Central issues among coastal Muslims needed to be resolved internally before there
would be a chance of getting a grip on the fundamental problems. Stambuli and
Abubakar demanded mutual respect to be shown by all in these discussions, and
they themselves acted as role models, dealing politely with every caller and letting them finish their points. They patiently handled a couple of emotional out-
bursts and charged accusations by callers (against the United States and its war
in Iraq, or the Israelis in Palestine) while keeping control of the conversations.
They followed up with precise questions in response, asking some of the callers
advocating violence to clarify their position by argument.

Stambuli also described a scenario of intense global migration that meant
many Kenyan Muslims had relatives living in countries around the world, including in economically attractive Western countries (where, he said, they were safe,
given care, housing, and money, before they had contributed a thing).

> Our brothers and sisters who are in London these days, how are they? And
> those who are in Dubai and Saudi Arabia, what about them? Those in Canada
> or Ireland, how are they? They were chased away, they fled, they were wel-
> comed over there, they were given money before getting a job, they were taken
> care of until they got jobs and accomodation by social services.
>
> *Ndugu zetu wako London sasa hivi wako vipi? Walioko Madubai, Saudia
> wakoje? Canada, Ireland wako vipi? Walifukuzwa, walikimbia, wakapokewa
> kule, wakapawa pesa kabla hajapata kazi, akawaangaliwa mpaka akapata kazi
> na nyumba ya social services.*

As migrants, Kenyan Muslims had become part of these societies, which, as one
caller argued, could be seen as acceptable targets for violent attacks, in retali-
ation for Muslim suffering in Iraq, Afghanistan, and Palestine. Stambuli and
Abubakar responded to callers who advocated violence by putting them on the
spot, asking them whether they could really advocate the likely deaths of innocent women and children, or of Muslim peers and even relatives who were living
abroad. Callers' reactions to these carefully formulated questions were evasive,
and male and female advocates of violence alike seemed, by the sound of their
voices, to be tightening up, forcing themselves to be "hard" and unsympathetic
to victims belonging to other groups. They answered that while it was not commendable that innocent and helpless people (especially Muslims) were to become
victims, this was a lamentable but ultimately inevitable risk under the circumstances. To them, this dilemma was a result of the persistent attacks by the enemy
forces, attacks to which they felt the need to respond in kind: "An eye for an eye,
and a tooth for a tooth," as one of them quoted the Qur'an. The "enemies" mentioned specifically were, again and again, the USA and Israel, who were seen to
drive fellow Muslims to the most desperate acts. While Stambuli and Abubakar

expressed understanding and did not deny the need for compassion and solidarity with Palestinians, Iraqis, and others, they continued to argue that deliberate killing of innocent people could not be justifiable by Islam—and that the bigger and most important *jihad* lay in rebuilding Muslim society properly. In response, one caller advocating violence actually conceded that in order to focus on a forceful military response to the oppressors, "we need to put Islam aside" (*Islam tuweke kando*); only then could the situation be addressed in adequate practical and strategic terms, and not in religious terms (anymore). The moderators rejected his stance, while highlighting that this comment was evidence that Islam could not be used to justify terrorist acts.

In the discussions, a remarkable (but perhaps not surprising) regional differentiation was flagged up by several callers who emphasized a contrast of outlook and mentality between East African Muslims and Middle Eastern ones—distinguishing supposedly more peaceful "Africans" from bellicose "Arabs." Some callers blamed Middle Easterners for their rigid and strict interpretation of Islam and their violent tendencies, and even for being less humane on the whole. They pointed out that "Arabs" seemed racist and behaved arrogantly toward Africans (whether fellow Muslims or not). They were cast as the more likely perpetrators of the acts of destruction that fall under *ugaidi*—in contrast to supposedly more docile East Africans. Other callers asked why certain Muslim countries in the Middle East were not affected by the Western onslaught on Islam. They blamed those countries for collaborating with the West, for becoming its aides against their Muslim brothers and sisters. And they particularly blamed the Kenyan government for collaborations it had cultivated with the USA in its so-called war on terror. Indeed, they claimed that since then, Kenyan Muslims (a demographic minority of somewhere between 10 percent and 20 percent of Kenya's population) not only had lived as second-class citizens in their own country, but were even cast and targeted generally as potential terrorist suspects by their own government, a government that was ready to ignore their basic human rights and pass them on to external authorities.[20]

Throughout the program, Stambuli held the focus of discussion on the main question: whether terrorist acts (*ugaidi*) could really be justified with reference to *jihad*. While this seemed to be commonly assumed by some callers, it was rejected by others, including Stambuli himself, who also explained his position. Addressing all this in an open public discussion among local Muslims made it possible that people's arguments could be engaged with and scrutinized. In this spirit Stambuli called upon people to participate widely in this discussion and to phone in. He pointed to the right (*haki*) of all Muslims to speak up and be heard, even if their opinions were not popular with some listeners. In the progression of this discussion, he made sure people could express their opinions, as long as this was done respectfully and in appropriate terms. But this did not mean that he (and Abubakar) simply accepted any opinion; they spoke up and challenged contributions they found problematic, asking critical questions of those who advocated violence.

In his introductory speech to the second leg of discussion, Stambuli looked back on the previous day's experiences and commented on the contributions and reactions to the program, as a way to return to and extend the discussion. Since a flow of reactions had come in during and after the broadcast on the previous day, some critical of such a discussion as such, he made a point of emphasizing that whatever he had said (and all he would say today) was his personal opinion and did not represent the position of Radio Rahma. Beyond that, he reminded people of his own limitations. He did not pose as a sheikh and pretend to have an authority he did not have, but his intentions and his work were directed to facilitate debate among his people:

> I think many could join in and others did not, they stayed listening in. Some of them thought all was fine, and others became alarmed that perhaps we were against Muslims dedicating themselves to *jihad*. Therefore, there were those who spoke to us on the side, and others who spoke to us on the phone, and others who could send us a text message. We did not have the time to read out all the text messages. But there were those who said it would be better to legalize eating pork than to let us speak like we did. There are those who sent us short messages to tell us that they now thought this radio station was one of *fitna* (divisive actions).
>
> *Nafikiri wengi waliweza kuchangia na wengine hawakuchangia, wakaa wamekaa tu kusikiliza, wako walioelewa sawasawa na wako ambao wali-kuwa na hamaki wakiona pengine tuwapinga Waislamu [1:04] kufanya juhudi au kutekeleza jihadi. Kwa hivyo wako wale waliotuzungumza kando na wale wanaweza kutuambia kwa simu, walioweza kuleta ujumbe mfupi. Katika mijumbe mifupi mengine hatukupata wasaa kuisoma. Kuna waliosema afadh-ali tungehalalisha kula nguruwe kuliko hali tuliosema. Kuna wale waliotuletea ujumbe mfupi wakatuambia sasa tunaona idhaa hii ikuwa ni idhaa ya fitina.*
>
> I want to take this opportunity to explain that anything I said here should not be understood as the position of the radio station. If anything has been said, it is the opinion of Stambuli, not the radio. And many times I have said this already, every day, and what I talk about I always try to prove as much as I can . . . and I am a human being. I'm not a prophet, I'm not an angel, nor am I among those who are counted as sheikhs and bound by knowledge. I have not reached that level, I am your fellow Muslim, but I like if I look at an issue and problematize it a little bit, to bring it to a radio station like this one, so that we have the opportunity to discuss together.
>
> *Mimi nataka kuchukua fursa hii kueleza kwa lolote ninalosema hapa isifa-hamike kuwa ndiyo maoni ya idhaa. Kama kuna kitu kimesemekana ni maoni ya Stambuli, si ya idhaa. Na mara nyingi huwa kama nilivyosema kila siku na nililozungumza nitajaribu ninawezavyo kuthibitisha. Ala kulli hali, na mimi*

ni mwanadamu, mimi si mtume, mimi si malaika, wala katika watu wanaohis-
abiwa kuwa masheikh waliobobea kwenye elimu. Mimi sijafikia kiwango hicho,
mimi mi mwislamu mwenzenu lakini napenda jambo ikiwe nimeliona na lali-
tatiza kidogo nilileta kwenye idhaa kama hiyo, fursa kama hiyo ili tulijadili
pamoja [3:01].

There is no perfect human being, and we cannot debate [lit., negotiate]
about everything. There will be things we will be debating with each other and
others that we won't be debating intellectually [lit., in our thoughts].

Hakuna mwanadamu kamili na hatuwezi kubadiliana kwa kila kitu.
Utakuwa mambo tutakubadiliana na mengine hatutakubadiliana kifikra.

So, Stambuli addressed his position as an engaged layman who values open discussion and seeks to facilitate it within his community, employing the means
he has at hand. An implicit conviction is indicated here, that open debate per se
is a good thing—even if all debate has its limits, and perhaps some convictions
cannot be challenged by reason or openly discussed. The exchange of arguments
and the negotiation of convictions already counts for much to Stambuli and his
broadcast, in that potentially problematic issues for the community were brought
to light and discussed together, in mutual debate with each other—and every-
body could call in.

In this respect, he expressed delight about the fact that the day before, so
many people had participated and spoken their minds: "It was all in the open,
everyone said what they felt" (*kulikuwa na uwazi, kila mtu alisema hisia zake*).
And he reminded his audience of another important point made the previous day
(by someone he recalled by name and location): that the big challenge for coastal
Muslims, and the big struggle (*jihadi*) to engage in, was actually to redress their
political and economic situation:

> And when he joined in, I explained that I agreed with him 100% because he
> said that now the struggle (*juhudi*; like *jihadi*) that should be performed is
> changing the lives of Muslims more than anything else, since we as Muslims
> had stayed behind economically and politically, especially in our country. *We*
> *were not left behind, we stayed behind!* I use the word "we stayed" because
> we Muslims have the liberty to do whatever we want. In economic terms we
> can act like we want, and in politics we can either agree to enter politics or
> if we don't want that, we can do as we like, and often we have already given
> examples of some communities who have no MPs, who have nothing, but they
> conduct and run their own affairs and nobody interferes (my emphasis, KK).
>
> *Na yeye alipochangia nilieleza kuwa nimekubadiliana naye mia afili*
> *mia kwa sababu alisema sasa hivi juhudi zifanywe katika kugeuza maisha ya*
> *waislamu zaidi kwa sababu waislamu kiuchumi, kisiasa haswa humu nchini*
> *mwetu tumebakia nyuma. Hatukuatwa nyuma, tumebakia nyuma! Natu-*
> *mia neno tumebakia kwa sababu waislamu tunao uhuru wa kufanya mambo*
> *yetu tutakavyo, kama uchumi tutaweza kupeleka tutakavyo, kama ni siasa*

tutaweza aidha kukubali kuendelea kuingia kwenye mambo ya siasi au kama hatutaki tukafanya tutakavyo na mara nyingi tushatoa mifano ya baadhi ya jamii ambazo hazina wabunge, hazina lolote lakini mambo yao wayapeleka na hakuna naye waingilia (5:15).

"We were not *left* behind, we *stayed* behind!" (*Hatukuatwa nyuma, tumebakia nyuma!*). For Stambuli, the contrastive emphasis here between passive and active voice was immensely important. It implied an emphasis on agency and therefore also on the responsibility of coastal Muslims for their own situation—they had been regarded as "backward" and "behind" in comparison to "upcountry" regions (and particularly Nairobi) for many decades now. A recognition of responsibility here was the crucial and necessary point of departure from which real change for the better could be initiated, by coastal Muslims themselves. Therefore, Stambuli applauded the call to invest all one's energy into the struggle of working on this kind of change, with the goal of bringing coastal Muslims forward again. It was this struggle that he returned to later on in discussion, calling it "the greater *jihad*" (*jihadi kuu*) and referring to it as the most important struggle, which can make a true difference to the lives of Muslims. He contrasted this kind of *jihad* with a lesser one (of violence and combat) and asked the audience whether, if it came to that decision, they really could agree that innocent Kenyans (no matter what religion, race, or origin) would be killed as part of the efforts of self-defense against superior powers. Would they not prefer that greater *jihad*, of a struggle toward long-lasting. meaningful social change, to this one "of machetes"? His appeal that they should do so, at least, was clear.

> If things were so? Do you think we should start that greater *jihad*, or do you think we should start this one of machetes (*pangas*)?
>
> *Hali ikiwa hivi? Mnaona tuanze ili jihadi kuu au mnaona tuanze hii hii ya mapanga?*

He narrated an episode of Prophet Muhammad's life, illustrating how the Prophet himself had pointedly resisted attacking others for a long time, despite all agony and suffering, even though he would have had the means to do so.

> Now Prophet Muhammad (p.b.u.h.) [peace be upon him], I explain again, was the situation he was in like this? He was able to fight but he didn't, he waited to be directed in a certain way. We were not present at the time when Prophet Muhammad built his followers around him. It was not as if God gave clear orders that we had to carry out, no!—But let us go to the bridge, let us build ourselves economically, let us build ourselves socially, let us be unified.
>
> *Sasa Bwana Mtume Mohammed (s.a.w.) naeleza tena, hali ilipokuwa hivi? Yeye alikuwa aweza kupigana lakini hakupigana, alingoja, akalekezwa njia. Sisi hatukuweko wakati bwana mtume Mohammed (s.a.w.), akijenga suhaba*

zake. [16:01] *Si kwamba na amri alizotoa mungu basi sisi tekelezwe, la!—Lakini twendeni kwa daraja, tujijengeni waislamu kiutumi, tujijengeni kijamii tuwe kitu kimoja.*

Otherwise, if we were not unified, he said, the "others" (*wasio sisi*, lit. "those who are not us") would continue to take over our things, while we were busy separating ourselves from each other (*tunavyokhitilafiana*) and arguing with each other (*tunavyozozana*). The "Bridge" here reinvoked an image he had described earlier, of the daily masses of poor laborers commuting across Nyali Bridge (and Likoni Ferry, and Makupa Causeway) every morning and evening, referring to ordinary people's daily challenges (of commute, earning money, and providing food for their families). This image also stood for the kind of true concern for the people and a commitment to joint communal effort and social struggle for the better. In this way, he implored listeners to look around themselves in Mombasa and think of all the many ordinary citizens and poor people who were struggling to make ends meet, on a daily basis in their everyday lives, not knowing in the morning whether they would have enough shillings for an evening tea at the end of the day, or the next breakfast:

> Have you already come to the Bridge to see how people are going to town by foot, and you don't know how many children they have, or what worries? Have you stood at Makupa Causeway there at Kibarani and looked at the people, by foot in the mornings and by foot in the evenings? They don't know what they will eat. And maybe, if perhaps you are one of the rich, one of those laborers you have given a wage of three thousand shillings, and he has four children and a wife and siblings who depend on him. A small room downstairs for five hundred shillings (a month), and four children. Let's say they may need even only a hundred shillings every day. Will he really last until the end of the month?
>
> [15:04] *Ushakuja bridge ukaangalia watu wanavyokwenda town na miguu na hujui ana watoto wangapi, ana uzito gani? Ushasimama Makupa Causeway pale Kibarani ukiangalia watu, asubuhi kwa miguu, jioni kwa miguu? Hajui atakula nini. Na wewe pengine tajiri ni mmoja katika unayewapa mshahara ya elfu tatu, na ana watoto wanne na mke na ndugu wamtegemea yeye. Nyumba chini kichumba shilingi mia tano, watoto wanne we pima hata kama shilingi mia mia kila siku. Huyu atafika mwisho wa mwezi kweli?*

As Stambuli covered sensitive material in his broadcast discussions (especially this one), he made sure to cover his ground well, choosing his words carefully and referring to the Qur'an (the accepted source of authority) in matters of advice, critique, or reflection that may have been seen as controversial. A common rhetorical pattern he employed was to present a particular Qur'anic quotation, comment on its meaning, and then point out that what he was arguing for was not his own spontaneous idea but God's word in the Qur'an. Another one was to invoke the role model of Prophet Muhammad (the other generally accepted reference point). If Stambuli could in this way affirm the reasonability and moreover the necessity of his own position, this could then become a position, or even a path, to be taken by others as well.

> These are not the words of Stambuli. Open up sura 13, aya 11 (sura al-Ra'ad). Open it up and see, and then ask yourself: are you smart/knowledgeable (*mwerevu*)? Yesterday when we were talking about these things and we said that it had (OR: there were) other conditions/stipulations; others attacked us and said we should not mislead people. We do not mislead! Prophet Muhammad was not a coward. And there was a time when his mothers [sic] got killed . . . there were Africans, Ethiopians who got killed. And he could not fight either (at that time). He waited until he went to Medina, where he was followed by people, and then he was given the order (to fight), but he was told not to overstep the limits: fight with the one who fights you.
>
> *Si maneno ya Stambuli, fungua sura ya kumi na tatu, aya ya kumi na moja (13:11): Sura Al-Ra'ad: Fungua na uangalie, halafu ujiuliza: wewe u mwerevu? Jana tulipozungumza mambo haya tukasema ina masharti yake wengine wali-turukia kama tuache kupotosha watu. Hatupotoshi! Bwana mtume Muham-mad (s.a.w.) alikuwa si mwoga. Na walipokuwa wakiuliwa mama zake . . . ambao ni waafrika, Ethiopa, wakiuliwa. Yaani haweza kupigana vile vile. Akangoja mpaka alipokuwa kwenda zake Madina kule alipofuatwa akato-kozwa ndiyo akapawa amri lakini akaambiwa usipite mipaka [12:06]. Pigana na yule akupigae.*

Here Prophet Muhammad is shown as a role model who endured much pain and still resisted the urge to attack and kill in revenge, waiting for proper advice and signs to indicate to him when the right time would be. Endurance and patience (*ustahiki; subira*) were the qualities shown by the Prophet back then, and they may still be the recommendable virtues for people today. The point was to listen and wait, as there might be a moment when God would communicate that the time to use violence against one's attackers or oppressors had come. But even then, he said, it was only admissable within certain boundaries and restrictions: you should fight only with the one who fights you (*pigana na yule akupigae*), and not extend your violence to the unarmed or his children or kin. Indeed, he implored his listeners to consider imagining themselves on the receiving end of a terrorist attack, which was not inconceivable given the circumstances, even here in Kenya.

> And if Abubakar comes here and he causes horror (commits terror) without any consultations with Muslims here, and then goes away, what would we say? How would we judge this? Our mothers, grandmothers, sisters in their houses when such a thing would happen. Who would defend them? Or would we leave this to God alone? Again, my elders, my siblings, and my mothers, if I have faulted you or if I have spoken badly, please forgive me. My position is that

we still have a long way, us Muslims, especially here in Kenya, to the degree that I can understand.

[17:10] *Na Abubakar akija hapa akafanya kituko bila na kushauriana na waislamu hapa, halafu akienda zake. Huwa sisi tutapima vipi? Mama zetu, nyanya zetu, dada zetu manyumbani pakitokizea wala tokezea. Nani atawasimamia hawa? Au tumwachia mungu tu? Tena wazee wangu, ndugu zangu, mama zangu kama nawakosea au kama nitawaeleka vibaya watanisamehe. Msimamo wangu ni kuwa tuna njia ndefu sisi waislamu haswa hapa Kenya, kiwango ambacho mimi naelewa.*

In the end, then, does the advocacy of violence (in principle) not lead to a situation of everyday experience in fear of potential attacks from anywhere? Such is the big question brought up by Stambuli here. For if we have to reckon with the presence of such attackers—like "Abubakar" here, an arbitrary Muslim name, who could be anyone (*mtu fulani*)—we can never be sure our sisters and mothers are safe. With his own Swahili imagery, Stambuli here referred to a fundamentally unsettled, worried, and unsafe society that was created, in a kind of vicious circle, by a (general) readiness of people to use violence as a means of addressing social problems and dealing with social tensions. This is a pattern we can probably identify in the United States and Israel, and also increasingly in European countries. But these issues, in Stambuli's opinion, need to be taken on and worked through by way of a "greater *jihad*," through social engagement with people in the community, for a possible solution to be reached. And it is in this direction, as he said, that he still envisaged a long way and much work ahead for Kenyan Muslims.

We can see that after presenting his own stance or making a point, Stambuli frequently turned to address his audience as a constituency of elders and siblings, according to the conventions of politeness and by means of rhetorical gestures that express humility and recognize his own limitations (of knowledge; of status), but also to the sincerity of his good motivations for his actions. As he said elsewhere in the program, "without respecting people, you will wrong them" (*bila kuwaheshimu watu utawakosea*). In short, Stambuli sought to represent himself here—or even personify the idea of a morally upright struggle—as a well-informed citizen and committed Muslim spokesperson who is himself only an ordinary layman from among the people.

The Special Guest: Professor Muhammad Hyder

The special guest for the second of the two broadcasts on "terror" (*ugaidi*) was Prof. Muhammad Hyder, a prominent local intellectual and a retired professor of zoology of the University of Nairobi, with a doctorate from the University of St Andrews. He had written a series of articles on science and the Qur'an for *Sauti ya Haki* during the 1970s (chapter 4), and he was a long-standing Muslim activist who was still running NGO projects focusing, for instance, on local educational development. He was also a major figure behind the enthusiastic but ultimately unsuccessful campaign for a Muslim university in Mombasa (until now, Mombasa had no university proper, only branch campuses and a polytechnical college). He complemented Stambuli and Abubakar well in this program, with comments and insights that drew from a wealth of experience, and as a good speaker and comfortable narrator live on air.

The notorious lack of leadership on the coast was among the first points to come up for him to comment upon. This was a regrettable and long-term "wound" (*kidonda*) of the Kenyan Muslim community, he said. "We do not have leadership" (*Hatuna uwongozi*), he said, and there was no reliable guidance available by Kenyan *ulama* (8:20). This was an ongoing point of discontent and frustration among coastal Muslims, who felt, as Prof. Hyder said, that they were "always behind" (*siku zote tuko nyuma*). Coastal leaders, it was known, had never spoken up with enough determination and engagement on behalf of their people vis-à-vis the government to make a difference. Indeed, part of Stambuli's agenda for his broadcast programs in *"Elimika na Stambuli"* was a critique of the Muslim elites, who had done well for themselves but not looked at the well-being of others, or the common good of their community.

In response to a caller who contested the term "Islamic terrorism" and pointed to current and historical acts of violent destruction committed by the United States and other Western powers that, he said, might well be called "terrorism" (like carpet bombing, or the use of nuclear bombs), Stambuli reminded his audience of the historical context and the coming-into-being of the current groups committing terror in the name of Islam, which had little to do with religion as such.

> Stambuli:[21] Thank you. Here there is something that I would like to comment on so that we understand each other well. For instance, many people know nowadays that "terrorism" has to do with Osama bin Laden. But there are things that even if we talk about them, we don't like to name them. For instance, that Osama bin Laden long ago met with Russians who came from Afghanistan. Turki al-Faisal introduced him to the Americans and they gave him "training" and after giving him "training" and money, he was then given fighters by the Americans, to fight the Russians until they left Afghanistan. Only then they started to come together as a group of their own. It is not right that we talk about these things, but otherwise we don't understand these things widely enough [in context] so that people will understand them well, especially our Kenyan friends.[22] My question, for instance, is about that person, our fellow Muslim, when he was dealing with those Americans in order to fight the Russians and push them out of Afghanistan—did he not know they were enemies? These kinds of things we should ask each other, and inform each other about. . . . But are these things talked about?

> *Ahsante.* [21:00] *Hapa wajua kuna kitu ambacho mie kidogo nataka tuelewane. Kwa mfano watu wengi wajua sasa hivi terrorism inahusishwa na Osama bin Laden. Lakini kuna mambo ambayo hata tukiyazungumza hatupendi kuyataja. Kwa mfano Osama bin Laden iliyopo akutana na warusi watokea Afghanistan, Turki al-Faisal aliyemjulisha kwa waamerika na Amerika wakampa training na baada kumpa training na mapesa akawa yatoka, wakapawa wapigana na Russia mpaka wakaitoka Afghanistan. Halafu wakaanza kupambana yenyewe. Si haki kwamba tutakuwa tutazungumza jambo hili lakini hatueleweki kwa upana ili watu watakaelewa haswa waKenya wenzetu. Swala langu kwa mfano huyu huyu ndugu yetu, mwislamu mwenzetu, alipokuwa alishirikiana na hao waamerika kumtoa mrussia pale Afghanistan* [22:05]. *Je alikuwa hajui kama hawa ni maadui? Vitu kama hivi tuulizane, tuambiane ni kweli. . . . Mambo kama haya je yazungumzwa?*[23]

In response to a caller who argued against the use of the (popular) term "Islamic terrorism," Prof. Hyder agreed and rejected the term, just like he rejected the term "Christian terrorism" (though historically, he said it was possible to entertain this idea, looking for instance at medieval church history). He also pointed to the phenomenon of "state-sponsored terrorism" that could be seen across the world, and he briefly contemplated historical versions of "church-sponsored terrorism" that might share common features with what was nowadays called "Islamic terrorism," the enactment of violent terror and destruction while (wrongfully) invoking religion.

> Doctor Ali, I would like to briefly say here that you said that the Americans, when they attacked Afghanistan or when they went to attack Iraq, whether that should be called "terrorism"? That is called "state-sponsored terrorism." When they coined this term "state-sponsored terrorism" they were about to attack Libya but they didn't want that to be seen.
> *Dokta Ali nataka kidogo kusema hapa kwamba umesema waamerika walipokuwa wamepiga Afghanistan au walipokwenda kupiga Iraq je utaja ili ni terrorism? Ile itwa state-sponsored terrorism. Walipotunga neno hili ya state-sponsored terrorism walikuwa kupiga Libya lakini wao hawataki kuona yao* [24:04].[24]

With this, he turned to speak about Noam Chomsky, the world-famous linguist and philosopher, as a politically engaged Jewish American intellectual and remarkable critic of his own country, and even more so, his own community. Prof. Hyder introduced Chomsky as an exceptional role model of a knowledgeable critic who fearlessly spoke truth to power, but whose voice was suppressed in the American public. As Prof. Hyder summarized it, Chomsky had argued that the United States (and other countries) have long engaged in what may well be called politics of "state-sponsored-terrorism." Chomsky, Hyder said, at the age of over eighty, still published one critical political commentary every week, in which he critiqued US governmental politics and how they contributed to increase global injustice (especially with a view to the Israeli-Palestinian conflict and the US role in it) (23:50).

> But there is an American called Noam Chomsky who doesn't give them oppor-
> tunity. Noam Chomsky is one of the best brains in America. He is a mathema-
> tician, a linguist—he does many things we could talk about, but every week
> he writes an article saying that among all the terrorists in the whole world,
> terrorist number one is America.
>> And he himself is American?
>> Yes, he's American.
>> *Lakini wako Amerika mmoja ni Noam Chomsky ambaye hawapi nafasi.*
>> *Noam Chomsky ni mmoja katika one of the best brains leo katika Amerika.*
>> *Ni mtu ni mathematician, ni linguist—anafanya nyingi ambazo ile lakini kila*
>> *wiki huandika article ya kusema: katika terrorist katika dunia nzima terrorist*
>> *number one ni Amerika.*
>> *Na ni mwamerika?*
>> *Eh, ni mwamerika.*[25]

Indeed, Chomsky spoke and wrote (after 9/11 and before) about systematic US strategies and implementation of Latin American regimes subservient to US interests (and dependent on US support), from the 1970s to 1990s, which involved strategic use of violence that by all definitions of the term deserved the name "terrorism." Chomsky clearly laid out the foundations and continuities between an initial US conception and practice of a "war on terror" as begun under Ronald Reagan and the more recent initiative by George W. Bush, who used some of the same main advisers (Chomsky 2003, 48–76). Prof. Hyder pointed to the admirable activity of critique that Chomsky had been pursuing, critical of his own government, and against the (supposed) interests of his own religious community, the American Jews. By doing so, Chomsky could almost be seen as a role model for what it meant for someone to engage in proper *jihad*. For Prof. Hyder, this was in the first instance an internal struggle within oneself (*jihad kubwa ni ya sisi wenyewe*), about dedication and self-discipline in working with one's full conviction for a good cause.

As for the United States and its allies (after September 11, 2001, and before the Iraq war in March 2003), Prof. Hyder made sure to provide information on the historical context and background, for those listeners who might not be aware (anymore): the United States had been wanting to invade Iraq and pushed for it with all means, including making the crucial rhetorical link between President Saddam Hussein and Osama bin Laden's al-Quaeda terrorist network—a link that subsequently was admitted to be invented.

> They themselves these days say that Saddam and Osama are like "cotton and
> fire" [a dangerous combination; they are incompatible]. That is why you can-
> not use Saddam, because the reason for attacking Saddam was that he was

working together with Osama. 9/11 has nothing to do with it, they themselves agree "publicly" now. It has nothing to do with Iraq or Saddam. But those same people, the group around Rumsfeld, if you go and look at the pictures when (earlier on) they went to Saddam to offer him all kinds of technologies. At that time, what were they waiting to do? They wanted to go to war.

Na wao wenyewe wakubali sasa watakavyosema kwamba Saddam na Osama ni pamba na moto [25:09]. Kwa hivyo huwezi kutumia—Saddam kwamba—sababu ya kumpiga Saddam kwa sababu kwamba ya kwa sababu yeye anafungamana na Osama. 9/11 haihusiani wakubali wao publicly sasa. Haihusiani hata kidogo na Iraq wala Saddam. Lakini hawa hawa akina Rumsfeld ukienda utaziona picha wamekwenda kuzungumza na Saddam na kumoffer kila kina namna vifaa. Wakati ule wamengoja kufanya nini? Wataka kupigana.

The United States had collected all kinds of intelligence and was ready to provide it, he said. They had prepared everything, and were waiting for other people to fight their wars for them. Ultimately, and here he agreed with a previous caller, this was all about oil, and access to the available resources for the US economy. "Democracy?," he asked. "Yes, we all want democracy—but who brings democracy by force? That is a clear lie." With these kinds of comments, Prof. Hyder acted as a kind of public adviser to the coastal Muslim audience, giving his opinions in context and providing knowledge about links and historical background that was accessible in the public realm but not known to everyone. He was a critical mind, who, throughout the postcolonial decades had lent his voice and expertise to the agenda of consciousness-building and social reform, on the side of Sheikh Muhammad Kasim Mazrui and Sheikh Abdalla Saleh Farsy—indeed, writing for *Sauti ya Haki*, as we saw in the previous chapter, as a scientist presenting arguments for the compatibility of science and the Qur'an.

At the time of Stambuli's radio broadcasts, Prof. Hyder was also in charge of the Muslim Civic Educational Trust (MCET), a small NGO seeking to boost educational development among coastal Muslims and bringing out weekly double-sided pamphlets in English—similar to the *Sahifa* pamphlets by Sheikh Al-Amin Mazrui (chapter 3)—called *Kenya waislamu waitakavyo* (Kenya How the Muslims Want It). These pamphlets, written in English and published between 2002 and 2004, focused on two or three topics of discussion each issue. These constituted commentaries on contemporary Kenya from a Muslim perspective that advocated human rights and better education and engaged in discussions about the improvement of democracy in Kenya, the status of women, proper ways of dressing, and the fight against corruption—which, in this early phase of the Kibaki government in the post-Moi era, was high on the national agenda. Last but not least, Prof. Hyder was also a great-uncle to Stambuli, as part of a wider network of (intellectually active) family members who engaged in education and politics, religion and literature.

Listening 2: The Concluding Minutes and Professor Hyder's Vote of Thanks

I now zoom in on a final "close listening" exercise, by focusing atttention on the concluding part of the discussion on *ugaidi* (terrorism). Some core elements of the program can be exemplified by listening to these last four minutes of the broadcast: commentary contributions by listeners, both as callers and by text message, responding to earlier points made in the discussion and seeking either to emphasize a certain point or to mediate between conflicting statements made by previous callers. We also gain a sense of how the moderators worked in mediating, summarizing, and passing on the word between callers and the visiting speaker. Finally, important reflections on the fundamental relevance of the program for the community were presented by Prof. Hyder in his concluding vote of thanks, about the great value of an accessible and open discursive space being provided for internal discussions.

> **Final caller:** Since September 11, all Muslims in the whole world have been mistreated. Why were those Arab Muslims not mistreated by the Americans and the British, why not?
>   *Tangu Septemba 11, waislamu wote ulimwenguni mzima walinyanyaswa. Mbona wale waislamu wa Arabuni hawakunyanyaswa na waamerika na waingereza, kwa sababu gani?* (1:10:20)

The final caller (a middle-aged male, from what we can judge) goes on talking fast and agitated, and the gist of his contribution is about how Arab Muslims have failed the wider global Muslim community. They did not show solidarity with their suffering Muslim peers around the world, but they collaborated with the United States and other Western powers, benefiting economically and politically for themselves, and thereby broke their bonds with their Muslim brothers and sisters around the world. Even though Muhammad the Prophet came from among them and the Qur'an was presented to Muslims in their language, the caller says that these "Arab Muslims" were hypocritical and actually "*makafiri wachafu*" (dirty infidels)—in contrast to the suffering African Muslims and particularly the East African Muslims who, from their own perspective, should try to clean Islam from within, away from the "*chafu*" (dirt) that "these people" (*watu hawa*)—Arab terrorists, and Arab collaborators with Western powers—have cast upon Islam and the *umma*.

Listening to the caller in his role as host and co-moderator, Stambuli made audible sounds expressing acknowledgment and attention while keeping his distance. He then announced the next day's program, which would continue discussing this topic once more (as a rare exception). Afterward Abubakar read out a text message comment, and he reiterated his previous plea that people should provide their proper names with their comments when writing or phoning in, as there should be nothing secretive about participating in such a discussion. Then Stambuli read out a final text message, which turned out to consist of a general appeal:

> May peace be with you! The reconciliation is that we should live in the Islamic way, following the Qur'an and the *sunna*, and we should love each other and respect each other, and command good of each other and forbid evil.
>
> *Salaam aleikum! suluhisho ni sisi tuishi kiislamu na tujivunia tufuate kuran na suna, na tupendane na tuheshiame, na tuamrishane mema na tukatazane maovu.*

The declatory tone here fit the message—to do good and avoid evil—also as a concluding act to the broadcast, and so this quote invoked a common moral ground among the listeners, by reiterating a shared discursive reference point. Stambuli then was asked to conclude, and he expressed his thanks to all the listeners and the special guest, Prof. Hyder, for their participation in the program. He mentioned the specifics of his own individual take on things, as a motivation for this particular topical program, and his limitations as a human being in trying to make the kind of vision he had in mind come true.

Abubakar, the moderator, then asked Prof. Muhammad Hyder to speak his closing words. I quote these in full here, as they convey a good sense of a senior assured speaker, his flow of diction, and the patterns of reasoning and rhetoric involved. Next to other tropes and idioms of speech that we encountered already (in the course of these chapters), he also invoked Islamic history and the role model of Prophet Muhammad and his companions, before turning to his points of advice to listeners in the here and now. As is common in Swahili lectures and advisory or admonishing texts and discourses within the community—and as we have seen in Sheikh Al-Amin's pamphlets above—a rhetorical "we" (*sisi*) is used, to include oneself and one's audience (as one's peers) as one.

Prof. Hyder's Closing Address (1:14:00)

> I am very happy to have been here with you. Our time is up, and we have been able to talk about many things. We have seen there have been some very hot and contested issues touched upon, for sure, and that one can sit here for two hours and benefit a lot from listening to the people, and become engaged in many discussions.
>
> *Nimefurahi sana kuwa nanyi. Wakati umepita, mengi tumeweza kusema. Inaonyesha kwamba mambo chemchem, kwa hakika, na mtu aweza kuketi kwa masaa mawili hapa, na akapata faidi kuwasikiza watu, na akaweza kujibizana kwa mambo mengi.*
>
> But I would like to say first of all: if we talk about the topic of *jihad*, we should remember that the *big jihad* is the one that you fight against yourself (your own will), to compare yourself with God (his demands) so that you orientate/adjust yourself with a view to God in everything that you do. If you

take that (*jihad*) on, then you know that the *second jihad* is about taking care of your own people, so that we can make sure, in a joint effort, that we are all Muslims; so that we can enable them to reach that level. Because when we take care of our people, we learn how to take care of an ill person, and how to attend to a poor person.

Lakini napenda kusema mwanzo: tukisema mada ya jihadi, tukumbuke kwamba jihadi kubwa ni ile ya wewe upigania na nafsi yako, kujilinganisha na Mwenyezi Mungu ili wewe umwelekee Mwenyezi Mungu katika mambo yako yote. Ukitukua ile utajua basi katika jihadi ya pili ni kuwatazama wale watu wako: ili tufungamane zote wawe Waislamu, ili tuawaweze tuwaenua. Kwamba tukisimamisha wale watu wetu tukatazama mgonjwa kwa vipi, maskini tunamtazama kwa vipi.

Islam in the ninth year, meaning since Medina, "the first city state of Islam," had no poor people. And we should ask ourselves, how could they achieve that then? They did not go to the World Bank, nor anywhere else; they started then and there on the basis of *zakat*, and they helped people.

Uislamu katika mwaka tisia, maana kuanzia Medina, the first city state of Islam, kulikuwako hakuna maskini. Tujiuliza walifanya vipi? Hawakwenda kwa world bank, hawakwenda kwenye nini. Walianza palepale kwa njia za zaka, na walisadia watu.

Well, perhaps we could use such ways too instead of strapping bombs to our bodies and going to blow ourselves up in order to attack others. That is terrorism—and it is not terrorism about which we can say it is Islamic. If we want to spread Islam further, the first thing is to clean up ourselves (our thoughts and feelings); the second is to take care of our people and our families, to bring them into a position in which they can acquire a certain standard of living; we assist to provide them with education, we give them some property and get them into a situation so that they get a job so that they can move forward by themselves, so that they can progress.

Je sisi tunaweza kutumia njia zile badala ya kujifungua mabomu, na kwenda kujipasua na kwenda kuwapigana: ule ni ugaidi—na si ugaidi ambao tuaweza kusema ni ya kiislamu. Kwa sababu sisi tuataka kueleza Uislamu, jambo la kwanza ni kujisafisha sisi nafsi zetu; jambo la pili ni kuwatukua wale jamaa zetu kuwatukua katika hali, tuwape ilmu, tuwape mali, kuwaenua katika hali wapate kazi, wapate njia za wao ili wao waweza kujiendeleza mbele. Ili wao waweza kuwaendelea.

And in our ongoing discussions with each other (we can develop ourselves), if God wishes, by discussing more and more amongst ourselves about matters such as those (covered today). Radio Rahma has given people a chance to be able to exchange (and possibly change each other's) thoughts about such matters. And I would like to congratulate you. I am happy to have been able to be with you here today.

Na sisi inshallah katika kujadiliana, na kujadiliana zaidi, kuhusu mambo kama haya. Radio Rahma imewapa watu nafasi ya kuweza kubadilishana fikra kwa mambo kama haya. Na napenda kuwapa pongezi, nafurahi sana kuweza kuwa pamoja na nanyi siku ya leo.

Concluding Reflections on Discursive Space

What Prof. Hyder highlighted in his closing comments should also be emphasized here in conclusion: that the *"Elimika na Stambuli!"* broadcasts provided
an important platform for open discussion among fellow Muslims, so that their
respective opinions could be developed and shaped, questioned or confirmed (or
rejected) in interaction with each other, as standpoints to be tested and strengthened. This was, Hyder said, what Stambuli and Abubakar should be congratulated for most. Prof. Hyder emphasized the fundamental value of engaging in
discussion as such, as it provided the opportunity for learning in mutual interaction. He praised the makers of the program for their provision of an open discursive space for such difficult and important discussions as they had just had, which
forced participants and listeners to test their own thinking, and to reconsider and
reshape it. Prof. Hyder here took on the role of an adviser to all listeners. At no
point was he telling them what to do or what to think, though he was providing
guidance on what to avoid and how to position oneself. His emphasis was on the
value of an openly accessible space for discussion, which holds the possibility of
change, and this indicated a strong appreciation of intellectual exchange in its
own right.

This corresponds to the enthusiastic way in which this show was received,
from its maiden broadcast (March 2005) onward. Mutual self-education
(*-jielimisha*) or teaching each other (*-elimishana*) was at the center of the program throughout, as well as speaking up against common malpractices, as the
program was building a dedicated discursive community of followers. An egalitarian kind of "forbidding wrong from below" was practiced here, one could
say—having in mind also the quotidian and "democratic" features that have
been linked to this command (Cook 2000, 584).[26] And Prof. Hyder's final commentary on the value and importance of discursive space for the discussion of
sensitive and fundamental issues in society can be understood as a thoughtful
discursive impersonation, a personal enactment of the moral obligation to provide guidance, by emphasizing the peaceful dynamics of open discussion that
may eventually facilitate change.

Reflecting on the discussions summarized here as well as other broadcasts of
the same show, as characterized above, we might say that the *"Elimika na Stambuli"* sessions represent something of an exercise in reappropriating public discursive space for the cultivation of critical internal debate and, in a wider sense,
of educational as well as political discussions that address matters of concern for
the coastal Muslim community directly, as part of an intracommunal assessment
and reorientation.

Apart from the crucial feature of open accessibility of the genre and media
employed—a live on-air phone-in discussion on radio—which facilitated the

possible participation by anyone willing, able, and motivated to call in, we also observe the effort put in by the organizers of the show to invite the right kinds of guest speakers for the envisaged topics of discussion. Such figures were qualified by the specific experience and knowledge they brought. As we have seen, this applies to senior notable members of the coastal Muslim community, who were then engaged in focused and often sensitive yet informal discussions, similar to the kind we encounter in *baraza* settings, characterized by mutual familiarity, recognition, respect, and a basic consensus or unity of shared belonging, shared concerns (or vulnerabilities), and shared aspirations (or future goals), though with potentially vastly diverging opinions of how to aim for some of them, or how to draw from others.

More generally, and in comparison with the above-mentioned women's forum (*Ukumbi wa Mamama*) program that also aired on Radio Rahma (Alidou 2013, 156–70), there is a common point here about employing a radio broadcast as a "creative space" (168–69) in which marginalized or underprivileged groups can virtually convene and discuss, freely and in public, topics that would usually be deemed too sensitive, divisive, or daring to cover (as seen above). This became possible because of the guarded space that radio provides while at the same time being (easily) accessible, for moderators as well as for callers and listeners. Many of the sanctions and limitations for polite interaction (according to age, status, or gender) that commonly apply for direct interaction in shared space—like prohibitions against looking at each other, or talking to each other only in certain prescribed ways and sequences—did not apply here in the same way. Female or junior callers could make their points without bowing to social hierarchies, and male elders and youngsters could benefit from listening in to ladies' programs, even calling in to engage in discussion. The resultant gains were remarkable, in terms of better mutual understanding between social subgroups who are not usually equal partners in conversation but kept apart (according to gender, age, ethnicity, or social status) and whose public interaction is highly regulated. Similar to my observations about the importance of intracommunal discussions of sensitive topics, Alidou's research on Radio Rahma's women's broadcast showed how sensitive and contested topics of a sexual, legal, or political nature were vividly discussed (e.g., AIDS: how to deal with its risks and realities, especially in marital relationships; rape: how to define it, and how to campaign for legal amendments to definitions of it and penalties for it; sexual practices: how habits and conventions were linked to risks and dangers of either of the above). This took place in a direct yet respectful manner for which the female moderators acted as role models (Alidou 2013, 156–70), and with a silent male audience listening in and learning.

Callers and listeners of both programs seemed to latch on quickly to the opportunity of such frank internal debates (as they were needed), and we might say—along with Prof. Hyder—that through them, people engaged with the chance to develop and boost their insight and mutual understanding, and thereby to reimagine their own community and potentially change and thus reshape it (see Mandaville 2001; Meyer 2009). Sensitive and contested topics— whether terrorism or rape or polygamy—thereby marked or constituted the discursive fields through which such creative dispute could be performed, by means of critical questioning and response. Such topics are fundamentally dilemmatic, in that there is no painless, clear, and easy way to address, negotiate, or resolve the presence of the issues around them, or how they are rhetorically invoked. Yet in addressing them on a common public platform for many diverse kinds of people who shape the community, opportunity is thereby gained also to reshape the community itself.

A Note on the Oral Word and the Written

In the previous chapter on the *Sauti ya Haki* newspaper, we saw that the representatives of one of the main groups involved in regional debates about Islamic propriety, the Alawiyya *masharifu*, were reluctant to engage in a print debate with their opponents, the reformists in charge of the newspaper, a new medium for public religious discourse in the Swahili region at the time. At the same time, apparently, they were active in responding orally, in their speeches and classes, to the points and critiques with which reformists addressed them.[27] Conversely, oral narratives (*kisa*) were integrated into *Sauti ya Haki* articles, as a means to convey important didactic points to the audience in a lively and humorous way that, as the editors knew, would be appreciated by the readership—also, I suggest, because the oral mode of interaction was the most common and natural to all.

In the discursive interactions of Stambuli's radio program, one could witness a remarkable ability to speak well in public, to use clear formulations, and to make considered arguments or point people in an appropriate direction, even while live on air and audible to a large public. (This is, in my experience, much different in Western contexts and surely the German one, where many callers would mumble, stutter, or otherwise display insecurities about what they say or how to say it when speaking in public). Even if I cannot go deeper into the exploration of the whys and hows of this rhetorical confidence and clarity here, this is a remarkable phenomenon that deserves recognition. Indeed, I hardly recall any callers to "*Elimika na Stambuli!*"—young or old, female or male, and with or without formal education—who presented their thoughts in a confusing or insecure manner.

In short, this may indicate that people on the whole (here, the range of coastal Muslims on air) seem confident and in their natural element when speaking, that is when expressing and presenting their thinking orally (as complex, critical, and questioning as it may be). With a view to social actors as agents of intellectual practice, this means that as researchers, we need to keep up our knowledge and awareness about direct interactions and the dimensions of social embeddedness and the social competence of speakers. As we could see here, with reference to the sample of a local radio station on the Swahili coast in the early twenty-first century, the relevance of orality in society is by no means receding (see Furniss 2004).

What interests me most in terms of questions to ask of these discussions, is the character of the thinking displayed here by engaged Muslim individuals, male or female, who were (to some extent) successful in publicly discussing fundamental and sensitive matters of social and political concern to the Muslim community. For Stambuli, for instance, the fact that he was a religious layman, an engaged, self-taught, and somewhat hands-on activist who could show that he had acquired a good measure of Islamic knowledge while not being closely associated with any of the major organized Islamic groups fighting for ideological supremacy, was surely essential for his (relative) success. He (re)presented the discontent and frustration of ordinary Muslims with the elites, and brought this to public expression. The elites had not managed to improve the status of Muslims in the country (or even the region) over the four decades since Independence. The questions and demands that he raised in his program were grounded in recognizable everyday experiences of ordinary Muslims, and as he spoke in a simple language that all could understand, he struck a chord with many listeners.

But ultimately, this ability may also have led to the discontinuation of the show, as the resultant popularity led to too much of a critical potential. The broadcast had been privately funded by sponsors (whom Stambuli had found), as Radio Rahma charged 30,000 shillings per hour for it. In 2007 the donors withdrew their monies, apparently under pressure by local politicians and members of the elite who resented Stambuli's critical agenda. Radio Rahma did not give the program another chance, despite its popular success. And so, the program ended. With this, a small but locally significant public forum for open debate also ceased to exist.[28] (Abdulswamad Nassir, son of Shariff Nassir, the previous political "king of the coast" under President Moi, was to begin his political career shortly after, and has in the meantime become the local member of parliament. He still owns Radio Rahma.)

It might make sense to consider further the features of what one might call "postcolonial thinking" here, drawing from these examples, and to reflect upon why this term may be useful to think with. For one, the kind of textual ethnography employed here draws us into people's social experience, and it makes us read (or listen) along, "tuned in," so to say, to their perspectives—which are both confrontational and conciliatory—and thus we are rereading and understanding society and the life-world here through the ways it has been (and continues to be) contested among coastal Muslims in Kenya. While the term "coastal Muslims" signifies a complex historical amalgam of subgroups from East Africa and connected Indian Ocean littorals, they are also citizens in a country where, as we have seen discussed even by Minister Balala on a broadcast show (see also Nassir 2008), even getting ID cards (let alone passports) is incredibly difficult for them. And general conditions of experience such as these shape the kind of fragile, vulnerable, enduring, yet creative postcolonial experience in a wider (and representative) sense than I have investigated and analyzed here and in the previous chapters.

In the internal debates among coastal Muslims who are positioned in a kind of tension-laden "double periphery" with a view to the global Muslim *umma* and the Kenyan postcolonial state (Kresse 2009; Kresse 2013), needing to justify and prove themselves vis-à-vis both of them, we can observe a remarkable double awareness or dual sensitivity that speaks volumes about discontent on the one side and social responsibility on the other. This was visible, for instance, in the ways in which Stambuli balanced and measured his expressions when addressing his listening public at the beginning and end of each show. Not only did he raise and engage critical perspectives on society by addressing practical matters and social concerns from within but he also added loops of self-critical reflection on top of this. Stambuli's thinking as seen here, maneuvering and mediating between vastly different members of his community, represents a kind of model perspective that stands for a flexible, critical, and well-grounded view, by ordinary self-educated Muslims, on their fragile postcolonial life-world, which is local, translocal, and transregional at the same time. And this thinking seems stimulated, unified, and fortified by drawing flexibly from its combined resources of social experience, moral commitment, and individual creativity. It can be understood as a specific kind of local cosmopolitanism, linked to the character and scope of experience of particular postcolonial subjects, and their creative efforts in endurance and resilience.

Notes

1. Stambuli Abdilahi Nassir and Abubakar Amin are their full names. I already knew Stambuli well before becoming interested in covering his (then new) radio broadcast as part of my research, and I got to know Abubakar during my visits to Mombasa in 2005 and 2006. Both invited and encouraged me to engage with their program then, and I had many conversations with each of them about it, also collecting materials and information. In recent communications, after having read a draft of this chapter which I sent them, both indicated (separately from each other) that they wanted their full real names to be used in publication. At time of finalization of this book, Stambuli was recently made Productions Manager of the new Sauti ya Pwani Radio Station in Mombasa, and Abubakar has been General Manager of Operations for Radio Maarifa in Tanga, Tanzania, for seven years.

2. There was a fatal bomb attack on a tourist hotel north of Mombasa, one frequented at the time by Israeli tourists. Thirteen people were killed, ten Kenyans and three Israelis. In parallel, there was a failed attempt to shoot down an Israeli Boeing 757 airplane loaded with tourists that was in the process of taking off at the Mombasa airport. See, for example, the *New York Times*, November 30, 2002.

3. The social dynamics of engaged "community radio" projects of different kinds have been covered for other African countries, in Muslim as well as non-Muslims contexts; see, for example, Haron 2015; Brigalia 2007; Graetz 2014; Furniss and Fardon 2000; Njogu and Middleton 2009.

4. The range was increased years later, and in 2012 I easily tuned in to Radio Rahma when visiting Lamu.

5. Stambuli discussed this historical case openly during another program. On MIOME, see also Chanfi 2008.

6. *"Lengo ni juzana-kujua kuhusu mazingira."* "The goal is to inform each other—to know (more) about the (social) environment" (39:00—Stambuli comments on the qualifications of Prof. Hyder, why he is good to listen to, highlighting his knowledge, his extensive education, and his experience of living abroad in West).

7. In my account of him then, I gave him the pseudonym "Saidi."

8. This early dating is correct, also according to another standard reference work (Horton and Middleton 2000).

9. In Annex C of the *Report of the Kenya Coastal Strip Conference* (Colonial Office 1962, 29–30).

10. Such rumors may have been strengthened when Sheikh Abdilahi decided, after this defeat, to remain politically active and join KANU in order to pursue coastal interests from within the national ruling party (after some time, however, he resigned from politics and turned to publishing).

11. In pre-Independence political debates in Parliament, Sheikh Abdilahi Nassir, as representative for Mombasa's Mvita district, had responded to Tom Mboya's call for Swahilis to "return to Arabia" by saying, "Luos should return to Sudan," referring to the historical migration of the Nilotic Luo southward, which historically came after the establishment of Swahili culture and society (between the ninth and twelfth centuries CE). See Prestholdt (2014); also personal communications with Sheikh Abdilahi, since 1998.

12. Police forces have been known, for years now, to be arresting them arbitrarily under the pretense of looking for terrorist suspects while actually looking for substantial bribes from those whom they held at random. The danger of being detained under these circumstances gradually increased with the "war on terror" activities, and after the new Uhuru Kenyatta government's line of military strikes on al-Shabab in Somalia and the responding (ever larger) terrorist attacks. It reached a point, in summer 2014, when several of my coastal Muslim interlocutors said they, as well as their peers, refrained from leaving their houses in the evenings, for fear of being randomly picked up by police.

13. Nevertheless, of course, Pwani University in Kilifi (north of Mombasa) had been founded, first as a branch of Nairobi-based Kenyatta University and subsequently as an independent institution.

14. For a wider critical discussion, see Mamdani 2005 (esp. 45–62; 249–260); see also Presbey 2007. For East Africa see Becker 2006, Prestholdt 2011; Mwakimako and Willis 2014, 2016; Seesemann 2007; see also issues of the *Friday Bulletin* throughout 2014.

15. Roxanne Euben has argued that violent *jihad* (whatever else may be said about it—and she goes into an extensive historical contextualization of meanings) "is a form of political action" (2002, 9) that, while it may "kill" politics, is also seen to make politics possible (27) (see also Asad 2007, 56–58). For a more recent study discussing the supposedly low numbers of Muslim terrorists in context, also with a view to Middle Eastern perspectives, see Kurzman 2011.

16. As Euben explains, referring to a historical dictionary, in Arabic, the term derives from the verb *jahada* (to exert, struggle, or strive), and it literally means "exerting one's utmost power, efforts, endeavours or ability in contending with an object of disapprobation" (Euben 2002, 12).

17. Here he used Abubakar as a placeholder name, like "so-and-so"; using the name of his co-moderator also meant to bring home the point about a fundamental internal division being pushed by such actions.

18. *Swala yangu, je wewe waona hapo nje, ni sawa yeyote awe apigana kiislamu au si kiislamu aje aingie nchini Kenya kuharibu, aende zake watu wafe.* [20:01] *Waliobakia nyuma iwe shauri yao watajua wenyewe. We waunga mkono? . . . Je, tubaguane sisi wenyewe likiwa kwa kuwa akina Abubakar si langu, ikiwa kwetu sisi ndiyo mimi nataka Abubakar kama hakunisaidia basi nimponde. Je, lilipomfika Abubakar we ulimsaidia? Kwani ramu wazee wangu, mama zangu, ndugu zangu, tupige simu, tujadili mambo haya, kwa nidhamu ya dini. Mimi nakubali na nafikiri ndugu yangu Abubakar mpaka sasa ashazoea, ashakufa ganzi moyo na kichwa. Hata ukitaka kutukashifu pia piga.* [21:01] *Hii ndiyo sera ya idhaa, piga hata ukitaka kutukashifu, utufanye wajinga, piga kwa hisani yako. Kama wewe mwislamu, kama wewe si mwislamu : piga! Kama wewe mchina, wewe mwafrika, wewe mzungu: piga kwa hisani yako! Tueleze maoni yako kuhusu mada tunayozungumza.*

19. *We mwenzangu mwanadamu unayo haki kuniona mimi na kosa na sipingi kama nilivyoambia jana naheshimu maoni yenu. Lakini unavyo ulivyoelewa dini na mimi nipe ile haki hata kama wanichukia na mimi ninavyoelewa ile dini. Waweza kuwanishinda naweza mimi nakushinda.*

20. See Seesemann 2007; Prestholdt 2011. This also comes out in the historical overviews by Branch (2011) and Hornsby (2012).

21. He was responding to a caller by the name of Dokta Ali, saying the following: "*Kwani kufanya* carpet bombing *vile walifanya. Hiyo ndiyo ni* terrorism *ya aina gani?* [20:07] *Na ni kusema mtu ambaye alitumia* weapon *ya* mass destruction *mwanzo mwanzo alikuwa ni mwamerica aliyefikwa bomu ya* nuclear *huku Hiroshima na Nagasaki. Je mbona watu hawataki kumwambia huyu* terrorist *ya mwanzo. Kwa sababu* media *ni mikononi kwake na vile sasa hivi ulisema kuwa waislamu tunao pesa wameweka kwenye benki za America.*"

22. Here he refers to the common convention that it is not good to talk in detail in public about bad deeds of others.

23. He continues, "*Kwa sababu aya za qur'an na hadithi za mtume zimekuja kabla ya yeye kuzaliwa. Yeye alipokuwa akishirikiana na wale kama nduguze mpaka wakawa watamtoa mrusi, yeye alikuwa hakuziona hizi aya na hadithi? Si masallah ya kuwa tuwajaribu kuambiziana waislamu kuwalaza. Hatulazi mtu.*"

24. Note that the Kenyan philosopher Henry Odera Oruka already discussed state or state-sponsored terrorism (with a view on postcolonial Africa) in his book *Punishment and Terrorism in Africa* early on (Oruka 1985).

25. He goes on to refer to the military invasions and involvements by the United States of Granada, Nicaragua, and Panama as examples.

26. Note that Cook also calls this an "intellectual tradition" that he seeks to explore within the society where it flourished, also to see what difference it may have made in the streets (Cook 2000, xiii).

27. I heard this also from personal conversations with interlocutors from Lamu.

28. Information confirmed by Stambuli A. Nassir in May 2017. Then, Stambuli still continued to give talks and lectures throughout the region and on social media. He remains a popular speaker, and he has a strong voice in the Swahili community, including the diaspora.

6 Conclusion

Toward the Understanding of Understanding: Elements of a Swahili Intellectual Tradition

IN THE PRECEDING chapters, I have shed light on the ways in which urban coastal Muslims in postcolonial Kenya (beginning in the British colonial era) debate among themselves and engage in renegotiations of their own self-positioning within the Kenyan postcolony. The chapters discussed them both as community members and as engaged individuals, in challenging and precarious conditions that saw the former Arab Swahili elite vastly diminished in their political status and influence. Never quite in a position to actively shape the political conditions or possibilities of their experience, they act as highly ambivalent social actors, often seen as subservient, accepting and willing to please, yet also continuously discontented citizens, in a national political scenario. Herein, they have to position and prove themselves, both vis-à-vis external impositions and expectations by the postcolonial state (as Kenyans) and vis-à-vis internal rivalries, demands, and challenges that often, but by no means always, relate to conflicting interpretations of Islam.

Having to make do with a peripheral positioning in society does not necessarily mean accepting or confirming for oneself a position as inferior or weaker—though this may indeed often happen. This appears to apply to many coastal Muslims in Kenya, as a mass of people that have been regarded as calculable, and to be steered and reckoned with by those in power. Political rulers like President Moi demanded of them to stay as they are (*wabakiye hivyo hivyo*), as quiet, docile, and enduring citizens. From another perspective, however, a peripheral position can also be seen as a "privileged locus" (Lambek 1990, 26)—for analysis and critique of the wider social world of which one is part, and for engagement within it, in response to the challenges that one is facing. There are "peripheral visions" of national and global politics that can provide stimulating perspectives on lifeworlds in their transregional entanglements (Wedeen 2008).

The exposure to a wider range of experiences that one is subjected to in such a position (also and especially through the externally imposed frames of meaning) also opens up the opportunity to use this as an extended resource to draw from, for one's own thinking and doing. Thus, being situated in a peripheral position (as in the colonial and postcolonial constellations witnessed here) also leads to a wider resourcefulness to handle situations, not only in terms of endurance and resilience, but also in terms of alternate paradigms and systems of knowledge and education, or behavioral social skills (linked to different cultural traditions and their relevant languages). This enables certain individuals, who are resilient and determined enough, to build and shape creative ways to address and negotiate the social pressures and confrontations around them.

The case studies explored above can be read in this way, and the media and publics shaped by such individuals then are accessible platforms for the mediation and negotiation of social meaning, within a wider "struggle for orientation" (Loimeier 2009, 8) in a heterogenous and internally strained regional religious community that lacks a clear shared sense of unity.[1] Thus there is continuous striving for moral guidance and normative orientation that shapes the dynamics of interaction within the community, and this is performed especially through public debate. The discursive means that this entails is the use of rhetoric and genres and idioms of speech, whereby classical forms and strategies are continued while at the same time new ones are coined, adapted, and integrated. In these lively debates, as we could see, the whole realm of accessible resources (old and new) can be brought into play, for the form and content of public reasoning and self-positioning. The writers' and speakers' skills of navigating the world are exhibited as part of these debates, and the guidance they can provide to their peers to navigate it better is taken on, assessed, and appreciated or criticized.

Hereby, the need for orientation is responded to differently by different social actors at different points in time, as we have seen in the three main case studies. Yet fundamentally, in each case, a basic connection between the experience of individuals and their ways of grappling with things, under adverse conditions, is visible. In the chapters above, I have been following closely, ethnographically and by means of textual readings and narrative examples, the ways in which individuals engage in these struggles. Some show determination in actively reshaping their living conditions and their community, through endurance and strategies of resilience, by navigating the difficult social reality they are facing in the best available ways they can see. My discussion shows how they are conscious of the obligations they feel they need to fulfill as Muslims, and thus as members of the *umma*, a locally based yet globally connected community of believers. Its regional internal divisions were clearly visible in the *Sauti ya Haki* newspaper, for instance, whose agenda of modernization and social reform was pitched in direct opposition to its Sufi-oriented rivals, who were clearly identified and criticized throughout the publication period (chapter 4). The agenda of reform entailed negative effects, as its goals were presented in ways that were destructive to regional Muslim unity. Pursuing the task of reforming the community inherently emphasized existent splits and caused new ones. Internal divisions were enforced by fundamentally criticizing one's opponents as wrong and their leaders as "mis-leaders." And while *Sauti ya Haki* was used as a public platform by the reformers, some Sufi Alawiyya leaders from their side used sermons, classes, and lecture events as their own (more conventional oral) public platforms from which to defend and reassert themselves, stirring up resentment against reformers.[2] The power dynamics within the regional Muslim community may be cast in terms of a dialectical back-and-forth, whereby liberating moments, operating in adverse conditions and the resentment of a sizable group of opponents, alternated with and fed into dogmatic and potentially oppressive ones.[3]

In the case of *Sauti ya Haki*, this is a time when the term "Wahhabi" was (or became) commonly employed as a derogatory label for local Salafi-oriented reformists in response to what was perceived as their moral policing and self-righteous pious critique of others. In response to such insults, the editor, Sheikh Muhammad Kasim, called upon his followers not to become upset when being called "Wahhabi." After all, this could be seen as indirect praise, as it confirmed that those who were insulted like this were doing the right thing. He compared this to a time in the past, when pious young men who went to mosque were mocked in the same kind of ironic and dismissive way as *walii* (saints), by local "good-for-nothing youths' (*vijana wa kihuni*) who were not concerning themselves with religion and sought to embarrass others who did (M. K. Mazrui 1971, 19–20). Persistent mutual attacks like these make a pronounced conscious Islamic conduct of one's life in peaceful cohabitation with others difficult to near impossible for anyone, when public critique was lurking at every corner. If, what one group understands as pious may be deemed illegitimate and "un-Islamic" by the other, conflict becomes pervasive in everyday life. This ties in with my ethnographic observations since the late 1990s. Despite invocations of "Muslim unity" from both sides, the impression was that individual believers were often pushed to identify as members of either one or the other of two groups poised against each other, while their convictions and social allegiances may have linked them to both.[4] The effect for the self-positioning of many ordinary Muslims seemed to be that they either became insecure about how to behave and what really mattered in being a "good" Muslim (as previous paradigms seemed unacceptable), or they engaged in a somewhat hardened, emboldened, and combative attitude of self-presentation that pledged unquestionable allegiance to the ideological position of their group (and against the other). Thus evolved a gradually increasing sense of unease and uncertainty about how to conduct oneself in everyday life, and of mutual stand-off between the two major groups of regional Muslims. Among other aspects, this constellation, and the situation it created—of personal insecurity about the proper basics of Islam and discontent and apprehensiveness with the ways Muslim leaders handled controversies—also contributed to the emerging possibility of success for a slow but significant growth of coastal East African Shii converts.[5]

Mediated Immediacy and Discursive Space

The Islamic radio broadcast sessions discussed above revolved around the provision of an open and inclusive discursive space, mediating an immediate presence of callers who participated in social debates live on air. The radio broadcasts were accessible and liberating, and they encouraged free discussion, *kujadiliana* (the mutual exchange of thoughts and arguments). Transmission by radio, as a form of discursive dissemination, enabled the safe expression of critique among community members in public, without the common burden of social status (gender, age, ethnicity, education) obstructing people's participation. Without any filtering processes involved to this end, the program was egalitarian in outlook and pushed for a more egalitarian social reality for the coastal Muslim community on the whole, in the "real-life" scenarios that were discussed. Listening to the discussions pursued in this program, and considering the (sometimes highly controversial) themes selected and the (unusually open) ways in which they were discussed, one could not help but think of the reflexive discursive processes facilitated here as possible beginnings of fundamental transformation processes, of which the weekly *"Elimika"* broadcasts were indicative signs or premonitions— similar to Sheikh Al-Amin Mazrui's essays in his time. This points more generally to the presence of a "potential of self-transformation" as a feature of Swahili Muslim publics (at least this one)—a feature that Habermas (1989, 20) saw as distinct to the social history of the emergence of the European bourgeois public that he analyzed.[6]

As we have seen for the radio broadcasts, many callers appreciated and took advantage of the remarkable opportunities for open interaction that the easily accessible discursive space provided. Being able to conduct controversial, difficult, and painful discussions about such sensitive yet pressing topics as terrorism (*ugaidi*), within a community that had itself been collectively treated as suspected of terrorism by the state, was a remarkable achievement during such testing times, which honored the moderators and was acknowledged by the callers. The moderators' attempts at keeping such a discussion balanced and focused required high sensitivity, alertness, and discursive agility. Its live, on-air performance, then, proved not only the possibility of discussing such contested matters with each other (within a strained discursive unity of sorts), but also the value of having such an open joint discursive space for such discussions in the first place. This is what Prof. Hyder highlighted in his concluding speech. In fact, the way in which he spoke during his vote of thanks at the end of the show convincingly pointed to the value of the broadcast as an important and open—indeed, liberating—space that could facilitate social change. As Hyder said, by continuing to exchange arguments with each other, change—or the realization of the potential of communal self-transformation—became possible, in nonviolent ways. Similar observations have been made for a live discussion program on a new Arab satellite TV channel, which was also conceived to facilitate direct, immediate discussions and confront invited guests with questions by an audience that participated by means of telephone calls (Eickelman 2005, 47–50).[7]

From a different angle, and less bound to a fragile society and the idea of the possibility of change, the value of such an accessible discursive space can be considered as a provision that responds to a fundamental human need for expression. Being able to be heard and to express one's anxieties (and thus, in a way, relieve oneself and let go of them) is itself, at times, an existential human desire. And in this regard, too, the discursive opportunity to participate and "ex-press" (press meaning out of) oneself in the radio show, which was designed to be open-access and live, provided a liberating and cathartic space for those who called:

> When human beings seek guidance, illumination, or advice, it is not necessarily the content of what is said in response by an expert, or the content of a tradition or text, that is important. Rather *it is the process and action of being free to voice one's concern and be listened to that matters*, for in speaking or acting out one effectively externalizes what is on one's mind or in one's heart, and this alone transforms one's experience of the quandary, lifts the burden, restores a sense of agency, and lessens one's solitude. In short, speaking and acting are an ethical good in their own right, irrespective of what is spoken or what follows from one's action. (Jackson 2013, 265; my emphasis)

Speaking out is already an act of relief and thus can be seen as beginning self-liberation, as the pressures of meaning upon oneself are released in the act of speaking. One can see a meaningful historical continuum emerging here, between very different kinds of mediating technologies or scenarios in society that provide and facilitate such existential relief, by means of providing space and opportunity for expression: from ritual sessions of speaking out (and prayer itself) to technologically advanced, guarded public spaces such as the radio, in which people "ex-press" themselves and seek to "im-press" each other, to modern therapeutic sessions. Each case illustrates the fundamental social embeddedness of discursive action and acts of seeking guidance or advice, which again are common motifs in many forms of intellectual practice. Each time, the linguistic, performative, and discursive forms in which this is pursued correlate to the kinds of sociality among people, their mutual interrelatedness (*ihr Aufeinanderbezogen-Sein*), an aspect I highlighted in chapter 1.

While, as we have been able to see in each of the chapters, such basic mutual relatedness is emphatically felt to be present in the Muslim Swahili context by social actors, this is by no means an exclusive feature of Muslim sociality, but it can also be linked to Swahili-speaking social interactions far inland. In fact, the Swahili word for the (morally obligatory) act of mutually reminding each other within a community, *kukumbushana*, was identified as a central keyword for the Central African indigenous Christian Jamaa movement (lit., "community"). This movement was founded by the Belgian priest Placide Tempels and used Shaba Swahili as the lingua franca among its members (Fabian 2007, 75; see Fabian 1971).[8] The members of this movement, at a fundamental level, remind each other of their humanity (*umuntu*) and, by extension, of the kinds of mutual moral obligations that arise from that. Uttering or pronouncing the commonly invoked social obligation to remind each other (*kukumbushana*) already as part of a performance of reminding each other, or educating each other (*kuelimishana*), or, along the same lines, forbidding each other (*kukanyana*), makes present and explicitly noticeable the kind of silent and inherent moral obligations that coastal Muslim social actors also acknowledge as being at work between them, embedded in mutual webs of social interrelations.

As "reminding" refers to a mediation process of "making present (again)" to a fellow human being the knowledge or experience that he or she already has, we are speaking about a merging process of knowledge and morality. We could call this a morally driven process of "re-presencing," the mediation of a conscious sense of a moral knowledge that is already there. Now, such processes of recurrent (re-)presencing, making present (again), may constitute not only ways of remembering and reminding others, but also forms of critique (just like how "forbidding," in its deictic negative capacity, is also a warning): "Could it not be said that 'critique'—in its concrete meaning of a practical/political attitude and a discursive strategy—is nothing but a way of remembering and reminding? Critique, being an exercise of an intellectual capacity, it is not something one does or advocates 'above and beyond,' 'outside of' or 'against' whatever critique is applied to" (Fabian 2007, 139).[9]

The point here is that critique is performative, embedded, and pointing to an already existent shared set of (moral) knowledge and obligations. Placing critique in this field of mutual concern and moral relevance more generally is useful to think with, as it is always embedded in and emerges out of dynamics of mutually directed social interactions. It is worthwhile to think with this field of mutually directed relations of knowledge and moral obligation that are (or can become) contested. And then, it can become useful (and is consistent with this framework) to understand "critique" as a particular performative form of responsible and responsive mutual interrelatedness of a fundamental moral nature, which goes together with and triggers performances or speech acts of warning, teaching, and so on, directed at one's peers.

Discursive Agency, Obligation, and Experience

This brings us back to deliberations about shared norms and values in "ordinary ethics" (Lambek 2010 and 2015; Das 2015), with a view as to how people behave morally toward each other in everyday life, in acts of promising or reminding each other, as they are embedded in meaningful webs of mutual interaction within which they operate and express themselves. This has become especially visible here for our main figures of interest discussed in this book, as the public discursive agents that they are. In Stambuli's efforts, for instance, when he raised the issue of "terror" (*ugaidi*) for a necessary frank and critical public discussion, we can see this kind of ethical commitment in play, a commitment that may involve putting oneself into a difficult position, exposing oneself and making oneself vulnerable by addressing issues and asking questions that many would prefer to avoid. Indeed, it is worthwhile to reflect on why Stambuli needed to do this; why did he decide to endure such difficult confrontational situations on air? He had taken on an obligation that he firmly believed in, as a kind of promise he had publicly given his coastal peers as well as himself, so much so that he was ready to endure much friction in the process. His mission was to speak out critically on any issues that needed attention, and to give voice to those whose opinions often remained unheard (indeed, letting them speak for themselves).

Uncomfortable questions and sensitive issues that are of fundamental concern to everyone individually and to the community on the whole, such as terrorism/*ugaidi* here, need to be addressed not only within social communities, but also in academia. As an informed and critical element within society on a global scale, academia is an institutionalized platform for mediating knowledge and informing the wider public, and it has an obligation to society at large. This should include exploring how conceptions of violence, terror, and religious struggle are controversially discussed in the world, among Muslims and beyond (e.g., Euben 2002; Asad 2007; Kurzman 2011). Making our readings of such internal debates mutually accessible from various regional perspectives can enable us, as researchers, to work more dialogically toward a substantial transregional debate. Thinking about my own ethnographic practice in relation to Stambuli's efforts and their discussion in context, I saw it as my obligation to follow and comment on this discussion as it reflects tensions and struggles internal to the coastal Muslim community. I would like to argue that, once we have "listened in" carefully and become sensitive to the motives and ethical dimensions involved in the life-worlds of the actors we give account of, a focus on intellectual practice can enable us to exercise responsibly the discursive agency we have acquired through our ethnographies (as part of a promise we give ourselves and our interlocutors).

It became my self-ascribed task, as ethnographer, to write an informed and sensitized account of this local (yet also translocal) internal discussion of *ugaidi*—and to listen and endure in the process, somewhat in parallel to Stambuli. By doing so, I could convey a sense of the value of an insight into the complex internal dynamics of the negotiation of such a sensitive and contested topic, including (perhaps most importantly) a sense of Stambuli's achievement in creating a discursive space for such a discussion to take place.[10] On a meta level, it may be productive to think further about how the doing and writing of ethnography provides us as researchers with discursive agency, which we acquire in the process (through shared experiences in fieldwork and dialogical reflections on it). Ethnography gives voice to us as anthropologists, while we (as writers) "create" it in the first place, giving voice to our interlocutors as the central subjects of our ethnographic narratives, through which we then pass on what we learned by thinking about how they acted.

Based on close readings, the discursive case studies above have explored further the webs of mutual relatedness, to see how patterns of social interaction and discursive performance, in printed and spoken exchange, relate to the "thinking of" society, also as "internal criticism" (flagged up for Muslim societies by Zaman 2012) and "internal pluralism" (flagged up for African societies by Hountondji 1983 and 1996). It is also worthwhile to determine how these normative and performative loops of "presencing" (of making present), as they point to and reinvoke a mutually constituted moral sphere (or moral economy), relate to a social experience that is specifically "postcolonial" in character. In coastal Kenya (and elsewhere) this may be an experience that is entangled in existential loops of a tense *past present continuous* whereby, at the same time, in remembering and making present, layers of (past) experience and (future) anticipation are intertwined. This resonates with Achille Mbembe's reflections on experiential time in postcolonial Africa. He points out that "the present *as experience of a time* is precisely that moment when different forms of absence become mixed together: absence of those presences that are no longer so and that one remembers (the past), and absence of those others that are yet to come and are anticipated (the future)" (Mbembe 2001, 16).

Overlaps and interplays also come into play, again and again, between the negotiation and invocation of knowledge (*elimu*) and religion (*dini*) in social life, and in the tackling of moral obligations, responsibilities, and dilemmas. In the preceding chapters, we have also seen this in repeated utterances, invocations, and reminders formulated as Islamic appeals and commitments couched in Swahili idioms and phrases that emphasized mutual attention and concern for each other, and for unity (*umoja*) among members of the Muslim community. Such emphasis on the need for unity may, however, have been a reflection of actual internal disunity and rivalry. While social unity is precarious, fragile, or even absent, it needs to be invoked emphatically, in order to be achieved by common effort that relies on active mutual attention among all involved. Unexamined religious practice and blind following of habitual patterns of behavior has been criticized as quasi-"tribal" in nature by local reformists. "Islam for us is tribalism!" (*Uislamu kwetu sisi ni ukabila!*), as Sheikh Abdilahi Nassir commented critically in a Ramadhan lecture I attended in January 1999. This is a phrase I have heard several times since, and in a country with a bad record of inter-ethnic violence and political tribalism, it carries a meaningful critical edge. It casts doubt on the character of the religious commitment of people, and thereby also invokes a comparison with non-Muslim mono-ethnic communities that often seem to be defined (and define themselves) through their ethnicity or tribalism (*ukabila*). Local, regional, and national politics in Kenya have continued to include a struggle with, and about, ethnicity or ethnic identity (*ukabila*) throughout the postcolonial era, and the Muslim community is no exception where and when it treats Islam reductively as (a customary attitude of) tribalism.

Understanding *ukabila* as ambivalent, and consciously seeing both sides of this ambivalence (following John Lonsdale), may be productive to think with here: on the one hand, a shared moral and conceptual framework of lived sociality, and on the other the potential political (mis-)use of ethnically focused identity of a group, "tribalism." Both meanings point to the common normative framework of the group and the correlative responsibility that group members are understood to have for each other, but they are interpreted in different ways. Thus, thinking of *ukabila* as a kind of moral underpinning of ethnic identity (in terms of mutual obligations) may also point at a way forward, a constructive alternative to uncritical and exclusive *ukabila*. "Moral ethnicity," as John Lonsdale calls the other side of "political tribalism," is "the publicly known moral economy of the small community" (Lonsdale 1992a, 10).[11] On this basis, he sees it as providing a potentially workable mechanism for responsible political rule. One could try to rethink (and try to resolve) the dynamics of *ukabila* within regional Islam along parallel lines, with a view to the diverse and different takes by engaged individuals explored in the chapters above.

Self-Critique and Self-Positioning, Embedded in Experience

Over the course of this book, I have been interested in forms, motifs, and contents of critique, self-critique, and creative meaningful discursive interaction within the regional Muslim community. We have explored how ideas are expressed and mediated in different genres at different historical points in time, as part of fundamental self-positioning processes, correlative to attempts of orientation within the (overlapping) political, religious, and moral scope of a sense of self that social actors (need to) develop as a credible basis from which to (inter)act, speak to others, and engage in everyday life, or in particular efforts (of critique, expression, etc.) that may go far beyond the everyday. A combination of basic aspects that make (social and individual) experience possible and shape it (as it comes into being) were sounded out and brought in as contextual features to the discursive analysis. In the case of the experiences observed and discussed here, social and political contexts, as inherent features of the media concerned, have to be taken on board, in order to consider how they feed into the processes of shaping or reshaping actual experience. Along these lines, the analytic process here has been concerned with "seeing through" intellectual practice, using it as a lens to understand the social processes, actors, and conceptual frameworks that have shaped it in the first place.[12] To reflect upon the processes that produced observable social phenomena—actual performances of intellectual practice—and understand their becoming in relation to the aspects and efforts that were central in their constitution, makes us, as observers, recall and reformulate (relive and rephrase) the process of experience-making in terms of that experience itself. In so doing, we are entering and following the hermeneutic circles of understanding of our main social actors, in reverse, counter to their original flow of experience (and their understanding of their experience), to gain a clearer understanding of their understanding.

In programmatic terms, this may be characterized as a critical hermeneutical anthropology dedicated to the understanding of conceptual and interactive aspects of internal debates, while drawing from the conceptual frameworks and the dynamic features of the regional intellectual traditions (central to which are discursive traditions linking up past, present, and future) for the analytic language used. Here, this means involving the Swahili conceptual framework and its terms, idioms, and phrases for the analysis of the negotiation of social relationships. Reflecting on the conditions of possibility of experience also leads us to issues of framing and expressing experiences, as it happens within society and by social actors—to matters of how the shared conceptual framework in Swahili relates to the specific options and choices for individual and specific expressions.

My ethnographic accounts and discussions in this book are intended to enable readers to access and reflect upon the internal debates covered here, to participate in reading and listening processes that are linked to, and part of, wider, mutually confronting and challenging processes of interaction, between rival groups seeking to dominate (chapter 4), or between leading figures (chapter 3) or facilitating figures (chapter 5) of critique, reform, and social change. All of these were taking place in public and mediated by different locally based media that were "Islamic" in their self-understanding. The discursive kinds of interactions between self and other all had to do with the negotiation of knowledge and normative standards and, in relation to that, power and social status, among coastal Muslims. These were meaningful and (to a larger or smaller extent) open processes of public self-positioning (*Selbstverortung*) and self-assurance (*Selbstvergewisserung*), which local audiences were exposed to and also invited to participate in (again, to different extents).[13]

In a similar spirit and from the perspective of Islamic studies, a recent comprehensive and conceptually oriented study of Islam can be drawn upon here, as it makes the case for understanding Islam "as hermeneutical engagement" (Ahmed 2016, 345). This is a process of "meaning-making for the Self" within the experiential confines of its "human and historical reality" and its internal contradictions, through a focus on "the social and discursive means by which Muslims entertain and maintain contradiction" (ibid., 544).[14] Inherently, the thematic issues seen contested here within society and the ways in which they are contested, through invocations of knowledge (Islamic and other), through rhetoric and sometimes blunt polemics, had to do with contested knowledge/power relationships within the Muslim community that were negotiated in public. In the Swahili context, as elsewhere, becoming knowledgeable is also becoming empowered, and it is in this sense that knowledge is sought, as a powerful tool and means to negotiate and possibly change and reform social reality, seeking to improve one's own terms within it. The Islamic reformers seen here use their command of both Islamic and secular knowledge as powerful means to present and propagate a vision of society that follows a modernizing and Islamic agenda at the same time. When considering ways and role models, they are not restricting themselves to "Islamic" cases, as the references to figures like Noam Chomsky (for his critical political engagement) and Thomas Lipton (for his philanthropy) illustrate.

Postcolonial Thinking

"Postcolonial thinking" strikes me as a befitting term for a certain type of intellectual negotiation of social reality that I found in the ethnographic descriptions that I provided here. It points to specific ways in which individuals perform intellectual practice in context, in terms of their creative processes of thinking, reasoning, and rhetoric, under conditions and within the scope of their postcolonial experience. Seeking to understand such flexible and streetwise thinking as "postcolonial thinking" may prove valuable, through the focus on ethnographic specificity and creative situated agency under conditions of endurance and resilience, as described earlier—somewhat in contrast to established "postcolonial thought," which seems more abstract and generalizing, and less specific and flexible. In other words, my sense is that engaged postcolonial thinking that is embedded in local life-worlds is (necessarily) fast and flexible, adaptable to situations and thinking on one's feet. This can be seen to be marked by its active "-ing" form that emphasizes ongoing processes of striving, struggling, improvising, and adjusting being performed, in precarious times and under uncertain circumstances. In contrast, postcolonial thought appears more passive and abstract, generalizing and academically established as a category, and further removed from lived experience. One could say it follows the guarded "ought" of given normative patterns and pathways it already stands for—almost as a self-circular label of sorts.

In pursuing an ethnography of postcolonial experience with a view to its intellectual as well as experiential levels, this book has responded to earlier calls from within anthropology to engage with general statements and reflections about postcoloniality or the postcolonial condition. The specific ethnographic accounts then feed into and underpin richer and more appropriate (re)conceptualizations of the postcolonial character of the societies and human experiences we are dealing with. Keeping in mind that the phrase "past present continuous" expresses a *leitmotif* or characteristic mode of postcolonial experience well beyond the East African context—as existential interrelated periods that are connected through personal experience and imagination—it makes sense, for each specific case study, to look closely at the ways in which experiences of the present and past feed into anticipations of future experiences for the social community.[15] Such imaginative, loaded circles between anticipation and realization, based on earlier experiences, may assist our understanding of local narrow-mindedness (also an expression of postcolonial self-positioning), as regional forms of parochialism or traditionalism that follow patterns of self-verification—and that may as such best be identified and analyzed further by ethnographic means. Such attitudes, captured well for instance by the Swahili label *sisi kwa sisi* ("us for ourselves"), can be explored further comparatively.[16] Internally, *sisi kwa sisi* can express a sense of frustration, such as "Nothing gets done in Mombasa," as Sheikh Al-Amin Mazrui criticized his townsmen in the colonial period (chapter 3). Linked to wider global debates about progress and modernization, education, colonial rule, and religious purification at the time, he coined and performed a form of flexible and critical "colonial thinking" that influenced the "postcolonial thinking" that followed more recently.[17]

Reflecting upon the kinds of postcolonial thinking encountered in the ethnographic accounts here, it seems useful to note specific and characteristic features in the performances of individuals. Depending on situation and context, these are often flexible, yet they also follow established pathways of expression and patterns of reasoning, building on existent continuities of intellectual practice, as they draw from shared reservoirs of meaning, conceptual "pools" that they adjust for ready use. As flexible performers in challenging situations, people participate in, and reshape, living discursive traditions, in their negotiation and self-positioning processes in society.[18]

We could see this in Stambuli's performances as host and moderator of his program on Radio Rahma. While he used established rhetorical patterns of speech (as did callers to the program)—the invocations of mutual reminding (-*kumbushana*) and forbidding (-*kanyana*), for instance—he also introduced the academic convention of providing references as proof of knowledge when one makes claims. Also, while he did not hide his status as a mere layman in religious knowledge, he invoked Islamic knowledge frequently and carefully, through references to the Qur'an (less so to the *hadith*). Two further sources that he drew from for his repertoire were historical knowledge and political critique (of the political elite, and of those who did not show any engagement). And he selected visiting speakers according to the relevance of what they would have to say, to the audience, at that particular difficult point in time. His invited guests represented an illustrative mix of the kind of knowledge and experience that Stambuli found useful to build on and draw from: progressive, modern, and cosmopolitan in outlook (underpinned by personal experience), critical and at the same time religiously conscious. This was a mix of features and qualifications that he wanted to induce and encourage among his listeners as well.

His guest Professor Hyder represents such a mix very well. In his case, the important sub-discussion of Noam Chomsky, the renowned linguist and outspoken political critic of US policies who is himself Jewish American, brought in new angles of discussion. Even simply knowing that someone like Chomsky existed and was profoundly critical of his own government was stimulating to the local audience. Hyder was also a retired university professor of zoology and a prominent social activist who had contributed to *Sauti ya Haki* in the 1970s; at the time he was still running a Muslim NGO that facilitated debates and formulated visions for the future, circulating a regular pamphlet called "Kenya How the Muslims Want It" (*Kenya Waislamu waitakavyo*). This indicates one type of role model that Stambuli wanted to present to his community.

Showing that one could, and should, be drawing from science, modern sources, or Western role models (like Chomsky) as well as from the Qur'an, *hadith*, and local political histories was an important effect that Stambuli's program (with Bwana Abubakar's help) sought to have. Yet Stambuli was not the first to offer this kind of approach to the local Swahili Muslim community. As we have seen, Sheikh Al-Amin Mazrui, over seventy years before, already showed a similar mix of critical food for thought for local Muslims in his essays: for him, Western role models (e.g., Thomas Lipton) and transregional political histories and perspectives on colonial empires came in. As we saw, he observed East Asia through Western impressions as they were mediated in the Arab world, and then he adapted such a lens to comment critically on his own coastal Muslim society; Islamic history, the *hadith*, and the Qur'an were also part of the mix of subjects he examined for his readers. Sheikh Al-Amin included critical perspectives on society (in Mombasa, Europe, and elsewhere), for instance on modern technologies and their social effects, and drew from and also engaged in larger transregional comparisons. Similarly, Sheikh Muhammad Kasim Mazrui, as editor of *Sauti ya Haki*, brought into play (unexpectedly, for local readers then, and academic readers now) a deep knowledge of recent academic publications on Islam in East Africa. In an article in response to attacks by his opponents, he quoted the latest works by Jan Knappert (a leading European scholar on Swahili literature) and John Mbiti (an East African theologian whose book *African Religions and Philosophy*, quoted here, made him famous in Africanist circles).

These examples show the scope of knowledge, the intellectual flexibility, and the adaptive sense of these local thinkers, authors, and publicists. They are tuned in well to the relevant social and academic discourse of globally dominant Westerners, like Sheikh Al-Amin Mazrui before and Prof. Hyder after them. Their possibilities of "navigating the world," a complex and politically tense but resoundingly interconnected (colonial and postcolonial) world, includes a wide range of repertoires and resources from, potentially, any other connected and accessible source.[19] This scope of locally specific, resourceful possibilities for addressing and responding to issues may be said to qualify "postcolonial thinking" in its ready flexibility. It is underpinned also by a multilingualism of local actors, and by knowledge of how things work and "tick" for people on the privileged side of the postcolonial world.

The dynamics of this resourcefulness need to be reckoned with and deserve to be explored more in future studies. One can build on earlier work on the creativity of social and political critique despite existent rigid constraints of all kinds, including on expression (e.g., Mbembe 1992 and 2001; de Boeck 1996; de Boeck and Plissart 2004), feeding into a characteristic "politics of striving" (Chabal 2009, 106–26) that goes well beyond the economic and had begun well before Independence. With a well-grounded sense of what is actually going on locally, ethnographic-cum-textual studies such as this one can contribute to a more widely and more deeply informed "postcolonial critique," responding to anthropological criticisms of "postcolonialism" as often insufficiently grounded in firsthand experience of non-Western postcolonial life-worlds; and also, as a largely europhone enterprise, insufficiently equipped linguistically, to acquire and interact with the kinds of local knowledge and expertise that are needed for original and constructive input (Barber 2007, 222–223; Mbembe 2001:, 7–9; Werbner 1996, 6–7, 22–23).

"Provincializing the social sciences," to pick up on an evocative phrase, expresses a critical project of overcoming the central dominance of Eurocentric conceptual frameworks for understanding and analyzing the human social world. Putting them in their place relativizes their significance, as only one strand among a wide range of historically grown and regionally grounded approaches. Recognizing different and diverse regional traditions of conceptualizing society,[20] of understanding the world, being in place, enables us, as researchers in the social sciences and humanities, to explore these traditions with a view to their ways of thinking "the human," "society," and "communicative interaction"; the corresponding Swahili webs of meaning, for instance, would be ranked around *utu*, *jamii,* and *mawasaliano.* Taking these traditions and their key concepts seriously in their own right as sociological thought puts these (thus far underrepresented) approaches in their proper place too.[21] Chakrabarty's call for "provincializing Europe" derives from what he described programmatically (2007, xiv, 16) as the tension between the indispensability and the inadequacy of "European thought" for understanding social life (the political or the historical) elsewhere, particularly in former colonial societies. As long as "the European intellectual tradition" is seen as the only paradigmatic one in the social sciences, as Chakrabarty says (2007, 5), this is an obstacle to the understanding of human society on the whole. The European is "one model among many," as can be established through work from within as well as outside the Western tradition (Taylor 2004, 196). Alternative regional intellectual traditions to think with, while not reverting to a simple relativism or laissez-faire of ideas, are urgently needed.

Chakrabarty cast European thought as indispensable since it had fundamentally shaped the conditions of the experience that was to be analyzed, and thus it needed to be kept on board for the analysis. At the same time, it was inadequate for this task because its lens, its perspective on social life elsewhere, was from the outset both incapable and insufficient to understand and represent it in appropriate and acceptable terms. Knowing about the conditions of experience for social actors, and being able to relate them to the conceptual apparatus that they use to talk about their experiences, enables us to understand their reasoning and arguing processes in social context. Focused on the discursive contents mediated by them as well as the social practices by which they are mediated, "thick descriptions" of intellectual practice can be undertaken that are also sensitized to the historical contexts and power relations influencing the range of experiences to be had.[22]

The chapters above have sought to provide such accounts, by means of a contextualizing anthropological focus on texts and internal debate. We have been able to see how a certain conceptual apparatus, in terms of recurrent key terms, phrases, and idioms and patterns of arguing and reasoning, is used by our writers and speakers to make their points. Sheikh Al-Amin Mazrui built and employed a reservoir of key terms that stood for his agenda of internal critique and commitment to social change, in that it verbally embodied the performative, striving nature of working toward a certain vision of society that was yet to be realized. For instance, he discussed the features of *ghera* (zeal), *kazi* (work), and *kitendo* (action), on which a reputation of *fahari* (pride or fame) could then be built. Knowledge and education (*ujuzi; elimu*) needed to be cultivated and disseminated, against the ignorance (*ujinga*) of opponents. Sheikh Al-Amin's essays can be seen to use these keywords as pillars or cornerstones for the conceptual critique or future vision they sought to present. This resource of terms, again, had obvious resonance with a set of related Arabic terms, employed by arabophone writers at the time for a similar reformist project elsewhere, as we saw for a work by Shakib Arslan (chapter 3). Sheikh Al-Amin's students and followers drew from this same conceptual reservoir he had put in place, for their public reformative agenda a generation later, pushed through *Sauti ya Haki* (chapter 4). Another one or two generations later, some of this regional conceptual repertoire for reform was still in place, now used by Stambuli and others in radio discussions during the post-Moi era (chapter 5). The idea of waking up (-*amsha*) one's fellow Muslims, and to strive and put effort into what one does (-*jitahidi; -fanya bidii*), for instance, were terms of ongoing significance. They were not per se the meaningful property of one particular group in social interaction, but they were reappropriated according to perspectives and chances within the dynamics of social life at certain points in time.

Each of the three case studies covered in detail here provided insights into the flexible social dynamics of negotiating Islam in the Kenyan coastal region, by means of worldly and religious knowledge in practice.[23] Hereby, constancy and continuity are visible in the use of discursive forms of mutuality that are invoked in social discourse and discussion, and that designate implicit social obligations and responsibilities, in relation to one's status in terms of education or seniority. Moral terms and normative concepts, usually cast as abstract nouns, such as *utu* (humaneness, morality), *wema* (goodness, kindness) or *uungwana* or *ustaarabu* (both: civilization, proper behavior) also seem to designate continuity. But as we have seen, the common understanding with which they are employed may well have changed over different generations. For instance, the fact that both Sheikh Al-Amin Mazrui in the 1930s and then Minister Najib Balala in 2006 stressed the point that *ustaarabu* (civilization) was not equivalent with *uArabu* (Arabness) shows that in both these periods, this was still a relevant (and perhaps even prevalent) understanding of the term. The commonly assumed contents or characteristics of goodness and kindness may change too—and it is the fascinating task of ethnographically and historically contextualizing readings to find out about the specific features of such changes, or indeed their continuities (as applicable in specific, and partly individually determined, situations).

Returning to the notion of "provincializing the social sciences," this means, analytically, to go beyond a Western-fabricated and objectifying lens on the social world that invented images and conceptions of other regions and presented its idea to the West, in narratives of "Orientalism" (Said 1978) or "Africanism" (Mudimbe 1988 and 1994); it also means to have provided ethnographic accounts mediating a sense of the internal dynamics that matter for social interaction and self-conceptualization. The task thus becomes not discarding the social sciences but rather renewing them, through specific conceptual perspectives from elsewhere, "from and for the margins"—in this case, the East African Swahili coast. Restructuring our disciplinary and interdisciplinary work by reconceptualizing possible ways in which "society," or "a vision of the human" (Chakrabarty 2007, 16, 4) can be thought, drawing from conceptual frameworks from elsewhere, builds on and takes further the critique of Eurocentrism as a process of provincialization, diminishing its analytic dominance. To further pursue the study of alternative conceptual frameworks and theoretical perspectives in non-Western regions will lead to a more adequate and well-rounded understanding of social actors in their respective life-worlds. In addition, these frameworks offer new, meaningful orientation and intellectual stimulation for the humanities and social sciences, the disciplines seeking to understand those life-worlds.

Regional Intellectual Tradition and a Swahili Conceptual Framework

This study has sought to make accessible to a wider readership some contours and aspects of a conceptual framework for thinking "the human" and "society" from the Swahili coast, from diverse vantage points of engaged individuals. Drawing on the ethnography pursued here, this book contributes toward such a larger project, analyzing the internal dynamics of intellectual practice—the negotiation of knowledge in social practice—in Swahili Muslim publics at different points in time. We can conceive of this in terms of a "regional tradition" of intellectual practice that underpins and feeds into regional intellectual history. This again is linked to and ranked around the cultural and political history of the Swahili region as a culturally and linguistically unified (or at least interconnected) social sphere, with a shared conceptual framework of key concepts.[24] Documenting such regional traditions of intellectual practice in Africa and elsewhere, in their historical and contemporary dimensions, by attention to texts as well as ethnographic means, is valuable in its own right (because we largely still lack such accounts).[25] Moreover, such work is needed in order to progress with the said project of "provincializing" and overcoming Eurocentrism. It needs to be pursued by means of corresponding regionally specific epistemological and methodological guidelines, following Paulin Hountondji's argument to take evidence of internal traditions of "endogenous knowledge" as point of orientation (Hountondji 1997).

This also resonates with Ousmane Kane's project of documenting non-europhone intellectual histories in Africa, with the intention to capture and reconstruct a rich sense of precolonial patterns and clusters of Africa's intellectual history through the focus on Muslim intellectuals and their texts (Kane 2012; realized in Kane 2016). This is an argument that can and should be extended to the present. The study of Swahili intellectual practice here, focusing on Swahili Muslim media at diverse points in the colonial and postcolonial periods, has combined a look at engaged individuals in society (writers, authors, speakers, moderators) with a look at language use and discursive performance in social practice (in terms of genres, patterns and idioms of speech, ways of speaking, and key concepts).[26] This goes along with, and complements, the deep ethno-graphic study of intellectual culture and a "mindful life" (Marsden 2005) in its vivid everyday contexts and negotiations that we need to see more of, in the study of Africa and elsewhere. Looked at from another angle, this study also comple-ments those studies on African philosophy and intellectual history that carve out notable particularities of knowledge production and thinking in social contexts, with a look at the links between epistemology, morality, and aesthetics; or with a look at the performative processes of what a good life means.[27] Beyond that, of course, this study also picks up on and feeds back into the agenda of conceptual decolonization that has been raised from different angles in African philosophy and literature (Wiredu 1995 and 1996; Ngũgĩ 1981, 1986, and 2009).

The question is not whether non-Europeans can think; but can Europeans, Westerners, listen (and read) and understand what is being thought and expressed elsewhere (Dabashi 2015, 1–43)? To engage in careful listening (and reading) pro-cesses that offer access to the internal negotiation of meaning in societies is a necessary and rewarding endeavor when seeking to understand how the world is thought, and human sociality and self-positioning performed in relation to this, in Africa or elsewhere.[28] It yields insights into the specific pathways in which knowledge and experience are conceived of and contested within the specific dynamics of social practice.

To conclude, the point of focusing on intellectual practice is that without a good understanding of this field of creative, knowledge-oriented, and intellectu-ally guided human practices in social interaction (including the political), and of the distinct genres and idioms of the cultural traditions they are part of, we cannot fully understand the richness of regional intellectual histories and the social relevance of intellectual traditions.[29] Both are underpinned and built by specific performances of individuals and groups, in particular social situations, when striving for orientation, and by means of established patterns of expression and ways of speaking, arguing, and reasoning. Knowing more about the concrete social contexts and personalities involved in these performances, all around the world, leads us to a richer picture of intellectual practice in society, and in social history.

To get there, we need to extend our perspectives on the internal dynam-ics of thinking and doing, and analyze the specific thickets of interrelationships between language use and social norms, the positionality and agency of indi-viduals, and how knowledge and religion matter for and are invoked by them. Thus the focus on intellectual practice advocated and pursued here needs to stay connected with the study of regional intellectual traditions and intellectual history. As we have seen, linking oneself to the study of discursive traditions and the internal dynamics of debate in society is fruitful. This book, of course, can only go so far in pursuing this project, as part of a long ongoing process to be continued. Our knowledge about the specific dynamics of how knowledge is created and qualified, questioned and justified, and contested and negotiated across the world – in and beyond Africa and the Muslim world – still needs to be enriched and extended much more, and connected, in critical comparison with established social and intellectual regional and transregional histories, to reflect a common mutual concern with the wider world.

***

As for a concluding comment on the specific recurrent loops of postcolonial experience that continue being cast and recast between past and present—indeed, "interlocking" pasts, presents, and futures (Mbembe 2001, 16)—it is appropriate to turn to a voice from coastal Kenya. Recall that the poet and political activist Abdilatif Abdalla had been imprisoned in 1968 for calling Jomo Kenyatta's KANU government "dictatorial," in a political pamphlet that condemned the ruling "black Boers" as worse than the colonial masters (Abdalla 2016; Kresse 2016). In 2012, Abdalla remarked that Kenya still seemed worse off than during colonial rule, and Kenyans themselves were to blame for this, as for too long they had been allowing their votes to be bought. In principle, things had not really changed much since then, he said (*hakuna mabadiliko mengi*). The ruling elite consisted of the same people (*watu ni walewale*), and their thoughts were the same (*fikra zao ni zilezile*). He concluded, "Their God is wealth—and their religion is to oppress their fellow human beings" (*Mungu yao ni mali, na dini yao ni kudhulumu wenzao*), and it was up to Kenyans themselves to change things.

Notes

1. In his long-term study on Islamic education on Zanzibar, Loimeier (2009) introduced a sense of the dynamic "negotiation of Islam" in East Africa within an internally diverse demographic constituency. Thus, diverse kinds of social and marketable skills linked to wider bodies of knowledge and practice navigating religion and the world (*dini na dunia*) become central. On the heterogeneous and strained unity, see, for example, the wide-ranging research literature on "Swahili" urban identity since the 1970s (e.g., Salim 1976; Ranger 1975; Strobel 1976; Mazrui and Shariff 1994; summary in Kresse 2007, 36–44).

2. This could go as far as painting their leaders as opposing God's will, as we can gather from the *Sauti ya Haki* readings above, and from what I could gather from informal personal conversations with members of the older generation in Lamu and Mombasa who remembered their experiences at the time.

3. For internal negotiations of Islam on the Swahili coast, we can see such dynamics in play in different historical contexts; see, for example, Farsy 1972; el-Zein 1974; Pouwels 1987; Bakari 1995; Bang 2003 and 2014; Loimeier 2009; Kresse 2003 and 2008.

4. See, for example, Parkin 1995; Purpura 1997; Beckerleg 1995.

5. See Kresse 2008 and 2009a; also Nassir 1989a, 1989b, 1990, 2003a, and 2003b.

6. Habermas understood this in contrast to Foucault's analysis of earlier "traditional" European publics, which regarded "the rules of formation of a discourse in power as mechanisms of exclusion that constitute their respective 'other'" (Habermas 1989, 20; my translation), thus the conflicting interest groups shared no common discursive space and could not productively interact. In contrast, Habermas sees the inclusive (and consciously self-referential, or self-aware) character of European bourgeois public discourse qualified by a fundamental receptiveness to critique from within society, "the potential of self-transformation." Without venturing here into a comparative discussion of these two imposing thinkers who have reflected on European history from mutually incompatible vantage points, it is nevertheless important to point to the fact that we can, for the postcolonial East African context, identify this potential too. For further conceptual discussion, see Calhoun 1992; Taylor 2004; Tayob 2007; Schulz 2007 (the last two on African Muslim publics, Schulz with a thorough view on Habermas).

7. Surveying and judging "new media" in Africa and the Muslim world with a view to the prospects for a more open society (as Eickelman does), or "democratization" processes, has become common in recent literature. See also Seib 2007; Njogu and Middleton 2009.

8. See also Tempels' famous book on Bantu philosophy (1959; orig. 1945), for which Tempels was banned from reentering the Belgian Kongo after an absence of illness in Belgium. The book claimed to present a close and realistic portrayal of a "dynamic" and life force–oriented Central African ontology and ethics, and it was either celebrated or sharply criticized by academic African theologians and philosophers.

9. For anthropology, Fabian sees a fundamental task in critique, yet in terms of features of a general "critical" approach and not a new and separate subdiscipline of sorts (Fabian 2001, xii).

10. If it is a "key task" for anthropologists "to take seriously points of view and visions of life they do not share" and even strongly disagree with (Schielke 2014, 13), this challenge was also mastered by Stambuli here.

11. See also his wider argument on the Kikuyu moral economy, and the tensions and potentials of moral ethnicity and political tribalism vis-à-vis each other (Lonsdale 1992b). His work is also an illustration for how regional political histories and intellectual practice are intertwined and have to be studied in interrelation. On this, see also Peterson 2004. Chabal has repeatedly expressed admiration for Lonsdale's approach and pointed at its potential to overcome "tribalism" more widely (e.g., 2009, 104–5, 67). Chabal discusses morality as an overlapping interrelationship between aspects of religion, tradition, and obligation ("three of its central components"). For related work that may contribute toward such a reconceptualization of Scott's (1976) "moral economy" in Muslim contexts, see Lambek 2010; Tripp 2006; more generally, Laidlaw 2014; see also the "moral imaginary" as coined by Wedeen (2008, 187). On the whole, mutually directed "sociality" stays central to the analysis here (see Long and Moore 2013).

12. In this, I have followed Randall Collins, whose sociological research on intellectual history and philosophy influenced how I think about the research conducted here. He described his "sociological task" in the following way: "to see through intellectual history to the network of links and energies that shaped its emergence in time" (Collins 1998, 15).

13. This could be played through even further, with the term *Selbstvergegenwärtigung* (becoming aware of one's own presence; becoming part of the present; making oneself present in the here and now), also with a view to the processes of "re-presencing" discussed

above, and in conversation with Fabian's leitmotif of "remembering the present" for an anthropology in dialogue with interlocutors (e.g., Fabian 1996, 2000, and 2007).

14. While I appreciate the constructive critical thrust of Ahmed's study (where I see a related agenda in my own work), I think he is overstating the case of what "Islamic" means (or should mean), as ultimately he wants us "to recognize that all acts and statements of meaning making for the Self by Muslims and non-Muslims that are carried out in terms of Islam" should be called "Islamic" (2016, 544)

15. We have already seen that the pamphlets "The Black Peril!" (*Khatari nyeusi!*, from 1930) by Sheikh Al-Amin Mazrui, written at the peak of British colonialism, and "Kenya: Where Are We Heading?' (*Kenya: Twendapi?*, from 1968) by Abdilatif Abdalla, opposing Jomo Kenyatta's KANU regime, both express a sense of almost prophetic anticipation about the political future. This is based on sensitive observations of recent developments in the present that stand for social and political change. In very different ways, they address power relationships, social hierarchies, and oppression in society.

16. See Kresse 2009a; also the lead article in *Sauti ya Haki*, October 1974. Cross-culturally, for instance, this Swahili expression *sisi kwa sisi* seems an almost exact equivalent of the Bavarian *mia san mia* (we are we)—which continues to be used as a major identity marker also, for example, by the German football club Bayern München. Such locally well-known customary yet regularly re-endorsed communal slogans (or expressions) are similarly invoked (ritually and rhetorically) by both groups to reinforce a sense of unity and common strength, against social others and outsiders.

17. See, for example, Shakib Arslan (2004; orig. 1930) reflected in Sheikh Al-Amin's pamphlets; see also Kresse 2017. More generally, see Kurzman 2002.

18. These traditions build upon the strategies of resilience employed by particular social actors who had the confidence to speak out in public.

19. See Kresse 2012 and 2013, discussing and problematizing "cosmopolitanism" for Mombasa and the Swahili coast, building on Simpson and Kresse 2008; Kresse and Simpson 2011; also Marsden 2005.

20. In parallel with various (more and less scholarly) regional traditions of writing about society (Fardon 1990).

21. There have been recurrent efforts in anthropology during the postcolonial period (and before) to work in this direction (e.g., Rosaldo 1980; MacGaffey 1983, 1986, and 2000; Moore 1996), which to my mind takes on Fabian's (1983) critical guidance to place anthropologists and their interlocutors as "coeval" partners (or rivals), even in terms of theorizing. See especially also the evocative approach by the Comaroffs, toward exploring and articulating "theory from the south" in a neoliberal world, which in part resonates well with my interests here (Comaroff and Comaroff 2012).

22. See Geertz's (1973) famous take on Ryle, but especially also Ryle himself (1971a and 1971b), whose reflections on "thinking," pondering, and learning processes in social context show how the internal projections of meaning-making (unobservable from an external observer's perspective that is not clued into the additional information mentioned here) are central to a proper understanding of what is actually going on from an actor's point of view. See also the work of Roxanne Euben (1999), who worked on what she calls "thick descriptions" of Islamic political thought.

23. See Loimeier 2009 and Asad 1986, for emphasis on the aspects of negotiating Islam through aspects of knowledge and skill, and within a contested and heterogeneous wider dynamic of transregional Islam as discursive tradition.

24. With this conception of a regional tradition, I am following Wyatt MacGaffey. Based on his long-term anthropological and historical research on the Bakongo region, he presented a case for a Central African "regional tradition" (2000, 7) that is worked out conceptually as an endogenous intellectual tradition of thought and practice. It is grounded in a long-grown cultural unity, with shared conceptual features and endogenous key concepts that correspond to an overarching cosmology. The regional tradition marks (or underpins) a common translocal "political culture" for social actors—for which MacGaffey shows how, in the Bakongo case, the presumed "religious" is actually the "political" (occult power, *kindoki* or "witchcraft," is key to an understanding of "the political"). The conceptual framework marking the cosmology and cultural unity of the regional tradition (MacGaffey 2000, esp. 5–7, 203–205) is extendable to a discussion of regional intellectual practice and regional intellectual history. There is also resonance with Richard Fardon's use of "regional traditions of ethnographic writing," referring to knowledge production processes in anthropology, in relation to such conceptual regional traditions and within histories of power relations (Fardon 1990).

25. See also Diagne (2008), with a view to West African intellectual history.

26. It might be difficult, for the purposes of this project here, to speak of a "Swahili episteme," in the Foucauldian sense of the term in which Mudimbe talked about an "African episteme" (1988 and 1994) and which Brenner (2001) used to frame his historical reconstruction of educational knowledge–power relationships for the colonial French Sudanic sphere, differentiating between "rationalist" and "esoteric" epistemic types. However, features of a Swahili conceptual frame, dynamic yet with a limited scope, can be sketched out as a kind of "Swahili model" to think with on a pathway toward overcoming analytic Eurocentrism, as I touched on above. For an inspiring fundamental study of knowledge–power relationships within processes of colonial reordering, see Mitchell 1988.

27. See Hallen and Sodipo 1997; Hallen 2000. Having laid out clear epistemological differences in ordinary language usage between Yoruba and English, with the common conventions in speaking being more strict and critical in Yoruba, Hallen (2000, 34) reiterates the pressing necessity to challenge the assumption and self-presentation of Western thought as "universalist" as fundamental to the cause of reconstructing African conceptual frameworks and their universalist impetus in perspective. On performance and a good life, see Diagne (2008, 8), and Oruka's sage philosophy project (Oruka 1990).

28. See Janz 2009 (esp. 243–248); Lambek 1993 (introduction); Kimmerle 1994 (pointing to a "philosophy of listening"; *Philosophie des Hoerens*).

29. See, for example, Peterson 2004 and MacGaffey 2000, complementing Asad 1986 and Barber 2007. Also, the study of intellectuals and the intellectual field elsewhere breaks down and diminishes a sense of binary opposition between (usually Western) researchers and (supposedly easily categorizable) researched people elsewhere (Feierman 1990, 38–39).

References

[Abdalla, Abdilatif]. (1968) 2016. "Kenya: Twendapi?" Unpublished political pamphlet. Translated by Kai Kresse as "Kenya: Where Are We Heading?" (Reprinted as appendix to Kresse 2016, 23–32).

———. 1973. *Sauti ya dhiki.* Nairobi: Oxford University Press.

Abdulaziz, Mohamed H. 1979. *Muyaka: Swahili Popular Poetry, 19th Century.* Nairobi: Kenya Literature Bureau.

Abiodun, Rowland. *Yoruba Art and Language: Seeking the African in African Art.* New York: Cambridge University Press.

Abu Khalil, Asad, and Mahmoud Haddad. 2016. "Islah." In *Oxford Encylopedia of the Islamic World.* Oxford Islamic Studies Online. http://www.oxfordislamicstudies.com/Public /book_oeiw.html. Accessed June 24, 2018.

Ahmed, Shahab. 2016. *What Is Islam? The Importance of Being Islamic.* Princeton, NJ: Princeton University Press.

Alidou, Ousseina D. 2013. *Muslim Women in Postcolonial Kenya: Leadership, Representation, and Social Change.* Madison: University of Wisconsin Press.

Al Jazeera English. "Africa Investigates: Inside Kenya's Death Squads." December 7, 2014. https://www.youtube.com/watch?v=lUjOdjdH8Uk. Accessed June 24, 2018.

Allen, John Willoughby Tarleton. 1971. *Tendi: Six Examples of a Swahili Classical Verse Form.* Nairobi: Ibadan; London: Heinemann.

Anderson, Benedict R. 1991. *Imagined Communities: Reflections on the Origin and Spread of Nationalism.* Rev. and extended ed. London: Verso.

Anderson, David M., and Jacob McKnight. 2014. "Kenya at War: Al-Shabaab and Its Enemies in Eastern Africa." *African Affairs* 114 (454), 1–27.

Appiah, Anthony. 1992. *In My Father's House: Africa in the Philosophy of Culture.* New York: Oxford University Press.

Arslan, Shakib. (1930) 2004. *Our Decline: Its Causes and Remedies.* Reprint, Kuala Lumpur: Islamic Book Trust.

Asad, Talal. 1986. *The Idea of an Anthropology of Islam.* Occasional papers series. Washington, DC: Center for Contemporary Arab Studies, Georgetown University.

———. 2007. *On Suicide Bombing.* New York: Columbia University Press.

Askew, Kelly M. 2002. *Performing the Nation: Swahili Music and Cultural Politics in Tanzania.* Chicago, IL: University of Chicago Press.

Badawy, Ahmad A. [1966?]. *Dhul-Faqaar.* Malindi and Lamu.

———. 1970. *Fimbo ya Musa: sehemu ya kwanza.* Lamu.

Bakari, Mohamed. 1995. "The New 'Ulama' in Kenya." In *Islam in Kenya*, edited by M. Bakari and S. S. Yahya, 168–93. Nairobi: MEWA.

Bakari, Mohamed, and S. S. Yahya, eds. 1995. *Islam in Kenya.* Nairobi: MEWA.

Baldauf, Ingeborg. 2001. "Jadidism in Central Asia within Reformism and Modernism in the Muslim World." *Die Welt des Islams, New Series* 41 (1): 72–88.

Bang, Anne K. 2003. *Sufis and Scholars of the Sea: Family Networks in East Africa, 1860–1925*. London: Routledge.

———. 2014. *Islamic Sufi Networks in the Western Indian Ocean (c. 1880–1940): Ripples of Reform*. Leiden: Brill.

———. 2011. "Authority and Piety, Writing and Print: A Preliminary Study of the Circulation of Islamic Texts in Late Nineteenth- and Early Twentieth-Century Zanzibar." *Africa: Journal of the International African Institute* 81 (1): 89–107.

Barber, Karin. 2007. *The Anthropology of Texts, Persons and Publics: Oral and Written Culture in Africa and Beyond*. New Departures in Anthropology. Cambridge, UK: Cambridge University Press.

———, ed., transl. 2012. *Print Culture and the First Yoruba Novel: I. B. Thomas's "Life Story of Me, Ṣẹgilọla" and Other Texts*. Leiden: Brill.

Bayart, Jean-François. (1993) 2000. *The State in Africa: The Politics of the Belly*. London: Longman.

Becker, Felicitas. 2006. "Rural Islamism during the 'War on Terror': A Tanzanian Case Study." *African Affairs* 105 (421): 583–603.

Beckerleg, Susan. 1995. "'Brown Sugar' or Friday Prayers: Youth Choices and Community Building in Coastal Kenya." *African Affairs* 94: 23–38.

Berg, Fred J. 1968. "The Swahili Community of Mombasa, 1500–1900." *Journal of African History* 1: 35–56.

———. 1971. "Mombasa under the Busaidi Sultanate: The City and Its Hinterlands in the 19th Century." PhD diss., University of Wisconsin.

Biersteker, Ann. 1991. "Language, Poetry, and Power: A Reconsideration of 'Utendi wa Mwana Kupona'." In *Faces of Islam in African Literature*, edited by Kenneth W. Harrow, 59–77. London: James Currey.

———. 1996. *Kujibizana: Questions of Language and Power in 19th- and 20th-Century Poetry in Kiswahili*. East Lansing: Michigan State University Press.

Biersteker, Ann, and Ibrahim Noor Shariff, eds. 1995. *Mashairi ya vita vya Kuduhu: War Poetry in Kiswahili Exchanged at the Time of the Battle of Kuduhu*. East Lansing: Michigan State University Press.

Bissel, William C. 2011. *Urban Design, Chaos, and Colonial Power in Zanzibar*. Bloomington: Indiana University Press.

Boeck, Filip de, and Marie-Françoise Plissart. 2004. *Kinshasa: Tales of the Invisible City*. Tervuren: Royal Museum for Central Africa.

Boeck, Filip de. 1996. "Postcolonialism, Power and Identity: Local and Global Perspectives from Zaire." In *Postcolonial Identities in Africa*, edited by Richard P. Werbner and T. O. Ranger, 75–106. London: Zed Books.

Bowen, John R. 1993. *Muslims through Discourse: Religion and Ritual in Gayo Society*. Princeton, NJ: Princeton University Press.

Boyd, Allen W. 1981. "To Praise the Prophet: A Processual Symbolic Analysis of 'Maulidi', a Muslim Ritual in Lamu, Kenya." PhD diss., Indiana University.

Branch, Daniel. 2011. *Kenya: Between Hope and Despair, 1963–2011*. New Haven, CT: Yale University Press.

Brennan, James R. 2008. "Lowering the Sultan's Flag: Sovereignty and Decolonization in Coastal Kenya." *Comparative Studies in Society and History* 50 (4): 831–61.

———. 2011. "Politics and Business in the Indian Newspapers of Colonial Tanganyika." *Africa: Journal of the International African Institute* 81 (1): 42–67.

———. 2015. "A History of *Sauti ya Mvita* ('Voice of Mombasa'): Radio, Public Culture, and Islam in Coastal Kenya, 1947–1966." In *New Media and Religious Transformations in Africa*, edited by Rosalind I. J. Hackett and Benjamin F. Soares, 19–38. Bloomington: Indiana University Press.

Brenner, Louis. 2001. *Controlling Knowledge: Religion, Power, and Schooling in a West African Muslim Society.* Bloomington: Indiana University Press.

Brigalia, Andrea. 2007. "The Radio Kaduna Tafsir (1978–1992) and the Construction of Public Images of Muslim Scholars in the Nigerian Media." *Journal for Islamic Studies* 27 (Thematic Issue on Islam and African Muslim Publics): 73–210.

Bromber, Katrin. 2006. "*Ustaarabu*: A Conceptual Change in Tanganyikan Newspaper Discourse in the 1920s." In *The Global Worlds of the Swahili: Interfaces of Islam, Identity and Space in 19th and 20th Century East Africa*, edited by R. Loimeier and R. Seesemann, 67–81. Berlin: Lit-Verlag.

———. 2009. *Imperiale Propaganda. Die ostafrikanische Militärpresse im Zweiten Weltkrieg*, ZMO-Studien 28. Berlin: Klaus Schwarz Verlag.

Calhoun, Craig. 1992. "Introduction: Habermas and the Public Sphere." In *Habermas and the Public Sphere*, edited by C. Calhoun, 1–48. Cambridge, MA: MIT Press.

Calvert, John. 2010. *Sayyid Qutb and the Origins of Radical Islamism.* London: Hurst.

Carmichael, Tim. 1997. "British 'Practice' Towards Islam in the East Africa Protectorate: Muslim Officials, Waqf Administration, and Secular Education in Mombasa and Environs, 1895–1920." *Journal of Muslim Minority Affairs* 17 (2): 293–309.

Caruso, Yuusuf. 2012. "Mazrui, Sheikh Al-Amin." In *Dictionary of African Biography*, edited by L. Gates Jr. and E. K. Akyeampong, vol. 1, 144–46. Oxford, UK: Oxford University Press.

Cassirer, Ernst. 1944. *An Essay on Man.* New Haven, CT: Yale University Press.

Chabal, Patrick. 2009. *Africa: The Politics of Suffering and Smiling.* London: Zed Books.

Chabal, Patrick, and Jean-Pascal Daloz. 1999. *Africa Works: Disorder as Political Instrument.* Bloomington: Indiana University Press.

Chakrabarty, Dipesh. (2000) 2007. *Provincializing Europe: Postcolonial Thought and Historical Difference.* Reprint, Princeton, NJ: Princeton University Press.

Chanfi, Ahmed. 2008. "Das Mombasa Institute of Muslim Education als Bildungseinrichtung und Erinnerungsort der waMwambao in Kenia." In *Erinnerungsräume und Wissenstransfer: Beiträge zur afrikanischen Geschichte*, edited by W. Speitkamp, 95–103. Goettingen: V&R Unipress.

Chomsky, Noam. 2003. *Power and Terror: Post-9/11 Talks and Interviews.* Edited by John Junkerman and Takei Masakazu. New York: Seven Stories Press.

Cleveland, William L. 1985. *Islam against the West: Shakib Arslan and the Campaign for Islamic Nationalism.* Austin: University of Texas Press.

Cohen, David W., and E. S. Atieno Odhiambo. 2004. *The Risks of Knowledge: Investigations into the Death of the Hon. Minister John Robert Ouko in Kenya, 1990.* Athens: Ohio University Press.

Colonial Office. 1961. *The Kenya Coastal Strip: Report of the Commissioner.* London: Her Majesty's Stationary Office.

Colonial Office. 1962. *Report of the Kenya Coastal Strip Conference, 1962.* London: Her Majesty's Stationery Office.

Collins, Randall. 1998. *The Sociology of Philosophies: A Global Theory of Intellectual Change.* Cambridge, MA: Harvard University Press.

Comaroff, Jean, and John L. Comaroff. 2012. *Theory from the South: Or, How Euro-America Is Evolving toward Africa*. Boulder, CO: Paradigm Publishers.

Cook, Michael. 2000. *Commanding Right and Forbidding Wrong in Islamic Thought*. Cambridge, UK: Cambridge University Press.

———. 2003. *Forbidding Wrong in Islam: An Introduction*. Cambridge, UK: Cambridge University Press.

Cooper, Frederick. 1980. *From Slaves to Squatters: Plantation Labor and Agriculture in Zanzibar and Coastal Kenya, 1890–1925*. New Haven, CT: Yale University Press.

———. 1987. *On the African Waterfront: Urban Disorder and the Transformation of Work in Colonial Mombasa*. New Haven, CT: Yale University Press.

———. 2002. *Africa since 1940: The Past of the Present*. Cambridge, UK: Cambridge University Press.

———. 2005. *Colonialism in Question: Theory, Knowledge, History*. Berkeley: University of California Press.

Coupland, Reginald. (1938) 1965. *East Africa and Its Invaders: From the Earliest Times to the Death of Seyyid Said in 1856*. Reprint, New York: Russell and Russell.

Cruise O'Brien, Donal B. 1995. "Coping with the Christians: The Muslim Predicament in Kenya." In *Religion and Politics in East Africa: The Period since Independence*, edited by Holger B. Hansen and Michael Twaddle, 200–219. Athens: Ohio University Press.

Dabashi, Hamid. 2009. *Post-Orientalism: Knowledge and Power in Time of Terror*. New Brunswick: Transaction Publishers.

———. 2015. *Can Non-Europeans Think?* London: Zed Books.

Dale, Godfrey. 1923. *Tafsiri ya Kurani ya kiArabu kwa lugha ya kiSwahili, pamoja na maelezo machache (The Qur'an in Swahili)*. London: Society for Promoting Christian Knowledge.

Das, Veena. 2015. "What Does Ordinary Ethics Look Like?" In Michael Lambek, Veena Das, Didier Fassin, and Webb Keane, *Four Lectures on Ethics: Anthropological Perspectives*, 53–125. Chicago, IL: HAU Books.

Deutsch, Jan-Georg. 2002. "The Indian Ocean and a Very Small Place in Zanzibar." In *Space on the Move: Transformations of the Indian Ocean Seascape in the Nineteenth and Twentieth Century*, edited by Jan-Georg Deutsch and Brigitte Reinwald, 61–73. Berlin: Klaus Schwarz Verlag.

Diagne, Souleyman Bachir. 2008. "Toward an Intellectual History of West Africa: The Meaning of Timbuktu." In *The Meanings of Timbuktu*, edited by Shamil Jeppie and S. B. Diagne, 19–27. Cape Town: HSRC Press.

Dumila, Faraj, ed. 1971. *Wasifu wa Kenyatta*. Nairobi: Jomo Kenyatta Foundation.

———, ed. 1978. *Wasifu wa Moi*. Nairobi: Kenya Literature Bureau.

Eastman, Carol M. 1994. "Service, Slavery ("Utumwa") and Swahili Social Reality." *Swahili Forum: Afrikanistische Arbeitspapiere* 37: 87–107.

Eickelman, Dale F. 1985. *Knowledge and Power in Morocco: The Education of a Twentieth-Century Notable*. Princeton, NJ: Princeton University Press.

———. 2005. "New Media in the Arab Middle East and the Emergence of Open Societies." In *Remaking Muslim Publics: Pluralism, Contestation, Democratization*, edited by R. W. Hefner. Princeton, NJ: Princeton University Press, 37–59.

Eickelman, Dale F., and Jon W. Anderson, eds. 2003. *New Media in the Muslim World: The Emerging Public Sphere*. 2nd ed. Bloomington: Indiana University Press.

Eickelman, Dale F., and James P. Piscatori, eds. 1996. *Muslim Politics*. Princeton, NJ: Princeton University Press.

el-Masri, F. H. 1987. "Sheikh Al-Amin b. Ali el-Mazrui and the Islamic Intellectual Tradition in East Africa." *Journal of Muslim Minority Affairs* 8 (2): 229–37.

el-Zein, Abdul Hamid M. 1974. *The Sacred Meadows: A Structural Analysis of Religious Symbolism in an East African Town*. Evanston, IL: Northwestern University Press.

Euben, Roxanne L. 1999. *Enemy in the Mirror: Islamic Fundamentalism and the Limits of Modern Rationalism*. Princeton, NJ: Princeton University Press.

———. 2002. "Killing for Politics: *Jihad*, Martyrdom, and Political Action." *Political Theory* 30 (1): 4–35.

Fabian, Johannes. 1971. *Jamaa: A Charismatic Movement in Katanga*. Evanston, IL: Northwestern University Press.

———. 1983. *Time and the Other: How Anthropology Makes Its Object*. New York: Columbia University Press.

———. 1986. *Language and Colonial Power: The Appropriation of Swahili in the Former Belgian Congo, 1880–1938*. Cambridge, UK: Cambridge University Press.

———. 1990. *Power and Performance: Ethnographic Explorations through Proverbial Wisdom and Theater in Shaba, Zaire*. Madison: University of Wisconsin Press.

———. 1996. *Remembering the Present: Painting and Popular History in Zaire*. Berkeley: University of California Press.

———. 2000. *Out of Our Minds: Reason and Madness in the Exploration of Central Africa: The Ad. E. Jensen Lectures at the Frobenius Institut, University of Frankfurt*. Berkeley: University of California Press.

———. 2001. *Anthropology with an Attitude: Critical Essays*. Palo Alto, CA: Stanford University Press.

———. 2007. *Memory against Culture: Arguments and Reminders*. Durham, NC: Duke University Press.

Fair, Laura. 2001. *Pastimes and Politics: Culture, Community, and Identity in Post-Abolition Urban Zanzibar, 1890–1945*. Athens: Ohio University Press.

Fardon, Richard. 1990. "General Introduction." In *Localizing Strategies: Regional Traditions of Ethnographic Writing*, edited by R. Fardon, 1–34. Edinburgh: Scottish Academic Press.

Fardon, Richard, and Graham Furniss, eds. 2000. *African Broadcast Cultures: Radio in Transition*. London: James Currey.

Farsy, Abadalla Saleh. 1942. *Seyyid Said bin Sultan*. Zanzibar: Mwongozi Printing Press.

———. 1969. *Qurani Takatifu*. Nairobi: Islamic Foundation.

———. 1972. *Baadhi ya Wanavyuoni wa Kishafi wa Mashariki ya Afrika*. Mombasa: Adam Traders. [See Farsy 1989.]

———. 1989. *The Shafi'i Ulama of East Africa, ca. 1830–1960: A Hagiographic Study*. Translated and annotated by Randal Pouwels. Madison: University of Wisconsin Press. Originally published as *Baadhi ya Wanavyuoni wa Kishafi wa Mashariki ya Afrika* (Mombasa: Adam Traders, 1972).

———. 1999a (1979). *Maisha ya Sayyidna Hasan*. Mombasa: Adam Traders.

———. 1999b (1980). *Maisha ya Sayyidna Huseyn*. Mombasa: Adam Traders.

Fassin, Didier. 2014. "The Ethical Turn in Anthropology: Promises and Uncertainties." In *HAU: Journal of Ethnographic Theory* 4 (1): 429–35.

Feierman, Steven. 1990. *Peasant Intellectuals: Anthropology and History in Tanzania.* Madison: University of Wisconsin Press.

Fuchs, H., F. de Jong, and J. Knappert. 2007. "Mawlid (a.), or Mawlūd." In *Encyclopedia of Islam,* edited by P. Bearman, Th. Bianquis, C. E. Bosworth, E. van Donzel, and W. P. Heinrichs. 2nd ed. Leiden: Brill Online.

Furniss, Graham. 2004. *Orality: The Power of the Spoken Word.* New York: Palgrave Macmillan.

Geertz, Clifford. 1973. "Thick Description: Toward an Interpretive Theory of Culture." In *The Interpretation of Cultures: Selected Essays,* 3–30. New York: Basic Books.

Gelvin, James L., and Nile Green, eds. 2013. *Global Muslims in the Age of Steam and Print.* Berkeley: University of California Press.

Ghazal, Amal N. 2010a. *Islamic Reform and Arab Nationalism: Expanding the Crescent from the Mediterranean to the Indian Ocean (1880s–1930s).* New York: Routledge.

———. 2010b. "The Other Frontiers of Arab Nationalism: Ibadis, Berbers, and the Arabist-Salafi Press in the Interwar Period." *Journal of Middle Eastern Studies* 42 (1): 105–22.

Ghedira, A. 2012. "Sahifa." In *Encyclopedia of Islam,* edited by P. Bearman, Th. Bianquis, C. E. Bosworth, E. van Donzel, and W. P. Heinrichs. 2nd ed. Leiden: Brill Online.

Gilsenan, Michael. 2005. *Recognizing Islam.* London: I. B. Tauris.

Glassman, Jonathon. 1995. *Feasts and Riots: Revelry, Rebellion, and Popular Consciousness on the Swahili Coast, 1856–1888.* London: J. Currey.

Godia, George. 1984. *Understanding Nyayo: Principles and Policies in Contemporary Kenya.* Nairobi: Transafrica.

Goffman, Erving. 1967. *Interaction Ritual: Essays on Face-to-Face Behavior.* Garden City, NY: Anchor Books.

Goldsmith, Paul. 2011. *The Mombasa Republican Council Conflict Assessment: Threats and Opportunities for Engagement.* Financed by USAID. Nairobi: Kenya Civil Society Strengthening Programme.

Goldsmith, Paul, Mohammed Shamuti, and Saleh Islam. 2011. "Overview of the Land Problem in Lamu." In *Kiswahili Research and Development in Eastern Africa,* edited by R. Chimera et al., 45–77. Mombasa: RISSEA and National Museums of Kenya.

Goodman, Nelson. 1978. *Ways of Worldmaking.* Indianapolis, IN: Hackett.

Gräf, Bettina. 2010. *Medien-Fatwas @ Yusuf al-Qaradawi: Die Popularisierung des islamischen Rechts.* Berlin: Klaus Schwarz Verlag.

Graetz, Tilo. 2014. *Technologische Dramen: Radiokulturen und Medienwandel in Benin (Westafrika).* Berlin: Transkript.

Green, Nile. 2011. *Bombay Islam: The Religious Economy of the West Indian Ocean, 1840–1915.* Cambridge, MA: Cambridge University Press.

Habermas, Juergen. 1989. *Strukturwandel der Oeffentlichkeit: Untersuchungen zu einer Kategorie der buergerlichen Gesellschaft.* Frankfurt: Suhrkamp.

Hackett, Rosalind I. J., and Benjamin F. Soares, eds. 2015. *New Media and Religious Transformations in Africa.* Bloomington: Indiana University Press.

Haj, Samira. 2009. *Reconfiguring Islamic Tradition: Reform, Rationality, and Modernity.* Cultural Memory in the Present. Palo Alto, CA: Stanford University Press.

Hallen, Barry. 2000. *The Good, the Bad, and the Beautiful: Discourse about Values in Yoruba Culture.* Bloomington: Indiana University Press.

Hallen, Barry, and J. O. Sodipo. (1986) 1997. *Knowledge, Belief and Witchcraft: Analytic Experiments in African Philosophy.* Reprint, Palo Alto, CA: Stanford University Press.

Hamdun, Said, and Noel King. 1994. *Ibn Battuta in Black Africa*. With a new foreword by Ross Dunn. Princeton, NJ: Markus Wiener.

Hamzah, Dyala, ed. 2013. *The Making of the Arab Intellectual: Empire, Public Sphere and the Colonial Coordinates of Selfhood*. London: Routledge.

Hansen, Holger B., and Michael Twaddle, eds. 1995. *Religion & Politics in East Africa: The Period since Independence*. Eastern African Studies. Athens: Ohio University Press.

Haron, Muhammed. 2015. "Muslim Community Radio Stations: Constructing and Shaping Identities in a Democratic South Africa." In Hackett, Rosalind I. J., and Benjamin F. Soares, eds. 2015. *New Media and Religious Transformations in Africa*, 82–96. Bloomington: Indiana University Press.

Hefner, Robert W. 2000. *Civil Islam: Muslims and Democratization in Indonesia*. Princeton Studies in Muslim Politics. Princeton, NJ: Princeton University Press.

———. ed. 2005. *Remaking Muslim Publics: Pluralism, Contestation, Democratization*. Princeton, NJ: Princeton University Press.

Heidegger, Martin. 1963. *Sein und Zeit*. Tuebingen: Niemeyer.

Hillewaert, Sarah. 2016. "'Whoever Leaves Their Tradition Is a Slave': Contemporary Notions of Servitude in an East African Town." *Africa: Journal of the International African Institute* 86 (3): 425–46.

Hirji, Zulfikar. 2012. *Between Empires: Sheikh-Sir Mbarak al-Hinawy (1896–1959)*. London: Azimuth Editions.

Hirsch, Susan F. 2008. *In the Moment of Greatest Calamity: Terrorism, Grief, and a Victim's Quest for Justice*. Princeton, NJ: Princeton University Press.

Hirschkind, Charles. 2006. *The Ethical Soundscape: Cassette Sermons and Islamic Counterpublics*. New York: Columbia University Press.

Ho, Engseng. 2006. *The Graves of Tarim: Genealogy and Mobility across the Indian Ocean*. Berkeley: University of California Press.

Hodgson, Marshall G. S. 1977. *The Venture of Islam: Conscience and History in a World Civilization*. Vol. 1: The Classical Age of Islam. Chicago, IL: University of Chicago Press.

Hofmeyr, Isabel. 2013. *Gandhi's Printing Press: Experiments in Slow Reading*. Cambridge, MA: Harvard University Press.

Hofmeyr, Isabel, P. Kaarsholm, and B. F. Frederiksen. 2011. "Introduction: Print Cultures, Nationalisms and Publics of the Indian Ocean." *Africa: Journal of the International African Institute* 81 (1): 1–22.

Hornsby, Charles. 2012. *Kenya: A History since Independence*. New York: I. B. Tauris.

Horton, Mark. 1987. "The Swahili Corridor." *Scientific American* 257 (3): 86–93.

Horton, Mark, and John Middleton. 2000. *The Swahili: The Social Landscape of a Mercantile Society*. Oxford, UK: Blackwell.

Horton, Robin. 1970. "African Traditional Thought and Western Science." In B. R. Wilson (ed.), *Rationality*. Oxford, UK: Blackwell.

Hountondji, Paulin J. 1983. "Reason and Tradition." In *Philosophy and Cultures: Proceedings of 2nd Afro-Asian Philosophy Conference, Nairobi, October/November 1981*, edited by H. O. Oruka and D. A. Masolo, 132–39. Nairobi: Bookwise.

———. 1990. "Scientific Dependence in Africa Today." *Research in African Literatures* 21(3): 5–15.

———. 1991. "Occidentalism, Elitism: Answer to Two Critiques." In *Philosophie, Ideologie und Gesellschaft in Afrika: Wien 1989*, edited by Christian Neugebauer. Frankfurt: Peter Lang.

———. 1995. "Producing Knowledge in Africa Today." *African Studies Review* 38 (3): 1–10.

———. (1976) 1996. *African Philosophy: Myth and Reality.* Translated by Henri Evans. First published in English 1983. 2nd ed. Bloomington: Indiana University Press.

———, ed. 1997. *Endogenous Knowledge: Research Trails.* Dakar: CODESRIA.

Hourani, Albert H. (1962) 1983. *Arabic Thought in the Liberal Age: 1798–1939.* Reissued with new preface. Cambridge, UK: Cambridge University Press.

Jackson, Michael. 2013. *Lifeworlds: Essays in Existential Anthropology.* Chicago, IL: University of Chicago Press.

Janmohamed, Karim K. 1978. "A History of Mombasa 1895–1939: Some Aspects of Economic and Social Life in an East African Port Town during Colonial Rule." PhD diss., Northwestern University.

James, Wendy. 1989. *The Listening Ebony.* Oxford, UK: Oxford University Press.

Janz, Bruce. 2009. *Philosophy in an African Place.* New York: Lexington.

Janzen, John M. 1992. *Ngoma: Discourses of Healing in Central and Southern Africa.* Berkeley: University of California Press.

Jeffers, Chike, ed. 2013. *Listening to Ourselves: A Multilingual Anthology of African Philosophy.* Albany: State University of New York Press.

Johnson, D. H. 1994. *Nuer Prophets.* Oxford, UK: Clarendon Press.

Kane, Ousmane. 2012. *Non-Europhone Intellectuals.* Dakar: CODESRIA.

———. 2016. *Beyond Timbuktu. An Intellectual History of Muslim West Africa.* Cambridge, MA: Harvard University Press.

Kant, Immanuel. (1781) 1930. *Kritik der reinen Vernunft.* Edited by R. Schmidt. Reprint, Hamburg: Meiner.

———. (1783) 1988. *Prolegomena zu einer jeden kuenftigen Metaphysik, die als Wissenschaft wird auftreten koennen.* Reprint, Erlangen: Fischer.

———. (1784) 1913. "Beantwortung der Frage: Was ist Aufklaerung?" In *Immanuel Kants Werke. Band IV. Schriften von 1783–1788,* edited by Artur Buchenau and Ernst Cassirer, 167–76. Berlin: Bruno Cassirer.

———. (1786) 1913. "Was heisst: sich im Denken orientieren?" In *Immanuel Kants Werke. Band IV. Schriften von 1783–1788,* edited by Artur Buchenau and Ernst Cassirer, 349–66. Berlin: Bruno Cassirer.

Kenya Human Rights Commission (KHRC). 1997. *Kayas Revisited: A Post-Election Balance Sheet.* Nairobi: Kenya Human Rights Commission.

———. 1998. *Killing the Vote: State Sponsored Violence and Flawed Elections in Kenya.* Nairobi: Kenya Human Rights Commission.

———. n.d. *The Political Economy of Ethnic Clashes: A Report of the International Commission of Jurists (Kenya Section).* Nairobi: Kenya Human Rights Commission.

Kenyatta, Jomo. 1968. *Suffering without Bitterness.* Nairobi: East African Publishing House.

———. 1971. *The Challenge of Uhuru: The Progress of Kenya, 1968 to 1970; Selected and Prefaced Extracts from the Public Speeches of His Excellency Mzee Jomo Kenyatta, President of the Republic of Kenya.* Nairobi: East African Publishing House.

Khadduri, M. 2007. "Maslaha." In *Encyclopedia of Islam,* edited by P. Bearman, Th. Bianquis, C. E. Bosworth, E. van Donzel, and W. P. Heinrichs. 2nd ed. Leiden: Brill Online.

Khitamy, Ahmed bin Sumeit. 1995. "The Role of the Riyadha Mosque-College in Enhancing the Islamic Identity in Kenya." In *Islam in Kenya,* edited by M. Bakari and S. S. Yahya, 269–76. Nairobi: MEWA.

Khuchi, Abubakar. [ca. 2010–2011.] "Majimbo: uhuru kamili kuwaokoa wapwani." Undated typescript. Lamu: n.p.

Kimmerle, Heinz. 1994. *Die Dimension des Interkulturellen.* Amsterdam: Rodopi.

Kindy, Hyder. 1972. *Life and Politics in Mombasa.* Nairobi: East African Publishing House.

Knappert, Jan. 1971. *Swahili Islamic Poetry.* Leiden: Brill.

Kresse, Kai. 2003. "'Swahili Enlightenment'? East African Reformist Discourse at the Turning Point: The Example of Sheikh Muhammad Kasim Mazrui." In "Islamic Thought in 20th-Century Africa," special issue, *Journal of Religion in Africa* 33 (3): 279–309.

———. 2004. "Making People Think: The Ramadhan Lectures of Sheikh Abdilahi Nassir in Mombasa, 1419 A. H." In *The Transmission of Learning in Islamic Africa,* edited by Scott S. Reese, 212–43. Leiden: Brill.

———. 2005. "At the *Baraza*: Socializing and Intellectual Practice at the Swahili Coast." In *Christianity and Social Change in Africa,* edited by T. Falola, 613–31. Durham, NC: Carolina Academic Press.

———. 2006. "Debating Maulidi: Ambiguities and Transformations of Muslim Identity along the Kenyan Swahili Coast." In *The Global Worlds of the Swahili: Interfaces of Islam, Identity and Space in 19th- and 20th-Century East Africa,* edited by R. Loimeier and R. Seesemann, 209–28. Berlin: Lit-Verlag.

———. 2007. *Philosophising in Mombasa: Knowledge, Islam and Intellectual Practice on the Swahili Coast.* Edinburgh: Edinburgh University Press for the International African Institute.

———. 2008. "The Uses of History: Rhetorics of Muslim Unity and Difference on the Kenyan Swahili Coast." In *Struggling with History: Islam and Cosmopolitanism in the Western Indian Ocean,* edited by E. Simpson and K. Kresse, 223–60. New York: Columbia University Press.

———. 2009a. "Muslim Politics in Postcolonial Kenya: Negotiating Knowledge on the Double-Periphery." *Journal of the Royal Anthropological Institute,* n.s., 15: 76–94.

———. 2009b. "Knowledge and Intellectual Practice in a Swahili Context: 'Wisdom' and the Social Dimensions of Knowledge." In *Africa: Journal of the International African Institute* 79 (1), special issue on *Knowledge in Practice: Expertise and the Transmission of Knowledge,* edited by K. Kresse and T. Marchand, 148–67.

———. 2011. "African Humanism and a Case Study from the Swahili Coast." In *Humanistic Ethics in the Age of Globality,* edited by C. Dierksmeier et al., 246–65. London: Palgrave Macmillan.

———. 2012. "Interrogating 'Cosmopolitanism' in an Indian Ocean Setting: Thinking through Mombasa on the Swahili Coast." In *Cosmopolitanism in Muslim Contexts,* edited by D. N. MacLean and S. Ahmed, 31–50. Edinburgh: Edinburgh University Press.

———. 2013. "On the Skills to Navigate the World, and Religion, for Coastal Muslims in Kenya." In *Articulating Islam: Anthropological Approaches to Muslim Worlds,* edited by M. Marsden and K. Retsikas, 77–99. Amsterdam: Springer Press.

———. 2016. "*Kenya: Twendapi?*: Re-Reading Abdilatif Abdalla's Pamphlet Fifty Years after Independence." *Africa: Journal of the International African Institute* 86 (1): 1–32.

———. 2017. "Introduction: *Guidance* and Social Critique: Mombasa through the Eyes of Sheikh Al-Amin Mazrui, 1930–1932." In *Guidance (Uwongozi) by Sheikh Al-Amin Mazrui: Selections from the First Swahili Islamic Newspaper,* edited by K. Kresse, translated by K. Kresse and H. Mwakimako, 1–29. Swahili-English edition. Leiden: Brill.

Kresse, Kai, and Edward Simpson. 2011. "Thinking Comparatively across the Western Indian Ocean." *ZMO Working Papers* 5: 1–15. http://d-nb.info/101656516X/34.

Kurzman, Charles. 2002. "Introduction." In *Modernist Islam, 1840–1940: A Sourcebook*, edited by C. Kurzman. Oxford: Oxford University Press.

———. 2011. *The Missing Martyrs: Why There Are So Few Muslim Terrorists*. New York: Oxford University Press.

Lacunza Balda, Justo. 1990. "Islamic Literature in Swahili." PhD diss., University of London.

———. 1997. "Translations of the Qur'an into Swahili, and Contemporary Islamic Revival in East Africa." In *African Islam and Islam in Africa*, edited by D. Westerlund and E. E. Rosander, 95–126. London: Hurst.

Laidlaw, James A. 2014. *The Subject of Virtue: An Anthropology of Ethics and Freedom*. Cambridge, UK: Cambridge University Press.

Lambek, Michael. 1990. "Certain Knowledge, Contestable Authority: Power and Practice on the Islamic Periphery." *American Ethnologist* 17 (1): 23–40.

———. 1993. *Knowledge and Practice in Mayotte: Local Discourses of Islam, Sorcery and Spirit Possession*. Toronto: University of Toronto Press.

———. 2010. *Ordinary Ethics: Anthropology, Language, and Action*. Edited by M. Lambek. New York: Fordham University Press. See esp. introduction and pp. 39–63, "Towards an Ethics of the Act."

———. 2015. "Living As If It Mattered." In Michael Lambek, Veena Das, Didier Fassin, and Webb Keane, *Four Lectures on Ethics: Anthropological Perspectives*. Chicago, IL: HAU Books, 5–51.

Lambek, Michael, Veena Das, Didier Fassin, and Webb Keane. 2015. *Four Lectures on Ethics: Anthropological Perspectives*. Chicago, IL: HAU Books.

Larkin, Brian. 2009. "Islamic Renewal, Radio, and the Surface of Things." In *Aesthetic Formations: Media, Religion, and the Senses*, edited by B. Meyer, 117–36. New York: Palgrave Macmillan.

———. 2015. "Binary Islam: Media and Religious Movements in Nigeria." In *New Media and Religious Transformations in Africa*, edited by Rosalind I. J. Hackett and B. Soares, 64–81. Bloomington: Indiana University Press.

Lauziere, Henri. 2010. "The Construction of Salafiyya: Reconsidering Salafism from the Perspective of Conceptual History." *International Journal of Middle Eastern Studies* 42 (3): 369–89.

Lewis, Ioan, ed. 1966. *Islam in Tropical Africa* (Studies presented and discussed at the fifth International African Seminar, Ahmadu Bello University, Zaria, January 1964, Volume 5). London: Oxford University Press for the International African Institute.

Lienhardt, Peter. 1959. "The Mosque College in Lamu and Its Social Background." *Tanganyika Notes and Records* 53: 228–42.

Limbert, Mandana. 2014. "Caste, Ethnicity, and the Politics of Arabness in Southern Arabia." *Comparative Studies in South Asia, Africa and the Middle East* 34 (3): 590–98.

Loimeier, Roman. 2007. "Sit Local, Think Global: The *Baraza* in Zanzibar." *Journal of Islamic Studies* 27: 16–38.

———. 2009. *Between Social Skills and Marketable Skills: The Politics of Islamic Education in 20th Century Zanzibar*. Leiden: Brill.

Loimeier, Roman, and Rüdiger Seesemann, eds. 2006. *The Global Worlds of the Swahili: Interfaces of Islam, Identity and Space in 19th- and 20th-Century East Africa*. Berlin: Lit-Verlag.

Long, Nicholas J., and Henrietta L. Moore, eds. 2013. *Sociality: New Directions*. New York: Berghahn Books.

Lonsdale, John. 1992a. *The Political Culture of Kenya*. Occasional Paper No. 37. Edinburgh: Edinburgh University Centre of African Studies.

———. 1992b. "The Moral Economy of Mau Mau: The Problem." In *Unhappy Valley: Conflict in Kenya and Africa*, edited by Bruce Berman and Jon Lonsdale, 265–314. Athens: Ohio University Press.

MacGaffey, Wyatt. 1983. *Modern Kongo Prophets: Religion in a Plural Society*. African Systems of Thought. Bloomington: Indiana University Press.

———. 1986. *Religion and Society in Central Africa: The BaKongo of Lower Zaire*. Chicago, IL: University of Chicago Press.

———. 2000. *Kongo Political Culture: The Conceptual Challenge of the Particular*. Bloomington: Indiana University Press.

MacMahon, Elizabeth. 2013. *Slavery and Emancipation in Islamic East Africa: From Honor to Respectability*. Cambridge, UK: Cambridge University Press.

Mamdani, Mahmood. 1996. *Citizen and Subject*. Princeton, NJ: Princeton University Press.

———. 2005. *Good Muslim, Bad Muslim: America, the Cold War, and the Roots of Terror*. New York: Three Leaves Press.

Mandaville, Peter G. 2001. *Transnational Muslim Politics: Reimagining the Umma*. London: Routledge.

Marsden, Magnus. 2005. *Living Islam: Muslim Religious Experience in Pakistan's North-West Frontier*. Cambridge, UK: Cambridge University Press.

Marsden, Magnus, and Konstantinos Retsikas, eds. 2013. *Articulating Islam: Anthropological Approaches to Muslim Worlds*. Dordrecht: Springer.

Martin, B. G. 1971. "Notes on Some Members of the Learned Classes of Zanzibar and East Africa in the 19th Century." *African Historical Studies* 4 (3): 525–45.

Masquelier, Adeline M. 2009. *Women and Islamic Revival in a West African Town*. Bloomington: Indiana University Press.

Matthews, Nathaniel. 2013. "Imagining Arab Communities: Colonialism, Islamic Reform, and Arab Identity in Mombasa, 1897–1933." *Islamic Africa* 4 (2): 135–63.

Maududi, Sayyid Abul Al'a. 1974. *Katika kufahamu Uislamu* [Toward Understanding Islam]. Translated by Shihabuddin Chiraghdin. Nairobi: The Islamic Foundation.

Mauss, Marcel. 1967. *The Gift: Forms and Functions of Exchange in Archaic Societies*. New York: Norton.

Mazrui, Alamin, and Hammad Muhammad Kasim Mazrui. 2017. "Foreword." In *Guidance (Uwongozi) by Sheikh Al-Amin Mazrui: Selections from the First Swahili Islamic Newspaper*, edited by K. Kresse, translated by K. Kresse and H. Mwakimako. Swahili-English edition. Leiden: Brill.

Mazrui, Alamin, and Ibrahim N. Shariff. 1994. *The Swahili: Idiom and Identity of an African People*. Trenton, NJ: Africa World Press.

Mazrui, Alamin M. 2007. *Swahili beyond the Boundaries: Literature, Language, and Identity*. Athens: Ohio University Press.

Mazrui, Ali A. 1993. "The Black Intifadah? Religion and Rage at the Kenya Coast." *Journal of Asian and African Affairs* 4 (2): 87–93.

Mazrui, Al-Amin bin Ali. n.d. *Hadithi Zilizochaguliwa: kimekusanya hadithi za Mtume: mia na thalathini za hikima na adabu na tabia njema* [Undated bilingual edition of 130 selected hadiths, selected and translated into Swahili]. With the assistance of M. K. Mazrui. Mombasa: Haji Mohamed & Sons.

———. n.d. *Hidayatul Atfal.* Mombasa: n.p.

———. 1939. *Dini ya Islamu* [The Religion of Islam]. Mombasa: East African Muslim Welfare Society.

———. (1944) 1955. *Uwongozi* [Guidance]. Reprint, Mombasa: East African Muslim Welfare Society (EAMWS). [See Mazrui 2017].

———. 1950. *Je, Ahmadiya ni Waislamu?* [Are the Ahmadiyas Muslims?]. Mombasa: n.p.

———. 1980. *Tafsiri ya Qur'ani tukufu: Al-Faatihah - Al-Baqarath.* Nairobi: Shungwaya.

———. 1981. *Tafsiri ya Qur'ani tukufu: Aali Imraan - An-Nisaa.* Nairobi: Shungwaya.

———. 1995. *The History of the Mazru'i Dynasty of Mombasa.* Translated by J. M. Ritchie. Fontes Historiae Africanae. Oxford, UK: Oxford University Press for the British Academy.

———. 2017. *Guidance (Uwongozi) by Sheikh Al-Amin Mazrui: Selections from the First Swahili Islamic Newspaper,* edited by K. Kresse, translated by K. Kresse and H. Mwakimako. Swahili-English edition. Leiden: Brill.

Mazrui, Muhammad K. 1958. *Maisha ya Assidik Abubakar.* Mombasa: Adam Traders.

———. 1962. *Maisha ya Alfaaruq Umar: Khalifa wa Pili.* Mombasa: H. O. Adam & Sons.

———. 1964. *Maisha ya Dhin-Nurain Uthman.* Mombasa: Adam Traders.

———. (1965) 1973. *Maisha ya al-Imam Ali.* 2nd ed. Mombasa: Adam Traders.

———. 1970. *Historia ya Utumwa Katika Uislamu na Dini Nyingine.* Nairobi: The Islamic Foundation.

———. [1970]. *Hukumu za sharia.* Vol. 1. Mombasa: Adam Traders.

———. [1971]. *Hukumu za sharia.* Vols. 2–3. Mombasa: H. O. Adam & Sons.

———. 1980. "Dibaji: Tarjama ya Sheikh Al-Amin bin Ali Kwa Ufupi." In *Tafsiri ya Qur'ani tukufu: Al-Faatihah - Al-Baqarath,* edited by Al-Amin bin Ali Mazrui, ix–xii. Nairobi: Shungwaya.

———. 1995. "A Biographical Sketch of the Author." In Al-Amin bin Ali Mazrui, *The History of the Mazru'i Dynasty of Mombasa,* 1–3. Translated by J. M. Ritchie. Fontes Historiae Africanae. Oxford, UK: Oxford University Press for the British Academy.

Mbembe, Achille. 1992. "Provisional Notes on the Postcolony." *Africa* 62 (1): 3–37.

———. 2001. *On the Postcolony.* Berkeley: University of California Press.

Mbiti, John S. 1969. *African Religions and Philosophy.* New York: Praeger.

McIntosh, Janet. 2004. "Reluctant Muslims: Embodied Hegemony and Moral Resistance in a Giriama Spirit Possession Complex." *Journal of the Royal Anthropological Institute* 10 (1): 91–112.

———. 2009. *The Edge of Islam: Power, Personhood, and Ethnoreligious Boundaries on the Kenya Coast.* Durham, NC: Duke University Press.

Messick, Brinkley M. 1993. *The Calligraphic State: Textual Domination and History in a Muslim Society.* Berkeley: University of California Press.

Meyer, Birgit. 2009. "Introduction." In *Aesthetic Formations: Media, Religion, and the Senses,* edited by M. Birgit. New York: Palgrave Macmillan.

Meyer, Birgit, and Annelies Moors, eds. 2006. *Religion, Media, and the Public Sphere.* Bloomington: Indiana University Press.

Middleton, John. 1992. *The World of the Swahili: An African Mercantile Civilization.* New Haven, CT: Yale University Press.

Miehe, Gudrun, and Katrin Bromber, eds. 2002. *Kala Shairi: German East Africa in Swahili Poems*. Köln: Köppe.

Miller, Daniel. 2015. "The Tragic Denouement of English Sociality." *Cultural Anthropology* 30 (2): 336–57.

Mirza, Sarah, and Strobel, Margaret, eds., transl. 1989. *Three Swahili Women: Life Histories from Mombasa, Kenya*. Bloomington: Indiana University Press.

Mitchell, Timothy. 1988. *Colonizing Egypt*. Berkeley: University of California Press.

Moi, Daniel arap. 1982. *Continuity and Consolidation in Kenya: Selected Speeches, December 1979–July 1981*. Nairobi: East African Publishing House.

———. 1986. *Kenya African Nationalism: Nyayo Philosophy and Principles*. London: Macmillan.

Mokoena, Hlonipha. 2011. *Magema Fuze: The Making of a Kholwa Intellectual*. Scottsville, South Africa: University of KwaZulu-Natal Press.

Moore, Henrietta. 1996. "The Changing Nature of Anthropological Knowledge." In *The Future of Anthropological Knowledge*, edited by H. Moore, 1–16. London: Routledge.

Mraja, M. 2011. "Sheikh Al-Amin Mazrui (1891–1947) and the Dilemma of Islamic Law in the Kenyan Legal System in the 21st Century." *Journal for Islamic Studies* 31: 60–74.

Mombasa Republican Council (MRC). 2010. *Manifesto*. Mombasa: n.p. Serial no. MRC/0016/01/01/2011.

Mudimbe, V. Y. 1988. *The Invention of Africa: Gnosis, Philosophy, and the Order of Knowledge*. Bloomington: Indiana University Press.

———. 1994. *The Idea of Africa*. Bloomington: Indiana University Press; London: James Currey.

Mulokozi, M. M., and Tigiti S. Y Sengo. 1995. *History of Swahili Poetry, A. D. 1000–2000: A Report*. Dar es Salaam, Tanzania: Institute of Kiswahili Research, University of Dar es Salaam.

Mwakimako, Hassan. 2010. "Conflicts and Tensions in the Appointment of Chief Kadhi in Colonial Kenya, 1898–1960s." In *Contemporary Muslim Societies: Muslim Family Law in Sub-Saharan Africa: Colonial Legacies and Postcolonial Challenges*, edited by Shamil Jeppie, Ebrahim Moosa, and Richard Roberts, 109–34. Amsterdam: Amsterdam University Press.

Mwakimako, Hassan, and J. Willis. 2014. "Islam, Politics, and Violence on the Kenya Coast." In *Observatoire des Enjeux Politiques et Sécuritaires dans la Corne de l'Afrique*, Note 4. Working Paper. SciencesPo. http://www.lam.sciencespobordeaux.fr/sites/lam/files /note4_observatoire.pdf. Accessed July 1, 2018.

Mwakimako, Hassan, and Justin Willis. 2016. "Islam and Democracy: Debating Electoral Involvement on the Kenyan Coast." *Islamic Africa* 7: 1–25.

Nassir, Ahmad Juma Bhalo. 1979. *Utenzi wa mtu ni utu*. Nairobi: Macmillan.

Nassir, Abdalla bin Ali. 1977. *Al-Inkishafi: Catechism of a Soul*. Translated by James de Vere Allen. Nairobi: East African Literature Bureau.

Nassir, Abdilahi. 1989a. *Shia na hadith: majibu na maelezo*. Mombasa: n.p.

———. 1989b. *Shia na Qur'ani: majibu na maelezo*. Mombasa: n.p.

———. 1990. *Shia na sahaba: majibu na maelezo*. Mombasa: n.p.

———. 2003a. *Shia na taqiya*. Mombasa: Markazi ya Ahlul Bayt.

———. 2003b. *Yazid hakuwa Amiirul-muminin*. Mombasa: Bilal Muslim Mission.

———. 2008. "Kenyan Muslims and the Righting of Historical Injustices: The Case of Mwambao." Lecture given at Zentrum Moderner Orient (ZMO), Berlin, July

2008. Unpublished transcript. Audio recording available at https://www.zmo.de /veranstaltungen/2008/dokumentationswahilinight.html. Accessed May 19, 2018.

Ndzovu, Hassan. 2014. *Muslims in Kenyan Politics*. Evanston, IL: Northwestern University Press.

Neugebauer, Christian, ed. 1991. *Philosophie, Ideologie und Gesellschaft in Afrika: Wien 1989*. Frankfurt: Peter Lang.

Ngũgĩ wa Thiong'o. 1981. *Writers in Politics*. London: Heinemann.

———. 1986. *Decolonising the Mind: The Politics of Language in African Literature*. Nairobi: East African Educational Publishers.

———. 1987. *Matigari*. Oxford, UK: Heinemann.

———. 1993. *Moving the Centre: The Struggle for Cultural Freedoms*. London: James Currey.

———. 1998. *Penpoints, Gunpoints, and Dreams: Towards a Critical Theory of the Arts and the State in Africa*. Oxford, UK: Clarendon Press.

———. 2009. *Something Torn and New: An African Renaissance*. New York: Basic Books.

———. 2013. "Tongue and Pen: A Challenge to Philosophers from Africa." *African Cultural Studies* 25 (2): 158–63.

———. 2016. "Abdilatif Abdalla and the Voice of Prophecy." In *Abdilatif Abdalla: Poet in Politics*, edited by R. M. Beck and K. Kresse, 11–18. Dar es Salaam, Tanzania: Mkuki na Nyota.

Njiru, Lee, and Browne Kutswa, eds. 1997. *Which Way Africa?* Selected speeches by President Daniel arap Moi. Nairobi: Government Press.

Njogu, Kimani. 2004. *Reading Poetry as Dialogue*. Nairobi: Jomo Kenyatta Foundation.

Njogu, Kimani, and John Middleton, eds. 2009. *Media and Identity in Africa*. Edinburgh: Edinburgh University Press.

Oded, Arye. 1996. "Islamic Extremism in Kenya: The Rise and Fall of Sheikh Khalid Balala." *Journal of Religion in Africa* 26: 406–15.

——— 2000. *Islam and Politics in Kenya*. London: Lynne Rienner.

Odinga, Oginga. 1968. *Not Yet Uhuru: The Autobiography of Oginga Odinga*. Nairobi: Heineman.

Oruka, Henry Odera. 1985. *Punishment and Terrorism in Africa*. Nairobi: Kenyan Literature Bureau.

———. 1990. *Sage Philosophy: Indigenous Thinkers and Modern Debate on African Philosophy*. Leiden: Brill.

———. 1997. "Philosophy and Humanism in Africa." In *Practical Philosophy: In Search of an Ethical Minimum*, 138–45. Nairobi: East African Educational Publishers.

Oruka, H. Odera, and D. A. Masolo, eds. 1983. *Philosophy and Cultures: Proceedings of 2nd Afro-Asian Philosophy Conference, Nairobi, October/November 1981*. Nairobi: Bookwise.

Ostebo, Terje. 2012. *Localising Salafism: Religious Change among Oromo Muslims in Bale, Ethiopia*. Leiden: Brill.

Parkin, David. 1984. "Being and Selfhood among Intermediary Swahili." In *Swahili Language and Society*, edited by Joan Maw and David J. Parkin, 247–60. Vienna: Afro-Pub.

———. 1991. *Sacred Void: Spatial Images of Work and Ritual among the Giriama of Kenya*. Cambridge, UK: Cambridge University Press.

———. 1995. "Blank Banners and Islamic Consciousness in Zanzibar." In *Questions of Consciousness*, edited by A. P. Cohen and N. Rapport, 198–216. London: Routledge.

Pearson, M. N. 2006. "Littoral Society: The Concept and the Problems." *Journal of World History* 17 (4): 353–73.

Peterson, Derek. 2004. *Creative Writing: Translation, Bookkeeping, and the Work of Imagination in Colonial Kenya*. Portsmouth, NH: Heinemann.

Peterson, Derek R., Emma Hunter, and Stephanie Newell, eds. 2015. *African Print Cultures: Newspapers and Their Publics in the Twentieth Century*. Ann Arbor: University of Michigan Press.

Pollock, Sheldon I. 2015. "Introduction." In *World Philology*, edited by S. Pollock, B. A. Elman, and K. K. Chang. Cambridge, MA: Harvard University Press.

Pouwels, R. L. 1981. "Sheikh Al-Amin bin Ali Mazrui and Islamic Modernism in East Africa, 1875–1947." *International Journal of Middle Eastern Studies* 13 (3): 329–45.

———. 1987. *Horn and Crescent: Cultural Change and Traditional Islam on the East African Coast, 800–1900*. Cambridge, UK: Cambridge University Press.

Presbey, Gail M., ed. 2007. *Philosophical Perspectives on the 'War on Terrorism.'* New York: Rodopi.

Prestholdt, Jeremy. 2008. *Domesticating the World: African Consumerism and the Genealogies of Globalization*. Berkeley: University of California Press.

———. 2011. "Kenya, the United States, and Counterterrorism." *Africa Today* 57 (4): 2–27.

———. 2014. "Politics of the Soil: Separatism, Autochtony, and Decolonization at the Kenyan Coast." *Journal of African History* 55: 249–70.

Prins, A. H. J. 1965. *Sailing from Lamu: A Study of Maritime Culture in Islamic East Africa*. Assen, Netherlands: Van Gorcum.

Purpura, Allyson. 1997. "Knowledge and Agency: The Social Relations of Islamic Expertise in Zanzibar." PhD diss., City University of New York.

Quayson, Ato. 2003. *Calibrations: Reading for the Social*. Minneapolis: University of Minnesota Press.

Quṭb, Sayyid. 2000. *Social Justice in Islam*. Rev. ed. Oneonta, NY: Islamic Publications International.

Ranger, Terence O. 1975. *Dance and Society in Eastern Africa, 1890–1970: The Beni Ngoma*. London: Heinemann.

Reese, Scott S. 2004. "The Adventures of Abu Harith: Muslim Travel Writing and Navigating the Modern in Colonial East Africa." In *The Transmission of Learning in Islamic Africa*, edited by S. S. Reese, 244–56. Leiden: Brill.

———. 2008. *Renewers of the Age: Holy Men and Social Discourse in Colonial Benaadir*. Leiden: Brill.

———. 2015. "Shaykh Abdullahi al-Qutbi and the Pious Believer's Dilemma: Local Moral Guidance in an Age of Global Islamic Reform." *Journal of Eastern African Studies* 9 (3): 488–504.

Rettová, Alena. 2007. *Afrophone Philosophies: Reality and Challenge*. Středokluky, Czech Republic: Zdeněk Susa.

Ricard, Alain. 2004. *The Languages and Literatures of Africa*. Trenton, NJ: Africa World Press.

Robinson, Francis. 1993. "Technology and Religious Change: Islam and the Impact of Print." *Modern Asian Studies* 27 (1): 229–51.

Romero, Patricia. 1997. *Lamu: History, Society, and Family in an East African Port City*. Princeton, NJ: Markus Wiener.

Rosaldo, Michelle Z. 1980. *Knowledge and Passion: Ilongot Notions of Self and Social Life.* Cambridge, UK: Cambridge University Press.

Rutten, Marcel, and Alamin Mazrui, eds. 1997. *Out for the Count: The 1997 General Elections and Prospects for Democracy in Kenya.* Kampala: Fountain.

Ryad, Umar. 2008. "Islamic Reformism and Christianity: A Critical Reading of the Works of Muhammad Rashid Rida and His Associates (1898–1935)." PhD diss., University of Leiden.

Ryle, Gilbert. 1971a. "The Thinking of Thoughts: What is 'le Penseur' Doing?" In *Collected Papers,* vol. 2, 480–96. New York: Barnes and Noble.

———. 1971b. "Thinking and Self-Teaching." *Journal of Philosophy of Education* 5 (2): 216–28.

Saavedra Casco, José A. 2007. *Utenzi, War Poems, and the German Conquest of East Africa: Swahili Poetry as a Historical Source.* Trenton, NJ: Africa World Press.

Sadgrove, Philip. 2004. "From Wadi Mizab to Unguja: Zanzibar's Scholarly Links." In *The Transmission of Learning in Islamic Africa,* edited by S. S. Reese. Leiden: Brill

Said, Edward W. 1978. *Orientalism.* New York: Pantheon.

———. 1984. "Travelling Theory." In *The World, the Text, and the Critic.* Cambridge, MA: Harvard University Press.

Sajid, Mehdi. 2015. *Muslime im Zwischenkriegseuropa und die Dekonstruktion der Faszination vom Westen: eine kritische Auseinandersetzung mit Sakib Arslans Artikeln in der aegyptischen Zeitschrift al-Fath (1926–1935).* Berlin: EBV Verlag.

Salim, Ahmed I. 1970. "The Movement for 'Mwambao' or Coast Autonomy in Kenya, 1956–63." In *Hadith 2: Proceedings of the 1968 Conference of the Historical Association of Kenya,* edited by B. A. Ogot and A. Brockett, 210–28. Nairobi: East African Publishing House.

———. 1973. *The Swahili-Speaking Peoples of Kenya's Coast, 1895–1965.* Nairobi: East African Publishing House.

———. 1976. "Native or Non-Native? The Problem of Identity and Social Stratification of the Arab-Swahili of Kenya." In *Hadith 6: History and Social Change in East Africa,* edited by B. A. Ogot, 65–85. Nairobi: East African Literature Bureau.

———. 1987. "Sheikh Al-Amin bin Ali Mazrui: un reformiste modern au Kenya." In *Les voies de l'Islam en Afrique orientale,* edited by F. Constantin, 59–71. Paris: Karthala.

Salim, Swalha. 1985. "A Modern Reformist among the Sunni Ulama in East Africa." MA thesis, Institute of Islamic Studies, McGill University.

Salvatore, Armando, and Dale F. Eickelman. 2006. Preface to *Public Islam and the Common Good,* edited by A. Salvatore and D. F. Eickelman. Leiden: Brill.

Samsom, Ridder. 1996. "Tungo za kujibizana: 'Kuambizana ni sifa ya kupendana'." *Swahili Forum* 3: 1–10.

Schielke, Samuli. 2014. "There Will Be Blood: Expecting Violence in Egypt, 2011–2013." *ZMO Working Papers* no. 11, 1–16.

Schmidt-Glintzer, Helwig. 2014. "Die gelbe Gefahr." *Merkur: Zeitschrift fuer Ideengeschichte* 8 (1): 43–58.

Schulz, Dorothea. 2007. "Evoking Moral Community, Fragmenting Muslim Discourse: Sermon Audio-Recordings and the Reconfiguration of Public Debate in Mali." *Journal of Islamic Studies* 27: 39–72.

———. 2012. *Muslims and New Media in West Africa: Pathways to God.* Bloomington: Indiana University Press.

Schulze, Reinhard. 1996. "Was ist die islamische Aufklaerung?" *Welt des Islams* 36 (3): 276–325.

———. 2000. *A Modern History of the Islamic World*. New York: I. B. Tauris.

Scott, James C. 1976. *Weapons of the Weak: Everyday Forms of Peasant Resistance*. New Haven, CT: Yale University Press.

Sedgwick, Mark J. 2010. *Muhammad Abduh*. New York: Oneworld.

Seesemann, Ruediger. 2007. "Kenyan Muslims, the Aftermath of 9/11, and the 'War on Terror'." In *Islam and Muslim Politics in Africa*, edited by B. F. Soares and R. Otayek, 157–76. London: Palgrave Macmillan. Seib, Philip. 2007. "New Media and Prospects for Democratization." In *New Media and the New Middle East*, edited by P. Seib, 1–17. London: Palgrave MacMillan.

Sengo, T. S. Y., and M. M. Mulokozi. 1994. *Research on the History of Kiswahili Poetry A. D. 1000–2000: Final Report*. Dar es Salaam, Tanzania: Institute of Kiswahili Research, University of Dar es Salaam.

Shariff, Ibrahim N. 1988. *Tungo zetu: Msingi wa mashairi na tungo nyinginezo*. Trenton, NJ: Red Sea Press.

Simpson, E., and K. Kresse. 2008. "Cosmopolitanism Contested: Anthropology and History in the Western Indian Ocean." In *Struggling with History: Islam and Cosmopolitanism in the Western Indian Ocean*, edited by E. Simpson and K. Kresse, 1–41. New York: Columbia University Press.

Soares, Benjamin F. 2005. *Islam and the Prayer Economy: History and Authority in a Malian Town*. Ann Arbor: University of Michigan Press.

Soghayroun, Ibrahim E. 2001. "The Arab and Swahili Culture in Historical Perspective: Some Important Links in 'The History of the Mazrū'īs in East Africa' by Shaykh Al-Amīn B. 'Alī Al-Mazrū'ī." *Sudanic Africa* 12: 15–32.

Strandes, Justus. (1899) 1961. *The Portuguese Period in East Africa*. Reprint, Nairobi: Kenya Literature Bureau.

Stren, Richard E. 1977. *Housing the Urban Poor in Africa: Policy, Politics, and Bureaucracy in Mombasa*. Institute of International Studies, Research Series 34. Berkeley: Institute of International Studies, University of California.

Strobel, Margaret. 1976. "From *Lelemama* to Lobbying: Women's Associations in Mombasa, Kenya." In *Hadith 6: History and Social Change in East Africa*, edited by B. A. Ogot, 107–135. Nairobi: East African Literature Bureau.

———. 1979. *Muslim Women in Mombasa, 1890–1975*. New Haven: Yale University Press.

Subiri, Obwogo. 1999. *The Bombs That Shook Nairobi and Dar: A Story of Pain and Betrayal*. Nairobi: Obwogo and Family.

Swaleh, Kadara. 2012. "Islamic Proselytising between Lamu and Mozambique: The Case of Kizingitini Village." *Social Dynamics* 38 (3): 398–418.

Tamim, Ghalib Y. 2006. *Maisha ya Sheikh Al-Amin bin Ali Mazrui*. Nairobi: Signal Press.

———. 2013. "Sheikh Ali bin Abdalla bin Naf'i Mazrui (1825–1894): The Pioneering Role Model of East African Reformers." Paper presented at workshop Religious Leadership in East Africa: Christian Evangelism and Islamic Reform, Kenya, July 2.

Taylor, Charles. 2004. *Modern Social Imaginaries*. Durham, NC: Duke University Press.

Tayob, Abdulkader. 2007. "Muslim Publics: Contents and Discontents." In "Thematic Issue on Islam and African Muslim Publics," edited by A. Tayob, special issue, *Journal for Islamic Studies* 27: 1–15.

Tempels, Placide. (1945) 1959. *Bantu Philosophy*. Paris: Présence Africaine.

Tolmacheva, Marina, C. H. Stigand, Dagmar Weiler, M. Heepe, and Alfred Voeltzkow. 1993. *The Pate Chronicle: Edited and Translated from MSS 177, 321, 344, and 358 of the Library of the University of Dar es Salaam*. East Lansing: Michigan State University Press.

Topan, Farouk M. 1992. "Swahili as a Religious Language." *Journal of Religion in Africa* 22 (4): 331–49.

Trimingham, J. S. 1964. *Islam in East Africa*. Oxford, UK: Clarendon Press.

Tripp, Charles. 2006. *Islam and the Moral Economy: The Challenge of Capitalism*. Cambridge, UK: Cambridge University Press.

Triulzi, Alessandro 1981. *Salt, Gold and Legitimacy: Prelude to the History of a No-Man's Land, Bela Shangul, Ethiopia*. Naples: Instituto Universitario Orientale.

Unified Movement for Democracy in Kenya (UMOJA). 1989. *Moi's Reign of Terror: A Decade of Nyayo Crimes Against the People of Kenya*. Background documentation No. 2. London: UMOJA.

Vail, Leroy, and Landeg White. 1991. *Power and the Praise Poem: Southern African Voices in History*. London: James Currey.

Van Binsbergen, Wim. 2005. "'An Incomprehensible Miracle'—Central African Clerical Intellectualism versus African Historic Religion: A Close Reading of Valentin Mudimbe's 'Tales of Faith'." *Journal of African Cultural Studies* 17 (1): 11–65.

Vierke, Clarissa. 2011. *On the Poetics of the Utendi: A Critical Edition of the 19th Century Poem "Utendi wa Haudaji" Together with a Stylistic Analysis*. Berlin: Lit-Verlag.

Voll, John O. 1996. "Abduh and the Transvaal Fatwa: The Neglected Question." In *Islam and the Question of Minorities*, edited by T. Sonn, 27–40. Atlanta, GA: Scholars Press.

Warner, Michael. 2005. *Publics and Counterpublics*. New York: Zone Books.

Wedeen, Lisa. 2008. *Peripheral Visions: Publics, Power and Performance in Yemen*. Chicago, IL: University of Chicago Press.

Werbner, Richard P. 1996. "Introduction: Multiple Identities, Plural Arenas." In *Postcolonial Identities in Africa*, edited by R. P. Werbner and T. O. Ranger, 1–25. London: Zed Books.

———, ed. 1998. *Memory and the Postcolony: African Anthropology and the Critique of Power*. London: Zed Books.

———, ed. 2000. *Postcolonial Subjectivities*. London: Zed Books.

White, Luise. 2000. *Speaking with Vampires: Rumor and History in Colonial Africa*. Berkeley: University of California Press.

Willis, Justin. 1993. *Mombasa, the Swahili, and the Making of the Mijikenda*. Oxford: Clarendon Press.

Wiredu, Kwasi 1980. "How Not to Compare African Traditional Thought and Western Thought." In *Philosophy and an African Culture*. Cambridge, UK: Cambridge University Press.

———. 1995. *Conceptual Decolonization in African Philosophy: Four Essays*. Edited by Olusegun Oladipo. Ibadan: Hope.

———. 1996. *Cultural Universals and Particulars: An African Perspective*. Bloomington: Indiana University Press.

Wiredu, Kwasi, and Kai Kresse. 2000. "Language Matters: Decolonization, Multilingualism, and African Languages in the Making of African Philosophy." Dialogue conducted in 1996. In *Polylog: Forum for Intercultural Philosophy* 2. http://them.polylog.org/2/dwk-en.htm. Accessed July 25, 2016.

Wrong, Michela. 2009. *It's Our Turn to Eat: The Story of a Kenyan Whistle-Blower.* New York: Harper.

Yassin, Ahmed. 2004. *Conflict and Conflict Resolution among the Swahili of Kenya.* PhD diss., University of London.

Zaman, Muhammad Q. 2002. *The Ulama in Contemporary Islam: Custodians of Change.* Princeton Studies in Muslim Politics. Princeton, NJ: Princeton University Press.

———. 2012. *Modern Islamic Thought in a Radical Age: Religious Authority and Internal Criticism.* Cambridge, UK: Cambridge University Press.

Newspapers and Pamphlets

Sauti ya Haki. Mombasa (1972–1982).

The Message. Mombasa (ca. 1990–1992).

The Milestone. Mombasa (ca. 1990–1992).

An-Nuur. Dar es Salaam (since ca. 1994).

Friday Bulletin. Nairobi (since ca. 1996).

Kenya: Waislamu waitakavyo. Mombasa (ca. 2003–2005).

Index

Abdalla, Abdilatif, 10, 145n38, 208, 210n15
academia: African studies, 22–24, 125, 201; and eurocentrism, 5, 12, 26–27, 203–204, 206 (*see also* intellectual traditions, European); of languages, 23–24, 27; of terrorism and internal debates, 196
Abubakar Amin. *See* Baalawy, Abubakar Amin
Africanism, 23
Ahmadiyya, 65
al-Islah pamphlets, 67, 95, 97n17
al-Manar newspaper, 65, 69, 97n23, 116–17
anthropological research: *ix*, 37, 46, 209n10; and empirical conditions, 46, 55; critical anthropology, 46–47, 209n9; hermeneutical anthropology, 30n22, 199
Arabs, 4, 28n
Arabness (*U-Arabu*), 87, 162, 205
Arslan, Shakib, 69–70, 97n22
Asad, Talal, 21

Baalawy, Abubakar Amin, *xii*, *xvin3*, *101*, 147, 150, 153, 154–55, 156, 186n1
Balala, Najib, 158, 162–63
Barber, Karin, 21, 47
Basaddiq, Omar, *99*, 160
"The Black Peril!" (*Khatari Nyeusi!*), 72–73, 82–84, 97n25, 210n14
British colonialism: 3, 8, 63, 84, 86–87; anti-Islam prejudice, 129, 162; and colonial critique, 91; civilizing narratives of, 41–42, 68; industry and modernization under, 68, 89

change, 22, 35, 84–85, 139, 194
Chomsky, Noam, 176–77, 202
Christians: Christocentric politics, 3, 4, 43–44, 61, 126–27, 148; Swahili Qur'an translation, 65, 96n10, 98n42; Jamaa movement, 195; local schools, 74–75; Muslim perspective, 112

Chakrabarty, Dipesh, 11, 27, 204
"civilization" (*ustaarabu*), 87, 162–63, 205. *See also* Arabness
coastal independence movement (*mwambao*), 9–10, 29n18, *99*, 159–62
coastal people (*wapwani*); and government rule, 3–4, 6–7; and tensions with *wabara*, 9, 40, 45, 82–84, 93, 148; losing status, 68, 71–72, 72–73, 83; positioning identity, 6, 41–42, 72–73, 84, 190, 192; losing identity, 80–82
Collins, Randall, 13–14, 31n36, 209n12
community: 10, 31n37, 35–36; and mutual obligation, 16, 17–21, 50, 135, 194–95; interaction rituals of, 30n26, 31n37; of mindful interaction, 25; (re-)formation of, 36–37, 149
comparative reflections, 53–55, 93
conceptualizations, 25–27
conceptual frameworks: 10, 12, 26, 47, 199, 206; and Islam, 16, 32n52, 144n24, 210n14; of afrophone thinking, 27, 30n23, 204–205; of colonialism, 84, 85; of Swahili, 206–208, 212n26
creative agency: 43, 153, 184; processes, 55n1, 193; and imagination, 47

Dabashi, Hamid, 27
de Boeck, Filip, 42–43, 90
democratization, 164, 182
discontent: with elitism, 88, 185; with government, 5–7, 7–8, 9, 9–10, 28n6, 90; with local leadership, 175, 185; with Muslim world, 67, 70, 80–82, 88, 192–93; with post-independence, 90; with social standing, 42
discursive traditions: 10, 201; and Islam, 21–22, 140, 191
discursive community, 34, 182–84, 193–94, 196–97

education (*elimu*): against ignorance, 111; history of, 86–87, 152, 163; of language, 81; on Islam, 86–87, 112–13, 128; on technology, 83–84, 112; for performance, 85; on politics, 130

epistemes, African, 23, 26, 212n26

ethnography, 5, 25–26, 32n52, 35, 163–64, 196, 197

Europeans, imitation of: viii, 70, 72, 78–80; or, self-representation, 79

Fabian, Johannes, 46–47, 56n15, 209n9, 209–210n13, 211n21

Farsy, Sheikh Abdalla Saleh: 65, 105, 121, 135–36, 144–45n36; and Alawiyya, 105; and controversies, 133–36; and new *maulidi*, 133, 145n40; and Sheikh Ali Seneda (Gunda), 134–35; *fatwa* judgements of, 122–23; social critique of opponents, 135; death of, 109, 136–37

Friday Bulletin, ix–x

"Get Educated with Stambuli!" (*Elimika na Stambuli!*): xi–xii, 52–53, 185; and egalitarianism, 54, 182, 193; and historical consciousness, 152, 158–59, 159, 160, 161, 164; and mutual education, 151–53, 182; and Najib Balala, 162–63; 54, 150; and Sheikh Abdilahi Nassir, 159–62; and terrorism, 163–74, 174–78, 179–80; community impact of, 157, 158, 183–84, 193–94; engagement with, 150–51, 153, 179; form of discussion in, 159, 166–67; for Muslim unity (*umoja*), 152, 193; on "commanding right and forbidding wrong," 151, 165, 180, 182; on social equivalence, 93; rhetoric of, 151, 152–53, 155, 158, 172–73, 180, 201–202; topics of, 151–52, 157, 158–59, 166, 184

goodness (*utu*), 18, 107

Habermas, Jürgen, 32–33n56, 193, 209n6

hadith: 17, 21–22, 48; Swahili translation of, 66, 107, 114, 140

Hadrami Alawiyya: 51, 54, 65; and criticism of "modernists," 69, 86, 105–106, 134, 145n44; and Habib Saleh, 106; and media avoidance, 86, 96n10, 98n35, 121, 184; and

oral discourse, 142, 145n43, 192; and Sufi *masharifu*, 65, 87, 135

Haj, Samira, 22

Hodgson, Marshall, *vii, viii*; "islamicate," *xvi*n3

Hountondji, Paulin, 14, 23, 32n53

Hyder, Mohamed, 53, 113, 158, 174–78, 179–80, 180–81, 182, 202

ideological narratives, 42, 72–73

ignorance (*jahiliyya* [*ujinga*]), 70, 77, 84–85, 111, 115

intellectual culture, 12, 23, 207

intellectual practice: ix, 4, 10–11, 12, 13, 24, 32–33, 194, 207, 209n11; of Swahili, 13, 19–20; of *umma*, 21, 21–22; of "Voice of Justice," 140–41; seeing through, 199

intellectual rituals, 13,

intellectual traditions: 10, 57n20; African, 26–27, 211n24; European, 11, 204; Swahili, 12, 190, 206–208

internal pluralism, 23, 48, 197

Islam: 21–22; "as hermeneutical engagement," 200; diffusing of, 51, 126; mediation of, 38, 55n6, 155, 208n1; modernization and reform of, 38, 67, 92; vernacularization of, 35, 38; and violence, 165, 173, 175–76

Islamic Party of Kenya (IPK), 43, 56n12, 98n44, 146n51

jihad, 163, 165, 167–68, 188n15; a greater *jihad*, 168, 170–72, 174, 178, 180–81

"Justice up!" (*Haki juu!*), 123–128

Kane, Ousmane, 26, 206

Kenya People's Union (KPU), 10

Kenyatta, President Jomo, 30n20, 128–129, 131, 144–45n36

Kenyatta, President Uhuru, *100*, 147, 187n12

Kibaki, President Mwai, 147–48

Kilindini Harbour, 7, 71

knowledge (*elimu*): 11–12, 70, 93, 118, 138, 197, 200, 208; and moral obligation, 15–16, 107; and work, 80, 85, 94 of religion, 35, 38; social, 5, 81; sociology of, 13–14; status of, 54, 83–84; transregional flows of, 51–52, 92, 137–38

"Knowledge and Experts" (*Elimu na wataalamu*): 114–16, 116–17; of an ignorant sheikh, 114–15; on *Tafsir of Manar*, 116–17

Lancaster House Conference Agreement of 1963, 8, 9, 99, 160
language use: *ix*, 10, 85, 87, 206–207, 212n27; historical tensions of, 73; and sociality, 12, 15–16, 85; and ethics (*see* moral obligation, of ordinary ethics); and rhetoric (*see* rhetorical style and motifs)
Lambek, Michael, 18
Lamu: 5–8, *100*; Hadrami Alawiyya networks of, 65; Riyadha Mosque in, 96n11

maps of experience, 46, 118
maulidi: and Muslim identity, 120; controversies, 28n6–7, 119–20, 132–33, 154; coverage of, 120, 130, 154–55; in national politics, 130, 131; rituals of, 5, 6, 28n7, 119–20; a sermon, 5–7, 28n7; alternative ceremony, 133, 145n40
Mazrui family in Mombasa: 63–66; including Sheikh Ali bin Nafi, 63–64
Mazrui, Sheikh Al-Amin bin Ali: *ix–x*, 35, 38, 53–54, 62, *101*, 202; and Alawiyya, 69; colonial ambivalence of, 88–90; communal concern, 89; education and influences, 64–65, 66, 85; on forbidding wrong, 49–50, 53, 73–74, 82, 88; using Swahili language, 64, 86, 204–205; rhetorical speech of, 76, 85, 95, 204 (*see also* rhetorical style of anticipation); reform agenda of, 65–66, 68–69, 75–76, 77, 86; writings of, 66, 68; legacy of, 90–92, 105, 107, 108, 112–14, 114–16
Mazrui, Sheikh Muhammad Kasim: *x–xi*, 50–52, 54, 105, 202–203; reading of, 139; death of, 109, 136–138
Mbembe, Achille, *vii, vii–viii*, 197
mediation, 25, 36–37, 43, 69–70, 180, 186, 195
Meyer, Birgit, 35–36, 36
Mijikenda, 28n1, 92
Moi, President Daniel arap, 61, 131, 145n39
Mombasa (Mvita): as translocal space, 62–63, 64; history of, 62–63; labor

migrants in, 71, 72, 83; Makadara Grounds of, *103*, 153; Twelve Tribes of, 42; urban community of, 71–72, *102*
Mombasa Republican Council (MRC) manifesto, 8–9, 29n13, *99*
moral community: 18, 68; and common good, 18
"moral ethnicity," 198
moral obligation: 15–16, 20, 31n32, 48, 140, 182, 194, 196–98; and dilemmas, 164; and goodness is action (*utu ni kitendo*), 107; for commanding right (*kuamrishana wema*) and forbidding wrong (*kukatazana uovu*), 17, 32n46, 47–49, 49–50, 88, 123–28, 135, 151, 182; for financial investment, 75; of knowledge (*elimu*) and work (*kazi*), 80, 82, 85, 94; of ordinary ethics, 18–19, 50, 196; of reminding, 195; understandings of, 53, 205

Nahdy, Sheikh Nassor: 121; *fatwa* judgements of, 122–23
Nassir, Abdulswamad Shariff, 148, 149
Nassir, Sheikh Abdilahi: 4, 29, *99*, *103*, 136–37, 158, 187n2, 187n11; and Twelver Shiism, 160; on *Radio Rahma*, 159–62
Nassir, Stambuli Abdilahi: *xi–xii*, *xvin3*, 53, *103*, 147, 150, 156–58, 185, 186n1, 189n28, 201–202; on terrorism, 165–66, 169–70, 196; and Sheikh Abdilahi, 160
Nassir, Shariff, 90, 148, 149
Ngũgĩ wa Thiong'o, 26–27, 87

"The Obligations of Muslims Today," 73–78
orientation, struggle for, 191–92
Omani Arabs: 4, 28n1, 92, 96n7; integration with Sunni-Shafii, 64

"Past present continuous," 3, 4, 44, 47, 197, 201, 208
performance: 18, 31n37, 34–35; of action and work, 69–70, 80, 85; of critique, 195; of moral obligation, 107; performing *ustaarabu*, 87; speaking as, 18, 32–33n44, 184–85, 194, 206–207
philosophy: 13; African, 14, 23, 26, 33n59, 207

poetry: 20–21; Swahili genres: *utendi*, 7, 17, 20, 29n11; *kujibizana*, 31n35, 111; *shairi* and *nyimbo*, 20
political corruption: 130–31, 148; and propaganda, 131
postcolonial critique, 203
postcolonial experience: 42–44, 46–47, 90; features of, 62, 93
postcolonial state: 90; and Kenyatta government, 9, 28n6, 30n20, 145n38, 208 (*see also* President Jomo Kenyatta); and Moi government, 30n20, 61, 90, 147 (*see also* President Daniel arap Moi); of Kenya African National Union (KANU), 29n17, 128; of "*nyayo* politics," 147–48; of National Rainbow Coalition (NARC), 28n6, 148; post-Moi government, 147–48
postcolonial thinking: 24, 27, 185–86, 200–26; and regional languages, 47
provincializing Europe, 11, 27, 204
provincializing social sciences, 203–204, 205–206
publics: 14, 24–25, 32–33n56, 34–35, 191; media, 47–49, 55n6, 56n12, 87; Muslim, 17, 20, 45, 48; new media, 35–36, 39, 55n6; print and pamphlets, 37–38, 66–67, 74, 87–88, 138, 146n51, 178; radio, 54, 138, 147, 148–149, 155–56, 165, 182–84, 193–95; self-censoring, 128–130, 131–32, 145n37, 165

Qur'an: 17, 21–22, 48; vernacular translations of, 65, 66, 96n10, 98n42, 140; education of, 65, 74–75, 112, 127
Qutb, Seyid, *viii–ix*

racial prejudice: 40, 41–42, 97n29; between Arabs and Africans, 41, 72–73, 82–84, 162–63, 168, 180; between Arabs and Swahili, 41, 92, 128
Radio Rahma: *xi–xii*, 101–104, 148–151, 182–84; and "women's forum," 149, 183; as "virtual *baraza*," 150, 183; ideological directions of, 154–55, 185; public events of, 153–54; reservations against, 154–55
"Regionalism" (*Majimbo*), 7–8
resilience: 43–44; lack of, 92–95
"Religious Discord" (*Fitina ya dini*), 111–13

religious economy: 38–39, 121; and "knowledge economy," 107
religious innovations (*bidaa*), 28n7, 65, 105, 119, 126, 132–33
Ridha, Sayyid Muhammad Rashid, 97n23, 116, 117
rhetorical style: 54, 57n21; of anticipation, 82–97, 210n15; of collage and quotation, 132; of fear, 49, 50, 116; of humor and irony, 117–18; of mutual concern, 52, 95; open-access, 49, 52, 149, 182–84; oral narrative, 68, 116–18, 126, 184–86; self-questioning, 76; of shaming, 49
rhetorical motif: of causing disunity, 51, 115–16, 124, 125, 139; of commanding right and forbidding wrong, 49–50, 50–51, 52, 73–74, 123–28, 151, 180; of education against ignorance, 111; of goodness is action, 107; of knowledge and work, 80, 85; of polemics, 135–36; of Prophet Muhammad, 172–73; of unity (*umoja*), 70, 128, 138, 152; of wake-up calls, 43, 67, 73, 152–53, 166, 205; of "we are we" (*sisi ni sisi*), 6, 180; of "us for ourselves" (*sisi kwa sisi*), 201, 211n16

Saggaf, Mwalimu, 39, 40, 56n7, 97n22
Sahifa pamphlets: *ix–x*, 49–50, 54, 62, 65–66, 66–69, 95; and Arabic, 86; on Christian and Ahmadiyya threats, 65; internal critique of, 68, 94. See also *Uwongozi* (*Guidance*)
Salafi modernist reformism: 67, 69, 88, 142n1, 142–43n5, 154, 192; and egalitarianism, 86, 135; and pursuing independence, 75–76; and "Muslim awakening," 70, 98n45
self-positioning: 44–46, 72–73, 153, 198–200; and narratives of superiority, 72–73, 84, 111
slavery (*utumwa*): 40, 41–42, 63, 73; return of, 83, 84
Stambuli. See Nassir, Stambuli Abdilahi
Swahili corridor, 4
Swahili language: *viii*, 35, 85–86, 197–98; and moral speech, 140; and webs of meaning, 203–204; dialects of, 106; idioms of, 15, 18, 52, 80, 151; terms of, *xv*, 85, 140–41, 205–205

Swahili Muslims: as Kenyans, 6, 96n1, 129, 149, 162–63; and ethnic identity, 197–98; in "double peripheral," 4, 132, 186, 190–91; in "deep slumber," 72, 73, 83, 152–53; internal tensions of, 16, 45, 69, 70, 87, 97n29, 105, 164, 199; morality of, *see* moral obligations; postcolonial experience, 39–40

Swahili society: 4, 14–16; as "middlemen society," 4, 74

terrorism (*ugaidi*): 39, 163–74, 175–76, 178–80; and al-Qaeda bombings of 1998, 40, 148; and attacks of *9/11*, 148, 178–79, 180; and bombings in Mombasa of 2002, 148, 187n2; and regional differentiation, 168; justifications and *jihad*, 163, 164, 165–66 167–68, 168

textual study: 5, 25; of Arslan, 69–70; anthropology of, 37

tradition, 14, 22, 22–24, 80, 142n1

transnational Islam, 137–38

upcountry people (*wabara*): 3; rule by, 3, 40, 92; as "colonizers," 8–9, 61; gaining status, 68, 72–73, 83

umma: 2; reimagining of, 62, 66, 149, 183–84; emerging global community of, 62–63, 167; major events of, 132–33

Uwongozi (*Guidance*): ix–x, x, 62, 65, 94–95; on coastal marginalization, 74, 76–78, 83, 84, 94; a new public, 87–88; and "in religion and the world" (*dini na dunia*), 68, 75, 80, 82; on obligations, 73–78; racial undertones of, 73, 84; on western

influence, 78–80, 93. See also *Sahifa* pamphlets

"Voice of Justice" (*Sauti ya Haki*): 50–52, 54, 105, 108–110, 138–42; and community concerns, 118–19, 122–23; as "tongue of the community" (*ulimi wa umma*), 106, 108, 110, 120, 138; criticism and defense of, 51, 57n18, 106, 123–28, 133; dialogical dimensions of, 109–110; dual opposition between Alawiyya and modernists, 106–107, 123, 133–35, 142, 145n45, 192–93; for justice and truth (*haki*), 108, 111; in vernacular (Kimvita), 106, 108; on forbidding wrong, 138; public challenges, 109–110, 116, 121, 139; readership of, 110, 120; reform agenda of, 107, 110–14, 120, 139, 142, 191–92; sections of: *hadith*, 114; *fatawa*, 118–23, 144n24; "On Educating the Youth"; science and the Quran, 113; the golden tail, 109, 130

Wahhabi, 115, 138, 143nn22–23, 154–55, 192. *See also* Salafi reformism

"war on terror": 40, 148, 163, 174, 177–78; and Islamophobia, 148–49, 162–63, 187n12

Warner, Michael, 34, 148

Wiredu, Kwasi, 23

world philology, 27

"worldly glory" (*utukufu wa ulimwengu*), 112

"Zeal, People . . . ! !" (*Ghera jamani . . . ! !*), 76–78

KAI KRESSE is Professor of Social and Cultural Anthropology at Freie Universitaet Berlin, and Vice Director for Research at Leibniz Zentrum Moderner Orient (ZMO), Berlin. Before that, he was Associate Professor of African and Swahili Studies at Columbia University, and Lecturer of Social Anthropology at the University of St. Andrews. He is author of *Philosophizing in Mombasa: Knowledge, Islam, and Intellectual Practice on the Swahili Coast.*

www.ingramcontent.com/pod-product-compliance
Lightning Source LLC
Chambersburg PA
CBHW051959270326
41929CB00015B/2722